Julie Paschkis art—Uncle Sam on bike

J.F.

This book is
one of fifteen
awarded as
part of

the 2007
**We the People
Bookshelf**
on the
**Pursuit of
Happiness**

Presented by the National Endowment for the
Humanities (NEH) in cooperation with the American Library
Association (ALA). NEH and ALA gratefully acknowledge
support from Scholastic Inc. for the 2007 Bookshelf.

www.neh.gov   **www.ala.org**

LEAVES OF GRASS

WALT WHITMAN

LEAVES OF GRASS

GRASS

THE "DEATH-BED" EDITION

Introduction by William Carlos Williams

Notes by Meir Rinde, Brandeis University

THE MODERN LIBRARY

NEW YORK

Grateful acknowledgment is made to the following for permission
to reprint previously published material:

NICHOLAS HOWE, LITERARY EXECUTOR OF IRVING HOWE: Excerpt from
"Walt Whitman" from *Modern Literary Criticism: An Anthology* by
Irving Howe. Reprinted by permission of Nicholas Howe,
Literary Executor of Irving Howe.

NEW DIRECTIONS PUBLISHING CORPORATION: "An Essay on *Leaves of Grass*"
from *Unpublished Materials* by William Carlos Williams.
Copyright © 1955 by Florence H. Williams. Reprinted by permission
of New Directions Publishing Corporation.

NEW YORK UNIVERSITY PRESS: Excerpt from *The Walt Whitman Reader* by Gay
Wilson Allen, later editions published by New York University Press as
The New Walt Whitman Handbook. Reprinted by permission of
New York University Press.

The Yale Review: Excerpt from "Walt Whitman and the New Poetry"
by Amy Lowell. Originally published in *The Yale Review*, Vol. XVI,
No. 3, April 1927. Reprinted by permission of *The Yale Review*.

LIBRARY OF CONGRESS CATALOGING-IN-PUBLICATION DATA
Whitman, Walt, 1819–1892.
Leaves of grass/Walt Whitman; with an introduction by
William Carlos Williams.—"Death-bed" ed.
p.   cm.
ISBN 0-679-78342-3
I. Title.
PS3201   2000
811'.3—dc21   00-64572

Modern Library website address: www.modernlibrary.com

Printed in the United States of America

4 6 8 9 7 5

Walt Whitman

Walt Whitman was born on May 31, 1819, near Huntington, Long Island, New York. His father—a farmer turned carpenter from whom Whitman acquired his freethinking intellectual and political attitudes—moved his wife and nine children to Brooklyn in 1823. The young Whitman attended public schools until the age of eleven, when he was apprenticed to a printer. In 1835 he became a journeyman printer and spent the next decade working as a compositor, freelance writer, editor, and itinerant schoolteacher. But Whitman's fortunes changed in 1846 when he was named editor of the *Brooklyn Eagle*. However his "free soil" political beliefs cost him the editorship of the conservative paper two years later. Following his dismissal, Whitman traveled to New Orleans, where he was briefly editor of the New Orleans *Crescent*. Upon his return north in June 1848, he frequented the opera and museums, dabbled in politics, and immersed himself in the life of the streets. Although Whitman had earlier affected the mien of a dandy, he now dressed as a "rough" and became prominent among the bohemian element of New York. But the poems and stories he published in these years showed no hint of his future greatness.

The next five years (1850–1855), while outwardly undramatic, proved to be the most important period—intellectually and spiritually—in the life of Walt Whitman the poet. During this time he read avidly and kept a series of notebooks. Two novels by George Sand helped fix the direction of Whitman's thinking. One was *The Countess of Rudolstadt*, which featured a wandering bard and prophet who expounded the new religion of Humanity. The other was *The Journeyman Joiner*, the story of a proletarian philosopher who works as a carpenter with his father but also devotes time to reading, giving advice on art, and freely sharing the affection of friends. But of course it was Ralph Waldo Emerson's summons (in "The Poet") for a great American muse to step forward and celebrate the emerging nation that was pivotal to Whitman's future. On July 4, 1855, the first edition of *Leaves of Grass*, the volume of poems that for the next four decades would become his life's work, was placed on sale. Although some critics treated the volume as a joke and others were outraged by its unprecedented mixture of mysticism and earthiness, the book attracted the attention of some of the finest literary intelligences. "I greet you at the beginning of a great career," Emerson wrote to Whitman. "I find incomparable things said incomparably well."

The Civil War found Whitman working as an unofficial nurse to Northern and Southern soldiers in the army hospitals of Washington, D.C. His war poems appeared in *Drum-Taps* (1865) and were later incorporated into *Leaves of Grass*—as was "When Lilacs Last in the Dooryard Bloom'd," his elegy to the recently assassinated President Lincoln. After the war he became a clerk in the Indian Bureau of the Department of the Interior, from which he was shortly dismissed on the grounds that *Leaves of Grass* was an immoral book. (Whitman was soon reinstated in another government clerkship with the Department of Justice.) Despite such notoriety, his poetry slowly achieved a wide readership in America and in England, where he was praised by Swinburne and Tennyson. (D. H. Lawrence later referred to Whitman as the "greatest modern poet," and "the greatest of Americans.")

Whitman suffered a stroke in 1873 and was forced to retire to Camden, New Jersey, where he would spend the last twenty years of his life. There he continued to write poetry, and in 1881 the seventh edition of *Leaves of Grass* was published to generally favorable reviews. However, the book was soon banned in Boston on the grounds that it was "obscene literature." Whitman was in a precarious financial way in his remaining years, and such writers as Mark Twain, Henry James, and Robert Louis Stevenson contributed to his support. Rich admirers kept him supplied with oysters and champagne (he was fond of both). Whitman even received a visitation from Oscar Wilde, who later reported that "the good gray poet" made no effort to conceal his homosexuality from him. ("The kiss of Walt Whitman," Wilde said, "is still on my lips.")

In January 1892 the final "Death-bed Edition" of *Leaves of Grass* appeared on sale, and Whitman's life's work was complete. He died two months later on the evening of March 26, 1892, and was buried four days afterward at Harleigh Cemetery in Camden. "Most of the great poets are impersonal," Whitman once wrote of *Leaves of Grass.* "I am personal. . . . In my poems, all revolves around, concentrates in, radiates from myself. I have but one central figure, the general human personality typified in myself. But my book compels, absolutely necessitates, every reader to transpose himself or herself into the central position, and become the living fountain, actor, experiencer himself or herself, of every page, every aspiration, every line."

Contents

MEMORIES OF PRESIDENT LINCOLN

AUTUMN RIVULETS

WHISPERS OF HEAVENLY DEATH

FIRST ANNEX: SANDS AT SEVENTY

SECOND ANNEX: GOOD-BYE MY FANCY

Introduction

William Carlos Williams

Leaves of Grass! It was a good title for a book of poems, especially for a new book of American poems. It was a challenge to the entire concept of the poetic idea, and from a new viewpoint, a rebel viewpoint, an American viewpoint. In a word and at the beginning it enunciated a shocking truth, that the common ground is of itself a poetic source. There had been inklings before this that such was the case in the works of Robert Burns and the poet Wordsworth, but in this instance the very forms of the writing had been altered: it had gone over to the style of the words as they appeared on the page. Whitman's so-called "free verse" was an assault on the very citadel of the poem itself; it constituted a direct challenge to all living poets to show cause why they should not do likewise. It is a challenge that still holds good after a century of vigorous life during which it has been practically continuously under fire but never defeated.

From the beginning Whitman realized that the matter was largely technical. It had to be free verse or nothing with him and he seldom varied from that practice—and never for more than the writing of an occasional poem. It was a sharp break, and if he was to go astray he had no one but himself to blame for it. It was a technical matter, true enough, and he would stick it out to the end, but to do any more with it than simply to write the poems was beyond him.

He had seen a great light but forgot almost at once after the first revelation everything but his "message," the idea which originally set him in motion, the idea on which he had been nurtured, the idea of democracy—and took his eye off the words themselves which should have held him.

The point is purely academic—the man had his hands full with the conduct of his life and couldn't, if they had come up, be bothered with other matters. As a result, he made no further progress as an artist but, in spite of various topical achievements, continued to write with diminishing effectiveness for the remainder of his life.

He didn't know any better. He didn't have the training to construct his verses after a conscious mold which would have given him power over them to turn them this way, then that, at will. He only knew how to give them birth and to release them to go their own way. He was preoccupied with the great ideas of the time, to which he was devoted, but, after all, poems are made out of words not ideas. He never showed any evidence of knowing this and the unresolved forms consequent upon his beginnings remained in the end just as he left them.

Verses, in English, are frequently spoken of as measures. It is a fortunate designation as it gives us, in looking at them, the idea of elapsed time. We are reminded that the origin of our verse was the dance—and even if it had not been the dance, the heart when it is stirred has its multiple beats, and verse at its most impassioned sets the heart violently beating. But as the heart picks up we also begin to count. Finally, the measure for each language and environment is accepted. In English it is predominantly the iambic pentameter, but whether that is so for the language Whitman spoke is something else again. It is

a point worth considering, but apart from the briefest of
notices a point not to be considered here. It may be that
the essential pace of the English and the American lan-
guages is diametrically opposed each to the other and
that that is an important factor in the writing of their po-
etry, but that is for the coming generations to discover.
Certainly not only the words but the meter, the measure
that governed Whitman's verses, was not English. But
there were more pressing things than abstract discussions
of meter to be dealt with at that time and the poet soon
found himself involved in them.

Very likely the talk and the passionate talk about free-
dom had affected him as it had infected the French and
many others earlier. It is said that, when as a young man
he lived in New Orleans, he had fallen in love with a
beautiful octoroon but had allowed his friends and rela-
tives to break up the match. It is possible that the disap-
pointment determined the pattern of his later rebellion in
verse. Free verse was his great idea! *Versos sueltos* the
Spanish call them. It is not an entirely new idea, but it was
entirely new to the New York Yankee who was, so to
speak, waiting for it with open arms and an overcharged
soul and the example of Thomas Jefferson to drive him on.

But verse had always been, for Englishmen and the
colonials that imitated them, a disciplined maneuver of
the intelligence, as it is today, in which measure was pre-
dominant. They resented this American with his new
idea, and attacked him in a characteristic way—*on moral
grounds*. And he fell for it. He had no recourse but to de-
fend himself and the fat was in the fire. How could verse
be free without being immoral? There is something to it.
It is the same attack, with a more modern tilt to it, that un-

doubtedly bothers T. S. Eliot. He is one of the best in-
formed of our writers and would do us a great service, if
free verse—mold it as he will—is not his choice, to find us
an alternative. From the evidence, he has tried to come up
with just that, but up to the present writing he has not
brought the thing off.

The case of Mr. Eliot is in this respect interesting. He
began writing at Harvard from a thoroughly well-
schooled background and produced a body of verse that
was immediately so successful that when his poem *The
Waste Land* was published, it drove practically everyone
else from the field. Ezra Pound, who had helped him
arrange the poem on the page, was confessedly jealous.
Other American poets had to take second place. A new
era, under domination of a return to a study of the clas-
sics, was gratefully acknowledged by the universities,
and Mr. Eliot, not Mr. Pound, was ultimately given the
Nobel Prize. The drift was plainly away from all that was
native to America, Whitman among the rest, and toward
the study of the past and England.

Though no one realized it, a violent revolution had
taken place in American scholarship and the interests
from which it stemmed. Eliot had completely lost interest
in all things American, in the very ideology of all that
America stood for, including the idea of freedom itself in
any of its phases. Whitman as a symbol of indiscriminate
freedom was completely antipathetic to Mr. Eliot, who
now won the country away from him again. The ten-
dency toward freedom in the verse forms, which seemed
to be thriving among American poets, was definitely
checked and the stage was taken over for other things. I
shall never forget the impression created by *The Waste*

Land; it was as if the bottom had dropped out of everything. I had not known how much the spirit of Whitman animated us until it was withdrawn from us. Free verse became overnight a thing of the past. Men went about congratulating themselves as upon the disappearance of something that had disturbed their dreams; and indeed it was so—the dreams of right-thinking students of English verse had long been disturbed by the appearance among them of the horrid specter of Whitman's free verse. Now it was as if a liberator, a Saint George, had come just in the nick of time to save them. The instructors in all the secondary schools were grateful.

Meanwhile, Mr. Eliot had become a British subject and removed himself to England where he took up residence. He became a member of the Church of England. He was determined to make the break with America complete, as his fellow artist Henry James had done before him, and began to publish such poems as *Ash Wednesday* and the play *Murder in the Cathedral,* and the *Four Quartets.* Something had happened to him, something drastic, something to do, doubtless, with man's duty and his freedom in the world. It is a far cry from this to Whitman's thought of man as a free agent. The pendulum had gone the full swing.

It is inevitable for us to connect the happenings in the world generally with what takes place in the poem. When Mr. Eliot quit writing, when he quit writing poems, it looked as if he had got to a point where he had nowhere else to turn, and as if in his despair he had given up not only the poem but the world. A man as clever and well-informed as he was had the whole world at his feet, but the only conclusion that he reached was that he wanted none of it. Especially did he want none of the newer freedom.

Not that he didn't in his verse try it on, for size, let us say, in his later experiments, particularly in *Four Quartets*, but even there he soon came to the end of his rope. The accented strophe he had definitely given up, as Wagner in the prelude to *Parsifal* had done the same, but to infer from that fact that he had discovered the freedom of a new measure was not true. It looked to me, at least, as if there were some profound depth to his probing beyond which he dared not go without compromising his religious faith. He did not attempt it. It is useful to record the limits of his penetration and the point at which he gave up his attempts to penetrate further. Just how far shall we go in our search for freedom and, more importantly, how shall our efforts toward a greater freedom be conditioned in our verses? All these decisions, which must be reached in deciding what to do, have implications of general value in our lives.

The young men who are students of literature today in our universities do not believe in seeking within the literary forms, the lines, the foot, the way in which to expand their efforts to know the universe, as Whitman did, but are content to follow the theologians and Mr. Eliot. In that, they are children of the times; they risk nothing, for by risking an expanded freedom you are very likely to come a cropper. What, in the words of Hjalmar Ekdahl in *The Wild Duck,* are you going to invent?

Men, offering their heads, have always come up with new proposals, and the world of events waits upon them, and who shall say whether it were better to close one's eyes or go forward like Galileo to the light or wait content in the darkness like the man in the next county? Whitman went forward to what to him seemed desirable, and so if we are to reject him entirely we must at least follow him at the start to find out what his discoveries were intended to signify and what not to signify.

Certainly, we are in our day through with such loose freedom as he employed in his verses in the blind belief that it was all going to come out right in the end. We know now that it is not. But are we, because of that, to give up freedom entirely? Merely to put down the lines as they happen to come into your head will not make a poem, and if, as happened more than once in Whitman's case, a poem result, who is going to tell what he has made? The man knew what he was doing, but he did not know all he was doing. Much still remains to discover, but that freedom in the conduct of the verses is desirable cannot be questioned.

There is a very moving picture of Whitman facing the breakers coming in on the New Jersey shore, when he heard the onomatopoeic waves talk to him direct in a Shakespearean language which might have been Lear himself talking to the storm. But it was not what it seemed; it was a new language, an unnamed language which Whitman could not identify or control.

For as the English had foreseen, this freedom of which there had been so much talk had to have limits somewhere. If not, it would lead you astray. That was the problem. And there was at about that time a whole generation of Englishmen, prominent among whom was Frank Harris, whom it did lead astray in moral grounds, just as there were Frenchmen at the time of the French Revolution who were led astray and are still being led astray under the difficult conditions that exist today. It is the reaction against such patterns of thought that moved Eliot and that part of the present generation which is not swallowed up by its fascination with the scene which draws them to Paris whenever they get the opportunity to go there. For in your search for freedom—which is desirable—you must stop somewhere, but where exactly shall you stop? Whitman could not say.

To propose that the answer to the problem should lie in the verse itself would have been to those times an impertinence—and the same would be the case even now. The Greeks had their Dionysia in the spring of the year, when morals could be forgotten, and then the control of life resumed its normal course. In other words, they departmentalized their lives, being of an orderly cast of mind, but we do not lend ourselves easily to such a solution. With us it is all or nothing, provided we are not caught at it. Either we give ourselves to a course of action or we do not give ourselves. Either we are to be free men or not free men—at least in theory. Whitman, like Tom Paine, recognized no limits and that got him into trouble.

But the waves on the Jersey shore still came tumbling in, quieting him as their secret escaped him, isolating him and leaving him lonesome—but possessed by the great mystery which won the world to his side. For he was unquestionably the child of the years. What was the wave that moved the dawning century also moved him and demanded his recognition, and it was not to be denied. All the discoveries and inventions which were to make the twentieth century exceed all others, for better or worse, were implicit in his work. He surpassed the ritualistic centuries which preceded him, just as Ehrlich and Koch and finally Einstein were to exceed Goethe. It was destined to be so, and the New World of which he was a part gave him birth. He had invented a new way of assaulting fate. "Make new!" was to him as it was to Pound much later on an imperious command which completely controlled him.

If he was to enlarge his opportunity he needed room, in verse as in everything else. But there were to be no fundamental changes in the concepts that keep our lives going at an accepted pace and within normal limits. The line was still to be the line, quite in accord with the normal contours of our accepted verse forms. It is not so much that which brought Whitman's verse into question but the freedom with which he laid it on the page. There he had abandoned all sequence and all order. It was as if a tornado had struck.

A new order had hit the world, a relative order, a new measure with which no one was familiar. The thing that no one realized, and this includes Whitman himself, is that the native which they were dealing with was no longer English but a new language akin to the New World to which its nature accorded in subtle ways that they did not recognize. That made all the difference. And not only was it new to America—it was new to the world. There was to be a new measure applied to all things, for there was to be a new order operative in the world. But it has to be insisted on that it was not disorder. Whitman's verses seemed disorderly, but ran according to an unfamiliar and a difficult measure. It was an order which was essential to the new world, not only of the poem, but to the world of chemistry and physics. In this way, the man was more of a prophet than he knew. The full significance of his innovations in the verse patterns has not yet been fully disclosed.

The change in the entire aesthetic of American art as it began to differ not only from British but from all the art of the world up to this time was due to this tremendous change in measure, a relative measure, which he was the first to feel and to embody in his works. What he was leaving behind did not seem to oppress him, but it oppressed the others and rightly so.

It is time now to look at English and American verse at the time Whitman began to write, for only by so doing can we be led to discover what he did and the course that lay before him. He had many formidable rivals to face on his way to success. But his chief opponent was, as he well knew, the great and medieval Shakespeare. And if any confirmation of Shakespeare's sacrosanct position in the language is still sought it is easily to be obtained when anything is breathed mentioning some alteration in the verse forms which he distinguished by using them. He may be imitated as Christopher Fry imitates him, but to vary or depart from him is heresy. Taken from this viewpoint, the clinical sheets of Shakespeare as a writer are never much studied. That he was the greatest word-man that ever existed in the language or out of it is taken for granted but there the inquiry ends.

Shakespeare presented Whitman with a nut hard to crack. What to do with the English language? It was all the more of a problem since the elements of it could not be presented at all or even recognized to exist. As far as the English language was concerned, there was only to use it and to use it well according to the great tradition of the masters.

And indeed it was a magnificent tradition. At the beginning of the seventeenth century it had reached an apogee which it had, to a great extent, maintained to the present day and of which it was proud and jealous. But when Shakespeare wrote, the laurels were new and had so recently been attained and had come from such distinguished achievements that the world seemed to pause for breath. It was a sort of noon and called for a halt. The man himself seemed to feel it and during an entire lifetime did no more than develop to the full his talents. It was noon sure enough for him, and he had only to stretch out in the sun and expand his mood.

Unlike Whitman, he was or represented the culmination of a historic as well as literary past whose forms were just coming to a head after the great trials which were to leave their marks on the centuries. There had been Chaucer, but the language had come of age since then as had the country. Now America had been discovered and the world could not grow much larger. Further expansion, except in a limited degree, was unlikely, so that the poet was left free to develop his world of detail but was not called upon to extend it. More was not necessary than to find something to do and develop it for the entire span of a long life. But as always with the artist, selection was an important point in the development.

For instance, as his sonnets show, Shakespeare was an accomplished rhymer, but he gave it up early. The patches of heroic couplet which he wrote for the Players in *Hamlet* are among the best examples of that form. Yet his main reliance was on blank verse—though he did, on occasion, try his hand at a triple accent which he rejected without more than a thought. The demands of the age called for other things and he was, above everything else, a practical man.

Practicing for so long a time upon the iambic pentameter, he had the opportunity to develop himself prodigiously in it. Over the years he shows a technical advance, a certain impatience with restraint in his work which makes it loose and verges more toward the conformation of prose. There is a great difference between Shakespeare's earlier and later work, the latter being freer and more natural in tone.

A feeling for prose began to be felt all through his verse. But at his death the form began to lapse rapidly into the old restrictions. It got worse and worse with the years until all the Elizabethan tenor had been stripped away, or as Milton phrased it speaking of his illustrious predecessor:

> Sweetest Shakespeare, Nature's child,
> Warbled his native woodnotes wild.

With Milton came Cromwell and the English Revolution, and Shakespeare was forgotten, together with the secrets of his versification, just as Whitman today is likely to be forgotten and the example of his verses and all that refers to him.

The interest that drove Whitman on is the same one that drove Shakespeare at the end of his life in an attempt to enlarge the scope of written verse, to find more of expression in the forms of the language employed. But the consequences of such experimentation are always drastic and amount in the end to its suppression, which in the person of a supreme genius is not easy.

From what has been said thus far, you can see why it is impossible to imitate Shakespeare; he was part of a historic process which cannot repeat itself. All imitations of the forms of the past are meaningless, empty shells, which have merely the value of decorations. So that, if anything is now to be created, it must be in a new form. Whitman, if he was to do anything of moment, could not, no matter how much he may have bowed down to the master, imitate him. It would not have had any meaning at all. And his responsibility to the new language was such that he had no alternative but to do as it bade him.

Though he may not have known it, with Whitman the whole spirit of the age itself had been brought under attack. It was a blind stab which he could not identify any more than a child. How could he, no matter how acute his instincts were, have foreseen the discoveries in chemistry, in physics, in abnormal psychology, or even the invention of the telephone or the disclosure of our subterranean wealth in petroleum? He knew only, as did those who were disturbed by his free verse, that something had occurred to the normal structure of conventional aesthetic and that he could not accept it any longer. Therefore, he acted.

We have to acknowledge at once in seeking a meaning involving the complex concerns of the world that the philosophic, the aesthetic, and the mechanical are likely to stem in their development from the same root. One may be much in advance of the other in its discoveries, but in the end a great equalizing process is involved so that the discovery of the advance in the structure of the poetic line is equated by an advance in the conception of physical facts all along the line. Man has no choice in these matters; the only question is, will he recognize the changes that are taking place in time to make the proper use of them? And when time itself is conceived of as relative, no matter how abstruse that may sound, the constructions, the right constructions, cannot be accepted with a similar interpretation. It may take time to bring this about, but when a basic change has occurred in our underlying concern it brooks no interference in the way it will work itself out.

Whitman didn't know anything about this, nor does Mr. Eliot take it into his considerations nor Father Merton either, but if they had to construct a satisfactory poetic line it had and still has to be done according to this precept. For we have learned, if we have learned anything from the past, that the principles of physics are immutable. Best, if you do not approve of what writing has become, to follow in Mr. Eliot's footsteps.

For it is important to man's fate that these matters be—if anything is important to man's fate in this modern world. At least, you cannot retrace steps that have been taken in the past. And you don't know, you simply do not know, what may come of it. No more than Whitman knew what his struggle to free verse may have implied and may still imply for us no matter how, at the moment, the world may have forsaken him. The books are not closed even though the drift in the tide of our interest may at the moment be all the other way. It cannot so soon have reversed itself. Something is still pending, though the final shape of the thing has not yet crystallized. Perhaps that is the reason for the regression. There are too many profitable leads in other associated fields of the intelligence for us to draw back now.

Where have the leads which are *not* aesthetic tended to take us in the present century? By paying attention to detail and our telescopes and microscopes and the reinterpretations of their findings, we realize that man has long since broken from the confinement of the more rigid of his taboos. It is reasonable to suppose that he will in the future, in spite of certain setbacks, continue to follow the same course.

Man finds himself on the earth whether he likes it or not, with nowhere else to go. What then is to become of him? Obviously we can't stand still or we shall be destroyed. Then if there is no room for us on the outside we shall, in spite of ourselves, have to go *in:* into the cell, the atom, the poetic line, for our discoveries. We have to break the old apart to make room for ourselves, whatever may be our tragedy and however we may fear it. By making room within the line itself for his inventions, Whitman revealed himself to be a worthy and courageous man of his age and, to boot, a farseeing one.

LEAVES OF GRASS

Come, said my Soul,
Such verses for my Body let us write, (for we are one,)
That I should after death invisibly return,
Or, long, long hence, in other spheres,
There to some group of mates the chants resuming,
(Tallying Earth's soil, trees, winds, tumultuous waves,)
Ever with pleas'd smile I may keep on,
Ever and ever yet the verses owning—as, first, I here and now,
Signing for Body and Soul, set them to my name,

Walt Whitman

* INSCRIPTIONS.

ONE'S-SELF I SING.

One's-self I sing, a simple separate person,
Yet utter the word Democratic, the word En-Masse.

Of physiology from top to toe I sing,
Not physiognomy alone nor brain alone is worthy for the
    Muse, I say the Form complete is worthier far,
The Female equally with the Male I sing.

Of Life immense in passion, pulse, and power,
Cheerful, for freest action form'd under the laws divine,
The Modern Man I sing.

AS I PONDER'D IN SILENCE.

As I ponder'd in silence,
Returning upon my poems, considering, lingering long,
A Phantom arose before me with distrustful aspect,
Terrible in beauty, age, and power,
The genius of poets of old lands,
As to me directing like flame its eyes,
With finger pointing to many immortal songs,
And menacing voice, *What singest thou?* it said,

Know'st thou not there is but one theme for ever-enduring
      bards?
And that is the theme of War, the fortune of battles,
The making of perfect soldiers.

Be it so, then I answer'd,
I too haughty Shade also sing war, and a longer and greater one
      than any,
Waged in my book with varying fortune, with flight, advance
      and retreat, victory deferr'd and wavering,
(Yet methinks certain, or as good as certain, at the last,) the field
      the world,
For life and death, for the Body and for the eternal Soul,
Lo, I too am come, chanting the chant of battles,
I above all promote brave soldiers.

IN CABIN'D SHIPS AT SEA.

In cabin'd ships at sea,
The boundless blue on every side expanding,
With whistling winds and music of the waves, the large
      imperious waves,
Or some lone bark buoy'd on the dense marine,
Where joyous full of faith, spreading white sails,
She cleaves the ether mid the sparkle and the foam of day,
      or under many a star at night,
By sailors young and old haply will I, a reminiscence of
      the land, be read,
In full rapport at last.

Here are our thoughts, voyagers' thoughts,
Here not the land, firm land, alone appears, may then by them
    be said,
The sky o'erarches here, we feel the undulating deck beneath our
    feet,
We feel the long pulsation, ebb and flow of endless motion,
The tones of unseen mystery, the vague and vast suggestions
    of the briny world, the liquid-flowing syllables,
The perfume, the faint creaking of the cordage, the melancholy
    rhythm,
The boundless vista and the horizon far and dim are all here,
And this is ocean's poem.

Then falter not O book, fulfil your destiny,
You not a reminiscence of the land alone,
You too as a lone bark cleaving the ether, purpos'd I know
    not whither, yet ever full of faith,
Consort to every ship that sails, sail you!
Bear forth to them folded my love, (dear mariners, for you
    I fold it here in every leaf;)
Speed on my book! spread your white sails my little bark
    athwart the imperious waves,
Chant on, sail on, bear o'er the boundless blue from me
    to every sea,
This song for mariners and all their ships.

TO FOREIGN LANDS.

I heard that you ask'd for something to prove this puzzle
    the New World,
And to define America, her athletic Democracy,

Therefore I send you my poems that you behold in them
what you wanted.

TO A HISTORIAN.

You who celebrate bygones,
Who have explored the outward, the surfaces of the races,
the life that has exhibited itself,
Who have treated of man as the creature of politics, aggre-
gates, rulers and priests,
I, habitan of the Alleghanies, treating of him as he is in
himself in his own rights,
Pressing the pulse of the life that has seldom exhibited
itself, (the great pride of man in himself,)
Chanter of Personality, outlining what is yet to be,
I project the history of the future.

TO THEE OLD CAUSE.

To thee old cause!
Thou peerless, passionate, good cause,
Thou stern, remorseless, sweet idea,
Deathless throughout the ages, races, lands,
After a strange sad war, great war for thee,
(I think all war through time was really fought, and ever
will be really fought, for thee,)
These chants for thee, the eternal march of thee.

(A war O soldiers not for itself alone,
Far, far more stood silently waiting behind, now to
    advance in this book.)

Thou orb of many orbs!
Thou seething principle! thou well-kept, latent germ! thou
    centre!
Around the idea of thee the war revolving,
With all its angry and vehement play of causes,
(With vast results to come for thrice a thousand years,)
These recitatives for thee,—my book and the war are one,
Merged in its spirit I and mine, as the contest hinged on
    thee,
As a wheel on its axis turns, this book unwitting to itself,
Around the idea of thee.

EIDÓLONS.

    I met a seer,
Passing the hues and objects of the world,
The fields of art and learning, pleasure, sense,
    To glean eidólons.

    Put in thy chants said he,
No more the puzzling hour nor day, nor segments, parts,
    put in,
Put first before the rest as light for all and entrance-song
    of all,
    That of eidólons.

Ever the dim beginning,
Ever the growth, the rounding of the circle,
Ever the summit and the merge at last, (to surely start
     again,)
     Eidólons! eidólons!

Ever the mutable,
Ever materials, changing, crumbling, re-cohering,
Ever the ateliers, the factories divine,
     Issuing eidólons.

Lo, I or you,
Or woman, man, or state, known or unknown,
We seeming solid wealth, strength, beauty build,
     But really build eidólons.

The ostent evanescent,
The substance of an artist's mood or savan's studies long,
Or warrior's, martyr's, hero's toils,
     To fashion his eidólon.

Of every human life,
(The units gather'd, posted, not a thought, emotion, deed,
     left out,)
The whole or large or small summ'd, added up,
     In its eidólon.

The old, old urge,
Based on the ancient pinnacles, lo, newer, higher pinna-
     cles,
From science and the modern still impell'd,
     The old, old urge, eidólons.

The present now and here,
America's busy, teeming, intricate whirl,
Of aggregate and segregate for only thence releasing,
     To-day's eidólons.

These with the past,
Of vanish'd lands, of all the reigns of kings across the sea,
Old conquerors, old campaigns, old sailors' voyages,
     Joining eidólons.

. Densities, growth, façades,
Strata of mountains, soils, rocks, giant trees,
Far-born, far-dying, living long, to leave,
     Eidólons everlasting.

Exalté, rapt, ecstatic,
The visible but their womb of birth,
Of orbic tendencies to shape and shape and shape,
     The mighty earth-eidólon.

All space, all time,
(The stars, the terrible perturbations of the suns,
Swelling, collapsing, ending, serving their longer, shorter
     use,)
     Fill'd with eidólons only.

The noiseless myriads,
The infinite oceans where the rivers empty,
The separate countless free identities, like eyesight,
     The true realities, eidólons.

Not this the world,
Nor these the universes, they the universes,
Purport and end, ever the permanent life of life,
     Eidólons, eidólons.

Beyond thy lectures learn'd professor,
Beyond thy telescope or spectroscope observer keen,
     beyond all mathematics,
Beyond the doctor's surgery, anatomy, beyond the
     chemist with his chemistry,
     The entities of entities, eidólons.

Unfix'd yet fix'd,
Ever shall be, ever have been and are,
Sweeping the present to the infinite future,
     Eidólons, eidólons, eidólons.

The prophet and the bard,
Shall yet maintain themselves, in higher stages yet,
Shall mediate to the Modern, to Democracy, interpret yet
     to them,
     God and eidólons.

And thee my soul,
Joys, ceaseless exercises, exaltations,
Thy yearning amply fed at last, prepared to meet,
     Thy mates, eidólons.

Thy body permanent,
The body lurking there within thy body,
The only purport of the form thou art, the real I myself,
     An image, an eidólon.

Thy very songs not in thy songs,
No special strains to sing, none for itself,
But from the whole resulting, rising at last and floating,
   A round full-orb'd eidólon.

FOR HIM I SING.

For him I sing,
I raise the present on the past,
(As some perennial tree out of its roots, the present on the
      past,)
With time and space I him dilate and fuse the immortal
      laws,
To make himself by them the law unto himself.

WHEN I READ THE BOOK.

When I read the book, the biography famous,
And is this then (said I) what the author calls a man's life?
And so will some one when I am dead and gone write my
      life?
(As if any man really knew aught of my life,
Why even I myself I often think know little or nothing of
      my real life,
Only a few hints, a few diffused faint clews and indirec-
      tions
I seek for my own use to trace out here.)

BEGINNING MY STUDIES.

Beginning my studies the first step pleas'd me so much,
The mere fact consciousness, these forms, the power of
    motion,
The least insect or animal, the senses, eyesight, love,
The first step I say awed me and pleas'd me so much,
I have hardly gone and hardly wish'd to go any farther,
But stop and loiter all the time to sing it in ecstatic songs.

BEGINNERS.

How they are provided for upon the earth, (appearing at
    intervals,)
How dear and dreadful they are to the earth,
How they inure to themselves as much as to any—what
    a paradox appears their age,
How people respond to them, yet know them not,
How there is something relentless in their fate all times,
How all times mischoose the objects of their adulation
    and reward,
And how the same inexorable price must still be paid for
    the same great purchase.

TO THE STATES.

To the States or any one of them, or any city of the States,
    Resist much, obey little,

Once unquestioning obedience, once fully enslaved,
Once fully enslaved, no nation, state, city of this earth,
    ever afterward resumes its liberty.

ON JOURNEYS THROUGH THE STATES.

On journeys through the States we start,
(Ay through the world, urged by these songs,
Sailing henceforth to every land, to every sea,)
We willing learners of all, teachers of all, and lovers of all.

We have watch'd the seasons dispensing themselves and
        passing on,
And have said, Why should not a man or woman do as
    much as the seasons, and effuse as much?

We dwell a while in every city and town,
We pass through Kanada, the North-east, the vast valley
    of the Mississippi, and the Southern States,
We confer on equal terms with each of the States,
We make trial of ourselves and invite men and women to
    hear,
We say to ourselves, Remember, fear not, be candid, pro-
    mulge the body and the soul,
Dwell a while and pass on, be copious, temperate, chaste,
    magnetic,
And what you effuse may then return as the seasons
    return,
And may be just as much as the seasons.

TO A CERTAIN CANTATRICE.

Here, take this gift,
I was reserving it for some hero, speaker, or general,
One who should serve the good old cause, the great idea,
    the progress and freedom of the race,
Some brave confronter of despots, some daring rebel;
But I see that what I was reserving belongs to you just as
    much as to any.

ME IMPERTURBE.

Me imperturbe, standing at ease in Nature,
Master of all or mistress of all, aplomb in the midst of irra-
    tional things,
Imbued as they, passive, receptive, silent as they,
Finding my occupation, poverty, notoriety, foibles,
    crimes, less important than I thought,
Me toward the Mexican sea, or in the Mannahatta or the
    Tennessee, or far north or inland,
A river man, or a man of the woods or of any farm-life of
    these States or of the coast, or the lakes or Kanada,
Me wherever my life is lived, O to be self-balanced for
    contingencies,
To confront night, storms, hunger, ridicule, accidents,
    rebuffs, as the trees and animals do.

SAVANTISM.

Thither as I look I see each result and glory retracing itself
and nestling close, always obligated,
Thither hours, months, years—thither trades, compacts,
establishments, even the most minute,
Thither every-day life, speech, utensils, politics, persons,
estates;
Thither we also, I with my leaves and songs, trustful,
admirant,
As a father to his father going takes his children along
with him.

THE SHIP STARTING.

Lo, the unbounded sea,
On its breast a ship starting, spreading all sails, carrying
even her moonsails,
The pennant is flying aloft as she speeds she speeds so
stately below emulous waves press forward,
They surround the ship with shining curving motions
and foam.

I HEAR AMERICA SINGING.

I hear America singing, the varied carols I hear,
Those of mechanics, each one singing his as it should be
blithe and strong,
The carpenter singing his as he measures his plank or
beam,

The mason singing his as he makes ready for work, or
    leaves off work,
The boatman singing what belongs to him in his boat, the
    deckhand singing on the steamboat deck,
The shoemaker singing as he sits on his bench, the hatter
    singing as he stands,
The wood-cutter's song, the ploughboy's on his way in
    the morning, or at noon intermission or at sundown,
The delicious singing of the mother, or of the young wife
    at work, or of the girl sewing or washing,
Each singing what belongs to him or her and to none else,
The day what belongs to the day—at night the party of
    young fellows, robust, friendly,
Singing with open mouths their strong melodious songs.

WHAT PLACE IS BESIEGED?

What place is besieged, and vainly tries to raise the siege?
Lo, I send to that place a commander, swift, brave,
    immortal,
And with him horse and foot, and parks of artillery,
And artillery-men, the deadliest that ever fired gun.

STILL THOUGH THE ONE I SING.

Still though the one I sing,
(One, yet of contradictions made,) I dedicate to National-
    ity,
I leave in him revolt, (O latent right of insurrection! O
    quenchless, indispensable fire!)

SHUT NOT YOUR DOORS.

Shut not your doors to me proud libraries,
For that which was lacking on all your well-fill'd shelves,
    yet needed most, I bring,
Forth from the war emerging, a book I have made,
The words of my book nothing, the drift of it every thing,
A book separate, not link'd with the rest nor felt by the
    intellect,
But you ye untold latencies will thrill to every page.

POETS TO COME.

Poets to come! orators, singers, musicians to come!
Not to-day is to justify me and answer what I am for,
But you, a new brood, native, athletic, continental, greater
    than before known,
Arouse! for you must justify me.

I myself but write one or two indicative words for the
    future,
I but advance a moment only to wheel and hurry back in
    the darkness.

I am a man who, sauntering along without fully stopping,
    turns a casual look upon you and then averts his face,
Leaving it to you to prove and define it,
Expecting the main things from you.

TO YOU.

Stranger, if you passing meet me and desire to speak to
    me, why should you not speak to me?
And why should I not speak to you?

THOU READER.

Thou reader throbbest life and pride and love the same
    as I,
Therefore for thee the following chants.

*

STARTING FROM PAUMANOK.

1

Starting from fish-shape Paumanok where I was born,
Well-begotten, and rais'd by a perfect mother,
After roaming many lands, lover of populous pavements,
Dweller in Mannahatta my city, or on southern savannas,
Or a soldier camp'd or carrying my knapsack and gun, or
    a miner in California,
Or rude in my home in Dakota's woods, my diet meat,
    my drink from the spring,
Or withdrawn to muse and meditate in some deep recess,
Far from the clank of crowds intervals passing rapt and
    happy,

Aware of the fresh free giver the flowing Missouri, aware
    of mighty Niagara,
Aware of the buffalo herds grazing the plains, the hirsute
    and strong-breasted bull,
Of earth, rocks, Fifth-month flowers experienced, stars,
    rain, snow, my amaze,
Having studied the mocking-bird's tones and the flight
    of the mountain-hawk,
And heard at dawn the unrivall'd one, the hermit thrush
    from the swamp-cedars,
Solitary, singing in the West, I strike up for a New World.

2

Victory, union, faith, identity, time,
The indissoluble compacts, riches, mystery,
Eternal progress, the kosmos, and the modern reports.

This then is life,
Here is what has come to the surface after so many throes
    and convulsions.

How curious! how real!
Underfoot the divine soil, overhead the sun.

See revolving the globe,
The ancestor-continents away group'd together,
The present and future continents north and south, with
    the isthmus between.

See, vast trackless spaces,
As in a dream they change, they swiftly fill,

Countless masses debouch upon them,
They are now cover'd with the foremost people, arts,
      institutions, known.

See, projected through time,
For me an audience interminable.

With firm and regular step they wend, they never stop,
Successions of men, Americanos, a hundred millions,
One generation playing its part and passing on,
Another generation playing its part and passing on in its
      turn,
With faces turn'd sideways or backward towards me to
      listen,
With eyes retrospective towards me.

3

Americanos! conquerors! marches humanitarian!
Foremost! century marches! Libertad! masses!
For you a programme of chants.

Chants of the prairies,
Chants of the long-running Mississippi, and down to the
      Mexican sea,
Chants of Ohio, Indiana, Illinois, Iowa, Wisconsin and
      Minnesota,
Chants going forth from the centre from Kansas, and
      thence equidistant,
Shooting in pulses of fire ceaseless to vivify all.

4

Take my leaves America, take them South and take them
    North,
Make welcome for them everywhere, for they are your
    own offspring,
Surround them East and West, for they would surround
    you,
And you precedents, connect lovingly with them, for they
    connect lovingly with you.

I conn'd old times,
I sat studying at the feet of the great masters,
Now if eligible O that the great masters might return and
    study me.

In the name of these States shall I scorn the antique?
Why these are the children of the antique to justify it.

5

Dead poets, philosophs, priests,
Martyrs, artists, inventors, governments long since,
Language-shapers on other shores,
Nations once powerful, now reduced, withdrawn, or des-
    olate,
I dare not proceed till I respectfully credit what you have
    left wafted hither,
I have perused it, own it is admirable, (moving awhile
    among it,)
Think nothing can ever be greater, nothing can ever
    deserve more than it deserves,

Regarding it all intently a long while, then dismissing it,
I stand in my place with my own day here.

Here lands female and male,
Here the heir-ship and heiress-ship of the world, here the
    flame of materials,
Here spirituality the translatress, the openly-avow'd,
The ever-tending, the finale of visible forms,
The satisfier, after due long-waiting now advancing,
Yes here comes my mistress the soul.

6

The soul,
Forever and forever—longer than soil is brown and
    solid—longer than water ebbs and flows.

I will make the poems of materials, for I think they are to
    be the most spiritual poems,
And I will make the poems of my body and of mortality,
For I think I shall then supply myself with the poems of
    my soul and of immortality.

I will make a song for these States that no one State may
    under any circumstances be subjected to another
    State,
And I will make a song that there shall be comity by day
    and by night between all the States, and between any
    two of them,
And I will make a song for the ears of the President, full of
    weapons with menacing points,
And behind the weapons countless dissatisfied faces;

And a song make I of the One form'd out of all,
The·fang'd and glittering One whose head is over all,
Resolute warlike One including and over all,
(However high the head of any else that head is over all.)

I will acknowledge contemporary lands,
I will trail the whole geography of the globe and salute
     courteously every city large and small,
And employments! I will put in my poems that with you
     is heroism upon land and sea,
And I will report all heroism from an American point of
     view.

I will sing the song of companionship,
I will show what alone must finally compact these,
I believe these are to found their own ideal of manly love,
     indicating it in me,
I will therefore let flame from me the burning fires that
     were threatening to consume me,
I will lift what has too long kept down those smoulder-
     ing fires,
I will give them complete abandonment,
I will write the evangel-poem of comrades and of love,
For who but I should understand love with all its sorrow
     and joy?
And who but I should be the poet of comrades?

7

I am the credulous man of qualities, ages, races,
I advance from the people in their own spirit,
Here is what sings unrestricted faith.

Omnes! omnes! let others ignore what they may,
I make the poem of evil also, I commemorate that part
    also,
I am myself just as much evil as good, and my nation is—
    and I say there is in fact no evil,
(Or if there is I say it is just as important to you, to the
    land or to me, as any thing else.)

I too, following many and follow'd by many, inaugurate a
    religion, I descend into the arena,
(It may be I am destin'd to utter the loudest cries there, the
    winner's pealing shouts,
Who knows? they may rise from me yet, and soar above
    every thing.)

Each is not for its own sake,
I say the whole earth and all the stars in the sky are for
    religion's sake.

I say no man has ever yet been half devout enough,
None has ever yet adored or worship'd half enough,
None has begun to think how divine he himself is, and
    how certain the future is.

I say that the real and permanent grandeur of these States
    must be their religion,
Otherwise there is no real and permanent grandeur;
(Nor character nor life worthy the name without religion,
Nor land nor man or woman without religion.)

8

What are you doing young man?
Are you so earnest, so given up to literature, science, art,
    amours?
These ostensible realities, politics, points?
Your ambition or business whatever it may be?

It is well—against such I say not a word, I am their poet
    also,
But behold! such swiftly subside, burnt up for religion's
    sake,
For not all matter is fuel to heat, impalpable flame, the
    essential life of the earth,
Any more than such are to religion.

9

What do you seek so pensive and silent?
What do you need camerado?
Dear son do you think it is love?

Listen dear son—listen America, daughter or son,
It is a painful thing to love a man or woman to excess, and
    yet it satisfies, it is great,
But there is something else very great, it makes the whole
    coincide,
It, magnificent, beyond materials, with continuous hands
    sweeps and provides for all.

10

Know you, solely to drop in the earth the germs of a
    greater religion,
The following chants each for its kind I sing.

My comrade!
For you to share with me two greatnesses, and a third one
    rising inclusive and more resplendent,
The greatness of Love and Democracy, and the greatness
    of Religion.

Melange mine own, the unseen and the seen,
Mysterious ocean where the streams empty,
Prophetic spirit of materials shifting and flickering
    around me,
Living beings, identities now doubtless near us in the air
    that we know not of,
Contact daily and hourly that will not release me,
These selecting, these in hints demanded of me.

Not he with a daily kiss onward from childhood kissing
    me,
Has winded and twisted around me that which holds me
    to him,
Any more than I am held to the heavens and all the spiri-
    tual world,
After what they have done to me, suggesting themes.

O such themes—equalities! O divine average!
Warblings under the sun, usher'd as now, or at noon, or
    setting,

Strains musical flowing through ages, now reaching
  hither,
I take to your reckless and composite chords, add to them,
  and cheerfully pass them forward.

11

As I have walk'd in Alabama my morning walk,
I have seen where the she-bird the mocking-bird sat on
  her nest in the briers hatching her brood.

I have seen the he-bird also,
I have paus'd to hear him near at hand inflating his throat
  and joyfully singing.

And while I paus'd it came to me that what he really sang
  for was not there only,
Nor for his mate nor himself only, nor all sent back by the
  echoes,
But subtle, clandestine, away beyond,
A charge transmitted and gift occult for those being born.

12

Democracy! near at hand to you a throat is now inflating
  itself and joyfully singing.

Ma femme! for the brood beyond us and of us,
For those who belong here and those to come,
I exultant to be ready for them will now shake out carols
  stronger and haughtier than have ever yet been heard
  upon earth.

I will make the songs of passion to give them their way,
And your songs outlaw'd offenders, for I scan you with
    kindred eyes, and carry you with me the same as any.

I will make the true poem of riches,
To earn for the body and the mind whatever adheres and
    goes forward and is not dropt by death;
I will effuse egotism and show it underlying all, and I will
    be the bard of personality,
And I will show of male and female that either is but the
    equal of the other,
And sexual organs and acts! do you concentrate in me, for
    I am determin'd to tell you with courageous clear
    voice to prove you illustrious,
And I will show that there is no imperfection in the pre-
    sent, and can be none in the future,
And I will show that whatever happens to anybody it
    may be turn'd to beautiful results,
And I will show that nothing can happen more beautiful
    than death,
And I will thread a thread through my poems that time
    and events are compact,
And that all the things of the universe are perfect mira-
    cles, each as profound as any.

I will not make poems with reference to parts,
But I will make poems, songs, thoughts, with reference to
    ensemble,
And I will not sing with reference to a day, but with ref-
    erence to all days,
And I will not make a poem nor the least part of a poem
    but has reference to the soul,

Because having look'd at the objects of the universe, I find
    there is no one nor any particle of one but has refer-
    ence to the soul.

13

Was somebody asking to see the soul?
See, your own shape and countenance, persons, sub-
    stances, beasts, the trees, the running rivers, the rocks
    and sands.

All hold spiritual joys and afterwards loosen them;
How can the real body ever die and be buried?

Of your real body and any man's or woman's real body,
Item for item it will elude the hands of the corpse-cleaners
    and pass to fitting spheres,
Carrying what has accrued to it from the moment of birth
    to the moment of death.

Not the types set up by the printer return their impres-
    sion, the meaning, the main concern,
Any more than a man's substance and life or a woman's
    substance and life return in the body and the soul,
Indifferently before death and after death.

Behold, the body includes and is the meaning, the main
    concern, and includes and is the soul;
Whoever you are, how superb and how divine is your
    body, or any part of it!

14

Whoever you are, to you endless announcements!

Daughter of the lands did you wait for your poet?
Did you wait for one with a flowing mouth and indicative
    hand?
Toward the male of the States, and toward the female of
    the States,
Exulting words, words to Democracy's lands.

Interlink'd, food-yielding lands!
Land of coal and iron! land of gold! land of cotton, sugar,
    rice!
Land of wheat, beef, pork! land of wool and hemp! land of
    the apple and the grape!
Land of the pastoral plains, the grass-fields of the world!
    land of those sweet-air'd interminable plateaus!
Land of the herd, the garden, the healthy house of adobie!
Lands where the north-west Columbia winds, and where
    the south-west Colorado winds!
Land of the eastern Chesapeake! land of the Delaware!
Land of Ontario, Erie, Huron, Michigan!
Land of the Old Thirteen! Massachusetts land! land of
    Vermont and Connecticut!
Land of the ocean shores! land of sierras and peaks!
Land of boatmen and sailors! fishermen's land!
Inextricable lands! the clutch'd together! the passionate
    ones!
The side by side! the elder and younger brothers! the
    bony-limb'd!

The great women's land! the feminine! the experienced
 sisters and the inexperienced sisters!
Far breath'd land! Arctic braced! Mexican breez'd! the
 diverse! the compact!
The Pennsylvanian! the Virginian! the double Carolinian!
O all and each well-loved by me! my intrepid nations! O
 I at any rate include you all with perfect love!
I cannot be discharged from you! not from one any sooner
 than another!
O death! O for all that, I am yet of you unseen this hour
 with irrepressible love,
Walking New England, a friend, a traveler,
Splashing my bare feet in the edge of the summer ripples
 on Paumanok's sands,
Crossing the prairies, dwelling again in Chicago,
 dwelling in every town,
Observing shows, births, improvements, structures, arts,
Listening to orators and oratresses in public halls,
Of and through the States as during life, each man and
 woman my neighbor,
The Louisianian, the Georgian, as near to me, and I as
 near to him and her,
The Mississippian and Arkansian yet with me, and I yet
 with any of them,
Yet upon the plains west of the spinal river, yet in my
 house of adobie,
Yet returning eastward, yet in the Seaside State or in
 Maryland,
Yet Kanadian cheerily braving the winter, the snow and
 ice welcome to me,
Yet a true son either of Maine or of the Granite State, or
 the Narragansett Bay State, or the Empire State,

Yet sailing to other shores to annex the same, yet wel-
    coming every new brother,
Hereby applying these leaves to the new ones from the
    hour they unite with the old ones,
Coming among the new ones myself to be their compan-
    ion and equal, coming personally to you now,
Enjoining you to acts, characters, spectacles, with me.

15

With me with firm holding, yet haste, haste on.

For your life adhere to me,
(I may have to be persuaded many times before I consent
    to give myself really to you, but what of that?
Must not Nature be persuaded many times?)

No dainty dolce affettuoso I,
Bearded, sun-burnt, gray-neck'd, forbidding, I have
    arrived,
To be wrestled with as I pass for the solid prizes of the
    universe,
For such I afford whoever can persevere to win them.

16

On my way a moment I pause,
Here for you! and here for America!
Still the present I raise aloft, still the future of the States I
    harbinge glad and sublime,
And for the past I pronounce what the air holds of the red
    aborigines.

The red aborigines,
Leaving natural breaths, sounds of rain and winds, calls
  as of birds and animals in the woods, syllabled to us
  for names,
Okonee, Koosa, Ottawa, Monongahela, Sauk, Natchez,
  Chattahoochee, Kaqueta, Oronoco,
Wabash, Miami, Saginaw, Chippewa, Oshkosh, Walla-
  Walla,
Leaving such to the States they melt, they depart, charg-
  ing the water and the land with names.

17

Expanding and swift, henceforth,
Elements, breeds, adjustments, turbulent, quick and
  audacious,
A world primal again, vistas of glory incessant and
  branching,
A new race dominating previous ones and grander far,
  with new contests,
New politics, new literatures and religions, new inven-
  tions and arts.

These, my voice announcing—I will sleep no more but
  arise,
You oceans that have been calm within me! how I feel
  you, fathomless, stirring, preparing unprecedented
  waves and storms.

18

See, steamers steaming through my poems,

See, in my poems immigrants continually coming and
   landing,

See, in arriere, the wigwam, the trail, the hunter's hut, the
   flat-boat, the maize leaf, the claim, the rude fence, and
   the backwoods village,

See, on the one side the Western Sea and on the other the
   Eastern Sea, how they advance and retreat upon my
   poems as upon their own shores,

See, pastures and forests in my poems—see, animals wild
   and tame—see, beyond the Kaw, countless herds of
   buffalo feeding on short curly grass,

See, in my poems, cities, solid, vast, inland, with paved
   streets, with iron and stone edifices, ceaseless vehi-
   cles, and commerce,

See, the many-cylinder'd steam printing-press—see, the
   electric telegraph stretching across the continent,

See, through Atlantica's depths pulses American Europe
   reaching, pulses of Europe duly return'd,

See, the strong and quick locomotive as it departs, pant-
   ing, blowing the steam-whistle,

See, ploughmen ploughing farms—see, miners digging
   mines—see, the numberless factories,

See, mechanics busy at their benches with tools—see from
   among them superior judges, philosophs, Presidents,
   emerge, drest in working dresses,

See, lounging through the shops and fields of the States,
   me well-belov'd, close-held by day and night,

Hear the loud echoes of my songs there—read the hints
   come at last.

19

O camerado close! O you and me at last, and us two only.
O a word to clear one's path ahead endlessly!
O something ecstatic and undemonstrable! O music wild!
O now I triumph—and you shall also;
O hand in hand—O wholesome pleasure—O one more
    desirer and lover!
O to haste firm holding—to haste, haste on with me.

*

SONG OF MYSELF.

1

I celebrate myself, and sing myself,
And what I assume you shall assume
For every atom belonging to me as good belongs to you.

I loafe and invite my soul,
I lean and loafe at my ease observing a spear of summer
    grass.

My tongue, every atom of my blood, form'd from this
    soil, this air,
Born here of parents born here from parents the same,
    and their parents the same,
I, now thirty-seven years old in perfect health begin,
Hoping to cease not till death.

Creeds and schools in abeyance,
Retiring back a while suffic'd at what they are, but never
      forgotten,
I harbor for good or bad, I permit to speak at every haz-
      ard,
Nature without check with original energy.

2

Houses and rooms are full of perfumes, the shelves are
      crowded with perfumes,
I breathe the fragrance myself and know it and like it,
The distillation would intoxicate me also, but I shall not
      let it.

The atmosphere is not a perfume, it has no taste of the dis-
      tillation, it is odorless,
It is for my mouth forever, I am in love with it,
I will go to the bank by the wood and become undis-
      guised and naked,
I am mad for it to be in contact with me.
The smoke of my own breath,
Echoes, ripples, buzz'd whispers, love-root, silk-thread,
      crotch and vine,
My respiration and inspiration, the beating of my heart,
      the passing of blood and air through my lungs,
The sniff of green leaves and dry leaves, and of the shore
      and dark-color'd sea rocks, and of hay in the barn,
The sound of the belch'd words of my voice loos'd to the
      eddies of the wind,
A few light kisses, a few embraces, a reaching around of
      arms,

The play of shine and shade on the trees as the supple
    boughs wag,
The delight alone or in the rush of the streets, or along the
    fields and hill-sides,
The feeling of health, the full-noon trill, the song of me ris-
    ing from bed and meeting the sun.

Have you reckon'd a thousand acres much? have you
    reckon'd the earth much?
Have you practis'd so long to learn to read?
Have you felt so proud to get at the meaning of poems?

Stop this day and night with me and you shall possess the
    origin of all poems,
You shall possess the good of the earth and sun, (there are
    millions of suns left,)
You shall no longer take things at second or third hand,
    nor look through the eyes of the dead, nor feed on the
    spectres in books,
You shall not look through my eyes either, nor take things
    from me,
You shall listen to all sides and filter them from your self.

3

I have heard what the talkers were talking, the talk of the
    beginning and the end,
But I do not talk of the beginning or the end.

There was never any more inception than there is now,
Nor any more youth or age than there is now,

And will never be any more perfection than there is now,
Nor any more heaven or hell than there is now.

Urge and urge and urge,
Always the procreant urge of the world.
Out of the dimness opposite equals advance, always sub-
    stance and increase, always sex,
Always a knit of identity, always distinction, always a
    breed of life.

To elaborate is no avail, learn'd and unlearn'd feel that it
    is so.

Sure as the most certain sure, plumb in the uprights, well
    entretied, braced in the beams,
Stout as a horse, affectionate, haughty, electrical,
I and this mystery here we stand.

Clear and sweet is my soul, and clear and sweet is all that
    is not my soul.

Lack one lacks both, and the unseen is proved by the seen,
Till that becomes unseen and receives proof in its turn.

Showing the best and dividing it from the worst age vexes
    age,
Knowing the perfect fitness and equanimity of things,
    while they discuss I am silent, and go bathe and
    admire myself.

Welcome is every organ and attribute of me, and of any
    man hearty and clean,

Not an inch nor a particle of an inch is vile, and none shall
 be less familiar than the rest.

I am satisfied—I see, dance, laugh, sing;
As the hugging and loving bed-fellow sleeps at my side
 through the night, and withdraws at the peep of the
 day with stealthy tread,
Leaving me baskets cover'd with white towels swelling
 the house with their plenty,
Shall I postpone my acceptation and realization and
 scream at my eyes,
That they turn from gazing after and down the road,
And forthwith cipher and show me to a cent,
Exactly the value of one and exactly the value of two, and
 which is ahead?

4

Trippers and askers surround me,
People I meet, the effect upon me of my early life or the
 ward and city I live in, or the nation,
The latest dates, discoveries, inventions, societies, authors
 old and new,
My dinner, dress, associates, looks, compliments, dues,
The real or fancied indifference of some man or woman I
 love,
The sickness of one of my folks or of myself, or ill-doing
 or loss or lack of money, or depressions or exaltations,
Battles, the horrors of fratricidal war, the fever of doubtful
 news, the fitful events;
These come to me days and nights and go from me again,
But they are not the Me myself.

Apart from the pulling and hauling stands what I am,
Stands amused, complacent, compassionating, idle, unitary,
Looks down, is erect, or bends an arm on an impalpable certain rest,
Looking with side-curved head curious what will come next,
Both in and out of the game and watching and wondering at it.

Backward I see in my own days where I sweated through fog with linguists and contenders,
I have no mockings or arguments, I witness and wait.

5

I believe in you my soul, the other I am must not abase itself to you,
And you must not be abased to the other.

Loafe with me on the grass, loose the stop from your throat,
Not words, not music or rhyme I want, not custom or lecture, not even the best,
Only the lull I like, the hum of your valvéd voice.

I mind how once we lay such a transparent summer morning,
How you settled your head athwart my hips and gently turn'd over upon me,
And parted the shirt from my bosom-bone, and plunged your tongue to my bare-stript heart,

And reach'd till you felt my beard, and reach'd till you
    held my feet.

Swiftly arose and spread around me the peace and
    knowledge that pass all the argument of the earth,
And I know that the hand of God is the promise of my
    own,
And I know that the spirit of God is the brother of my
    own,
And that all the men ever born are also my brothers, and
    the women my sisters and lovers,
And that a kelson of the creation is love,
And limitless are leaves stiff or drooping in the fields,
And brown ants in the little wells beneath them,
And mossy scabs of the worm fence, heap'd stones, elder,
    mullein and poke-weed.

6

A child said *What is the grass?* fetching it to me with full
    hands;
How could I answer the child? I do not know what it is
    any more than he.

I guess it must be the flag of my disposition, out of hope-
    ful green stuff woven.

Or I guess it is the handkerchief of the Lord,
A scented gift and remembrancer designedly dropt,
Bearing the owner's name someway in the corners, that
    we may see and remark, and say *Whose?*

Or I guess the grass is itself a child, the produced babe of
    the vegetation.

Or I guess it is a uniform hieroglyphic,
And it means, Sprouting alike in broad zones and narrow
    zones,
Growing among black folks as among white,
Kanuck, Tuckahoe, Congressman, Cuff, I give them the
    same, I receive them the same.

And now it seems to me the beautiful uncut hair of
    graves.

Tenderly will I use you curling grass,
It may be you transpire from the breasts of young men,
It may be if I had known them I would have loved them,
It may be you are from old people, or from offspring
    taken soon out of their mothers' laps,
And here you are the mothers' laps.

This grass is very dark to be from the white heads of old
    mothers,
Darker than the colorless beards of old men,
Dark to come from under the faint red roofs of mouths.

O I perceive after all so many uttering tongues,
And I perceive they do not come from the roofs of mouths
    for nothing.

I wish I could translate the hints about the dead young
    men and women,

And the hints about old men and mothers, and the off-
spring taken soon out of their laps.

What do you think has become of the young and old
men?
And what do you think has become of the women and
children?

They are alive and well somewhere,
The smallest sprout shows there is really no death,
And if ever there was it led forward life, and does not
wait at the end to arrest it,
And ceas'd the moment life appear'd.

All goes onward and outward, nothing collapses,
And to die is different from what any one supposed, and
luckier.

7

Has any one supposed it lucky to be born?
I hasten to inform him or her it is just as lucky to die, and
I know it.

I pass death with the dying and birth with the new-
wash'd babe, and am not contain'd between my hat
and boots,
And peruse manifold objects, no two alike and every one
good,
The earth good and the stars good, and their adjuncts all
good.

I am not an earth nor an adjunct of an earth,
I am the mate and companion of people, all just as immor-
    tal and fathomless as myself,
(They do not know how immortal, but I know.)

Every kind for itself and its own, for me mine male and
    female,
For me those that have been boys and that love women,
For me the man that is proud and feels how it stings to be
    slighted,
For me the sweet-heart and the old maid, for me mothers
    and the mothers of mothers,
For me lips that have smiled, eyes that have shed tears,
For me children and the begetters of children.

Undrape! you are not guilty to me, nor stale nor dis-
    carded,
I see through the broadcloth and gingham whether or no,
And am around, tenacious, acquisitive, tireless, and can-
    not be shaken away.

8

The little one sleeps in its cradle,
I lift the gauze and look a long time, and silently brush
    away flies with my hand.

The youngster and the red-faced girl turn aside up the
    bushy hill,
I peeringly view them from the top.

The suicide sprawls on the bloody floor of the bedroom,
I witness the corpse with its dabbled hair, I note where the
    pistol has fallen.

The blab of the pave, tires of carts, sluff of boot-soles, talk
    of the promenaders,
The heavy omnibus, the driver with his interrogating
    thumb, the clank of the shod horses on the granite
    floor,
The snow-sleighs, clinking, shouted jokes, pelts of snow-
    balls,
The hurrahs for popular favorites, the fury of rous'd
    mobs,
The flap of the curtain'd litter, a sick man inside borne to
    the hospital,
The meeting of enemies, the sudden oath, the blows and
    fall,
The excited crowd, the policeman with his star quickly
    working his passage to the centre of the crowd,
The impassive stones that receive and return so many
    echoes,
What groans of over-fed or half-starv'd who fall sun-
    struck or in fits,
What exclamations of women taken suddenly who hurry
    home and give birth to babes,
What living and buried speech is always vibrating here,
    what howls restrain'd by decorum,
Arrests of criminals, slights, adulterous offers made,
    acceptances, rejections with convex lips,
I mind them or the show or resonance of them—I come
    and I depart.

9

The big doors of the country barn stand open and ready,
The dried grass of the harvest-time loads the slow-drawn
    wagon,
The clear light plays on the brown gray and green
    intertinged,
The armfuls are pack'd to the sagging mow.

I am there, I help, I came stretch'd atop of the load,
I felt its soft jolts, one leg reclined on the other,
I jump from the cross-beams and seize the clover and tim-
    othy,
And roll head over heels and tangle my hair full of wisps.

10

Alone far in the wilds and mountains I hunt,
Wandering amazed at my own lightness and glee,
In the late afternoon choosing a safe spot to pass the night,
Kindling a fire and broiling the fresh-kill'd game,
Falling asleep on the gather'd leaves with my dog and
    gun by my side.

The Yankee clipper is under her sky-sails, she cuts the
    sparkle and scud,
My eyes settle the land, I bend at her prow or shout joy-
    ously from the deck.

The boatmen and clam-diggers arose early and stopt for
    me,

I tuck'd my trouser-ends in my boots and went and had
    a good time;
You should have been with us that day round the chow-
    der-kettle.

I saw the marriage of the trapper in the open air in the far
    west, the bride was a red girl,
Her father and his friends sat near cross-legged and
    dumbly smoking, they had moccasins to their feet
    and large thick blankets hanging from their shoul-
    ders,
On a bank lounged the trapper, he was drest mostly in
    skins, his luxuriant beard and curls protected his
    neck, he held his bride by the hand,
She had long eyelashes, her head was bare, her coarse
    straight locks descended upon her voluptuous limbs
    and reach'd to her feet.

The runaway slave came to my house and stopt outside,
I heard his motions crackling the twigs of the woodpile,
Through the swung half-door of the kitchen I saw him
    limpsy and weak,
And went where he sat on a log and led him in and
    assured him,
And brought water and fill'd a tub for his sweated body
    and bruis'd feet,
And gave him a room that enter'd from my own, and
    gave him some coarse clean clothes,
And remember perfectly well his revolving eyes and his
    awkwardness,
And remember putting plasters on the galls of his neck
    and ankles;

He staid with me a week before he was recuperated and
    pass'd north,
I had him sit next me at table, my fire-lock lean'd in the
    corner.

11

Twenty-eight young men bathe by the shore,
Twenty-eight young men and all so friendly;
Twenty-eight years of womanly life and all so lonesome.

She owns the fine house by the rise of the bank,
She hides handsome and richly drest aft the blinds of the
    window.

Which of the young men does she like the best?
Ah the homeliest of them is beautiful to her.

Where are you off to, lady? for I see you,
You splash in the water there, yet stay stock still in your
    room.

Dancing and laughing along the beach came the twenty-
    ninth bather,
The rest did not see her, but she saw them and loved
    them.

The beards of the young men glisten'd with wet, it ran
    from their long hair,
Little streams pass'd all over their bodies.

An unseen hand also pass'd over their bodies,
It descended tremblingly from their temples and ribs.

The young men float on their backs, their white bellies
    bulge to the sun, they do not ask who seizes fast to
    them,
They do not know who puffs and declines with pendant
    and bending arch,
They do not think whom they souse with spray.

12

The butcher-boy puts off his killing-clothes, or sharpens
    his knife at the stall in the market,
I loiter enjoying his repartee and his shuffle and break-
    down.

Blacksmiths with grimed and hairy chests environ the
    anvil,
Each has his main-sledge, they are all out, there is a great
    heat in the fire.

From the cinder-strew'd threshold I follow their move-
    ments,
The lithe sheer of their waists plays even with their mas-
    sive arms,
Overhand the hammers swing, overhand so slow, over-
    hand so sure,
They do not hasten, each man hits in his place.

13

The negro holds firmly the reins of his four horses, the
    block swags underneath on its tied-over chain,
The negro that drives the long dray of the stone-yard,
    steady and tall he stands pois'd on one leg on the
    string-piece,
His blue shirt exposes his ample neck and breast and
    loosens over his hip-band,
His glance is calm and commanding, he tosses the slouch
    of his hat away from his forehead,
The sun falls on his crispy hair and mustache, falls on the
    black of his polish'd and perfect limbs.

I behold the picturesque giant and love him, and I do not
    stop there,
I go with the team also.

In me the caresser of life wherever moving, backward as
    well as forward sluing,
To niches aside and junior bending, not a person or object
    missing,
Absorbing all to myself and for this song.

Oxen that rattle the yoke and chain or halt in the leafy
    shade, what is that you express in your eyes?
It seems to me more than all the print I have read in my
    life.

My tread scares the wood-drake and wood-duck on my
    distant and day-long ramble,

They rise together, they slowly circle around.

I believe in those wing'd purposes,
And acknowledge red, yellow, white, playing within me,
And consider green and violet and the tufted crown
    intentional,
And do not call the tortoise unworthy because she is not
    something else,
And the jay in the woods never studied the gamut, yet
    trills pretty well to me,
And the look of the bay mare shames silliness out of me.

14

The wild gander leads his flock through the cool night,
Ya honk he says, and sounds it down to me like an invita-
    tion,
The pert may suppose it meaningless, but I listening close,
Find its purpose and place up there toward the wintry
    sky.

The sharp-hoof'd moose of the north, the cat on the
    house-sill, the chickadee, the prairie-dog,
The litter of the grunting sow as they tug at her teats,
The brood of the turkey-hen and she with her half-spread
    wings,
I see in them and myself the same old law.

The press of my foot to the earth springs a hundred affec-
    tions,
They scorn the best I can do to relate them.

I am enamour'd of growing out-doors,
Of men that live among cattle or taste of the ocean or
    woods,
Of the builders and steerers of ships and the wielders of
    axes and mauls, and the drivers of horses,
I can eat and sleep with them week in and week out.

What is commonest, cheapest, nearest, easiest, is Me,
Me going in for my chances, spending for vast returns,
Adorning myself to bestow myself on the first that will
    take me,
Not asking the sky to come down to my good will,
Scattering it freely forever.

15

The pure contralto sings in the organ loft,
The carpenter dresses his plank, the tongue of his fore-
    plane whistles its wild ascending lisp,
The married and unmarried children ride home to their
    Thanksgiving dinner,
The pilot seizes the king-pin, he heaves down with a
    strong arm,
The mate stands braced in the whale-boat, lance and har-
    poon are ready,
The duck-shooter walks by silent and cautious stretches,
The deacons are ordain'd with cross'd hands at the altar,
The spinning-girl retreats and advances to the hum of the
    big wheel,
The farmer stops by the bars as he walks on a First-day
    loafe and looks at the oats and rye,

The lunatic is carried at last to the asylum a confirm'd
  case,
(He will never sleep any more as he did in the cot in his
  mother's bed-room;)
The jour printer with gray head and gaunt jaws works at
  his case,
He turns his quid of tobacco while his eyes blurr with the
  manuscript;
The malform'd limbs are tied to the surgeon's table,
What is removed drops horribly in a pail;
The quadroon girl is sold at the auction-stand, the drunk-
  ard nods by the bar-room stove,
The machinist rolls up his sleeves, the policeman travels
  his beat, the gate-keeper marks who pass,
The young fellow drives the express-wagon, (I love him,
  though I do not know him;)
The half-breed straps on his light boots to compete in the
  race,
The western turkey-shooting draws old and young, some
  lean on their rifles, some sit on logs,
Out from the crowds steps the marksman, takes his posi-
  tion, levels his piece;
The groups of newly-come immigrants cover the wharf or
  levee,
As the woolly-pates hoe in the sugar-field, the overseer
  views them from his saddle,
The bugle calls in the ball-room, the gentlemen run for
  their partners, the dancers bow to each other,
The youth lies awake in the cedar-roof'd garret and harks
  to the musical rain,
The Wolverine sets traps on the creek that helps fill the
  Huron,

The squaw wrapt in her yellow-hemm'd cloth is offering
     moccasins and bead-bags for sale,
The connoisseur peers along the exhibition-gallery with
     half-shut eyes bent sideways,
As the deck-hands makes fast the steamboat the plank is
     thrown for the shore-going passengers,
The young sister holds out the skein while the elder sis-
     ter winds it off in a ball, and stops now and then for
     the knots,
The one-year wife is recovering and happy having a week
     ago borne her first child,
The clean-hair'd Yankee girl works with her sewing-
     machine or in the factory or mill,
The paving-man leans on his two-handed rammer, the
     reporter's lead flies swiftly over the note-book, the
     sign-painter is lettering with blue and gold,
The canal boy trots on the tow-path, the book-keeper
     counts at his desk, the shoemaker waxes his thread,
The conductor beats time for the band and all the per-
     formers follow him,
The child is baptized, the convert is making his first pro-
     fessions,
The regatta is spread on the bay, the race is begun, (how
     the white sails sparkle!)
The drover watching his drove sings out to them that
     would stray,
The pedler sweats with his pack on his back (the pur-
     chaser higgling about the odd cent;)
The bride unrumples her white dress, the minute-hand of
     the clock moves slowly,
The opium-eater reclines with rigid head and just open'd
     lips,

The prostitute draggles her shawl, her bonnet bobs on her
    tipsy and pimpled neck,
The crowd laugh at her blackguard oaths, the men jeer
    and wink to each other,
(Miserable! I do not laugh at your oaths nor jeer you;)
The President holding a cabinet council is surrounded by
    the great Secretaries,
On the piazza walk three matrons stately and friendly
    with twined arms,
The crew of the fish-smack pack repeated layers of halibut
    in the hold,
The Missourian crosses the plains toting his wares and his
    cattle,
As the fare-collector goes through the train he gives notice
    by the jingling of loose change,
The floor-men are laying the floor, the tinners are tinning
    the roof, the masons are calling for mortar,
In single file each shouldering his hod pass onward the
    laborers;
Seasons pursuing each other the indescribable crowd is
    gather'd, it is the fourth of Seventh-month, (what
    salutes of cannon and small arms!)
Seasons pursuing each other the plougher ploughs, the
    mower mows, and the winter-grain falls in the
    ground;
Off on the lakes the pike-fisher watches and waits by the
    hole in the frozen surface,
The stumps stand thick round the clearing, the squatter
    strikes deep with his axe,
Flatboatmen make fast towards dusk near the cotton-
    wood or pecan-trees,
Coon-seekers go through the regions of the Red river or

through those drain'd by the Tennessee, or through
those of the Arkansas,

Torches shine in the dark that hangs on the Chatta-
hoochee or Altamahaw,

Patriarchs sit at supper with sons and grandsons and
great-grandsons around them,

In walls of adobie, in canvas tents, rest hunters and trap-
pers after their day's sport,

The city sleeps and the country sleeps,

The living sleep for their time, the dead sleep for their
time,

The old husband sleeps by his wife and the young hus-
band sleeps by his wife;

And these tend inward to me, and I tend outward to them,

And such as it is to be of these more or less I am,

And of these one and all I weave the song of myself.

16

I am of old and young, of the foolish as much as the wise,

Regardless of others, ever regardful of others,

Maternal as well as paternal, a child as well as a man,

Stuff'd with the stuff that is coarse and stuff'd with the
stuff that is fine,

One of the Nation of many nations, the smallest the same
and the largest the same,

A Southerner soon as a Northerner, a planter nonchalant
and hospitable down by the Oconee I live,

A Yankee bound my own way ready for trade, my joints
the limberest joints on earth and the sternest joints on
earth,

A Kentuckian walking the vale of the Elkhorn in my deer-
      skin leggings, a Louisianian or Georgian,
A boatman over lakes or bays or along coasts, a Hoosier,
      Badger, Buckeye;
At home on Kanadian snow-shoes or up in the bush, or
      with fishermen off Newfoundland,
At home in the fleet of ice-boats, sailing with the rest and
      tacking,
At home on the hills of Vermont or in the woods of
      Maine, or the Texan ranch,
Comrade of Californians, comrade of free North-West-
      erners, (loving their big proportions,)
Comrade of raftsmen and coalmen, comrade of all who
      shake hands and welcome to drink and meat,
A learner with the simplest, a teacher of the thought-
      fullest,
A novice beginning yet experient of myriads of seasons,
Of every hue and caste am I, of every rank and religion,
A farmer, mechanic, artist, gentleman, sailor, quaker,
Prisoner, fancy-man, rowdy, lawyer, physician, priest.

I resist any thing better than my own diversity,
Breathe the air but leave plenty after me,
And am not stuck up, and am in my place.

(The moth and the fish-eggs are in their place,
The bright suns I see and the dark suns I cannot see are
      in their place,
The palpable is in its place and the impalpable is in its
      place.)

17

These are really the thoughts of all men in all ages and
    lands, they are not original with me,
If they are not yours as much as mine they are nothing,
    or next to nothing,
If they are not the riddle and the untying of the riddle
    they are nothing,
If they are not just as close as they are distant they are
    nothing.

This is the grass that grows wherever the land is and the
    water is,
This the common air that bathes the globe.

18

With music strong I come, with my cornets and my
    drums,
I play not marches for accepted victors only, I play
    marches for conquer'd and slain persons.

Have you heard that it was good to gain the day?
I also say it is good to fall, battles are lost in the same spirit
    in which they are won.

I beat and pound for the dead,
I blow through my embouchures my loudest and gayest
    for them.

Vivas to those who have fail'd!
And to those whose war-vessels sank in the sea!
And to those themselves who sank in the sea!
And to all generals that lost engagements, and all over-
come heroes!
And the numberless unknown heroes equal to the great-
est heroes known!

19

This is the meal equally set, this the meat for natural
hunger,
It is for the wicked just the same as the righteous, I make
appointments with all,
I will not have a single person slighted or left away,
The kept-woman, sponger, thief, are hereby invited;
The heavy-lipp'd slave is invited, the venerealee is
invited;
There shall be no difference between them and the rest.

This is the press of a bashful hand, this the float and odor
of hair,
This the touch of my lips to yours, this the murmur of
yearning,
This the far-off depth and height reflecting my own face,
This the thoughtful merge of myself, and the outlet again.

Do you guess I have some intricate purpose?
Well I have, for the Fourth month showers have, and the
mica on the side of a rock has.

Do you take it I would astonish?
Does the daylight astonish? does the early redstart twit-
    tering through the woods?
Do I astonish more than they?

This hour I tell things in confidence,
I might not tell everybody, but I will tell you.

20

Who goes there? hankering, gross, mystical, nude;
How is it I extract strength from the beef I eat?

What is a man anyhow? what am I? what are you?

All I mark as my own you shall offset it with your own,
Else it were time lost listening to me.

I do not snivel that snivel the world over,
That months are vacuums and the ground but wallow
    and filth.

Whimpering and truckling fold with powders for
    invalids, conformity goes to the fourth-remov'd,
I wear my hat as I please indoors or out.

Why should I pray? why should I venerate and be cere-
    monious?

Having pried through the strata, analyzed to a hair, coun-
    sel'd with doctors and calculated close,
I find no sweeter fat than sticks to my own bones.

In all people I see myself, none more and not one a barley-
     corn less,
And the good or bad I say of myself I say of them.

I know I am solid and sound,
To me the converging objects of the universe perpetually
     flow,
All are written to me, and I must get what the writing
     means.

I know I am deathless,
I know this orbit of mine cannot be swept by a carpenter's
     compass,
I know I shall not pass like a child's carlacue cut with a
     burnt stick at night.

I know I am august,
I do not trouble my spirit to vindicate itself or be under-
     stood,
I see that the elementary laws never apologize,
(I reckon I behave no prouder than the level I plant my
     house by, after all.)

I exist as I am, that is enough,
If no other in the world be aware I sit content,
And if each and all be aware I sit content.

One world is aware and by far the largest to me, and that
     is myself,
And whether I come to my own to-day or in ten thousand
     or ten million years,

I can cheerfully take it now, or with equal cheerfulness I
    can wait.

My foothold is tenon'd and mortis'd in granite,
I laugh at what you call dissolution,
And I know the amplitude of time.

21

I am the poet of the Body and I am the poet of the Soul,
The pleasures of heaven are with me and the pains of hell
    are with me,
The first I graft and increase upon myself, the latter I
    translate into a new tongue.

I am the poet of the woman the same as the man,
And I say it is as great to be a woman as to be a man,
And I say there is nothing greater than the mother of men.

I chant the chant of dilation or pride,
We have had ducking and deprecating about enough,
I show that size is only development.

Have you outstript the rest? are you the President?
It is a trifle, they will more than arrive there every one,
    and still pass on.

I am he that walks with the tender and growing night,
I call to the earth and sea half-held by the night.

Press close bare-bosom'd night—press close magnetic
    nourishing night!

Night of south winds—night of the large few stars!
Still nodding night—mad naked summer night.

Smile O voluptuous cool-breath'd earth!
Earth of the slumbering and liquid trees!
Earth of departed sunset—earth of the mountains misty-
    topt!
Earth of the vitreous pour of the full moon just tinged
    with blue!
Earth of shine and dark mottling the tide of the river!
Earth of the limpid gray of clouds brighter and clearer for
    my sake!
Far-swooping elbow'd earth—rich apple-blossom'd earth!
Smile, for your lover comes.

Prodigal, you have given me love—therefore I to you give
    love!
O unspeakable passionate love.

22

You sea! I resign myself to you also—I guess what you
    mean,
I behold from the beach your crooked inviting fingers,
I believe you refuse to go back without feeling of me,
We must have a turn together, I undress, hurry me out of
    sight of the land,
Cushion me soft, rock me in billowy drowse,
Dash me with amorous wet, I can repay you.

Sea of stretch'd ground-swells,
Sea breathing broad and convulsive breaths,

Sea of the brine of life and of unshovell'd yet always-
     ready graves,
Howler and scooper of storms, capricious and dainty sea,
I am integral with you, I too am of one phase and of all
     phases.

Partaker of influx and efflux I, extoller of hate and concil-
     iation,
Extoller of amies and those that sleep in each others'
     arms.

I am he attesting sympathy,
(Shall I make my list of things in the house and skip the
     house that supports them?)

I am not the poet of goodness only, I do not decline to be
     the poet of wickedness also.

What blurt is this about virtue and about vice?
Evil propels me and reform of evil propels me, I stand
     indifferent,
My gait is no fault-finder's or rejecter's gait,
I moisten the roots of all that has grown.

Did you fear some scrofula out of the unflagging preg-
     nancy?
Did you guess the celestial laws are yet to be work'd over
     and rectified?

I find one side a balance and the antipodal side a balance,
Soft doctrine as steady help as stable doctrine,

Thoughts and deeds of the present our rouse and early
    start.

This minute that comes to me over the past decillions,
There is no better than it and now.

What behaved well in the past or behaves well to-day is
    not such a wonder,
The wonder is always and always how there can be a
    mean man or an infidel.

23

Endless unfolding of words of ages!
And mine a word of the modern, the word En-Masse.

A word of the faith that never balks,
Here or henceforward it is all the same to me, I accept
    Time absolutely.

It alone is without flaw, it alone rounds and completes all,
That mystic baffling wonder alone completes all.

I accept Reality and dare not question it,
Materialism first and last imbuing.

Hurrah for positive science! long live exact demonstra-
    tion!
Fetch stonecrop mixt with cedar and branches of lilac,
This is the lexicographer, this the chemist, this made a
    grammar of the old cartouches,

These mariners put the ship through dangerous unknown
    seas.
This is the geologist, this works with the scalpel, and this
    is a mathematician.

Gentlemen, to you the first honors always!
Your facts are useful, and yet they are not my dwelling,
I but enter by them to an area of my dwelling.

Less the reminders of properties told my words,
And more the reminders they of life untold, and of free-
    dom and extrication,
And make short account of neuters and geldings, and
    favor men and women fully equipt,
And beat the gong of revolt, and stop with fugitives and
    them that plot and conspire.

24

Walt Whitman, a kosmos, of Manhattan the son,
Turbulent, fleshy, sensual, eating, drinking and breeding,
No sentimentalist, no stander above men and women or
    apart from them,
No more modest than immodest.

Unscrew the locks from the doors!
Unscrew the doors themselves from their jambs!

Whoever degrades another degrades me,
And whatever is done or said returns at last to me.

Through me the afflatus surging and surging, through me
    the current and index.

I speak the pass-word primeval, I give the sign of democ-
    racy,
By God! I will accept nothing which all cannot have their
    counter-part of on the same terms.

Through me many long dumb voices,
Voices of the interminable generations of prisoners and
    slaves,
Voices of the diseas'd and despairing and of thieves and
    dwarfs,
Voices of cycles of preparation and accretion,
And of the threads that connect the stars, and of wombs
    and of the father-stuff,
And of the rights of them the others are down upon,
Of the deform'd, trivial, flat, foolish, despised,
Fog in the air, beetles rolling balls of dung.

Through me forbidden voices,
Voices of sexes and lusts, voices veil'd and I remove the
    veil,
Voices indecent by me clarified and transfigur'd.

I do not press my fingers across my mouth,
I keep as delicate around the bowels as around the head
    and heart,
Copulation is no more rank to me than death is.

I believe in the flesh and the appetites,

Seeing, hearing, feeling, are miracles, and each part and
　　tag of me is a miracle.

Divine am I inside and out, and I make holy whatever I
　　touch or am touch'd from,
The scent of these arm-pits aroma finer than prayer,
This head more than churches, bibles, and all the creeds.

If I worship one thing more than another it shall be the
　　spread of my own body, or any part of it,
Translucent mould of me it shall be you!
Shaded ledges and rests it shall be you!
Firm masculine colter it shall be you!
Whatever goes to the tilth of me it shall be you!
You my rich blood! your milky stream pale strippings of
　　my life!
Breast that presses against other breasts it shall be you!
My brain it shall be your occult convolutions!
Root of wash'd sweet-flag! timorous pond-snipe! nest of
　　guarded duplicate eggs! it shall be you!
Mix'd tussled hay of head, beard, brawn, it shall be you!
Trickling sap of maple, fibre of manly wheat, it shall be
　　you!
Sun so generous it shall be you!
Vapors lighting and shading my face it shall be you!
You sweaty brooks and dews it shall be you!
Winds whose soft-tickling genitals rub against me it shall
　　be you!
Broad muscular fields, branches of live oak, loving
　　lounger in my winding paths, it shall be you!

Hands I have taken, face I have kiss'd, mortal I have ever
    touch'd, it shall be you.

I dote on myself, there is that lot of me and all so luscious,
Each moment and whatever happens thrills me with joy,
I cannot tell how my ankles bend, nor whence the cause of
    my faintest wish,
Nor the cause of the friendship I emit, nor the cause of the
    friendship I take again.

That I walk up my stoop, I pause to consider if it really be,
A morning-glory at my window satisfies me more than
    the metaphysics of books.

To behold the day-break!
The little light fades the immense and diaphanous shad-
    ows,
The air tastes good to my palate.

Hefts of the moving world at innocent gambols silently
    rising, freshly exuding,
Scooting obliquely high and low.

Something I cannot see puts upward libidinous prongs,
Seas of bright juice suffuse heaven.

The earth by the sky staid with, the daily close of their
    junction,
The heav'd challenge from the east that moment over my
    head,
The mocking taunt, See then whether you shall be master!

25

Dazzling and tremendous how quick the sun-rise would
    kill me,
If I could not now and always send sun-rise out of me.

We also ascend dazzling and tremendous as the sun,
We found our own O my soul in the calm and cool of the
    day-break.

My voice goes after what my eyes cannot reach,
With the twirl of my tongue I encompass worlds and vol-
    umes of worlds.

Speech is the twin of my vision, it is unequal to measure
    itself,
It provokes me forever, it says sarcastically,
Walt you contain enough, why don't you let it out then?

Come now I will not be tantalized, you conceive too much
    of articulation,
Do you not know O speech how the buds beneath you are
    folded?
Waiting in gloom, protected by frost,
The dirt receding before my prophetical screams,
I underlying causes to balance them at last,
My knowledge my live parts, it keeping tally with the
    meaning of all things,
Happiness, (which whoever hears me let him or her set
    out in search of this day.)

My final merit I refuse you, I refuse putting from me what
    I really am,
Encompass worlds, but never try to encompass me,
I crowd your sleekest and best by simply looking toward
    you.

Writing and talk do not prove me,
I carry the plenum of proof and every thing else in my
    face,
With the hush of my lips I wholly confound the skeptic.

26

Now I will do nothing but listen,
To accrue what I hear into this song, to let sounds con-
    tribute toward it.

I hear bravuras of birds, bustle of growing wheat, gossip
    of flames, clack of sticks cooking my meals,
I hear the sound I love, the sound of the human voice,
I hear all sounds running together, combined, fused or
    following,
Sounds of the city and sounds out of the city, sounds of
    the day and night,
Talkative young ones to those that like them, the loud
    laugh of work-people at their meals,
The angry base of disjointed friendship, the faint tones of
    the sick,
The judge with hands tight to the desk, his pallid lips pro-
    nouncing a death-sentence,
The heave'e'yo of stevedores unlading ships by the
    wharves, the refrain of the anchor lifters,

The ring of alarm-bells, the cry of fire, the whirr of swift-
    streaking engines and hose-carts with premonitory
    tinkles and color'd lights,
The steam-whistle, the solid roll of the train of approach-
    ing cars,
The slow march play'd at the head of the association
    marching two and two,
(They go to guard some corpse, the flag-tops are draped
    with black muslin.)

I hear the violoncello, ('tis the young man's heart's com-
    plaint,)
I hear the key'd cornet, it glides quickly in through my
    ears,
It shakes mad-sweet pangs through my belly and breast.

I hear the chorus, it is a grand opera,
Ah this indeed is music—this suits me.

A tenor large and fresh as the creation fills me,
The orbic flex of his mouth is pouring and filling me full.

I hear the train'd soprano (what work with hers is this?)
The orchestra whirls me wider than Uranus flies,
It wrenches such ardors from me I did not know I pos-
    sess'd them,
It sails me, I dab with bare feet, they are lick'd by the indo-
    lent waves,
I am cut by bitter and angry hail, I lose my breath,
Steep'd amid honey'd morphine, my windpipe throttled
    in fakes of death,

At length let up again to feel the puzzle of puzzles,
And that we call Being.

27

To be in any form, what is that?
(Round and round we go, all of us, and ever come back
    thither,)
If nothing lay more develop'd the quahaug in its callous
    shell were enough.

Mine is no callous shell,
I have instant conductors all over me whether I pass or
    stop,
They seize every object and lead it harmlessly through
    me.

I merely stir, press, feel with my fingers, and am happy,
To touch my person to some one else's is about as much
    as I can stand.

28

Is this then a touch? quivering me to a new identity,
Flames and ether making a rush for my veins,
Treacherous tip of me reaching and crowding to help
    them,
My flesh and blood playing out lightning to strike what
    is hardly different from myself,
On all sides prurient provokers stiffening my limbs,
Straining the udder of my heart for its withheld drip,
Behaving licentious toward me, taking no denial,

Depriving me of my best as for a purpose,
Unbuttoning my clothes, holding me by the bare waist,
Deluding my confusion with the calm of the sunlight and
    pasture-fields,
Immodestly sliding the fellow-senses away,
They bribed to swap off with touch and go and graze at
    the edges of me,
No consideration, no regard for my draining strength or
    my anger,
Fetching the rest of the herd around to enjoy them a
    while,
Then all uniting to stand on a headland and worry me.

The sentries desert every other part of me,
They have left me helpless to a red marauder,
They all come to the headland to witness and assist
    against me.

I am given up by traitors,
I talk wildly, I have lost my wits, I and nobody else am the
    greatest traitor,
I went myself first to the headland, my own hands carried
    me there.

You villain touch! what are you doing? my breath is tight
    in its throat,
Unclench your floodgates, you are too much for me.

29

Blind loving wrestling touch, sheath'd hooded sharp-
    tooth'd touch!
Did it make you ache so, leaving me?

Parting track'd by arriving, perpetual payment of perpet-
    ual loan,
Rich showering rain, and recompense richer afterward.

Sprouts take and accumulate, stand by the curb prolific
    and vital,
Landscapes projected masculine, full-sized and golden.

30

All truths wait in all things,
They neither hasten their own delivery nor resist it,
They do not need the obstetric forceps of the surgeon,
The insignificant is as big to me as any,
(What is less or more than a touch?)

Logic and sermons never convince,
The damp of the night drives deeper into my soul.

(Only what proves itself to every man and woman is so,
Only what nobody denies is so.)

A minute and a drop of me settle my brain,
I believe the soggy clods shall become lovers and lamps,
And a compend of compends is the meat of a man or
    woman,

And a summit and flower there is the feeling they have
    for each other,
And they are to branch boundlessly out of that lesson
    until it becomes omnific,
And until one and all shall delight us, and we them.

31

I believe a leaf of grass is no less than the journey-work
    of the stars,
And the pismire is equally perfect, and a grain of sand,
    and the egg of the wren,
And the tree-toad is a chef-d'œuvre for the highest,
And the running blackberry would adorn the parlors of
    heaven,
And the narrowest hinge in my hand puts to scorn all
    machinery,
And the cow crunching with depress'd head surpasses
    any statue,
And a mouse is miracle enough to stagger sextillions of
    infidels.

I find I incorporate gneiss, coal, long-threaded moss,
    fruits, grains, esculent roots,
And am stucco'd with quadrupeds and birds all over,
And have distanced what is behind me for good reasons,
But call any thing back again when I desire it.

In vain the speeding or shyness,
In vain the plutonic rocks send their old heat against my
    approach,

In vain the mastodon retreats beneath its own powder'd
    bones,
In vain objects stand leagues off and assume manifold
    shapes,
In vain the ocean settling in hollows and the great mon-
    sters lying low,
In vain the buzzard houses herself with the sky,
In vain the snake slides through the creepers and logs,
In vain the elk takes to the inner passes of the woods,
In vain the razor-bill'd auk sails far north to Labrador,
I follow quickly, I ascend to the nest in the fissure of the
    cliff.

32

I think I could turn and live with animals, they are so
    placid and self-contain'd,
I stand and look at them long and long.

They do not sweat and whine about their condition,
They do not lie awake in the dark and weep for their sins,
They do not make me sick discussing their duty to God,
Not one is dissatisfied, not one is demented with the
    mania of owning things,
Not one kneels to another, nor to his kind that lived thou-
    sands of years ago,
Not one is respectable or unhappy over the whole earth.

So they show their relations to me and I accept them,
They bring me tokens of myself, they evince them plainly
    in their possession.

I wonder where they get those tokens,
Did I pass that way huge times ago and negligently drop
    them?
Myself moving forward then and now and forever,
Gathering and showing more always and with velocity,
Infinite and omnigenous, and the like of these among
    them,
Not too exclusive toward the reachers of my remem-
    brancers,
Picking out here one that I love, and now go with him on
    brotherly terms.

A gigantic beauty of a stallion, fresh and responsive to my
    caresses,
Head high in the forehead, wide between the ears,
Limbs glossy and supple, tail dusting the ground,
Eyes full of sparkling wickedness, ears finely cut, flexibly
    moving.

His nostrils dilate as my heels embrace him,
His well-built limbs tremble with pleasure as we race
    around and return.

I but use you a minute, then I resign you, stallion,
Why do I need your paces when I myself out-gallop
    them?
Even as I stand or sit passing faster than you.

33

Space and Time! now I see it is true, what I guess'd at,
What I guess'd when I loaf'd on the grass,

What I guess'd while I lay alone in my bed,
And again as I walk'd the beach under the paling stars of
the morning.

My ties and ballasts leave me, my elbows rest in sea-gaps,
I skirt sierras, my palms cover continents,
I am afoot with my vision.

By the city's quadrangular houses—in log huts, camping
with lumbermen,
Along the ruts of the turnpike, along the dry gulch and
rivulet bed,
Weeding my onion-patch or hoeing rows of carrots and
parsnips, crossing savannas, trailing in forests,
Prospecting, gold-digging, girdling the trees of a new
purchase,
Scorch'd ankle-deep by the hot sand, hauling my boat
down the shallow river,
Where the panther walks to and fro on a limb overhead,
where the buck turns furiously at the hunter,
Where the rattlesnake suns his flabby length on a rock,
where the otter is feeding on fish,
Where the alligator in his tough pimples sleeps by the
bayou,
Where the black bear is searching for roots or honey,
where the beaver pats the mud with his paddle-
shaped tail;
Over the growing sugar, over the yellow-flower'd cotton
plant, over the rice in its low moist field,
Over the sharp-peak'd farm house, with its scallop'd
scum and slender shoots from the gutters,

Over the western persimmon, over the long-leav'd corn,
    over the delicate blue-flower flax,
Over the white and brown buckwheat, a hummer and
    buzzer there with the rest,
Over the dusky green of the rye as it ripples and shades in
    the breeze;
Scaling mountains, pulling myself cautiously up, holding
    on by low scragged limbs,
Walking the path worn in the grass and beat through the
    leaves of the brush,
Where the quail is whistling betwixt the woods and the
    wheat-lot,
Where the bat flies in the Seventh-month eve, where the
    great gold-bug drops through the dark,
Where the brook puts out of the roots of the old tree and
    flows to the meadow,
Where cattle stand and shake away flies with the tremu-
    lous shuddering of their hides,
Where the cheese-cloth hangs in the kitchen, where
    andirons straddle the hearth-slab, where cobwebs fall
    in festoons from the rafters;
Where trip-hammers crash, where the press is whirling its
    cylinders,
Wherever the human heart beats with terrible throes
    under its ribs,
Where the pear-shaped balloon is floating aloft, (floating
    in it myself and looking composedly down,)
Where the life-car is drawn on the slip-noose, where the
    heat hatches pale-green eggs in the dented sand,
Where the she-whale swims with her calf and never for-
    sakes it,

Where the steam-ship trails hind-ways its long pennant of
    smoke,
Where the fin of the shark cuts like a black chip out of the
    water,
Where the half-burn'd brig is riding on unknown cur-
    rents,
Where shells grow to her slimy deck, where the dead are
    corrupting below;
Where the dense-starr'd flag is borne at the head of the
    regiments,
Approaching Manhattan up by the long-stretching island,
Under Niagara, the cataract falling like a veil over my
    countenance,
Upon a door-step, upon the horse-block of hard wood
    outside,
Upon the race-course, or enjoying picnics or jigs or a good
    game of base-ball,
At he-festivals, with blackguard gibes, ironical license,
    bull-dances, drinking, laughter,
At the cider-mill tasting the sweets of the brown mash,
    sucking the juice through a straw,
At apple-peelings wanting kisses for all the red fruit I
    find,
At musters, beach-parties, friendly bees, huskings, house-
    raisings;
Where the mocking-bird sounds his delicious gurgles,
    cackles, screams, weeps,
Where the hay-rick stands in the barn-yard, where the
    dry-stalks are scatter'd, where the brood-cow waits in
    the hovel,

Where the bull advances to do his masculine work, where
the stud to the mare, where the cock is treading the
hen,
Where the heifers browse, where geese nip their food
with short jerks,
Where sun-down shadows lengthen over the limitless
and lonesome prairie,
Where herds of buffalo make a crawling spread of the
square miles far and near,
Where the humming-bird shimmers, where the neck of
the long-lived swan is curving and winding,
Where the laughing-gull scoots by the shore, where she
laughs her near-human laugh,
Where bee-hives range on a gray bench in the garden half
hid by the high weeds,
Where band-neck'd partridges roost in a ring on the
ground with their heads out,
Where burial coaches enter the arch'd gates of a cemetery,
Where winter wolves bark amid wastes of snow and ici-
cled trees,
Where the yellow-crown'd heron comes to the edge of the
marsh at night and feeds upon small crabs,
Where the splash of swimmers and divers cools the warm
noon,
Where the katy-did works her chromatic reed on the wal-
nut-tree over the well,
Through patches of citrons and cucumbers with silver-
wired leaves,
Through the salt-lick or orange glade, or under conical
firs,
Through the gymnasium, through the curtain'd saloon,
through the office or public hall;

Pleas'd with the native and pleas'd with the foreign,
pleas'd with the new and old,
Pleas'd with the homely woman as well as the handsome,
Pleas'd with the quakeress as she puts off her bonnet and
talks melodiously,
Pleas'd with the tune of the choir of the whitewash'd
church,
Pleas'd with the earnest words of the sweating Methodist
preacher, impress'd seriously at the camp meeting;
Looking in at the shop windows of Broadway the whole
forenoon, flatting the flesh of my nose on the thick
plate glass,
Wandering the same afternoon with my face turn'd up to
the clouds, or down a lane or along the beach,
My right and left arms round the sides of two friends, and
I in the middle;
Coming home with the silent and dark-cheek'd bush boy,
(behind me he rides at the drape of the day,)
Far from the settlements studying the print of animals'
feet, or the moccasin print,
By the cot in the hospital reaching lemonade to a feverish
patient,
Nigh the coffin'd corpse when all is still, examining with
a candle;
Voyaging to every port to dicker and adventure,
Hurrying with the modern crowd as eager and fickle as
any,
Hot toward one I hate, ready in my madness to knife him,
Solitary at midnight in my back yard, my thoughts gone
from me a long while,
Walking the old hills of Judæa with the beautiful gentle
God by my side,

Speeding through space, speeding through heaven and
    the stars,
Speeding amid the seven satellites and the broad ring,
    and the diameter of eighty thousand miles,
Speeding with tail'd meteors, throwing fire-balls like the
    rest,
Carrying the crescent child that carries its own full
    mother in its belly,
Storming, enjoying, planning, loving, cautioning,
Backing and filling, appearing and disappearing,
I tread day and night such roads.

I visit the orchards of spheres and look at the product,
And look at quintillions ripen'd and look at quintillions
    green.

I fly those flights of a fluid and swallowing soul,
My course runs below the soundings of plummets.

I help myself to material and immaterial,
No guard can shut me off, no law prevent me.

I anchor my ship for a little while only,
My messengers continually cruise away or bring their
    returns to me.

I go hunting polar furs and the seal, leaping chasms with
    a pike-pointed staff, clinging to topples of brittle and
    blue.

I ascend to the foretruck,
I take my place late at night in the crow's-nest,

We sail the arctic sea, it is plenty light enough,
Through the clear atmosphere I stretch around on the
     wonderful beauty,
The enormous masses of ice pass me and I pass them, the
     scenery is plain in all directions,
The white-topt mountains show in the distance, I fling out
     my fancies toward them,
We are approaching some great battle-field in which we
     are soon to be engaged,
We pass the colossal outposts of the encampment, we
     pass with still feet and caution,
Or we are entering by the suburbs some vast and ruin'd
     city,
The blocks and fallen architecture more than all the liv-
     ing cities of the globe.

I am a free companion, I bivouac by invading watchfires,
I turn the bridegroom out of bed and stay with the bride
     myself,
I tighten her all night to my thighs and lips.

My voice is the wife's voice, the screech by the rail of the
     stairs,
They fetch my man's body up dripping and drown'd.

I understand the large hearts of heroes,
The courage of present times and all times,
How the skipper saw the crowded and rudderless wreck
     of the steam-ship, and Death chasing it up and down
     the storm,
How he knuckled tight and gave not back an inch, and
     was faithful of days and faithful of nights,

And chalk'd in large letters on a board, *Be of good cheer,*
    we will not desert you;
How he follow'd with them and tack'd with them three
    days and would not give it up,
How he saved the drifting company at last,
How the lank loose-gown'd women look'd when boated
    from the side of their prepared graves,
How the silent old-faced infants and the lifted sick, and
    the sharp-lipp'd unshaved men;
All this I swallow, it tastes good, I like it well, it becomes
    mine,
I am the man, I suffer'd, I was there.

The disdain and calmness of martyrs,
The mother of old, condemn'd for a witch, burnt with dry
    wood, her children gazing on,
The hounded slave that flags in the race, leans by the
    fence, blowing, cover'd with sweat,
The twinges that sting like needles his legs and neck, the
    murderous buckshot and the bullets,
All these I feel or am.

I am the hounded slave, I wince at the bite of the dogs,
Hell and despair are upon me, crack and again crack the
    marksmen,
I clutch the rails of the fence, my gore dribs, thinn'd with
    the ooze of my skin,
I fall on the weeds and stones,
The riders spur their unwilling horses, haul close,
Taunt my dizzy ears and beat me violently over the head
    with whip-stocks.

Agonies are one of my changes of garments,
I do not ask the wounded person how he feels, I myself
    become the wounded person,
My hurts turn livid upon me as I lean on a cane and
    observe.

I am the mash'd fireman with breast-bone broken,
Tumbling walls buried me in their debris,
Heat and smoke I inspired, I heard the yelling shouts of
    my comrades,
I heard the distant click of their picks and shovels,
They have clear'd the beams away, they tenderly lift me
    forth.

I lie in the night air in my red shirt, the pervading hush is
    for my sake,
Painless after all I lie exhausted but not so unhappy,
White and beautiful are the faces around me, the heads
    are bared of their fire-caps,
The kneeling crowd fades with the light of the torches.

Distant and dead resuscitate,
They show as the dial or move as the hands of me, I am
    the clock myself.

I am an old artillerist, I tell of my fort's bombardment,
I am there again.

Again the long roll of the drummers,
Again the attacking cannon, mortars,
Again to my listening ears the cannon responsive.

I take part, I see and hear the whole,
The cries, curses, roar, the plaudits for well-aim'd shots,
The ambulanza slowly passing trailing its red drip,
Workmen searching after damages, making indispens-
    able repairs,
The fall of grenades through the rent roof, the fan-shaped
    explosion,
The whizz of limbs, heads, stone, wood, iron, high in the
    air.

Again gurgles the mouth of my dying general, he furi-
    ously waves with his hand,
He gasps through the clot *Mind not me—mind—the
entrenchments.*

34

Now I tell what I knew in Texas in my early youth,
(I tell not the fall of Alamo,
Not one escaped to tell the fall of Alamo,
The hundred and fifty are dumb yet at Alamo,)
'Tis the tale of the murder in cold blood of four hundred
    and twelve young men.

Retreating they had form'd in a hollow square with their
    baggage for breastworks,
Nine hundred lives out of the surrounding enemys, nine
    times their number, was the price they took in
    advance,
Their colonel was wounded and their ammunition gone,

They treated for an honorable capitulation, receiv'd writ-
ing and seal, gave up their arms and march'd back
prisoners of war.

They were the glory of the race of rangers,
Matchless with horse, rifle, song, supper, courtship,
Large, turbulent, generous, handsome, proud, and affec-
tionate,
Bearded, sunburnt, drest in the free costume of hunters,
Not a single one over thirty years of age.

The second First-day morning they were brought out in
squads and massacred, it was beautiful early sum-
mer,
The work commenced about five o'clock and was over by
eight.

None obey'd the command to kneel,
Some made a mad and helpless rush, some stood stark
and straight,
A few fell at once, shot in the temple or heart, the living
and dead lay together,
The maim'd and mangled dug in the dirt, the new-comers
saw them there,
Some half-kill'd attempted to crawl away,
These were despatch'd with bayonets or batter'd with the
blunts of muskets,
A youth not seventeen years old seiz'd his assassin till
two more came to release him,
The three were all torn and cover'd with the boy's blood.

At eleven o'clock began the burning of the bodies;
That is the tale of the murder of the four hundred and
    twelve young men.

35

Would you hear of an old-time sea fight?
Would you learn who won by the light of the moon and
    stars?
List to the yarn, as my grandmother's father the sailor
    told it to me.

Our foe was no skulk in his ship I tell you, (said he,)
His was the surly English pluck, and there is no tougher
    or truer, and never was, and never will be;
Along the lower'd eve he came horribly raking us.

We closed with him, the yards entangled, the cannon
    touch'd,
My captain lash'd fast with his own hands.

We had receiv'd some eighteen pound shots under the
    water,
On our lower-gun-deck two large pieces had burst at the
    first fire, killing all around and blowing up overhead.

Fighting at sun-down, fighting at dark,
Ten o'clock at night, the full moon well up, our leaks on
    the gain, and five feet of water reported,
The master-at-arms loosing the prisoners confined in the
    after-hold to give them a chance for themselves.

The transit to and from the magazine is now stopt by the
    sentinels,
They see so many strange faces they do not know whom
    to trust.

Our frigate takes fire,
The other asks if we demand quarter?
If our colors are struck and the fighting done?

Now I laugh content, for I hear the voice of my little cap-
    tain,
We have not struck, he composedly cries, *we have just begun
    our part of the fighting.*

Only three guns are in use,
One is directed by the captain himself against the enemy's
    main-mast,
Two well serv'd with grape and canister silence his mus-
    ketry and clear his decks.

The tops alone second the fire of this little battery, espe-
    cially the main-top,
They hold out bravely during the whole of the action.

Not a moment's cease,
The leaks gain fast on the pumps, the fire eats toward the
    powder-magazine.

One of the pumps has been shot away, it is generally
    thought we are sinking.

Serene stands the little captain,
He is not hurried, his voice is neither high nor low,
His eyes give more light to us than our battle-lanterns.

Toward twelve there in the beams of the moon they sur-
    render to us.

36

Stretch'd and still lies the midnight,
Two great hulls motionless on the breast of the darkness,
Our vessel riddled and slowly sinking, preparations to
    pass to the one we have conquer'd,
The captain on the quarter-deck coldly giving his orders
    through a countenance white as a sheet,
Near by the corpse of the child that serv'd in the cabin,
The dead face of an old salt with long white hair and care-
    fully curl'd whiskers,
The flames spite of all that can be done flickering aloft and
    below,
The husky voices of the two or three officers yet fit for
    duty,
Formless stacks of bodies and bodies by themselves, dabs
    of flesh upon the masts and spars,
Cut of cordage, dangle of rigging, slight shock of the
    soothe of waves,
Black and impassive guns, litter of powder-parcels, strong
    scent,
A few large stars overhead, silent and mournful shining,
Delicate sniffs of sea-breeze, smells of sedgy grass and
    fields by the shore, death-messages given in charge to
    survivors,

The hiss of the surgeon's knife, the gnawing teeth of his
    saw,
Wheeze, cluck, swash of falling blood, short wild scream,
    and long, dull, tapering groan,
These so, these irretrievable.

37

You laggards there on guard! look to your arms!
In at the conquer'd doors they crowd! I am possess'd!
Embody all presences outlaw'd or suffering,
See myself in prison shaped like another man,
And feel the dull unintermitted pain.

For me the keepers of convicts shoulder their carbines and
    keep watch,
It is I let out in the morning and barr'd at night.

Not a mutineer walks handcuff'd to jail but I am hand-
    cuff'd to him and walk by his side,
(I am less the jolly one there, and more the silent one with
    sweat on my twitching lips.)

Not a youngster is taken for larceny but I go up too, and
    am tried and sentenced.

Not a cholera patient lies at the last gasp but I also lie at
    the last gasp,
My face is ash-color'd, my sinews gnarl, away from me
    people retreat.

Askers embody themselves in me and I am embodied in
    them,
I project my hat, sit shame-faced, and beg.

38

Enough! enough! enough!
Somehow I have been stunn'd. Stand back!
Give me a little time beyond my cuff'd head, slumbers,
    dreams, gaping,
I discover myself on the verge of a usual mistake.

That I could forget the mockers and insults!
That I could forget the trickling tears and the blows of the
    bludgeons and hammers!
That I could look with a separate look on my own cruci-
    fixion and bloody crowning.

I remember now,
I resume the overstaid fraction,
The grave of rock multiplies what has been confided to it,
    or to any graves,
Corpses rise, gashes heal, fastenings roll from me.

I troop forth replenish'd with supreme power, one of an
    average unending procession,
Inland and sea-coast we go, and pass all boundary lines,
Our swift ordinances on their way over the whole earth,
The blossoms we wear in our hats the growth of thou-
    sands of years.

Eleves, I salute you! come forward!
Continue your annotations, continue your questionings.

39

The friendly and flowing savage, who is he?
Is he waiting for civilization, or past it and mastering it?

Is he some Southwesterner rais'd out-doors? is he Kana-
dian?
Is he from the Mississippi country? Iowa, Oregon, Cali-
fornia?
The mountains? prairie life, bush life? or sailor from the
sea?

Wherever he goes men and women accept and desire
him,
They desire he should like them, touch them, speak to
them, stay with them.

Behavior lawless as snow-flakes, words simple as grass,
uncomb'd head, laughter, and naiveté,
Slow-stepping feet, common features, common modes
and emanations,
They descend in new forms from the tips of his fingers,
They are wafted with the odor of his body or breath, they
fly out of the glance of his eyes.

40

Flaunt of the sunshine I need not your bask—lie over!
You light surfaces only, I force surfaces and depths also.

Earth! you seem to look for something at my hands,
Say, old top-knot, what do you want?

Man or woman, I might tell how I like you, but cannot,
And might tell what it is in me and what it is in you, but
    cannot,
And might tell that pining I have, that pulse of my nights
    and days.

Behold, I do not give lectures or a little charity,
When I give I give myself.

You there, impotent, loose in the knees,
Open your scarf'd chops till I blow grit within you,
Spread your palms and lift the flaps of your pockets,
I am not to be denied, I compel, I have stores plenty and to
    spare,
And any thing I have I bestow.

I do not ask who you are, that is not important to me,
You can do nothing and be nothing but what I will infold
    you.

To cotton-field drudge or cleaner of privies I lean,
On his right cheek I put the family kiss,
And in my soul I swear I never will deny him.

On women fit for conception I start bigger and nimbler
    babes,
(This day I am jetting the stuff of far more arrogant
    republics.)

To any one dying, thither I speed and twist the knob of
    the door,
Turn the bed-clothes toward the foot of the bed,
Let the physician and the priest go home.

I seize the descending man and raise him with resistless
    will,
O despairer, here is my neck,
By God, you shall not go down! hang your whole weight
    upon me.

I dilate you with tremendous breath, I buoy you up,
Every room of the house do I fill with an arm'd force,
Lovers of me, bafflers of graves.

Sleep—I and they keep guard all night,
Not doubt, not decease shall dare to lay finger upon you,
I have embraced you, and henceforth possess you to
    myself,
And when you rise in the morning you will find what I
    tell you is so.

41

I am he bringing help for the sick as they pant on their
    backs,
And for strong upright men I bring yet more needed help.
I heard what was said of the universe,
Heard it and heard it of several thousand years;
It is middling well as far as it goes—but is that all?

Magnifying and applying come I,

Outbidding at the start the old cautious hucksters,

Taking myself the exact dimensions of Jehovah,

Lithographing Kronos, Zeus his son, and Hercules his
grandson,

Buying drafts of Osiris, Isis, Belus, Brahma, Buddha,

In my portfolio placing Manito loose, Allah on a leaf, the
crucifix engraved,

With Odin and the hideous-faced Mexitli and every idol
and image,

Taking them all for what they are worth and not a cent
more,

Admitting they were alive and did the work of their days,

(They bore mites as for unfledg'd birds who have now to
rise and fly and sing for themselves,)

Accepting the rough deific sketches to fill out better in
myself, bestowing them freely on each man and
woman I see,

Discovering as much or more in a framer framing a
house,

Putting higher claims for him there with his roll'd-up
sleeves driving the mallet and chisel,

Not objecting to special revelations, considering a curl of
smoke or a hair on the back of my hand just as curi-
ous as any revelation,

Lads ahold of fire-engines and hook-and-ladder ropes no
less to me than the gods of the antique wars,

Minding their voices peal through the crash of destruc-
tion,

Their brawny limbs passing safe over charr'd laths, their
white foreheads whole and unhurt out of the flames;

By the mechanic's wife with her babe at her nipple inter-
ceding for every person born,

Three scythes at harvest whizzing in a row from three
    lusty angels with shirts bagg'd out at their waists,
The snag-tooth'd hostler with red hair redeeming sins
    past and to come,
Selling all he possesses, traveling on foot to fee lawyers
    for his brother and sit by him while he is tried for
    forgery;
What was strewn in the amplest strewing the square rod
    about me, and not filling the square rod then,
The bull and the bug never worshipp'd half enough,
Dung and dirt more admirable than was dream'd,
The supernatural of no account, myself waiting my time
    to be one of the supremes,
The day getting ready for me when I shall do as much
    good as the best, and be as prodigious;
By my life-lumps! becoming already a creator,
Putting myself here and now to the ambush'd womb of
    the shadows.

42

A call in the midst of the crowd,
My own voice, orotund sweeping and final.

Come my children,
Come my boys and girls, my women, household and inti-
    mates,
Now the performer launches his nerve, he has pass'd his
    prelude on the reeds within.

Easily written loose finger'd chords—I feel the thrum of
    your climax and close.

My head slues round on my neck,
Music rolls, but not from the organ,
Folks are around me, but they are no household of mine.

Ever the hard unsunk ground,
Ever the eaters and drinkers, ever the upward and down-
    ward sun, ever the air and the ceaseless tides,
Ever myself and my neighbors, refreshing, wicked, real,
Ever the old inexplicable query, ever that thorn'd thumb,
    that breath of itches and thirsts,
Ever the vexer's *hoot! hoot!* till we find where the sly one
    hides and bring him forth,
Ever love, ever the sobbing liquid of life,
Ever the bandage under the chin, ever the trestles of
    death.

Here and there with dimes on the eyes walking,
To feed the greed of the belly the brains liberally spoon-
    ing,
Tickets buying, taking, selling, but in to the feast never
    once going,
Many sweating, ploughing, thrashing, and then the chaff
    for payment receiving,
A few idly owning, and they the wheat continually claim-
    ing.

This is the city and I am one of the citizens,
Whatever interests the rest interests me, politics, wars,
    markets, newspapers, schools,
The mayor and councils, banks, tariffs, steamships, facto-
    ries, stocks, stores, real estate and personal estate.

The little plentiful manikins skipping around in collars
  and tail'd coats,
I am aware who they are, (they are positively not worms
  or fleas,)
I acknowledge the duplicates of myself, the weakest and
  shallowest is deathless with me,
What I do and say the same waits for them,
Every thought that flounders in me the same flounders in
  them.

I know perfectly well my own egotism,
Know my omnivorous lines and must not write any less,
And would fetch you whoever you are flush with myself.

Not words of routine this song of mine,
But abruptly to question, to leap beyond yet nearer bring;
This printed and bound book—but the printer and the
  printing-office boy?
The well-taken photographs—but your wife or friend
  close and solid in your arms?
The black ship mail'd with iron, her mighty guns in her
  turrets— but the pluck of the captain and engineers?
In the houses the dishes and fare and furniture—but the
  host and hostess, and the look out of their eyes?
The sky up there—yet here or next door, or across the
  way?
The saints and sages in history—but you yourself?
Sermons, creeds, theology—but the fathomless human
  brain,
And what is reason? and what is love? and what is life?

43

I do not despise you priests, all time, the world over,
My faith is the greatest of faiths and the least of faiths,
Enclosing worship ancient and modern and all between
     ancient and modern,
Believing I shall come again upon the earth after five
     thousand years,
Waiting responses from oracles, honoring the gods, salut-
     ing the sun,
Making a fetich of the first rock or stump, powowing with
     sticks in the circle of obis,
Helping the llama or brahmin as he trims the lamps of the
     idols,
Dancing yet through the streets in a phallic procession,
     rapt and austere in the woods a gymnosophist,
Drinking mead from the skull-cup, to Shastas and Vedas
     admirant, minding the Koran,
Walking the teokallis, spotted with gore from the stone
     and knife, beating the serpent-skin drum,
Accepting the Gospels, accepting him that was crucified,
     knowing assuredly that he is divine,
To the mass kneeling or the puritan's prayer rising, or sit-
     ting patiently in a pew,
Ranting and frothing in my insane crisis, or waiting dead-
     like till my spirit arouses me,
Looking forth on pavement and land, or outside of pave-
     ment and land,
Belonging to the winders of the circuit of circuits.

One of that centripetal and centrifugal gang I turn and
     talk like a man leaving charges before a journey.

Down-hearted doubters dull and excluded,
Frivolous, sullen, moping, angry, affected, dishearten'd,
    atheistical,
I know every one of you, I know the sea of torment,
    doubt, despair and unbelief.

How the flukes splash!
How they contort rapid as lightning, with spasms and
    spouts of blood!

Be at peace bloody flukes of doubters and sullen mopers,
I take my place among you as much as among any,
The past is the push of you, me, all, precisely the same,
And what is yet untried and afterward is for you, me, all,
    precisely the same.

I do not know what is untried and afterward,
But I know it will in its turn prove sufficient, and cannot
    fail.

Each who passes is consider'd, each who stops is con-
    sider'd, not a single one can it fail.

It cannot fail the young man who died and was buried,
Nor the young woman who died and was put by his side,
Nor the little child that peep'd in at the door, and then
    drew back and was never seen again,
Nor the old man who has lived without purpose, and
    feels it with bitterness worse than gall,
Nor him in the poor house tubercled by rum and the bad
    disorder,

Nor the numberless slaughter'd and wreck'd, nor the
    brutish koboo call'd the ordure of humanity,
Nor the sacs merely floating with open mouths for food to
    slip in,
Nor any thing in the earth, or down in the oldest graves of
    the earth,
Nor any thing in the myriads of spheres, nor the myriads
    of myriads that inhabit them.
Nor the present, nor the least wisp that is known.

44

It is time to explain myself—let us stand up.

What is known I strip away,
I launch all men and women forward with me into the
    Unknown.

The clock indicates the moment—but what does eternity
    indicate?

We have thus far exhausted trillions of winters and sum-
    mers,
There are trillions ahead, and trillions ahead of them.

Births have brought us richness and variety,
And other births will bring us richness and variety.

I do not call one greater and one smaller,
That which fills its period and place is equal to any.

Were mankind murderous or jealous upon you, my
    brother, my sister?
I am sorry for you, they are not murderous or jealous
    upon me,
All has been gentle with me, I keep no account with
    lamentation,
(What have I to do with lamentation?)

I am an acme of things accomplish'd, and I an encloser of
    things to be.

My feet strike an apex of the apices of the stairs,
On every step bunches of ages, and larger bunches
    between the steps,
All below duly travel'd, and still I mount and mount.

Rise after rise bow the phantoms behind me,
Afar down I see the huge first Nothing, I know I was even
    there,
I waited unseen and always, and slept through the lethar-
    gic mist,
And took my time, and took no hurt from the fetid car-
    bon.

Long I was hugg'd close—long and long.

Immense have been the preparations for me,
Faithful and friendly the arms that have help'd me.

Cycles ferried my cradle, rowing and rowing like cheerful
    boatmen,

For room to me stars kept aside in their own rings,
They sent influences to look after what was to hold me.

Before I was born out of my mother generations guided
     me,
My embryo has never been torpid, nothing could overlay
     it.

For it the nebula cohered to an orb,
The long slow strata piled to rest it on,
Vast vegetables gave it sustenance,
Monstrous sauroids transported it in their mouths and
     deposited it with care.

All forces have been steadily employ'd to complete and
     delight me,
Now on this spot I stand with my robust soul.

45

O span of youth! ever-push'd elasticity!
O manhood, balanced, florid and full.

My lovers suffocate me,
Crowding my lips, thick in the pores of my skin,
Jostling me through streets and public halls, coming
     naked to me at night,
Crying by day *Ahoy!* from the rocks of the river, swing-
     ing and chirping over my head,
Calling my name from flower-beds, vines, tangled under-
     brush,
Lighting on every moment of my life,

Bussing my body with soft balsamic busses,
Noiselessly passing handfuls out of their hearts and giv-
ing them to be mine.

Old age superbly rising! O welcome, ineffable grace of
dying days!

Every condition promulges not only itself, it promulges
what grows after and out of itself,
And the dark hush promulges as much as any.

I open my scuttle at night and see the far-sprinkled sys-
tems,
And all I see, multiplied as high as I can cipher edge but
the rim of the farther systems.

Wider and wider they spread, expanding, always
expanding,
Outward and outward and forever outward.

My sun has his sun and round him obediently wheels,
He joins with his partners a group of superior circuit,
And greater sets follow, making specks of the greatest
inside them.

There is no stoppage and never can be stoppage,
If I, you, and the worlds, and all beneath or upon their
surfaces, were this moment reduced back to a pallid
float, it would not avail in the long run,
We should surely bring up again where we now stand,
And surely go as much farther, and then farther and far-
ther.

A few quadrillions of eras, a few octillions of cubic
    leagues, do not hazard the span or make it impatient,
They are but parts, anything is but a part.

See ever so far, there is limitless space outside of that,
Count ever so much, there is limitless time around that.

My rendezvous is appointed, it is certain,
The Lord will be there and wait till I come on perfect
    terms,
The great Camerado, the lover true for whom I pine will
    be there.

46

I know I have the best of time and space, and was never
    measured and never will be measured.

I tramp a perpetual journey, (come listen all!)
My signs are a rain-proof coat, good shoes, and a staff cut
    from the woods,
No friend of mine takes his ease in my chair,
I have no chair, no church, no philosophy,
I lead no man to a dinner-table, library, exchange,
But each man and each woman of you I lead upon a knoll,
My left hand hooking you round the waist,
My right hand pointing to landscapes of continents and
    the public road.

Not I, not any one else can travel that road for you,
You must travel it for yourself.

It is not far, it is within reach,
Perhaps you have been on it since you were born and did
    not know,
Perhaps it is everywhere on water and on land.
Shoulder your duds dear son, and I will mine, and let us
    hasten forth,
Wonderful cities and free nations we shall fetch as we go.

If you tire, give me both burdens, and rest the chuff of
    your hand on my hip,
And in due time you shall repay the same service to me,
For after we start we never lie by again.

This day before dawn I ascended a hill and look'd at the
    crowded heaven,
And I said to my spirit *When we become the enfolders of those*
    orbs, and the pleasure and knowledge of every thing in
    them, shall we be fill'd and satisfied then?
And my spirit said *No, we but level that lift to pass and con-*
    tinue beyond.

You are also asking me questions and I hear you,
I answer that I cannot answer, you must find out for your-
    self.

Sit a while dear son,
Here are biscuits to eat and here is milk to drink,
But as soon as you sleep and renew yourself in sweet
    clothes, I kiss you with a good-by kiss and open the
    gate for your egress hence.

Long enough have you dream'd contemptible dreams,
Now I wash the gum from your eyes,
You must habit yourself to the dazzle of the light and of
    every moment of your life.

Long have you timidly waded holding a plank by the
    shore,
Now I will you to be a bold swimmer,
To jump off in the midst of the sea, rise again, nod to me,
    shout, and laughingly dash with your hair.

47

I am the teacher of athletes,
He that by me spreads a wider breast than my own
    proves the width of my own,
He most honors my style who learns under it to destroy
    the teacher.

The boy I love, the same becomes a man not through
    derived power, but in his own right,
Wicked rather than virtuous out of conformity or fear,
Fond of his sweetheart, relishing well his steak,
Unrequited love or a slight cutting him worse than sharp
    steel cuts,
First-rate to ride, to fight, to hit the bull's eye, to sail a
    skiff, to sing a song or play on the banjo,
Preferring scars and the beard and faces pitted with
    small-pox over all latherers,
And those well-tann'd to those that keep out of the sun.

I teach straying from me, yet who can stray from me?
I follow you whoever you are from the present hour,
My words itch at your ears till you understand them.

I do not say these things for a dollar or to fill up the time
    while I wait for a boat,
(It is you talking just as much as myself, I act as the
    tongue of you,
Tied in your mouth, in mine it begins to be loosen'd.)

I swear I will never again mention love or death inside a
    house,
And I swear I will never translate myself at all, only to
    him or her who privately stays with me in the open
    air.

If you would understand me go to the heights or water-
    shore,
The nearest gnat is an explanation, and a drop or motion
    of waves a key,
The maul, the oar, the hand-saw, second my words.

No shutter'd room or school can commune with me,
But roughs and little children better than they.

The young mechanic is closest to me, he knows me well,
The woodman that takes his axe and jug with him shall
    take me with him all day,
The farm-boy ploughing in the field feels good at the
    sound of my voice,
In vessels that sail my words sail, I go with fishermen and
    seamen and love them.

The soldier camp'd or upon the march is mine,
On the night ere the pending battle many seek me, and I
    do not fail them,
On that solemn night (it may be their last) those that
    know me seek me.

My face rubs to the hunter's face when he lies down alone
    in his blanket,
The driver thinking of me does not mind the jolt of his
    wagon,
The young mother and old mother comprehend me,
The girl and the wife rest the needle a moment and for-
    get where they are,
They and all would resume what I have told them.

48

I have said that the soul is not more than the body,
And I have said that the body is not more than the soul,
And nothing, not God, is greater to one than one's self is,
And whoever walks a furlong without sympathy walks to
    his own funeral drest in his shroud,
And I or you pocketless of a dime may purchase the pick
    of the earth,
And to glance with an eye or show a bean in its pod con-
    founds the learning of all times,
And there is no trade or employment but the young man
    following it may become a hero,
And there is no object so soft but it makes a hub for the
    wheel'd universe,
And I say to any man or woman, Let your soul stand cool
    and composed before a million universes.

And I say to mankind, Be not curious about God,
For I who am curious about each am not curious about
      God,
(No array of terms can say how much I am at peace about
      God and about death.)

I hear and behold God in every object, yet understand
      God not in the least,
Nor do I understand who there can be more wonderful
      than myself.

Why should I wish to see God better than this day?
I see something of God each hour of the twenty-four, and
      each moment then,
In the faces of men and women I see God, and in my own
      face in the glass,
I find letters from God dropt in the street, and every one
      is sign'd by God's name,
And I leave them where they are, for I know that where-
      soe'er I go,
Others will punctually come for ever and ever.

49

And as to you Death, and you bitter hug of mortality, it
      is idle to try to alarm me.

To his work without flinching the accoucheur comes,
I see the elder-hand pressing receiving supporting,
I recline by the sills of the exquisite flexible doors,
And mark the outlet, and mark the relief and escape.

And as to you Corpse I think you are good manure, but
    that does not offend me,
I smell the white roses sweet-scented and growing,
I reach to the leafy lips, I reach to the polish'd breasts of
    melons.

And as to you Life I reckon you are the leavings of many
    deaths,
(No doubt I have died myself ten thousand times before.)

I hear you whispering there O stars of heaven,
O suns—O grass of graves—O perpetual transfers and
    promotions,
If you do not say any thing how can I say any thing?

Of the turbid pool that lies in the autumn forest,
Of the moon that descends the steeps of the soughing twi-
    light,
Toss, sparkles of day and dusk—toss on the black stems
    that decay in the muck,
Toss to the moaning gibberish of the dry limbs.

I ascend from the moon, I ascend from the night,
I perceive that the ghastly glimmer is noonday sunbeams
    reflected,
And debouch to the steady and central from the offspring
    great or small.

50

There is that in me—I do not know what it is—but I know
    it is in me.

Wrench'd and sweaty—calm and cool then my body
becomes,
I sleep—I sleep long.

I do not know it—it is without name—it is a word unsaid,
It is not in any dictionary, utterance, symbol.

Something it swings on more than the earth I swing on,
To it the creation is the friend whose embracing awakes
me.

Perhaps I might tell more. Outlines! I plead for my broth-
ers and sisters.

Do you see O my brothers and sisters?
It is not chaos or death—it is form, union, plan—it is eter-
nal life—it is Happiness.

51

The past and present wilt—I have fill'd them, emptied
them.
And proceed to fill my next fold of the future.

Listener up there! what have you to confide to me?
Look in my face while I snuff the sidle of evening,
(Talk honestly, no one else hears you, and I stay only a
minute longer.)

Do I contradict myself?
Very well then I contradict myself,
(I am large, I contain multitudes.)

I concentrate toward them that are nigh, I wait on the
   door-slab.

Who has done his day's work? who will soonest be
   through with his supper?
Who wishes to walk with me?

Will you speak before I am gone? will you prove already
   too late?

52

The spotted hawk swoops by and accuses me, he com-
   plains of my gab and my loitering.

I too am not a bit tamed, I too am untranslatable,
I sound my barbaric yawp over the roofs of the world.

The last scud of day holds back for me,
It flings my likeness after the rest and true as any on the
   shadow'd wilds,
It coaxes me to the vapor and the dusk.

I depart as air, I shake my white locks at the runaway sun,
I effuse my flesh in eddies, and drift it in lacy jags.

I bequeath myself to the dirt to grow from the grass I love,
If you want me again look for me under your boot-soles.

You will hardly know who I am or what I mean,
But I shall be good health to you nevertheless,
And filter and fibre your blood.

Failing to fetch me at first keep encouraged,
Missing me one place search another,
I stop somewhere waiting for you.

CHILDREN OF ADAM.

TO THE GARDEN THE WORLD.

To the garden the world anew ascending,
Potent mates, daughters, sons, preluding,
The love, the life of their bodies, meaning and being,
Curious here behold my resurrection after slumber,
The revolving cycles in their wide sweep having brought
    me again,
Amorous, mature, all beautiful to me, all wondrous,
My limbs and the quivering fire that ever plays through
    them, for reasons, most wondrous,
Existing I peer and penetrate still,
Content with the present, content with the past,
By my side or back of me Eve following,
Or in front, and I following her just the same.

FROM PENT-UP ACHING RIVERS.

From pent-up aching rivers,
From that of myself without which I were nothing,
From what I am determin'd to make illustrious, even if I
    stand sole among men,
From my own voice resonant, singing the phallus,

Singing the song of procreation,
Singing the need of superb children and therein superb
    grown people,
Singing the muscular urge and the blending,
Singing the bedfellow's song, (O resistless yearning!
O for any and each the body correlative attracting!
O for you whoever you are your correlative body! O it,
    more than all else, you delighting!)
From the hungry gnaw that eats me night and day,
From native moments, from bashful pains, singing them,
Seeking something yet unfound though I have diligently
    sought it many a long year,
Singing the true song of the soul fitful at random,
Renascent with grossest Nature or among animals,
Of that, of them and what goes with them my poems
    informing,
Of the smell of apples and lemons, of the pairing of birds,
Of the wet of woods, of the lapping of waves,
Of the mad pushes of waves upon the land, I them chant-
    ing,
The overture lightly sounding, the strain anticipating,
The welcome nearness, the sight of the perfect body,
The swimmer swimming naked in the bath, or motionless
    on his back lying and floating,
The female form approaching, I pensive, love-flesh
    tremulous aching,
The divine list for myself or you or for any one making,
The face, the limbs, the index from head to foot, and what
    it arouses,
The mystic deliria, the madness amorous, the utter aban-
    donment,
(Hark close and still what I now whisper to you,

I love you, O you entirely possess me,

O that you and I escape from the rest and go utterly off,
    free and lawless,

Two hawks in the air, two fishes swimming in the sea not
    more lawless than we;)

The furious storm through me careering, I passionately
    trembling,

The oath of the inseparableness of two together, of the
    woman that loves me and whom I love more than my
    life, that oath swearing,

(O I willingly stake all for you,

O let me be lost if it must be so!

O you and I! what is it to us what the rest do or think?

What is all else to us? only that we enjoy each other and
    exhaust each other if it must be so;)

From the master, the pilot I yield the vessel to,

The general commanding me, commanding all, from him
    permission taking,

From time the programme hastening, (I have loiter'd too
    long as it is.)

From sex, from the warp and from the woof,

From privacy, from frequent repinings alone,

From plenty of persons near and yet the right person not
    near,

From the soft sliding of hands over me and thrusting of
    fingers through my hair and beard,

From the long sustain'd kiss upon the mouth or bosom,

From the close pressure that makes me or any man drunk,
    fainting with excess,

From what the divine husband knows, from the work of
    fatherhood,

From exultation, victory and relief, from the bedfellow's
　　embrace in the night,
From the act-poems of eyes, hands, hips and bosoms,
From the cling of the trembling arm,
From the bending curve and the clinch,
From side by side the pliant coverlet off-throwing,
From the one so unwilling to have me leave, and me just
　　as unwilling to leave,
(Yet a moment O tender waiter, and I return,)
From the hour of shining stars and dropping dews,
From the night a moment I emerging flitting out,
Celebrate you act divine and you children prepared for,
And you stalwart loins.

I SING THE BODY ELECTRIC.

1

I sing the body electric,
The armies of those I love engirth me and I engirth them,
They will not let me off till I go with them, respond to
　　them,
And discorrupt them, and charge them full with the
　　charge of the soul.

Was it doubted that those who corrupt their own bodies
　　conceal themselves?
And if those who defile the living are as bad as they who
　　defile the dead?
And if the body does not do fully as much as the soul?
And if the body were not the soul, what is the soul?

2

The love of the body of man or woman balks account, the
    body itself balks account,
That of the male is perfect, and that of the female is per-
    fect.

The expression of the face balks account,
But the expression of a well-made man appears not only
    in his face,
It is in his limbs and joints also, it is curiously in the joints
    of his hips and wrists,
It is in his walk, the carriage of his neck, the flex of his
    waist and knees, dress does not hide him,
The strong sweet quality he has strikes through the cotton
    and broadcloth,
To see him pass conveys as much as the best poem, per-
    haps more,
You linger to see his back, and the back of his neck and
    shoulder-side.

The sprawl and fulness of babes, the bosoms and heads of
    women, the folds of their dress, their style as we pass
    in the street, the contour of their shape downwards,
The swimmer naked in the swimming-bath, seen as he
    swims through the transparent green-shine, or lies
    with his face up and rolls silently to and fro in the
    heave of the water,
The bending forward and backward of rowers in row-
    boats, the horseman in his saddle,
Girls, mothers, house-keepers, in all their performances,

The group of laborers seated at noon-time with their open
dinner-kettles, and their wives waiting,
The female soothing a child, the farmer's daughter in the
garden or cow-yard,
The young fellow hoeing corn, the sleigh-driver driving
his six horses through the crowd,
The wrestle of wrestlers, two apprentice-boys, quite
grown, lusty, good-natured, native-born, out on the
vacant lot at sundown after work,
The coats and caps thrown down, the embrace of love and
resistance,
The upper-hold and under-hold, the hair rumpled over
and blinding the eyes;
The march of firemen in their own costumes, the play of
masculine muscle through clean-setting trowsers and
waist-straps,
The slow return from the fire, the pause when the bell
strikes suddenly again, and the listening on the alert,
The natural, perfect, varied attitudes, the bent head, the
curv'd neck and the counting;
Such-like I love—I loosen myself, pass freely, am at the
mother's breast with the little child,
Swim with the swimmers, wrestle with wrestlers, march
in line with the firemen, and pause, listen, count.

3

I knew a man, a common farmer, the father of five sons,
And in them the fathers of sons, and in them the fathers of
sons.
This man was of wonderful vigor, calmness, beauty of
person,

The shape of his head, the pale yellow and white of his
hair and beard, the immeasurable meaning of his
black eyes, the richness and breadth of his manners,
These I used to go and visit him to see, he was wise also,
He was six feet tall, he was over eighty years old, his sons
were massive, clean, bearded, tan-faced, handsome,
They and his daughters loved him, all who saw him loved
him,
They did not love him by allowance, they loved him with
personal love,
He drank water only, the blood show'd like scarlet
through the clear-brown skin of his face,
He was a frequent gunner and fisher, he sail'd his boat
himself, he had a fine one presented to him by a ship-
joiner, he had fowling-pieces presented to him by
men that loved him,
When he went with his five sons and many grand-sons to
hunt or fish, you would pick him out as the most
beautiful and vigorous of the gang,
You would wish long and long to be with him, you would
wish to sit by him in the boat that you and he might
touch each other.

4

I have perceiv'd that to be with those I like is enough,
To stop in company with the rest at evening is enough,
To be surrounded by beautiful, curious, breathing, laugh-
ing flesh is enough,

To pass among them or touch any one, or rest my arm
    ever so lightly round his or her neck for a moment,
    what is this then?
I do not ask any more delight, I swim in it as in a sea.

There is something in staying close to men and women
    and looking on them, and in the contact and odor of
    them, that pleases the soul well,
All things please the soul, but these please the soul well.

5

This is the female form,
A divine nimbus exhales from it from head to foot,
It attracts with fierce undeniable attraction,
I am drawn by its breath as if I were no more than a help-
    less vapor, all falls aside but myself and it,
Books, art, religion, time, the visible and solid earth, and
    what was expected of heaven or fear'd of hell, are
    now consumed,
Mad filaments, ungovernable shoots play out of it, the
    response likewise ungovernable,
Hair, bosom, hips, bend of legs, negligent falling hands all
    diffused, mine too diffused,
Ebb stung by the flow and flow stung by the ebb, love-
    flesh swelling and deliciously aching,
Limitless limpid jets of love hot and enormous, quivering
    jelly of love, white-blow and delirious juice,
Bridegroom night of love working surely and softly into
    the prostrate dawn,

Undulating into the willing and yielding day,
Lost in the cleave of the clasping and sweet-flesh'd day.

This the nucleus—after the child is born of woman, man is
    born of woman,
This the bath of birth, this the merge of small and large,
    and the outlet again.

Be not ashamed women, your privilege encloses the rest,
    and is the exit of the rest,
You are the gates of the body, and you are the gates of the
    soul.

The female contains all qualities and tempers them,
She is in her place and moves with perfect balance,
She is all things duly veil'd, she is both passive and active,
She is to conceive daughters as well as sons, and sons as
    well as daughters.

As I see my soul reflected in Nature,
As I see through a mist, One with inexpressible complete-
    ness, sanity, beauty,
See the bent head and arms folded over the breast, the
    Female I see.

6

The male is not less the soul nor more, he too is in his
    place,
He too is all qualities, he is action and power,
The flush of the known universe is in him,

Scorn becomes him well, and appetite and defiance
   become him well,
The wildest largest passions, bliss that is utmost, sorrow
   that is utmost become him well, pride is for him,
The full-spread pride of man is calming and excellent to
   the soul,
Knowledge becomes him, he likes it always, he brings
   every thing to the test of himself,
Whatever the survey, whatever the sea and the sail he
   strikes soundings at last only here,
(Where else does he strike soundings except here?)

The man's body is sacred and the woman's body is
   sacred,
No matter who it is, it is sacred—is it the meanest one in
   the laborers' gang?
Is it one of the dull-faced immigrants just landed on the
   wharf?
Each belongs here or anywhere just as much as the well-
   off, just as much as you,
Each has his or her place in the procession.

(All is a procession,
The universe is a procession with measured and perfect
   motion.)

Do you know so much yourself that you call the meanest
   ignorant?
Do you suppose you have a right to a good sight, and he
   or she has no right to a sight?

Do you think matter has cohered together from its diffuse
     float, and the soil is on the surface, and water runs
     and vegetation sprouts,
For you only, and not for him and her?

7

A man's body at auction,
(For before the war I often go to the slave-mart and watch
     the sale,)
I help the auctioneer, the sloven does not half know his
     business.

Gentlemen look on this wonder,
Whatever the bids of the bidders they cannot be high
     enough for it,
For it the globe lay preparing quintillions of years without
     one animal or plant,
For it the revolving cycles truly and steadily roll'd.

In this head the all-baffling brain,
In it and below it the makings of heroes.

Examine these limbs, red, black, or white, they are cun-
     ning in tendon and nerve,
They shall be stript that you may see them.

Exquisite senses, life-lit eyes, pluck, volition,
Flakes of breast-muscle, pliant backbone and neck, flesh
     not flabby, good-sized arms and legs,
And wonders within there yet.

Within there runs blood,
The same old blood! the same red-running blood!
There swells and jets a heart, there all passions, desires,
    reachings, aspirations,
(Do you think they are not there because they are not
    express'd in parlors and lecture-rooms?)

This is not only one man, this the father of those who shall
    be fathers in their turns,
In him the start of populous states and rich republics,
Of him countless immortal lives with countless embodi-
    ments and enjoyments.

How do you know who shall come from the offspring of
    his offspring through the centuries?
(Who might you find you have come from yourself, if you
    could trace back through the centuries?)

8

A woman's body at auction,
She too is not only herself, she is the teeming mother of
    mothers,
She is the bearer of them that shall grow and be mates to
    the mothers.

Have you ever loved the body of a woman?
Have you ever loved the body of a man?
Do you not see that these are exactly the same to all in all
    nations and times all over the earth?

If any thing is sacred the human body is sacred,
And the glory and sweet of a man is the token of man-
    hood untainted,
And in man or woman a clean, strong, firm-fibred body,
    is more beautiful than the most beautiful face.

Have you seen the fool that corrupted his own live body?
    or the fool that corrupted her own live body?
For they do not conceal themselves, and cannot conceal
    themselves.

9

O my body! I dare not desert the likes of you in other men
    and women, nor the likes of the parts of you,
I believe the likes of you are to stand or fall with the likes
    of the soul, (and that they are the soul,)
I believe the likes of you shall stand or fall with my
    poems, and that they are my poems,
Man's, woman's, child's, youth's, wife's, husband's,
    mother's, father's, young man's, young woman's
    poems,
Head, neck, hair, ears, drop and tympan of the ears,
Eyes, eye-fringes, iris of the eye, eyebrows, and the wak-
    ing or sleeping of the lids,
Mouth, tongue, lips, teeth, roof of the mouth, jaws, and
    the jaw-hinges,
Nose, nostrils of the nose, and the partition,
Cheeks, temples, forehead, chin, throat, back of the neck,
    neck-slue,
Strong shoulders, manly beard, scapula, hind-shoulders,
    and the ample side-round of the chest,

Upper-arm, armpit, elbow-socket, lower-arm, arm-
sinews, arm-bones,
Wrist and wrist-joints, hand, palm, knuckles, thumb, fore-
finger, finger-joints, finger-nails,
Broad breast-front, curling hair of the breast, breast-bone,
breast-side,
Ribs, belly, backbone, joints of the backbone,
Hips, hip-sockets, hip-strength, inward and outward
round, man-balls, man-root,
Strong set of thighs, well carrying the trunk above,
Leg-fibres, knee, knee-pan, upper-leg, under-leg,
Ankles, instep, foot-ball, toes, toe-joints, the heel;
All attitudes, all the shapeliness, all the belongings of my
or your body or of any one's body, male or female,
The lung-sponges, the stomach-sac, the bowels sweet and
clean,
The brain in its folds inside the skull-frame,
Sympathies, heart-valves, palate-valves, sexuality, mater-
nity,
Womanhood, and all that is a woman, and the man that
comes from woman,
The womb, the teats, nipples, breast-milk, tears, laughter,
weeping, love-looks, love-perturbations and risings,
The voice, articulation, language, whispering, shouting
aloud,
Food, drink, pulse, digestion, sweat, sleep, walking,
swimming,
Poise on the hips, leaping, reclining, embracing, arm-
curving and tightening,
The continual changes of the flex of the mouth, and
around the eyes,
The skin, the sunburnt shade, freckles, hair,

The curious sympathy one feels when feeling with the
    hand the naked meat of the body,
The circling rivers the breath, and breathing it in and out,
The beauty of the waist, and thence of the hips, and
    thence downward toward the knees,
The thin red jellies within you or within me, the bones
    and the marrow in the bones,
The exquisite realization of health;
O I say these are not the parts and poems of the body
    only, but of the soul,
O I say now these are the soul!

A WOMAN WAITS FOR ME.

A woman waits for me, she contains all, nothing is lack-
    ing,
Yet all were lacking if sex were lacking, or if the moisture
    of the right man were lacking.

Sex contains all, bodies, souls,
Meanings, proofs, purities, delicacies, results, promulga-
    tions,
Songs, commands, health, pride, the maternal mystery,
    the seminal milk,
All hopes, benefactions, bestowals, all the passions, loves,
    beauties, delights of the earth,
All the governments, judges, gods, follow'd persons of
    the earth,
These are contain'd in sex as parts of itself and justifica-
    tions of itself.

Without shame the man I like knows and avows the deli-
    ciousness of his sex,
Without shame the woman I like knows and avows hers.

Now I will dismiss myself from impassive women,
I will go stay with her who waits for me, and with those
    women that are warm-blooded and sufficient for me,
I see that they understand me and do not deny me,
I see that they are worthy of me, I will be the robust hus-
    band of those women.

They are not one jot less than I am,
They are tann'd in the face by shining suns and blowing
    winds,
Their flesh has the old divine suppleness and strength,
They know how to swim, row, ride, wrestle, shoot, run,
    strike, retreat, advance, resist, defend themselves,
They are ultimate in their own right—they are calm, clear,
    well-possess'd of themselves.

I draw you close to me, you women,
I cannot let you go, I would do you good,
I am for you, and you are for me, not only for our own
    sake, but for others' sakes,
Envelop'd in you sleep greater heroes and bards,
They refuse to awake at the touch of any man but me.

It is I, you women, I make my way,
I am stern, acrid, large, undissuadable, but I love you,
I do not hurt you any more than is necessary for you,
I pour the stuff to start sons and daughters fit for these
    States, I press with slow rude muscle,

I brace myself effectually, I listen to no entreaties,
I dare not withdraw till I deposit what has so long accu-
    mulated within me.

Through you I drain the pent-up rivers of myself,
In you I wrap a thousand onward years,
On you I graft the grafts of the best-beloved of me and
    America,
The drops I distil upon you shall grow fierce and athletic
    girls, new artists, musicians, and singers,
The babes I beget upon you are to beget babes in their
    turn,
I shall demand perfect men and women out of my love-
    spendings,
I shall expect them to interpenetrate with others, as I and
    you interpenetrate now,
I shall count on the fruits of the gushing showers of them,
    as I count on the fruits of the gushing showers I give
    now,
I shall look for loving crops from the birth, life, death,
    immortality, I plant so lovingly now.

SPONTANEOUS ME.

Spontaneous me, Nature,
The loving day, the mounting sun, the friend I am happy
    with,
The arm of my friend hanging idly over my shoulder,
The hillside whiten'd with blossoms of the mountain ash,
The same late in autumn, the hues of red, yellow, drab,
    purple, and light and dark green,

The rich coverlet of the grass, animals and birds, the pri-
    vate untrimm'd bank, the primitive apples, the peb-
    ble-stones,
Beautiful dripping fragments, the negligent list of one
    after another as I happen to call them to me or think
    of them,
The real poems, (what we call poems being merely pic-
    tures,)
The poems of the privacy of the night, and of men like me,
This poem drooping shy and unseen that I always carry,
    and that all men carry,
(Know once for all, avow'd on purpose, wherever are
    men like me, are our lusty lurking masculine poems,)
Love-thoughts, love-juice, love-odor, love-yielding, love-
    climbers, and the climbing sap,
Arms and hands of love, lips of love, phallic thumb of
    love, breasts of love, bellies press'd and glued
    together with love,
Earth of chaste love, life that is only life after love,
The body of my love, the body of the woman I love, the
    body of the man, the body of the earth,
Soft forenoon airs that blow from the south-west,
The hairy wild-bee that murmurs and hankers up and
    down, that gripes the full-grown lady-flower, curves
    upon her with amorous firm legs, takes his will of her,
    and holds himself tremulous and tight till he is satis-
    fied;
The wet of woods through the early hours,
Two sleepers at night lying close together as they sleep,
    one with an arm slanting down across and below the
    waist of the other,

The smell of apples, aromas from crush'd sage-plant,
    mint, birch-bark,
The boy's longings, the glow and pressure as he confides
    to me what he was dreaming,
The dead leaf whirling its spiral whirl and falling still and
    content to the ground,
The no-form'd stings that sights, people, objects, sting me
    with,
The hubb'd sting of myself, stinging me as much as it ever
    can any one,
The sensitive, orbic, underlapp'd brothers, that only priv-
    ileged feelers may be intimate where they are,
The curious roamer the hand roaming all over the body,
    the bashful withdrawing of flesh where the fingers
    soothingly pause and edge themselves,
The limpid liquid within the young man,
The vex'd corrosion so pensive and so painful,
The torment, the irritable tide that will not be at rest,
The like of the same I feel, the like of the same in others,
The young man that flushes and flushes, and the young
    woman that flushes and flushes,
The young man that wakes deep at night, the hot hand
    seeking to repress what would master him,
The mystic amorous night, the strange half-welcome
    pangs, visions, sweats,
The pulse pounding through palms and trembling encir-
    cling fingers, the young man all color'd, red,
    ashamed, angry;
The souse upon me of my lover the sea, as I lie willing and
    naked,

The merriment of the twin babes that crawl over the grass
in the sun, the mother never turning her vigilant eyes
from them,
The walnut-trunk, the walnut-husks, and the ripening or
ripen'd long-round walnuts,
The continence of vegetables, birds, animals,
The consequent meanness of me should I skulk or find
myself indecent, while birds and animals never once
skulk or find themselves indecent,
The great chastity of paternity, to match the great chastity
of maternity,
The oath of procreation I have sworn, my Adamic and
fresh daughters,
The greed that eats me day and night with hungry gnaw,
till I saturate what shall produce boys to fill my place
when I am through,
The wholesome relief, repose, content,
And this bunch pluck'd at random from myself,
It has done its work—I toss it carelessly to fall where it
may.

ONE HOUR TO MADNESS AND JOY.

One hour to madness and joy! O furious! O confine me
not!
(What is this that frees me so in storms?
What do my shouts amid lightnings and raging winds
mean?)

O to drink the mystic deliria deeper than any other man!
O savage and tender achings! (I bequeath them to you my
    children,
I tell them to you, for reasons, O bridegroom and bride.)

O to be yielded to you whoever you are, and you to be
    yielded to me in defiance of the world!
O to return to Paradise! O bashful and feminine!
O to draw you to me, to plant on you for the first time the
    lips of a determin'd man.

O the puzzle, the thrice-tied knot, the deep and dark pool,
    all untied and illumin'd!
O to speed where there is space enough and air enough
    at last!
To be absolv'd from previous ties and conventions, I from
    mine and you from yours!
To find a new unthought-of nonchalance with the best of
    Nature!
To have the gag remov'd from one's mouth!
To have the feeling to-day or any day I am sufficient as I
    am.

O something unprov'd! something in a trance!
To escape utterly from others' anchors and holds!
To drive free! to love free! to dash reckless and danger-
    ous!
To court destruction with taunts, with invitations!
To ascend, to leap to the heavens of the love indicated to
    me!
To rise thither with my inebriate soul!
To be lost if it must be so!

To feed the remainder of life with one hour of fulness and
    freedom!
With one brief hour of madness and joy.

OUT OF THE ROLLING OCEAN THE CROWD.

Out of the rolling ocean the crowd came a drop gently to
    me,
Whispering *I love you, before long I die,*
I have travel'd a long way merely to look on you to touch you,
For I could not die till I once look'd on you,
For I fear'd I might afterward lose you.

Now we have met, we have look'd, we are safe,
Return in peace to the ocean my love,
I too am part of that ocean my love, we are not so much
    separated,
Behold the great rondure, the cohesion of all, how perfect!
But as for me, for you, the irresistible sea is to separate us,
As for an hour carrying us diverse, yet cannot carry us
    diverse forever;
Be not impatient—a little space—know you I salute the
    air, the ocean and the land,
Every day at sundown for your dear sake my love.

AGES AND AGES RETURNING AT INTERVALS.

Ages and ages returning at intervals,
Undestroy'd, wandering immortal,

Lusty, phallic, with the potent original loins, perfectly
    sweet,
I, chanter of Adamic songs,
Through the new garden the West, the great cities calling,
Deliriate, thus prelude what is generated, offering these,
    offering myself,
Bathing myself, bathing my songs in Sex,
Offspring of my loins.

WE TWO, HOW LONG WE WERE FOOL'D.

We two, how long we were fool'd,
Now transmuted, we swiftly escape as Nature escapes,
We are Nature, long have we been absent, but now we
    return,
We become plants, trunks, foliage, roots, bark,
We are bedded in the ground, we are rocks,
We are oaks, we grow in the openings side by side,
We browse, we are two among the wild herds sponta-
    neous as any,
We are two fishes swimming in the sea together,
We are what locust blossoms are, we drop scent around
    lanes mornings and evenings,
We are also the coarse smut of beasts, vegetables, miner-
    als,
We are two predatory hawks, we soar above and look
    down,
We are two resplendent suns, we it is who balance our-
    selves orbic and stellar, we are as two comets,
We prowl fang'd and four-footed in the woods, we spring
    on prey,

We are two clouds forenoons and afternoons driving
    overhead,
We are seas mingling, we are two of those cheerful waves
    rolling over each other and interwetting each other,
We are what the atmosphere is, transparent, receptive,
    pervious, impervious,
We are snow, rain, cold, darkness, we are each product
    and influence of the globe,
We have circled and circled till we have arrived home
    again, we two,
We have voided all but freedom and all but our own joy.

O HYMEN! O HYMENEE!

O hymen! O hymenee! why do you tantalize me thus?
O why sting me for a swift moment only?
Why can you not continue? O why do you now cease?
Is it because if you continued beyond the swift moment
    you would soon certainly kill me?

I AM HE THAT ACHES WITH LOVE.

I am he that aches with amorous love;
Does the earth gravitate? does not all matter, aching,
    attract all matter?
So the body of me to all I meet or know.

NATIVE MOMENTS.

Native moments—when you come upon me—ah you are
    here now,
Give me now libidinous joys only,
Give me the drench of my passions, give me life coarse
    and rank,
To-day I go consort with Nature's darlings, to-night too,
I am for those who believe in loose delights, I share the
    midnight orgies of young men,
I dance with the dancers and drink with the drinkers,
The echoes ring with our indecent calls, I pick out some
    low person for my dearest friend,
He shall be lawless, rude, illiterate, he shall be one con-
    demn'd by others for deeds done,
I will play a part no longer, why should I exile myself
    from my companions?
O you shunn'd persons, I at least do not shun you,
I come forthwith in your midst, I will be your poet,
I will be more to you than to any of the rest.

ONCE I PASS'D THROUGH A POPULOUS CITY.

Once I pass'd through a populous city imprinting my
    brain for future use with its shows, architecture, cus-
    toms, traditions,
Yet now of all that city I remember only a woman I casu-
    ally met there who detain'd me for love of me,
Day by day and night by night we were together— all else
    has long been forgotten by me,

I remember I say only that woman who passionately
     clung to me,
Again we wander, we love, we separate again,
Again she holds me by the hand, I must not go,
I see her close beside me with silent lips sad and tremu-
     lous.

I HEARD YOU SOLEMN-SWEET PIPES OF THE ORGAN.

I heard you solemn-sweet pipes of the organ as last Sun-
     day morn I pass'd the church,
Winds of autumn, as I walk'd the woods at dusk I heard
     your long-stretch'd sighs up above so mournful,
I heard the perfect Italian tenor singing at the opera, I
     heard the soprano in the midst of the quartet singing;
Heart of my love! you too I heard murmuring low
     through one of the wrists around my head,
Heard the pulse of you when all was still ringing little
     bells last night under my ear.

FACING WEST FROM CALIFORNIA'S SHORES.

Facing west from California's shores,
Inquiring, tireless, seeking what is yet unfound,
I, a child, very old, over waves, towards the house of
     maternity, the land of migrations, look afar,
Look off the shores of my Western sea, the circle almost
     circled;

For starting westward from Hindustan, from the vales of
    Kashmere,
From Asia, from the north, from the God, the sage, and
    the hero,
From the south, from the flowery peninsulas and the
    spice islands,
Long having wander'd since, round the earth having
    wander'd,
Now I face home again, very pleas'd and joyous,
(But where is what I started for so long ago?
And why is it yet unfound?)

AS ADAM EARLY IN THE MORNING.

As Adam early in the morning,
Walking forth from the bower refresh'd with sleep,
Behold me where I pass, hear my voice, approach,
Touch me, touch the palm of your hand to my body as I
    pass,
Be not afraid of my body.

CALAMUS.

IN PATHS UNTRODDEN.

In paths untrodden,
In the growth by margins of pond-waters,
Escaped from the life that exhibits itself,
From all the standards hitherto publish'd, from the plea-
sures, profits, conformities,
Which too long I was offering to feed my soul,
Clear to me now standards not yet publish'd, clear to me
that my soul,
That the soul of the man I speak for rejoices in comrades,
Here by myself away from the clank of the world,
Tallying and talk'd to here by tongues aromatic,
No longer abash'd, (for in this secluded spot I can
respond as I would not dare elsewhere,)
Strong upon me the life that does not exhibit itself, yet
contains all the rest,
Resolv'd to sing no songs to-day but those of manly
attachment,
Projecting them along that substantial life,
Bequeathing hence types of athletic love,
Afternoon this delicious Ninth-month in my forty-first
year,
I proceed for all who are or have been young men,

To tell the secret of my nights and days,
To celebrate the need of comrades.

SCENTED HERBAGE OF MY BREAST.

Scented herbage of my breast,
Leaves from you I glean, I write, to be perused best after-
    wards,
Tomb-leaves, body-leaves growing up above me above
    death,
Perennial roots, tall leaves, O the winter shall not freeze
    you delicate leaves,
Every year shall you bloom again, out from where you
    retired you shall emerge again;
O I do not know whether many passing by will discover
    you or inhale your faint odor, but I believe a few will;
O slender leaves! O blossoms of my blood! I permit you to
    tell in your own way of the heart that is under you,
O I do not know what you mean there underneath your-
    selves, you are not happiness,
You are often more bitter than I can bear, you burn and
    sting me,
Yet you are beautiful to me you faint tinged roots, you
    make me think of death,
Death is beautiful from you, (what indeed is finally beau-
    tiful except death and love?)
O I think it is not for life I am chanting here my chant of
    lovers, I think it must be for death,
For how calm, how solemn it grows to ascend to the
    atmosphere of lovers,

Death or life I am then indifferent, my soul declines to
    prefer,
(I am not sure but the high soul of lovers welcomes death
    most,)
Indeed O death, I think now these leaves mean precisely
    the same as you mean,
Grow up taller sweet leaves that I may see! grow up out of
    my breast!
Spring away from the conceal'd heart there!
Do not fold yourself so in your pink-tinged roots timid
    leaves!
Do not remain down there so ashamed, herbage of my
    breast!
Come I am determin'd to unbare this broad breast of
    mine, I have long enough stifled and choked;
Emblematic and capricious blades I leave you, now you
    serve me not,
I will say what I have to say by itself,
I will sound myself and comrades only, I will never again
    utter a call only their call,
I will raise with it immortal reverberations through the
    States,
I will give an example to lovers to take permanent shape
    and will through the States,
Through me shall the words be said to make death exhil-
    arating,
Give me your tone therefore O death, that I may accord
    with it,
Give me yourself, for I see that you belong to me now
    above all, and are folded inseparably together, you
    love and death are,

Nor will I allow you to balk me any more with what I was
    calling life,
For now it is convey'd to me that you are the purports
    essential,
That you hide in these shifting forms of life, for reasons,
    and that they are mainly for you,
That you beyond them come forth to remain, the real real-
    ity,
That behind the mask of materials you patiently wait, no
    matter how long,
That you will one day perhaps take control of all,
That you will perhaps dissipate this entire show of
    appearance,
That may-be you are what it is all for, but it does not last
    so very long,
But you will last very long.

WHOEVER YOU ARE HOLDING ME NOW IN HAND.

Whoever you are holding me now in hand,
Without one thing all will be useless,
I give you fair warning before you attempt me further,
I am not what you supposed, but far different.

Who is he that would become my follower?
Who would sign himself a candidate for my affections?

The way is suspicious, the result uncertain, perhaps
    destructive,
You would have to give up all else, I alone would expect
    to be your sole and exclusive standard,

Your novitiate would even then be long and exhausting,
The whole past theory of your life and all conformity to
    the lives around you would have to be abandon'd,
Therefore release me now before troubling yourself any
    further, let go your hand from my shoulders,
Put me down and depart on your way.

Or else by stealth in some wood for trial,
Or back of a rock in the open air,
(For in any roof'd room of a house I emerge not, nor in
    company,
And in libraries I lie as one dumb, a gawk, or unborn, or
    dead,)
But just possibly with you on a high hill, first watching
    lest any person for miles around approach unawares,
Or possibly with you sailing at sea, or on the beach of the
    sea or some quiet island,
Here to put your lips upon mine I permit you,
With the comrade's long-dwelling kiss or the new hus-
    band's kiss,
For I am the new husband and I am the comrade.

Or if you will, thrusting me beneath your clothing,
Where I may feel the throbs of your heart or rest upon
    your hip,
Carry me when you go forth over land or sea;
For thus merely touching you is enough, is best,
And thus touching you would I silently sleep and be car-
    ried eternally.

But these leaves conning you con at peril,
For these leaves and me you will not understand,

They will elude you at first and still more afterward, I will
    certainly elude you,
Even while you should think you had unquestionably
    caught me, behold!
Already you see I have escaped from you.

For it is not for what I have put into it that I have written
    this book,
Nor is it by reading it you will acquire it,
Nor do those know me best who admire me and vaunt-
    ingly praise me,
Nor will the candidates for my love (unless at most a very
    few) prove victorious,
Nor will my poems do good only, they will do just as
    much evil, perhaps more,
For all is useless without that which you may guess at
    many times and not hit, that which I hinted at;
Therefore release me and depart on your way.

FOR YOU O DEMOCRACY.

Come, I will make the continent indissoluble,
I will make the most splendid race the sun ever shone
    upon,
I will make divine magnetic lands,
           With the love of comrades,
              With the life-long love of comrades.

I will plant companionship thick as trees along all the
    rivers of America, and along the shores of the great
    lakes, and all over the prairies,

I will make inseparable cities with their arms about each
　　other's necks.
　　　　　　By the love of comrades,
　　　　　　　　By the manly love of comrades.

For you these from me, O Democracy, to serve you ma
　　femme!
For you, for you I am trilling these songs.

THESE I SINGING IN SPRING.

These I singing in spring collect for lovers,
(For who but I should understand lovers and all their sor-
　　row and joy?
And who but I should be the poet of comrades?)
Collecting I traverse the garden the world, but soon I pass
　　the gates,
Now along the pond-side, now wading in a little, fearing
　　not the wet,
Now by the post-and-rail fences where the old stones
　　thrown there, pick'd from the fields, have accumu-
　　lated,
(Wild-flowers and vines and weeds come up through the
　　stones and partly cover them, beyond these I pass,)
Far, far in the forest, or sauntering later in summer, before
　　I think where I go,
Solitary, smelling the earthy smell, stopping now and
　　then in the silence,
Alone I had thought, yet soon a troop gathers around me,
Some walk by my side and some behind, and some
　　embrace my arms or neck,

They the spirits of dear friends dead or alive, thicker they
    come, a great crowd, and I in the middle,
Collecting, dispensing, singing, there I wander with them,
Plucking something for tokens, tossing toward whoever
    is near me,
Here, lilac, with a branch of pine,
Here, out of my pocket, some moss which I pull'd off a
    live-oak in Florida as it hung trailing down,
Here, some pinks and laurel leaves, and a handful of sage,
And here what I now draw from the water, wading in the
    pond-side,
(O here I last saw him that tenderly loves me, and returns
    again never to separate from me,
And this, O this shall henceforth be the token of com-
    rades, this calamus-root shall,
Interchange it youths with each other! let none render it
    back!)
And twigs of maple and a bunch of wild orange and
    chestnut,
And stems of currants and plum-blows, and the aromatic
    cedar,
These I compass'd around by a thick cloud of spirits,
Wandering, point to or touch as I pass, or throw them
    loosely from me,
Indicating to each one what he shall have, giving some-
    thing to each;
But what I drew from the water by the pond-side, that I
    reserve,
I will give of it, but only to them that love as I myself am
    capable of loving.

NOT HEAVING FROM MY RIBB'D BREAST ONLY.

Not heaving from my ribb'd breast only,
Not in sighs at night in rage dissatisfied with myself,
Not in those long-drawn, ill-supprest sighs,
Not in many an oath and promise broken,
Not in my wilful and savage soul's volition,
Not in the subtle nourishment of the air,
Not in this beating and pounding at my temples and
    wrists,
Not in the curious systole and diastole within which will
    one day cease,
Not in many a hungry wish told to the skies only,
Not in cries, laughter, defiances, thrown from me when
    alone far in the wilds,
Not in husky pantings through clinch'd teeth,
Not in sounded and resounded words, chattering words,
    echoes, dead words,
Not in the murmurs of my dreams while I sleep,
Nor the other murmurs of these incredible dreams of
    every day,
Nor in the limbs and senses of my body that take you and
    dismiss you continually—not there,
Not in any or all of them O adhesiveness! O pulse of my
    life!
Need I that you exist and show yourself any more than
    in these songs.

OF THE TERRIBLE DOUBT OF APPEARANCES.

Of the terrible doubt of appearances,
Of the uncertainty after all, that we may be deluded,
That may-be reliance and hope are but speculations after
    all,
That may-be identity beyond the grave is a beautiful fable
    only,
May-be the things I perceive, the animals, plants, men,
    hills, shining and flowing waters,
The skies of day and night, colors, densities, forms, may-
    be these are (as doubtless they are) only apparitions,
    and the real something has yet to be known,
(How often they dart out of themselves as if to confound
    me and mock me!
How often I think neither I know, nor any man knows,
    aught of them,)
May-be seeming to me what they are (as doubtless they
    indeed but seem) as from my present point of view,
    and might prove (as of course they would) nought of
    what they appear, or nought anyhow, from entirely
    changed points of view;
To me these and the like of these are curiously answer'd
    by my lovers, my dear friends,
When he whom I love travels with me or sits a long while
    holding me by the hand,
When the subtle air, the impalpable, the sense that words
    and reason hold not, surround us and pervade us,
Then I am charged with untold and untellable wisdom, I
    am silent, I require nothing further,
I cannot answer the question of appearances or that of
    identity beyond the grave,

But I walk or sit indifferent, I am satisfied,
He ahold of my hand has completely satisfied me.

THE BASE OF ALL METAPHYSICS.

And now gentlemen,
A word I give to remain in your memories and minds,
As base and finale too for all metaphysics.

(So to the students the old professor,
At the close of his crowded course.)

Having studied the new and antique, the Greek and Ger-
    manic systems,
Kant having studied and stated, Fichte and Schelling and
    Hegel,
Stated the lore of Plato, and Socrates greater than Plato,
And greater than Socrates sought and stated, Christ
    divine having studied long,
I see reminiscent to-day those Greek and Germanic sys-
    tems,
See the philosophies all, Christian churches and tenets
    see,
Yet underneath Socrates clearly see, and underneath
    Christ the divine I see,
The dear love of man for his comrade, the attraction of
    friend to friend,
Of the well-married husband and wife, of children and
    parents,
Of city for city and land for land.

RECORDERS AGES HENCE.

Recorders ages hence,
Come, I will take you down underneath this impassive
    exterior, I will tell you what to say of me,
Publish my name and hang up my picture as that of the
    tenderest lover,
The friend the lover's portrait, of whom his friend his
    lover was fondest,
Who was not proud of his songs, but of the measureless
    ocean of love within him, and freely pour'd it forth,
Who often walk'd lonesome walks thinking of his dear
    friends, his lovers,
Who pensive away from one he lov'd often lay sleepless
    and dissatisfied at night,
Who knew too well the sick, sick dread lest the one he
    lov'd might secretly be indifferent to him,
Whose happiest days were far away through fields, in
    woods, on hills, he and another wandering hand in
    hand, they twain apart from other men,
Who oft as he saunter'd the streets curv'd with his arm
    the shoulder of his friend, while the arm of his friend
    rested upon him also.

WHEN I HEARD AT THE CLOSE OF THE DAY.

When I heard at the close of the day how my name had
    been receiv'd with plaudits in the capitol, still it was
    not a happy night for me that follow'd,
And else when I carous'd, or when my plans were accom-
    plish'd, still I was not happy,

But the day when I rose at dawn from the be[...]
    health, refresh'd, singing, inhaling the ri[...]
    autumn,
When I saw the full moon in the west grow pale and dis-
    appear in the morning light,
When I wander'd alone over the beach, and undressing
    bathed, laughing with the cool waters, and saw the
    sun rise,
And when I thought how my dear friend my lover was on
    his way coming, O then I was happy,
O then each breath tasted sweeter, and all that day my
    food nourish'd me more, and the beautiful day pass'd
    well,
And the next came with equal joy, and with the next at
    evening came my friend,
And that night while all was still I heard the waters roll
    slowly continually up the shores,
I heard the hissing rustle of the liquid and sands as
    directed to me whispering to congratulate me,
For the one I love most lay sleeping by me under the same
    cover in the cool night,
In the stillness in the autumn moonbeams his face was
    inclined toward me,
And his arm lay lightly around my breast—and that night
    I was happy.

ARE YOU THE NEW PERSON DRAWN TOWARD ME?

Are you the new person drawn toward me?
To begin with take warning, I am surely far different from
    what you suppose;

Do you suppose you will find in me your ideal?
Do you think it so easy to have me become your lover?
Do you think the friendship of me would be unalloy'd
    satisfaction?
Do you think I am trusty and faithful?
Do you see no further than this façade, this smooth and
    tolerant manner of me?
Do you suppose yourself advancing on real ground
    toward a real heroic man?
Have you no thought O dreamer that it may be all maya,
    illusion?

ROOTS AND LEAVES THEMSELVES ALONE.

Roots and leaves themselves alone are these,
Scents brought to men and women from the wild woods
    and pond-side,
Breast-sorrel and pinks of love, fingers that wind around
    tighter than vines,
Gushes from the throats of birds hid in the foliage of trees
    as the sun is risen,
Breezes of land and love set from living shores to you on
    the living sea, to you O sailors!
Frost-mellow'd berries and Third-month twigs offer'd
    fresh to young persons wandering out in the fields
    when the winter breaks up,
Love-buds put before you and within you whoever you
    are,
Buds to be unfolded on the old terms,
If you bring the warmth of the sun to them they will open
    and bring form, color, perfume, to you,

If you become the aliment and the wet they will become
   flowers, fruits, tall branches and trees.

NOT HEAT FLAMES UP AND CONSUMES.

Not heat flames up and consumes,
Not sea-waves hurry in and out,
Not the air delicious and dry, the air of ripe summer,
   bears lightly along white down-balls of myriads of
   seeds,
Wafted, sailing gracefully, to drop where they may;
Not these, O none of these more than the flames of me,
   consuming, burning for his love whom I love,
O none more than I hurrying in and out;
Does the tide hurry, seeking something, and never give
   up? O I the same,
O nor down-balls nor perfumes, nor the high rain-emit-
   ting clouds, are borne through the open air,
Any more than my soul is borne through the open air,
Wafted in all directions O love, for friendship, for you.

TRICKLE DROPS.

Trickle drops! my blue veins leaving!
O drops of me! trickle, slow drops,
Candid from me falling, drip, bleeding drops,
From wounds made to free you whence you were
   prison'd,
From my face, from my forehead and lips,

From my breast, from within where I was conceal'd, press
   forth red drops, confession drops,
Stain every page, stain every song I sing, every word I
   say, bloody drops,
Let them know your scarlet heat, let them glisten,
Saturate them with yourself all ashamed and wet,
Glow upon all I have written or shall write, bleeding
   drops,
Let it all be seen in your light, blushing drops.

CITY OF ORGIES.

City of orgies, walks and joys,
City whom that I have lived and sung in your midst will
   one day make you illustrious,
Not the pageants of you, not your shifting tableaus, your
   spectacles, repay me,
Not the interminable rows of your houses, nor the ships at
   the wharves,
Nor the processions in the streets, nor the bright windows
   with goods in them,
Nor to converse with learn'd persons, or bear my share
   in the soiree or feast;
Not those, but as I pass O Manhattan, your frequent and
   swift flash of eyes offering me love,
Offering response to my own—these repay me,
Lovers, continual lovers, only repay me.

BEHOLD THIS SWARTHY FACE.

Behold this swarthy face, these gray eyes,
This beard, the white wool unclipt upon my neck,
My brown hands and the silent manner of me without
    charm;
Yet comes one a Manhattanese and ever at parting kisses
    me lightly on the lips with robust love,
And I on the crossing of the street or on the ship's deck
    give a kiss in return,
We observe that salute of American comrades land and
    sea,
We are those two natural and nonchalant persons.

I SAW IN LOUISIANA A LIVE-OAK GROWING.

I saw in Louisiana a live-oak growing,
All alone stood it and the moss hung down from the
    branches,
Without any companion it grew there uttering joyous
    leaves of dark green,
And its look, rude, unbending, lusty, made me think of
    myself,
But I wonder'd how it could utter joyous leaves standing
    alone there without its friend near, for I knew I could
    not,
And I broke off a twig with a certain number of leaves
    upon it, and twined around it a little moss,
And brought it away, and I have placed it in sight in my
    room,

:ded to remind me as of my own dear friends,
/e lately I think of little else than of them,)
Yet it remains to me a curious token, it makes me think of
    manly love;
For all that, and though the live-oak glistens there in
    Louisiana solitary in a wide flat space,
Uttering joyous leaves all its life without a friend a lover
    near,
I know very well I could not.

TO A STRANGER.

Passing stranger! you do not know how longingly I look
    upon you,
You must be he I was seeking, or she I was seeking, (it
    comes to me as of a dream,)
I have somewhere surely lived a life of joy with you,
All is recall'd as we flit by each other, fluid, affectionate,
    chaste, matured,
You grew up with me, were a boy with me or a girl with
    me,
I ate with you and slept with you, your body has become
    not yours only nor left my body mine only,
You give me the pleasure of your eyes, face, flesh, as we
    pass, you take of my beard, breast, hands, in return,
I am not to speak to you, I am to think of you when I sit
    alone or wake at night alone,
I am to wait, I do not doubt I am to meet you again,
I am to see to it that I do not lose you.

THIS MOMENT YEARNING AND THOUGHTFUL.

This moment yearning and thoughtful sitting alone,
It seems to me there are other men in other lands yearning
    and thoughtful,
It seems to me I can look over and behold them in Ger-
    many, Italy, France, Spain,
Or far, far away, in China, or in Russia or Japan, talking
    other dialects,
And it seems to me if I could know those men I should
    become attached to them as I do to men in my own
    lands,
O I know we should be brethren and lovers,
I know I should be happy with them.

I HEAR IT WAS CHARGED AGAINST ME.

I hear it was charged against me that I sought to destroy
    institutions,
But really I am neither for nor against institutions,
(What indeed have I in common with them? or what with
    the destruction of them?)
Only I will establish in the Mannahatta and in every city
    of these States inland and seaboard,
And in the fields and woods, and above every keel little
    or large that dents the water,
Without edifices or rules or trustees or any argument,
The institution of the dear love of comrades.

THE PRAIRIE-GRASS DIVIDING.

The prairie-grass dividing, its special odor breathing,
I demand of it the spiritual corresponding,
Demand the most copious and close companionship of
    men,
Demand the blades to rise of words, acts, beings,
Those of the open atmosphere, coarse, sunlit, fresh, nutri-
    tious,
Those that go their own gait, erect, stepping with freedom
    and command, leading not following,
Those with a never-quell'd audacity, those with sweet
    and lusty flesh clear of taint,
Those that look carelessly in the faces of Presidents and
    governors, as to say *Who are you?*
Those of earth-born passion, simple, never constrain'd,
    never obedient,
Those of inland America.

WHEN I PERUSE THE CONQUER'D FAME.

When I peruse the conquer'd fame of heroes and the vic-
    tories of mighty generals, I do not envy the generals,
Nor the President in his Presidency, nor the rich in his
    great house,
But when I hear of the brotherhood of lovers, how it was
    with them,
How together through life, through dangers, odium,
    unchanging, long and long,
Through youth and through middle and old age, how
    unfaltering, how affectionate and faithful they were,

Then I am pensive—I hastily walk away fill'd with the bit-
terest envy.

WE TWO BOYS TOGETHER CLINGING.

We two boys together clinging,
One the other never leaving,
Up and down the roads going, North and South excur-
sions making,
Power enjoying, elbows stretching, fingers clutching,
Arm'd and fearless, eating, drinking, sleeping, loving,
No law less than ourselves owning, sailing, soldiering,
thieving, threatening,
Misers, menials, priests alarming, air breathing, water
drinking, on the turf or the sea beach dancing,
Cities wrenching, ease scorning, statutes mocking, feeble-
ness chasing,
Fulfilling our foray.

A PROMISE TO CALIFORNIA.

A promise to California,
Or inland to the great pastoral Plains, and on to Puget
Sound and Oregon;
Sojourning east a while longer, soon I travel toward you,
to remain, to teach robust American love,
For I know very well that I and robust love belong among
you, inland, and along the Western sea;
For these States tend inland and toward the Western sea,
and I will also.

HERE THE FRAILEST LEAVES OF ME.

Here the frailest leaves of me and yet my strongest last-
    ing,
Here I shade and hide my thoughts, I myself do not
    expose them,
And yet they expose me more than all my other poems.

NO LABOR-SAVING MACHINE.

No labor-saving machine,
Nor discovery have I made,
Nor will I be able to leave behind me any wealthy bequest
    to found a hospital or library,
Nor reminiscence of any deed of courage for America,
Nor literary success nor intellect, nor book for the book-
    shelf,
But a few carols vibrating through the air I leave,
For comrades and lovers.

A GLIMPSE.

A glimpse through an interstice caught,
Of a crowd of workmen and drivers in a bar-room around
    the stove late of a winter night, and I unremark'd
    seated in a corner,
Of a youth who loves me and whom I love, silently
    approaching and seating himself near, that he may
    hold me by the hand,

A long while amid the noises of coming and going, of
    drinking and oath and smutty jest,
There we two, content, happy in being together, speak-
    ing little, perhaps not a word.

A LEAF FOR HAND IN HAND.

A leaf for hand in hand;
You natural persons old and young!
You on the Mississippi and on all the branches and bay-
    ous of the Mississippi!
You friendly boatmen and mechanics! you roughs!
You twain! and all processions moving along the streets!
I wish to infuse myself among you till I see it common for
    you to walk hand in hand.

EARTH, MY LIKENESS.

Earth, my likeness,
Though you look so impassive, ample and spheric there,
I now suspect that is not all;
I now suspect there is something fierce in you eligible to
    burst forth,
For an athlete is enamour'd of me, and I of him,
But toward him there is something fierce and terrible in
    me eligible to burst forth,
I dare not tell it in words, not even in these songs.

I DREAM'D IN A DREAM.

I dream'd in a dream I saw a city invincible to the attacks
    of the whole of the rest of the earth,
I dream'd that was the new city of Friends,
Nothing was greater there than the quality of robust love,
    it led the rest,
It was seen every hour in the actions of the men of that
    city,
And in all their looks and words.

WHAT THINK YOU I TAKE MY PEN IN HAND?

What think you I take my pen in hand to record?
The battle ship, perfect-model'd, majestic, that I saw pass
    the offing to-day under full sail?
The splendors of the past day? or the splendor of the
    night that envelops me?
Or the vaunted glory and growth of the great city spread
    around me?—no;
But merely of two simple men I saw to-day on the pier in
    the midst of the crowd, parting the parting of dear
    friends,
The one to remain hung on the other's neck and passion-
    ately kiss'd him,
While the one to depart tightly prest the one to remain in
    his arms.

TO THE EAST AND TO THE WEST.

To the East and to the West,
To the man of the Seaside State and of Pennsylvania,
To the Kanadian of the north, to the Southerner I love,
These with perfect trust to depict you as myself, the
  germs are in all men,
I believe the main purport of these States is to found a
  superb friendship, exalté, previously unknown,
Because I perceive it waits, and has been always waiting,
  latent in all men.

SOMETIMES WITH ONE I LOVE.

Sometimes with one I love I fill myself with rage for fear
  I effuse unreturn'd love,
But now I think there is no unreturn'd love, the pay is cer-
  tain one way or another,
(I loved a certain person ardently and my love was not
  return'd,
Yet out of that I have written these songs.)

TO A WESTERN BOY.

Many things to absorb I teach to help you become eleve of
  mine;
Yet if blood like mine circle not in your veins,
If you be not silently selected by lovers and do not silently
  select lovers,
Of what use is it that you seek to become eleve of mine?

FAST-ANCHOR'D ETERNAL O LOVE!

Fast-anchor'd eternal O love! O woman I love!
O bride! O wife! more resistless than I can tell, the thought
    of you!
Then separate, as disembodied or another born,
Ethereal, the last athletic reality, my consolation,
I ascend, I float in the regions of your love O man,
O sharer of my roving life.

AMONG THE MULTITUDE.

Among the men and women the multitude,
I perceive one picking me out by secret and divine signs,
Acknowledging none else, not parent, wife, husband,
    brother, child, any nearer than I am,
Some are baffled, but that one is not—that one knows me.

Ah lover and perfect equal,
I meant that you should discover me so by faint indirec-
    tions,
And I when I meet you mean to discover you by the like
    in you.

O YOU WHOM I OFTEN AND SILENTLY COME.

O you whom I often and silently come where you are that
    I may be with you,
As I walk by your side or sit near, or remain in the same
    room with you,

Little you know the subtle electric fire that for
  playing within me.

THAT SHADOW MY LIKENESS.

That shadow my likeness that goes to and fro seeking a
  livelihood, chattering, chaffering,
How often I find myself standing and looking at it where
  it flits,
How often I question and doubt whether that is really me;
But among my lovers and caroling these songs,
O I never doubt whether that is really me.

FULL OF LIFE NOW.

Full of life now, compact, visible,
I, forty years old the eighty-third year of the States,
To one a century hence or any number of centuries hence,
To you yet unborn these, seeking you.

When you read these I that was visible am become invis-
  ible,
Now it is you, compact, visible, realizing my poems, seek-
  ing me,
Fancying how happy you were if I could be with you and
  become your comrade;
Be it as if I were with you. (Be not too certain but I am now
  with you.)

SALUT AU MONDE!

1

O take my hand Walt Whitman!
Such gliding wonders! such sights and sounds!
Such join'd unended links, each hook'd to the next,
Each answering all, each sharing the earth with all.

What widens within you Walt Whitman?
What waves and soils exuding?
What climes? what persons and cities are here?
Who are the infants, some playing, some slumbering?
Who are the girls? who are the married women?
Who are the groups of old men going slowly with their
	arms about each other's necks?
What rivers are these? what forests and fruits are these?
What are the mountains call'd that rise so high in the
	mists?
What myriads of dwellings are they fill'd with dwellers?

2

Within me latitude widens, longitude lengthens,
Asia, Africa, Europe, are to the east—America is provided
	for in the west,
Banding the bulge of the earth winds the hot equator,
Curiously north and south turn the axis-ends,
Within me is the longest day, the sun wheels in slanting
	rings, it does not set for months,

Stretch'd in due time within me the midnight sun just
    rises above the horizon and sinks again,
Within me zones, seas, cataracts, forests, volcanoes,
    groups,
Malaysia, Polynesia, and the great West Indian islands.

3

What do you hear Walt Whitman?

I hear the workman singing and the farmer's wife singing,
I hear in the distance the sounds of children and of ani-
    mals early in the day,
I hear emulous shouts of Australians pursuing the wild
    horse,
I hear the Spanish dance with castanets in the chestnut
    shade, to the rebeck and guitar,
I hear continual echoes from the Thames,
I hear fierce French liberty songs,
I hear of the Italian boat-sculler the musical recitative of
    old poems,
I hear the locusts in Syria as they strike the grain and
    grass with the showers of their terrible clouds,
I hear the Coptic refrain toward sundown, pensively
    falling on the breast of the black venerable vast
    mother the Nile,
I hear the chirp of the Mexican muleteer, and the bells of
    the mule,
I hear the Arab muezzin calling from the top of the
    mosque,
I hear the Christian priests at the altars of their churches,
    I hear the responsive bass and soprano,

I hear the cry of the Cossack, and the sailor's voice putting
    to sea at Okotsk,
I hear the wheeze of the slave-coffle as the slaves march
    on, as the husky gangs pass on by twos and threes,
    fasten'd together with wrist-chains and ankle-chains,
I hear the Hebrew reading his records and psalms,
I hear the rhythmic myths of the Greeks, and the strong
    legends of the Romans,
I hear the tale of the divine life and bloody death of the
    beautiful God the Christ,
I hear the Hindoo teaching his favorite pupil the loves,
    wars, adages, transmitted safely to this day from
    poets who wrote three thousand years ago.

4

What do you see Walt Whitman?
Who are they you salute, and that one after another salute
    you?

I see a great round wonder rolling through space,
I see diminute farms, hamlets, ruins, graveyards, jails, fac-
    tories, palaces, hovels, huts of barbarians, tents of
    nomads upon the surface,
I see the shaded part on one side where the sleepers are
    sleeping, and the sunlit part on the other side,
I see the curious rapid change of the light and shade,
I see distant lands, as real and near to the inhabitants of
    them as my land is to me.

I see plenteous waters,
I see mountain peaks, I see the sierras of Andes where
    they range,
I see plainly the Himalayas, Chian Shahs, Altays, Ghauts,
I see the giant pinnacles of Elbruz, Kazbek, Bazardjusi,
I see the Styrian Alps, and the Karnac Alps,
I see the Pyrenees, Balks, Carpathians, and to the north
    the Dofrafields, and off at sea mount Hecla,
I see Vesuvius and Etna, the mountains of the Moon, and
    the Red mountains of Madagascar,
I see the Lybian, Arabian, and Asiatic deserts,
I see huge dreadful Arctic and Antarctic icebergs,
I see the superior oceans and the inferior ones, the
    Atlantic and Pacific, the sea of Mexico, the Brazilian
    sea, and the sea of Peru,
The waters of Hindustan, the China sea, and the gulf of
    Guinea,
The Japan waters, the beautiful bay of Nagasaki land-
    lock'd in its mountains,
The spread of the Baltic, Caspian, Bothnia, the British
    shores, and the bay of Biscay,
The clear-sunn'd Mediterranean, and from one to another
    of its islands,
The White sea, and the sea around Greenland.

I behold the mariners of the world,
Some are in storms, some in the night with the watch on
    the look-out,
Some drifting helplessly, some with contagious diseases.

I behold the sail and steamships of the world, some in
    clusters in port, some on their voyages,

Some double the cape of Storms, some cape Verde, oth-
    ers capes Guardafui, Bon, or Bajadore,
Others Dondra head, others pass the straits of Sunda, oth-
    ers cape Lopatka, others Behring's straits,
Others cape Horn, others sail the gulf of Mexico or along
    Cuba or Hayti, others Hudson's bay or Baffin's bay,
Others pass the straits of Dover, others enter the Wash,
    others the firth of Solway, others round cape Clear,
    others the Land's End,
Others traverse the Zuyder Zee or the Scheld,
Others as comers and goers at Gibraltar or the Dard-
    anelles,
Others sternly push their way through the northern win-
    ter-packs,
Others descend or ascend the Obi or the Lena,
Others the Niger or the Congo, others the Indus, the
    Burampooter and Cambodia,
Others wait steam'd up ready to start in the ports of Aus-
    tralia,
Wait at Liverpool, Glasgow, Dublin, Marseilles, Lisbon,
    Naples, Hamburg, Bremen, Bordeaux, the Hague,
    Copenhagen,
Wait at Valparaiso, Rio Janeiro, Panama.

5

I see the tracks of the railroads of the earth,
I see them in Great Britain, I see them in Europe,
I see them in Asia and in Africa.

I see the electric telegraphs of the earth,
I see the filaments of the news of the wars, deaths, losses,
    gains, passions, of my race.

I see the long river-stripes of the earth,
I see the Amazon and the Paraguay,
I see the four great rivers of China, the Amour, the Yellow
    River, the Yiang-tse, and the Pearl,
I see where the Seine flows, and where the Danube, the
    Loire, the Rhone, and the Guadalquiver flow,
I see the windings of the Volga, the Dnieper, the Oder,
I see the Tuscan going down the Arno, and the Venetian
    along the Po,
I see the Greek seaman sailing out of Egina bay.

6

I see the site of the old empire of Assyria, and that of Per-
    sia, and that of India,
I see the falling of the Ganges over the high rim of
    Saukara.

I see the place of the idea of the Deity incarnated by
    avatars in human forms,
I see the spots of the successions of priests on the earth,
    oracles, sacrifices, brahmins, sabians, llamas, monks,
    muftis, exhorters,
I see where druids walk'd the groves of Mona, I see the
    mistletoe and vervain,
I see the temples of the deaths of the bodies of Gods, I see
    the old signifiers.

I see Christ eating the bread of his last supper in the midst
    of youths and old persons,
I see where the strong divine young man the Hercules
    toil'd faithfully and long and then died,
I see the place of the innocent rich life and hapless fate of
    the beautiful nocturnal son, the full-limb'd Bacchus,
I see Kneph, blooming, drest in blue, with the crown of
    feathers on his head,
I see Hermes, unsuspected, dying, well-belov'd, saying
    to the people *Do not weep for me,*
This is not my true country, I have lived banish'd from my true
    country, I now go back there,
I return to the celestial sphere where every one goes in his turn.

7

I see the battle-fields of the earth, grass grows upon them
    and blossoms and corn,
I see the tracks of ancient and modern expeditions.

I see the nameless masonries, venerable messages of the
    unknown events, heroes, records of the earth.

I see the places of the sagas,
I see pine-trees and fir-trees torn by northern blasts,
I see granite bowlders and cliffs, I see green meadows and
    lakes,
I see the burial-cairns of Scandinavian warriors,
I see them raised high with stones by the marge of restless
    oceans, that the dead men's spirits when they wea-
    ried of their quiet graves might rise up through the

mounds and gaze on the tossing billows, and be
refresh'd by storms, immensity, liberty, action.

I see the steppes of Asia,
I see the tumuli of Mongolia, I see the tents of Kalmucks
and Baskirs,
I see the nomadic tribes with herds of oxen and cows,
I see the table-lands notch'd with ravines, I see the jungles
and deserts,
I see the camel, the wild steed, the bustard, the fat-tail'd
sheep, the antelope, and the burrowing wolf.

I see the highlands of Abyssinia,
I see flocks of goats feeding, and see the fig-tree,
tamarind, date,
And see fields of teff-wheat and places of verdure and
gold.

I see the Brazilian vaquero,
I see the Bolivian ascending mount Sorata,
I see the Wacho crossing the plains, I see the incompara-
ble rider of horses with his lasso on his arm,
I see over the pampas the pursuit of wild cattle for their
hides.

8

I see the regions of snow and ice,
I see the sharp-eyed Samoiede and the Finn,
I see the seal-seeker in his boat poising his lance,
I see the Siberian on his slight-built sledge drawn by dogs,

I see the porpoise-hunters, I see the whale-crews of the
　　south Pacific and the north Atlantic,
I see the cliffs, glaciers, torrents, valleys, of Switzerland—
　　I mark the long winters and the isolation.

I see the cities of the earth and make myself at random a
　　part of them,
I am a real Parisian,
I am a habitan of Vienna, St. Petersburg, Berlin, Constan-
　　tinople,
I am of Adelaide, Sidney, Melbourne,
I am of London, Manchester, Bristol, Edinburgh, Limer-
　　ick,
I am of Madrid, Cadiz, Barcelona, Oporto, Lyons, Brus-
　　sels, Berne, Frankfort, Stuttgart, Turin, Florence,
I belong in Moscow, Cracow, Warsaw, or northward in
　　Christiania or Stockholm, or in Siberian Irkutsk, or in
　　some street in Iceland,
I descend upon all those cities, and rise from them again.

10

I see vapors exhaling from unexplored countries,
I see the savage types, the bow and arrow, the poison'd
　　splint, the fetich, and the obi.

I see African and Asiatic towns,
I see Algiers, Tripoli, Derne, Mogadore, Timbuctoo, Mon-
　　rovia,
I see the swarms of Pekin, Canton, Benares, Delhi, Cal-
　　cutta, Tokio,

I see the Kruman in his hut, and the Dahoman and
　　Ashantee-man in their huts,
I see the Turk smoking opium in Aleppo,
I see the picturesque crowds at the fairs of Khiva and
　　those of Herat,
I see Teheran, I see Muscat and Medina and the interven-
　　ing sands,I see the caravans toiling onward,
I see Egypt and the Egyptians, I see the pyramids and
　　obelisks,
I look on chisell'd histories, records of conquering kings,
　　dynasties, cut in slabs of sand-stone, or on granite-
　　blocks,
I see at Memphis mummy-pits containing mummies
　　embalm'd, swathed in linen cloth, lying there many
　　centuries,
I look on the fall'n Theban, the large-ball'd eyes, the side-
　　drooping neck, the hands folded across the breast.

I see all the menials of the earth, laboring,
I see all the prisoners in the prisons,
I see the defective human bodies of the earth,
The blind, the deaf and dumb, idiots, hunchbacks,
　　lunatics,
The pirates, thieves, betrayers, murderers, slave-makers
　　of the earth,
The helpless infants, and the helpless old men and
　　women.

I see male and female everywhere,
I see the serene brotherhood of philosophs,
I see the constructiveness of my race,

I see the results of the perseverance and industry of my
   race,
I see ranks, colors, barbarisms, civilizations, I go among
   them, I mix indiscriminately,
And I salute all the inhabitants of the earth.

11

You whoever you are!
You daughter or son of England!
You of the mighty Slavic tribes and empires! you Russ in
   Russia!
You dim-descended, black, divine-soul'd African, large,
   fine-headed, nobly-form'd, superbly destin'd, on
   equal terms with me!
You Norwegian! Swede! Dane! Icelander! you Prussian!
You Spaniard of Spain! you Portuguese!
You Frenchwoman and Frenchman of France!
You Belge! you liberty-lover of the Netherlands! (you
   stock whence I myself have descended;)
You sturdy Austrian! you Lombard! Hun! Bohemian!
   farmer of Styria!
You neighbor of the Danube!
You working-man of the Rhine, the Elbe, or the Weser!
   you working-woman too!
You Sardinian! you Bavarian! Swabian! Saxon! Wal-
   lachian! Bulgarian!
You Roman! Neapolitan! you Greek!
You lithe matador in the arena at Seville!
You mountaineer living lawlessly on the Taurus or Cau-
   casus!

You Bokh horse-herd watching your mares and stallions
    feeding!

You beautiful-bodied Persian at full speed in the saddle
    shooting arrows to the mark!

You Chinaman and Chinawoman of China! you Tartar of
    Tartary!

You women of the earth subordinated at your tasks!

You Jew journeying in your old age through every risk to
    stand once on Syrian ground!

You other Jews waiting in all lands for your Messiah!

You thoughtful Armenian pondering by some stream of
    the Euphrates! you peering amid the ruins of Nin-
    eveh! you ascending mount Ararat!

You foot-worn pilgrim welcoming the far-away sparkle of
    the minarets of Mecca!

You sheiks along the stretch from Suez to Bab-el-mandeb
    ruling your families and tribes!

You olive-grower tending your fruit on fields of
    Nazareth, Damascus, or Lake Tiberias!

You Thibet trader on the wide inland or bargaining in the
    shops of Lassa!

You Japanese man or woman! you liver in Madagascar,
    Ceylon, Sumatra, Borneo!

All you continentals of Asia, Africa, Europe, Australia,
    indifferent of place!

All you on the numberless islands of the archipelagoes of
    the sea!

And you of centuries hence when you listen to me!

And you each and everywhere whom I specify not, but
    include just the same!

Health to you! good will to you all, from me and Amer-
    ica sent!

Each of us inevitable,
Each of us limitless—each of us with his or her right upon
    the earth,
Each of us allow'd the eternal purports of the earth,
Each of us here as divinely as any is here.

12

You Hottentot with clicking palate! you woolly-hair'd
    hordes!
You own'd persons dropping sweat-drops or blood-
    drops!
You human forms with the fathomless ever-impressive
    countenances of brutes!
You poor koboo whom the meanest of the rest look down
    upon for all your glimmering language and spiritu-
    ality!
You dwarf'd Kamtschatkan, Greenlander, Lapp!
You Austral negro, naked, red, sooty, with protrusive lip,
    groveling, seeking your food!
You Caffre, Berber, Soudanese!
You haggard, uncouth, untutor'd Bedowee!
You plague-swarms in Madras, Nankin, Kaubul, Cairo!
You benighted roamer of Amazonia! you Patagonian! you
    Feejeeman!
I do not prefer others so very much before you either,
I do not say one word against you, away back there where
    you stand,
(You will come forward in due time to my side.)

13

My spirit has pass'd in compassion and determination
    around the whole earth,
I have look'd for equals and lovers and found them ready
    for me in all lands,
I think some divine rapport has equalized me with them.

You vapors, I think I have risen with you, moved away
    to distant continents, and fallen down there, for rea-
    sons,
I think I have blown with you you winds;
You waters I have finger'd every shore with you,
I have run through what any river or strait of the globe
    has run through,
I have taken my stand on the bases of peninsulas and on
    the high embedded rocks, to cry thence:

Salut au monde!
What cities the light or warmth penetrates I penetrate
    those cities myself,
All islands to which birds wing their way I wing my way
    myself.

Toward you all, in America's name,
I raise high the perpendicular hand, I make the signal,
To remain after me in sight forever,
For all the haunts and homes of men.

＊

SONG OF THE OPEN ROAD.

1

Afoot and light-hearted I take to the open road,
Healthy, free, the world before me,
The long brown path before me leading wherever I
    choose.

Henceforth I ask not good-fortune, I myself am good-for-
    tune,
Henceforth I whimper no more, postpone no more, need
    nothing,
Done with indoor complaints, libraries, querulous criti-
    cisms,
Strong and content I travel the open road.

The earth, that is sufficient,
I do not want the constellations any nearer,
I know they are very well where they are,
I know they suffice for those who belong to them,

(Still here I carry my old delicious burdens,
I carry them, men and women, I carry them with me
    wherever I go,
I swear it is impossible for me to get rid of them
I am fill'd with them, and I will fill them in return.)

2

You road I enter upon and look around, I believe you are
    not all that is here,
I believe that much unseen is also here.

Here the profound lesson of reception, nor preference nor
    denial,
The black with his woolly head, the felon, the diseas'd,
    the illiterate person, are not denied;
The birth, the hasting after the physician, the beggar's
    tramp, the drunkard's stagger, the laughing party of
    mechanics,
The escaped youth, the rich person's carriage, the fop, the
    eloping couple,
The early market-man, the hearse, the moving of furni-
    ture into the town, the return back from the town,
They pass, I also pass, any thing passes, none can be inter-
    dicted,
None but are accepted, none but shall be dear to me.

3

You air that serves me with breath to speak!
You objects that call from diffusion my meanings and
    give them shape!
You light that wraps me and all things in delicate equable
    showers!
You paths worn in the irregular hollows by the roadsides!
I believe you are latent with unseen existences, you are so
    dear to me.

You flagg'd walks of the cities! you strong curbs at the
    edges!
You ferries! you planks and posts of wharves! you timber-
    lined sides! you distant ships!
You rows of houses! you window-pierc'd façades! you
    roofs!
You porches and entrances! you copings and iron guards!
You windows whose transparent shells might expose so
    much!
You doors and ascending steps! you arches!
You gray stones of interminable pavements! you trodden
    crossings!
From all that has touch'd you I believe you have imparted
    to yourselves, and now would impart the same
    secretly to me,
From the living and the dead you have peopled your
    impassive surfaces, and the spirits thereof would be
    evident and amicable with me.

4

The earth expanding right hand and left hand,
The picture alive, every part in its best light,
The music falling in where it is wanted, and stopping
    where it is not wanted,
The cheerful voice of the public road, the gay fresh senti-
    ment of the road.

O highway I travel, do you say to me Do not leave me?
Do you say *Venture not—if you leave me you are lost?*
Do you say *I am already prepared, I am well-beaten and unde-*
    nied, adhere to me?

O public road, I say back I am not afraid to leave you, yet
 I love you,
You express me better than I can express myself,
You shall be more to me than my poem.

I think heroic deeds were all conceiv'd in the open air,
 and all free poems also,
I think I could stop here myself and do miracles,
I think whatever I shall meet on the road I shall like, and
 whoever beholds me shall like me,
I think whoever I see must be happy.

5

From this hour I ordain myself loos'd of limits and imag-
 inary lines,
Going where I list, my own master total and absolute,
Listening to others, considering well what they say,
Pausing, searching, receiving, contemplating,
Gently, but with undeniable will, divesting myself of the
 holds that would hold me.

I inhale great draughts of space,
The east and the west are mine, and the north and the
 south are mine.

I am larger, better than I thought,
I did not know I held so much goodness.

All seems beautiful to me,
I can repeat over to men and women You have done such
 good to me I would do the same to you,

I will recruit for myself and you as I go,
I will scatter myself among men and women as I go,
I will toss a new gladness and roughness among them,
Whoever denies me it shall not trouble me,
Whoever accepts me he or she shall be blessed and shall
      bless me.

6

Now if a thousand perfect men were to appear it would
      not amaze me,
Now if a thousand beautiful forms of women appear'd it
      would not astonish me.

Now I see the secret of the making of the best persons,
It is to grow in the open air and to eat and sleep with the
      earth.

Here a great personal deed has room,
(Such a deed seizes upon the hearts of the whole race of
      men,
Its effusion of strength and will overwhelms law and
      mocks all authority and all argument against it.)

Here is the test of wisdom,
Wisdom is not finally tested in schools,
Wisdom cannot be pass'd from one having it to another
      not having it,
Wisdom is of the soul, is not susceptible of proof, is its
      own proof,
Applies to all stages and objects and qualities and is con-
      tent,

Is the certainty of the reality and immortality of things,
    and the excellence of things;
Something there is in the float of the sight of things that
    provokes it out of the soul.

Now I re-examine philosophies and religions,
They may prove well in lecture-rooms, yet not prove at all
    under the spacious clouds and along the landscape
    and flowing currents.

Here is realization,
Here is a man tallied—he realizes here what he has in
    him,
The past, the future, majesty, love—if they are vacant of
    you, you are vacant of them.

Only the kernel of every object nourishes;
Where is he who tears off the husks for you and me?
Where is he that undoes stratagems and envelopes for
    you and me?

Here is adhesiveness, it is not previously fashion'd, it is
    apropos;
Do you know what it is as you pass to be loved by
    strangers?
Do you know the talk of those turning eye-balls?

7

Here is the efflux of the soul,
The efflux of the soul comes from within through
    embower'd gates, ever provoking questions,

These yearnings why are they? these thoughts in the
  darkness why are they?
Why are there men and women that while they are nigh
  me the sunlight expands my blood?
Why when they leave me do my pennants of joy sink flat
  and lank?
Why are there trees I never walk under but large and
  melodious thoughts descend upon me?
(I think they hang there winter and summer on those trees
  and always drop fruit as I pass;)
What is it I interchange so suddenly with strangers?
What with some driver as I ride on the seat by his side?
What with some fisherman drawing his seine by the shore
  as I walk by and pause?
What gives me to be free to a woman's and man's good-
  will? what gives them to be free to mine?

8

The efflux of the soul is happiness, here is happiness,
I think it pervades the open air, waiting at all times,
Now it flows unto us, we are rightly charged.

Here rises the fluid and attaching character,
The fluid and attaching character is the freshness and
  sweetness of man and woman,
(The herbs of the morning sprout no fresher and sweeter
  every day out of the roots of themselves, than it
  sprouts fresh and sweet continually out of itself.)

Toward the fluid and attaching character exudes the
  sweat of the love of young and old,

From it falls distill'd the charm that mocks beauty and
    attainments,
Toward it heaves the shuddering longing ache of contact.

9

Allons! whoever you are come travel with me!
Traveling with me you find what never tires.

The earth never tires,
The earth is rude, silent, incomprehensible at first, Nature
    is rude and incomprehensible at first,
Be not discouraged, keep on, there are divine things well
    envelop'd,
I swear to you there are divine things more beautiful than
    words can tell.

Allons! we must not stop here,
However sweet these laid-up stores, however convenient
    this dwelling we cannot remain here,
However shelter'd this port and however calm these
    waters we must not anchor here,
However welcome the hospitality that surrounds us we
    are permitted to receive it but a little while.

10

Allons! the inducements shall be greater,
We will sail pathless and wild seas,
We will go where winds blow, waves dash, and the Yan-
    kee clipper speeds by under full sail.

Allons! with power, liberty, the earth, the elements,
Health, defiance, gayety, self-esteem, curiosity;
Allons! from all formules!
From your formules, O bat-eyed and materialistic priests.

The stale cadaver blocks up the passage—the burial waits
    no longer.

Allons! yet take warning!
He traveling with me needs the best blood, thews,
    endurance,
None may come to the trial till he or she bring courage
    and health,
Come not here if you have already spent the best of your-
    self,
Only those may come who come in sweet and determin'd
    bodies,
No diseas'd person, no rum-drinker or venereal taint is
    permitted here.

(I and mine do not convince by arguments, similes,
    rhymes,
We convince by our presence.)

11

Listen! I will be honest with you,
I do not offer the old smooth prizes, but offer rough new
    prizes,
These are the days that must happen to you:
You shall not heap up what is call'd riches,

You shall scatter with lavish hand all that you earn or
    achieve,
You but arrive at the city to which you were destin'd, you
    hardly settle yourself to satisfaction before you are
    call'd by an irresistible call to depart,
You shall be treated to the ironical smiles and mockings of
    those who remain behind you,
What beckonings of love you receive you shall only
    answer with passionate kisses of parting,
You shall not allow the hold of those who spread their
    reach'd hands toward you.

12

Allons! after the great Companions, and to belong to
    them!
They too are on the road—they are the swift and majestic
    men—they are the greatest women,
Enjoyers of calms of seas and storms of seas,
Sailors of many a ship, walkers of many a mile of land,
Habitués of many distant countries, habitués of far-dis-
    tant dwellings,
Trusters of men and women, observers of cities, solitary
    toilers,
Pausers and contemplators of tufts, blossoms, shells of the
    shore,
Dancers at wedding-dances, kissers of brides, tender
    helpers of children, bearers of children,
Soldiers of revolts, standers by gaping graves, lowerers-
    down of coffins,

Journeyers over consecutive seasons, over the years, the
    curious years each emerging from that which pre-
    ceded it,
Journeyers as with companions, namely their own
    diverse phases,
Forth-steppers from the latent unrealized baby-days,
Journeyers gayly with their own youth, journeyers with
    their bearded and well-grain'd manhood,
Journeyers with their womanhood, ample, unsurpass'd,
    content,
Journeyers with their own sublime old age of manhood or
    womanhood,
Old age, calm, expanded, broad with the haughty breadth
    of the universe,
Old age, flowing free with the delicious near-by freedom
    of death.

13

Allons! to that which is endless as it was beginningless,
To undergo much, tramps of days, rests of nights,
To merge all in the travel they tend to, and the days and
    nights they tend to,
Again to merge them in the start of superior journeys,
To see nothing anywhere but what you may reach it and
    pass it,
To conceive no time, however distant, but what you may
    reach it and pass it,
To look up or down no road but it stretches and waits for
    you, however long but it stretches and waits for you,
To see no being, not God's or any, but you also go thither,

To see no possession but you may possess it, enjoying all
     without labor or purchase, abstracting the feast yet
     not abstracting one particle of it,
To take the best of the farmer's farm and the rich man's
     elegant villa, and the chaste blessings of the well-mar-
     ried couple, and the fruits of orchards and flowers of
     gardens,
To take to your use out of the compact cities as you pass
     through,
To carry buildings and streets with you afterward wher-
     ever you go,
To gather the minds of men out of their brains as you
     encounter them, to gather the love out of their hearts,
To take your lovers on the road with you, for all that you
     leave them behind you,
To know the universe itself as a road, as many roads, as
     roads for traveling souls.

All parts away for the progress of souls,
All religion, all solid things, arts, governments—all that
     was or is apparent upon this globe or any globe, falls
     into niches and corners before the procession of souls
     along the grand roads of the universe.

Of the progress of the souls of men and women along the
     grand roads of the universe, all other progress is the
     needed emblem and sustenance.

Forever alive, forever forward,
Stately, solemn, sad, withdrawn, baffled, mad, turbulent,
     feeble, dissatisfied,

Desperate, proud, fond, sick, accepted by men, rejected by
    men,
They go! they go! I know that they go, but I know not
    where they go,
But I know that they go toward the best—toward some-
    thing great.

Whoever you are, come forth! or man or woman come
    forth!
You must not stay sleeping and dallying there in the
    house, though you built it, or though it has been built
    for you.

Out of the dark confinement! out from behind the screen!
It is useless to protest, I know all and expose it.

Behold through you as bad as the rest,
Through the laughter, dancing, dining, supping, of peo-
    ple,
Inside of dresses and ornaments, inside of those wash'd
    and trimm'd faces,
Behold a secret silent loathing and despair.

No husband, no wife, no friend, trusted to hear the con-
    fession,
Another self, a duplicate of every one, skulking and hid-
    ing it goes,
Formless and wordless through the streets of the cities,
    polite and bland in the parlors,
In the cars of railroads, in steamboats, in the public assem-
    bly,

Home to the houses of men and women, at the table, in
 the bedroom, everywhere,
Smartly attired, countenance smiling, form upright, death
 under the breast-bones, hell under the skull-bones,
Under the broadcloth and gloves, under the ribbons and
 artificial flowers,
Keeping fair with the customs, speaking not a syllable of
 itself,
Speaking of any thing else but never of itself.

14

Allons! through struggles and wars!
The goal that was named cannot be countermanded.

Have the past struggles succeeded?
What has succeeded? yourself? your nation? Nature?
Now understand me well—it is provided in the essence of
 things that from any fruition of success, no matter
 what, shall come forth something to make a greater
 struggle necessary.

My call is the call of battle, I nourish active rebellion,
He going with me must go well arm'd,
He going with me goes often with spare diet, poverty,
 angry enemies, desertions.

15

Allons! the road is before us!
It is safe—I have tried it—my own feet have tried it well—
 be not detain'd!

Let the paper remain on the desk unwritten, and the book
    on the shelf unopen'd!
Let the tools remain in the workshop! let the money
    remain unearn'd!
Let the school stand! mind not the cry of the teacher!
Let the preacher preach in his pulpit! let the lawyer plead
    in the court, and the judge expound the law.

Camerado, I give you my hand!
I give you my love more precious than money,
I give you myself before preaching or law;
Will you give me yourself? will you come travel with me?
Shall we stick by each other as long as we live?

*

CROSSING BROOKLYN FERRY.

1

Flood-tide below me! I see you face to face!
Clouds of the west—sun there half an hour high—I see
    you also face to face.

Crowds of men and women attired in the usual costumes,
    how curious you are to me!
On the ferry-boats the hundreds and hundreds that cross,
    returning home, are more curious to me than you
    suppose,

And you that shall cross from shore to shore years hence
are more to me, and more in my meditations, than
you might suppose.

2

The impalpable sustenance of me from all things at all
hours of the day,
The simple, compact, well-join'd scheme, myself disinte-
grated, every one disintegrated yet part of the
scheme,
The similitudes of the past and those of the future,
The glories strung like beads on my smallest sights and
hearings, on the walk in the street and the passage
over the river,
The current rushing so swiftly and swimming with me far
away,
The others that are to follow me, the ties between me and
them,
The certainty of others, the life, love, sight, hearing of oth-
ers.

Others will enter the gates of the ferry and cross from
shore to shore,
Others will watch the run of the flood-tide,
Others will see the shipping of Manhattan north and
west, and the heights of Brooklyn to the south and
east,
Others will see the islands large and small;
Fifty years hence, others will see them as they cross, the
sun half an hour high,

A hundred years hence, or ever so many hundred years
    hence, others will see them,
Will enjoy the sunset, the pouring in of the flood-tide, the
    falling-back to the sea of the ebb-tide.

3

It avails not, time nor place—distance avails not,
I am with you, you men and women of a generation, or
    ever so many generations hence,
Just as you feel when you look on the river and sky, so I
    felt,
Just as any of you is one of a living crowd, I was one of a
    crowd,
Just as you are refresh'd by the gladness of the river and
    the bright flow, I was refresh'd,
Just as you stand and lean on the rail, yet hurry with the
    swift current, I stood yet was hurried,
Just as you look on the numberless masts of ships and the
    thick-stemm'd pipes of steamboats, I look'd.

I too many and many a time cross'd the river of old,
Watched the Twelfth-month sea-gulls, saw them high in
    the air floating with motionless wings, oscillating
    their bodies,
Saw how the glistening yellow lit up parts of their bodies
    and left the rest in strong shadow,
Saw the slow-wheeling circles and the gradual edging
    toward the south,
Saw the reflection of the summer sky in the water,
Had my eyes dazzled by the shimmering track of beams,

Look'd at the fine centrifugal spokes of light round the
    shape of my head in the sunlit water,
Look'd on the haze on the hills southward and south-
    westward,
Look'd on the vapor as it flew in fleeces tinged with vio-
    let,
Look'd toward the lower bay to notice the vessels arriv-
    ing,
Saw their approach, saw aboard those that were near me,
Saw the white sails of schooners and sloops, saw the ships
    at anchor,
The sailors at work in the rigging or out astride the spars,
The round masts, the swinging motion of the hulls, the
    slender serpentine pennants,
The large and small steamers in motion, the pilots in their
    pilot-houses,
The white wake left by the passage, the quick tremulous
    whirl of the wheels,
The flags of all nations, the falling of them at sunset,
The scallop-edged waves in the twilight, the ladled cups,
    the frolicsome crests and glistening,
The stretch afar growing dimmer and dimmer, the gray
    walls of the granite storehouses by the docks,
On the river the shadowy group, the big steam-tug closely
    flank'd on each side by the barges, the hay-boat, the
    belated lighter,
On the neighboring shore the fires from the foundry
    chimneys burning high and glaringly into the night,
Casting their flicker of black contrasted with wild red and
    yellow light over the tops of houses, and down into
    the clefts of streets.

4

These and all else were to me the same as they are to you,
I loved well those cities, loved well the stately and rapid
    river,
The men and women I saw were all near to me,
Others the same—others who look back on me because I
    look'd forward to them,
(The time will come, though I stop here to-day and to-
    night.)

5

What is it then between us?
What is the count of the scores or hundreds of years
    between us?

Whatever it is, it avails not—distance avails not, and place
    avails not,
I too lived, Brooklyn of ample hills was mine,
I too walk'd the streets of Manhattan island, and bathed
    in the waters around it,
I too felt the curious abrupt questionings stir within me,
In the day among crowds of people sometimes they came
    upon me,
In my walks home late at night or as I lay in my bed they
    came upon me,
I too had been struck from the float forever held in solu-
    tion,
I too had receiv'd identity by my body,
That I was I knew was of my body, and what I should be
    I knew I should be of my body.

6

It is not upon you alone the dark patches fall,
The dark threw its patches down upon me also,
The best I had done seem'd to me blank and suspicious,
My great thoughts as I supposed them, were they not in
    reality meagre?
Nor is it you alone who know what it is to be evil,
I am he who knew what it was to be evil,
I too knitted the old knot of contrariety,
Blabb'd, blush'd, resented, lied, stole, grudg'd,
Had guile, anger, lust, hot wishes I dared not speak,
Was wayward, vain, greedy, shallow, sly, cowardly,
    malignant,
The wolf, the snake, the hog, not wanting in me,
The cheating look, the frivolous word, the adulterous
    wish, not wanting,
Refusals, hates, postponements, meanness, laziness, none
    of these wanting,
Was one with the rest, the days and haps of the rest,
Was call'd by my nighest name by clear loud voices of
    young men as they saw me approaching or passing,
Felt their arms on my neck as I stood, or the negligent
    leaning of their flesh against me as I sat,
Saw many I loved in the street or ferry-boat or public
    assembly, yet never told them a word,
Lived the same life with the rest, the same old laughing,
    gnawing, sleeping,
Play'd the part that still looks back on the actor or actress,
The same old role, the role that is what we make it, as
    great as we like,
Or as small as we like, or both great and small.

7

Closer yet I approach you,
What thought you have of me now, I had as much of
    you—I laid in my stores in advance,
I consider'd long and seriously of you before you were
    born.

Who was to know what should come home to me?
Who knows but I am enjoying this?
Who knows, for all the distance, but I am as good as look-
    ing at you now, for all you cannot see me?

8

Ah, what can ever be more stately and admirable to me
    than mast-hemm'd Manhattan?
River and sunset and scallop-edg'd waves of flood-tide?
The sea-gulls oscillating their bodies, the hay-boat in the
    twilight, and the belated lighter?
What gods can exceed these that clasp me by the hand,
    and with voices I love call me promptly and loudly by
    my nighest name as I approach?
What is more subtle than this which ties me to the woman
    or man that looks in my face?
Which fuses me into you now, and pours my meaning
    into you?

We understand then do we not?
What I promis'd without mentioning it, have you not
    accepted?

What the study could not teach—what the preaching
could not accomplish is accomplish'd, is it not?

9

Flow on, river! flow with the flood-tide, and ebb with the
ebb-tide!

Frolic on, crested and scallop-edg'd waves!

Gorgeous clouds of the sunset! drench with your splen-
dor me, or the men and women generations after me!

Cross from shore to shore, countless crowds of passen-
gers!

Stand up, tall masts of Mannahatta! stand up, beautiful
hills of Brooklyn!

Throb, baffled and curious brain! throw out questions and
answers!

Suspend here and everywhere, eternal float of solution!

Gaze, loving and thirsting eyes, in the house or street or
public assembly!

Sound out, voices of young men! loudly and musically
call me by my nighest name!

Live, old life! play the part that looks back on the actor or
actress!

Play the old role, the role that is great or small according
as one makes it!

Consider, you who peruse me, whether I may not in
unknown ways be looking upon you;

Be firm, rail over the river, to support those who lean idly,
yet haste with the hasting current;

Fly on, sea-birds! fly sideways, or wheel in large circles
high in the air;

Receive the summer sky, you water, and faithfully hold
    it till all downcast eyes have time to take it from you!
Diverge, fine spokes of light, from the shape of my head,
    or any one's head, in the sunlit water!
Come on, ships from the lower bay! pass up or down,
    white-sail'd schooners, sloops, lighters!
Flaunt away, flags of all nations! be duly lower'd at sun-
    set!
Burn high your fires, foundry chimneys! cast black shad-
    ows at nightfall! cast red and yellow light over the
    tops of the houses!
Appearances, now or henceforth, indicate what you are,
You necessary film, continue to envelop the soul,
About my body for me, and your body for you, be hung
    out divinest aromas,
Thrive, cities—bring your freight, bring your shows,
    ample and sufficient rivers,
Expand, being than which none else is perhaps more spir-
    itual,
Keep your places, objects than which none else is more
    lasting.

You have waited, you always wait, you dumb, beautiful
    ministers,
We receive you with free sense at last, and are insatiate
    henceforward,
Not you any more shall be able to foil us, or withhold
    yourselves from us,
We use you, and do not cast you aside—we plant you per-
    manently within us,
We fathom you not—we love you—there is perfection in
    you also,

You furnish your parts toward eternity,
Great or small, you furnish your parts toward the soul.

*

SONG OF THE ANSWERER.

1

Now list to my morning's romanza, I tell the signs of the
    Answerer,
To the cities and farms I sing as they spread in the sun-
    shine before me.

A young man comes to me bearing a message from his
    brother,
How shall the young man know the whether and when of
    his brother?
Tell him to send me the signs.

And I stand before the young man face to face, and take
    his right hand in my left hand and his left hand in my
    right hand,
And I answer for his brother and for men, and I answer
    for him that answers for all, and send these signs.

Him all wait for, him all yield up to, his word is decisive
    and final,
Him they accept, in him lave, in him perceive themselves
    as amid light,
Him they immerse and he immerses them.

Beautiful women, the haughtiest nations, laws, the land-
 scape, people, animals,
The profound earth and its attributes and the unquiet
 ocean, (so tell I my morning's romanza,)
All enjoyments and properties and money, and whatever
 money will buy,
The best farms, others toiling and planting and he
 unavoidably reaps,
The noblest and costliest cities, others grading and build-
 ing and he domiciles there,
Nothing for any one but what is for him, near and far are
 for him, the ships in the offing,
The perpetual shows and marches on land are for him if
 they are for anybody.

He puts things in their attitudes,
He puts to-day out of himself with plasticity and love,
He places his own times, reminiscences, parents, broth-
 ers and sisters, associations, employment, politics, so
 that the rest never shame them afterward, nor assume
 to command them.

He is the Answerer,
What can be answer'd he answers, and what cannot be
 answer'd he shows how it cannot be answer'd.

A man is a summons and challenge,
(It is vain to skulk—do you hear that mocking and laugh-
 ter? do you hear the ironical echoes?)

Books, friendships, philosophers, priests, action, pleasure,
 pride, beat up and down seeking to give satisfaction,

He indicates the satisfaction, and indicates them that beat
up and down also.

Whichever the sex, whatever the season or place, he may
go freshly and gently and safely by day or by night,
He has the pass-key of hearts, to him the response of the
prying of hands on the knobs.

His welcome is universal, the flow of beauty is not more
welcome or universal than he is,
The person he favors by day or sleeps with at night is
blessed.

Every existence has its idiom, every thing has an idiom
and tongue,
He resolves all tongues into his own and bestows it upon
men, and any man translates, and any man translates
himself also,
One part does not counteract another part, he is the joiner,
he sees how they join.

He says indifferently and alike *How are you friend?* to the
President at his levee,
And he says *Good-day my brother*, to Cudge that hoes in
the sugar-field,
And both understand him and know that his speech is
right.

He walks with perfect ease in the capitol,
He walks among the Congress, and one Representative
says to another, *Here is our equal appearing and new.*

Then the mechanics take him for a mechanic,
And the soldiers suppose him to be a soldier, and the
    sailors that he has follow'd the sea,
And the authors take him for an author, and the artists for
    an artist,
And the laborers perceive he could labor with them and
    love them,
No matter what the work is, that he is the one to follow it
    or has follow'd it,
No matter what the nation, that he might find his brothers
    and sisters there.

The English believe he comes of their English stock,
A Jew to the Jew he seems, a Russ to the Russ, usual and
    near, removed from none.

Whoever he looks at in the traveler's coffee-house claims
    him,
The Italian or Frenchman is sure, the German is sure, the
    Spaniard is sure, and the island Cuban is sure,
The engineer, the deck-hand on the great lakes, or on the
    Mississippi or St. Lawrence or Sacramento, or Hud-
    son or Paumanok sound, claims him.

The gentleman of perfect blood acknowledges his perfect
    blood,
The insulter, the prostitute, the angry person, the beggar,
    see themselves in the ways of him, he strangely trans-
    mutes them,
They are not vile any more, they hardly know themselves
    they are so grown.

2

The indications and tally of time,
Perfect sanity shows the master among philosophs,
Time, always without break, indicates itself in parts,
What always indicates the poet is the crowd of the pleas-
    ant company of singers, and their words,
The words of the singers are the hours or minutes of the
    light or dark, but the words of the maker of poems are
    the general light and dark,
The maker of poems settles justice, reality, immortality,
His insight and power encircle things and the human
    race,
He is the glory and extract thus far of things and of the
    human race.

The singers do not beget, only the Poet begets,
The singers are welcom'd, understood, appear often
    enough, but rare has the day been, likewise the spot,
    of the birth of the maker of poems, the Answerer,
(Not every century nor every five centuries has contain'd
    such a day, for all its names.)

The singers of successive hours of centuries may have
    ostensible names, but the name of each of them is one
    of the singers,
The name of each is, eye-singer, ear-singer, head-singer,
    sweet-singer, night-singer, parlor-singer, love-singer,
    weird-singer, or something else.

All this time and at all times wait the words of true
    poems,

The words of true poems do not merely please,
The true poets are not followers of beauty but the august
 masters of beauty;
The greatness of sons is the exuding of the greatness of
 mothers and fathers,
The words of true poems are the tuft and final applause of
 science.

Divine instinct, breadth of vision, the law of reason,
 health, rudeness of body, withdrawnness,
Gayety, sun-tan, air-sweetness, such are some of the
 words of poems.

The sailor and traveler underlie the maker of poems, the
 Answerer,
The builder, geometer, chemist, anatomist, phrenologist,
 artist, all these underlie the maker of poems, the
 Answerer.

The words of the true poems give you more than poems,
They give you to form for yourself poems, religions, pol-
 itics, war, peace, behavior, histories, essays, daily life,
 and every thing else,
They balance ranks, colors, races, creeds, and the sexes,
They do not seek beauty, they are sought,
Forever touching them or close upon them follows
 beauty, longing, fain, love-sick.

They prepare for death, yet are they not the finish, but
 rather the outset,
They bring none to his or her terminus or to be content
 and full,

Whom they take they take into space to behold the birth
    of stars, to learn one of the meanings,
To launch off with absolute faith, to sweep through the
    ceaseless rings and never be quiet again.

*

OUR OLD FEUILLAGE.

Always our old feuillage!
Always Florida's green peninsula—always the priceless
    delta of Louisiana— always the cotton-fields of
    Alabama and Texas,
Always California's golden hills and hollows, and the sil-
    ver mountains of New Mexico—always soft-breath'd
    Cuba,
Always the vast slope drain'd by the Southern sea, insep-
    arable with the slopes drain'd by the Eastern and
    Western seas,
The area the eighty-third year of these States, the three
    and a half millions of square miles,
The eighteen thousand miles of sea-coast and bay-coast
    on the main, the thirty thousand miles of river navi-
    gation,
The seven millions of distinct families and the same num-
    ber of dwellings— always these, and more, branching
    forth into numberless branches,
Always the free range and diversity—always the conti-
    nent of Democracy;
Always the prairies, pastures, forests, vast cities, travel-
    ers, Kanada, the snows;

Always these compact lands tied at the hips with the belt
    stringing the huge oval lakes;

Always the West with strong native persons, the increas-
    ing density there, the habitans, friendly, threatening,
    ironical, scorning invaders;

All sights, South, North, East—all deeds, promiscuously
    done at all times,

All characters, movements, growths, a few noticed, myr-
    iads unnoticed,

Through Mannahatta's streets I walking, these things
    gathering,

On interior rivers by night in the glare of pine knots,
    steamboats wooding up,

Sunlight by day on the valley of the Susquehanna, and on
    the valleys of the Potomac and Rappahannock and
    the valleys of the Roanoke and Delaware,

In their northerly wilds beasts of prey haunting the
    Adirondacks the hills or lapping the Saginaw waters
    to drink,

In a lonesome inlet a sheldrake lost from the flock sitting
    on the water rocking silently,

In farmers' barns oxen in the stable, their harvest labor
    done they rest standing, they are too tired,

Afar on arctic ice the she-walrus lying drowsily while her
    cubs play around,

The hawk sailing where men have not yet sail'd, the far-
    thest polar sea, ripply, crystalline, open, beyond the
    floes,

White drift spooning ahead where the ship in the tempest
    dashes,

On solid land what is done in cities as the bells strike mid-
    night together,

In primitive woods the sounds there also sounding, the
   howl of the wolf, the scream of the panther, and the
   hoarse bellow of the elk,
In winter beneath the hard blue ice of Moosehead lake, in
   summer visible through the clear waters, the great
   trout swimming,
In lower latitudes in warmer air in the Carolinas the large
   black buzzard floating slowly high beyond the tree
   tops,
Below, the red cedar festoon'd with tylandria, the pines
   and cypresses growing out of the white sand that
   spreads far and flat,
Rude boats descending the big Pedee, climbing plants,
   parasites with color'd flowers and berries enveloping
   huge trees,
The waving drapery on the live-oak trailing long and low,
   noiselessly waved by the wind,
The camp of Georgia wagoners just after dark, the sup-
   per-fires and the cooking and eating by whites and
   negroes,
Thirty or forty great wagons, the mules, cattle, horses,
   feeding from troughs,
The shadows, gleams, up under the leaves of the old
   sycamore-trees, the flames with the black smoke from
   the pitch-pine curling and rising;
Southern fishermen fishing, the sounds and inlets of
   North Carolina's coast, the shad-fishery and the her-
   ring-fishery, the large sweep-seines, the windlasses
   on shore work'd by horses, the clearing, curing, and
   packing houses;

Deep in the forest in piney woods turpentine dropping
    from the incisions in the trees, there are the turpentine
    works,
There are the negroes at work in good health, the ground
    in all directions is cover'd with pine straw;
In Tennessee and Kentucky slaves busy in the coalings,
    at the forge, by the furnace-blaze, or at the corn-
    shucking,
In Virginia, the planter's son returning after a long
    absence, joyfully welcom'd and kiss'd by the aged
    mulatto nurse,
On rivers boatmen safely moor'd at nightfall in their boats
    under shelter of high banks,
Some of the younger men dance to the sound of the banjo
    or fiddle, others sit on the gunwale smoking and talk-
    ing;
Late in the afternoon the mocking-bird, the American
    mimic, singing in the Great Dismal Swamp,
There are the greenish waters, the resinous odor, the plen-
    teous moss, the cypress-tree, and the juniper-tree;
Northward, young men of Mannahatta, the target com-
    pany from an excursion returning home at evening,
    the musket-muzzles all bear bunches of flowers pre-
    sented by women;
Children at play, or on his father's lap a young boy fallen
    asleep, (how his lips move! how he smiles in his
    sleep!)
The scout riding on horseback over the plains west of the
    Mississippi, he ascends a knoll and sweeps his eyes
    around;

California life, the miner, bearded, dress'd in his rude cos-
tume, the stanch California friendship, the sweet air,
the graves one in passing meets solitary just aside the
horse-path;
Down in Texas the cotton-field, the negro-cabins, drivers
driving mules or oxen before rude carts, cotton bales
piled on banks and wharves;
Encircling all, vast-darting up and wide, the American
Soul, with equal hemispheres, one Love, one Dilation
or Pride;
In arriere the peace-talk with the Iroquois the aborigines,
the calumet, the pipe of good-will, arbitration, and
indorsement,
The sachem blowing the smoke first toward the sun and
then toward the earth,
The drama of the scalp-dance enacted with painted faces
and guttural exclamations,
The setting out of the war-party, the long and stealthy
march,
The single file, the swinging hatchets, the surprise and
slaughter of enemies;
All the acts, scenes, ways, persons, attitudes of these
States, reminiscences, institutions,
All these States compact, every square mile of these States
without excepting a particle;
Me pleas'd, rambling in lanes and country fields, Pau-
manok's fields,
Observing the spiral flight of two little yellow butterflies
shuffling between each other, ascending high in the
air,

The darting swallow, the destroyer of insects, the fall trav-
    eler southward but returning northward early in the
    spring,
The country boy at the close of the day driving the herd of
    cows and shouting to them as they loiter to browse by
    the roadside,
The city wharf, Boston, Philadelphia, Baltimore,
    Charleston, New Orleans, San Francisco,
The departing ships when the sailors heave at the capstan;
Evening—me in my room—the setting sun,
The setting summer sun shining in my open window,
    showing the swarm of flies, suspended, balancing in
    the air in the centre of the room, darting athwart, up
    and down, casting swift shadows in specks on the
    opposite wall where the shine is;
The athletic American matron speaking in public to
    crowds of listeners,
Males, females, immigrants, combinations, the copious-
    ness, the individuality of the States, each for itself—
    the money-makers,
Factories, machinery, the mechanical forces, the windlass,
    lever, pulley, all certainties,
The certainty of space, increase, freedom, futurity,
In space the sporades, the scatter'd islands, the stars—on
    the firm earth, the lands, my lands,
O lands! all so dear to me—what you are, (whatever it is,)
    I putting it at random in these songs, become a part of
    that, whatever it is,
Southward there, I screaming, with wings slow flapping,
    with the myriads of gulls wintering along the coasts
    of Florida,

Otherways there atwixt the banks of the Arkansaw, the
Rio Grande, the Nueces, the Brazos, the Tombigbee,
the Red River, the Saskatchawan or the Osage, I with
the spring waters laughing and skipping and run-
ning,
Northward, on the sands, on some shallow bay of Pau-
manok, I with parties of snowy herons wading in the
wet to seek worms and aquatic plants,
Retreating, triumphantly twittering, the king-bird, from
piercing the crow with its bill, for amusement—and I
triumphantly twittering,
The migrating flock of wild geese alighting in autumn to
refresh themselves, the body of the flock feed, the sen-
tinels outside move around with erect heads watch-
ing, and are from time to time reliev'd by other
sentinels—and I feeding and taking turns with the
rest,
In Kanadian forests the moose, large as an ox, corner'd by
hunters, rising desperately on his hind feet, and
plunging with his fore-feet, the hoofs as sharp as
knives—and I, plunging at the hunters, corner'd and
desperate,
In the Mannahatta, streets, piers, shipping, store-houses,
and the countless workmen working in the shops,
And I too of the Mannahatta, singing thereof—and no less
in myself than the whole of the Mannahatta in itself,
Singing the song of These, my ever-united lands— my
body no more inevitably united, part to part, and
made out of a thousand diverse contributions one
identity, any more than my lands are inevitably
united and made ONE IDENTITY;
Nativities, climates, the grass of the great pastoral Plains,

Cities, labors, death, animals, products, war, good and
    evil—these me,
These affording, in all their particulars, the old feuillage to
    me and to America, how can I do less than pass the
    clew of the union of them, to afford the like to you?
Whoever you are! how can I but offer you divine leaves,
    that you also be eligible as I am?
How can I but as here chanting, invite you for yourself to
    collect bouquets of the incomparable feuillage of
    these States?

※

A SONG OF JOYS.

O to make the most jubilant song!
Full of music—full of manhood, womanhood, infancy!
Full of common employments—full of grain and trees.

O for the voices of animals—O for the swiftness and bal-
    ance of fishes!
O for the dropping of raindrops in a song!
O for the sunshine and motion of waves in a song!

O the joy of my spirit—it is uncaged—it darts like light-
    ning!
It is not enough to have this globe or a certain time,
I will have thousands of globes and all time.

O the engineer's joys! to go with a locomotive!
To hear the hiss of steam, the merry shriek, the steam-
     whistle, the laughing locomotive!
To push with resistless way and speed off in the distance.

O the gleesome saunter over fields and hillsides!
The leaves and flowers of the commonest weeds, the
     moist fresh stillness of the woods,
The exquisite smell of the earth at daybreak, and all
     through the forenoon.

O the horseman's and horsewoman's joys!
The saddle, the gallop, the pressure upon the seat, the
     cool gurgling by the ears and hair.

O the fireman's joys!
I hear the alarm at dead of night,
I hear bells, shouts! I pass the crowd, I run!
The sight of the flames maddens me with pleasure.

O the joy of the strong-brawn'd fighter, towering in the
     arena in perfect condition, conscious of power, thirst-
     ing to meet his opponent.

O the joy of that vast elemental sympathy which only the
     human soul is capable of generating and emitting in
     steady and limitless floods.

O the mother's joys!
The watching, the endurance, the precious love, the
     anguish, the patiently yielded life.

O the joy of increase, growth, recuperation,
The joy of soothing and pacifying, the joy of concord and
  harmony.

O to go back to the place where I was born,
To hear the birds sing once more,
To ramble about the house and barn and over the fields
  once more,
And through the orchard and along the old lanes once
  more.

O to have been brought up on bays, lagoons, creeks, or
  along the coast,
To continue and be employ'd there all my life,
The briny and damp smell, the shore, the salt weeds
  exposed at low water,
The work of fishermen, the work of the eel-fisher and
  clam-fisher;
I come with my clam-rake and spade, I come with my eel-
  spear,
Is the tide out? I join the group of clam-diggers on the
  flats,
I laugh and work with them, I joke at my work like a met-
  tlesome young man;
In winter I take my eel-basket and eel-spear and travel out
  on foot on the ice—I have a small axe to cut holes in
  the ice,
Behold me well-clothed going gayly or returning in the
  afternoon, my brood of tough boys accompanying
  me,

My brood of grown and part-grown boys, who love to be
    with no one else so well as they love to be with me,
By day to work with me, and by night to sleep with me.

Another time in warm weather out in a boat, to lift the
    lobster-pots where they are sunk with heavy stones, (I
    know the buoys,)
O the sweetness of the Fifth-month morning upon the
    water as I row just before sunrise toward the buoys,
I pull the wicker pots up slantingly, the dark green lob-
    sters are desperate with their claws as I take them out,
    I insert wooden pegs in the joints of their pincers,
I go to all the places one after another, and then row back
    to the shore,
There in a huge kettle of boiling water the lobsters shall be
    boil'd till their color becomes scarlet.

Another time mackerel-taking,
Voracious, mad for the hook, near the surface, they seem
    to fill the water for miles;
Another time fishing for rock-fish in Chesapeake bay, I
    one of the brown-faced crew;
Another time trailing for blue-fish off Paumanok, I stand
    with braced body,
My left foot is on the gunwale, my right arm throws far
    out the coils of slender rope,
In sight around me the quick veering and darting of fifty
    skiffs, my companions.

O boating on the rivers,
The voyage down the St. Lawrence, the superb scenery,
    the steamers,

The ships sailing, the Thousand Islands, the occasional
    timber-raft and the raftsmen with long-reaching
    sweep-oars,
The little huts on the rafts, and the stream of smoke when
    they cook supper at evening.

(O something pernicious and dread!
Something far away from a puny and pious life!
Something unproved! something in a trance!
Something escaped from the anchorage and driving free.)

O to work in mines, or forging iron,
Foundry casting, the foundry itself, the rude high roof,
    the ample and shadow'd space,
The furnace, the hot liquid pour'd out and running.

O to resume the joys of the soldier!
To feel the presence of a brave commanding officer—to
    feel his sympathy!
To behold his calmness—to be warm'd in the rays of his
    smile!
To go to battle—to hear the bugles play and the drums
    beat!
To hear the crash of artillery—to see the glittering of the
    bayonets and musket-barrels in the sun!
To see men fall and die and not complain!
To taste the savage taste of blood—to be so devilish!
To gloat so over the wounds and deaths of the enemy.

O the whaleman's joys! O I cruise my old cruise again!
I feel the ship's motion under me, I feel the Atlantic
    breezes fanning me,

I hear the cry again sent down from the mast head,
    There—she blows!
Again I spring up the rigging to look with the rest—we
    descend, wild with excitement,
I leap in the lower'd boat, we row toward our prey where
    he lies,
We approach stealthy and silent, I see the mountainous
    mass, lethargic, basking,
I see the harpooner standing up, I see the weapon dart
    from his vigorous arm;
O swift again far out in the ocean the wounded whale, set-
    tling, running to windward, tows me,
Again I see him rise to breathe, we row close again,
I see a lance driven through his side, press'd deep, turn'd
    in the wound,
Again we back off, I see him settle again, the life is leaving
    him fast,
As he rises he spouts blood, I see him swim in circles nar-
    rower and narrower, swiftly cutting the water—I see
    him die,
He gives one convulsive leap in the centre of the circle,
    and then falls flat and still in the bloody foam.

O the old manhood of me, my noblest joy of all!
My children and grand-children, my white hair and
    beard,
My largeness, calmness, majesty, out of the long stretch of
    my life.

O ripen'd joy of womanhood! O happiness at last!
I am more than eighty years of age, I am the most vener-
    able mother,

How clear is my mind—how all people draw nigh to me!
What attractions are these beyond any before? what
    bloom more than the bloom of youth?
What beauty is this that descends upon me and rises out
    of me?

O the orator's joys!
To inflate the chest, to roll the thunder of the voice out
    from the ribs and throat,
To make the people rage, weep, hate, desire, with your-
    self,
To lead America—to quell America with a great tongue.

O the joy of my soul leaning pois'd on itself, receiving
    identity through materials and loving them, observ-
    ing characters and absorbing them,
My soul vibrated back to me from them, from sight, hear-
    ing, touch, reason, articulation, comparison, memory,
    and the like,
The real life of my senses and flesh transcending my
    senses and flesh,
My body done with materials, my sight done with my
    material eyes,
Proved to me this day beyond cavil that it is not my mate-
    rial eyes which finally see,
Nor my material body which finally loves, walks, laughs,
    shouts, embraces, procreates.

O the farmer's joys!
Ohioan's, Illinoisian's, Wisconsinese', Kanadian's, Iowan's,
    Kansian's, Missourian's, Oregonese' joys!
To rise at peep of day and pass forth nimbly to work,

To plough land in the fall for winter-sown crops,
To plough land in the spring for maize,
To train orchards, to graft the trees, to gather apples in the
    fall.

O to bathe in the swimming-bath, or in a good place along
    shore,
To splash the water! to walk ankle-deep, or race naked
    along the shore.

O to realize space!
The plenteousness of all, that there are no bounds,
To emerge and be of the sky, of the sun and moon and fly-
    ing clouds, as one with them.

O the joy of a manly self-hood!
To be servile to none, to defer to none, not to any tyrant
    known or unknown,
To walk with erect carriage, a step springy and elastic,
To look with calm gaze or with a flashing eye,
To speak with a full and sonorous voice out of a broad
    chest,
To confront with your personality all the other personali-
    ties of the earth.

Know'st thou the excellent joys of youth?
Joys of the dear companions and of the merry word and
    laughing face?
Joy of the glad light-beaming day, joy of the wide-
    breath'd games?

Joy of sweet music, joy of the lighted ball-room and the
     dancers?
Joy of the plenteous dinner, strong carouse and drinking?

Yet O my soul supreme!
Know'st thou the joys of pensive thought?
Joys of the free and lonesome heart, the tender, gloomy
     heart?
Joys of the solitary walk, the spirit bow'd yet proud, the
     suffering and the struggle?
The agonistic throes, the ecstasies, joys of the solemn mus-
     ings day or night?
Joys of the thought of Death, the great spheres Time and
     Space?
Prophetic joys of better, loftier love's ideals, the divine
     wife, the sweet, eternal, perfect comrade?
Joys all thine own undying one, joys worthy thee O soul.

O while I live to be the ruler of life, not a slave,
To meet life as a powerful conqueror,
No fumes, no ennui, no more complaints or scornful crit-
     icisms,
To these proud laws of the air, the water and the ground,
     proving my interior soul impregnable,
And nothing exterior shall ever take command of me.

For not life's joys alone I sing, repeating—the joy of death!
The beautiful touch of Death, soothing and benumbing a
     few moments, for reasons,
Myself discharging my excrementitious body to be
     burn'd, or render'd to powder, or buried,
My real body doubtless left to me for other spheres,

My voided body nothing more to me, returning to the
    purifications, further offices, eternal uses of the earth.

O to attract by more than attraction!
How it is I know not—yet behold! the something which
    obeys none of the rest,
It is offensive, never defensive—yet how magnetic it
    draws.

O to struggle against great odds, to meet enemies
    undaunted!
To be entirely alone with them, to find how much one can
    stand!
To look strife, torture, prison, popular odium, face to face!
To mount the scaffold, to advance to the muzzles of guns
    with perfect nonchalance!
To be indeed a God!

O to sail to sea in a ship!
To leave this steady unendurable land,
To leave the tiresome sameness of the streets, the side-
    walks and the houses,
To leave you O you solid motionless land, and entering a
    ship,
To sail and sail and sail!

O to have life henceforth a poem of new joys!
To dance, clap hands, exult, shout, skip, leap, roll on, float
    on!
To be a sailor of the world bound for all ports,

A ship itself, (see indeed these sails I spread to the sun
   and air,)
A swift and swelling ship full of rich words, full of joys.

❋

SONG OF THE BROAD-AXE.

1

Weapon shapely, naked, wan,
Head from the mother's bowels drawn,
Wooded flesh and metal bone, limb only one and lip only
   one,
Gray-blue leaf by red-heat grown, helve produced from
   a little seed sown,
Resting the grass amid and upon,
To be lean'd and to lean on.

Strong shapes and attributes of strong shapes, masculine
   trades, sights and sounds,
Long varied train of an emblem, dabs of music,
Fingers of the organist skipping staccato over the keys of
   the great organ.

2

Welcome are all earth's lands, each for its kind,
Welcome are lands of pine and oak,
Welcome are lands of the lemon and fig,
Welcome are lands of gold,

Welcome are lands of wheat and maize, welcome those
    of the grape,
Welcome are lands of sugar and rice,
Welcome the cotton-lands, welcome those of the white
    potato and sweet potato,
Welcome are mountains, flats, sands, forests, prairies,
Welcome the rich borders of rivers, table-lands, openings,
Welcome the measureless grazing-lands, welcome the
    teeming soil of orchards, flax, honey, hemp;
Welcome just as much the other more hard-faced lands,
Lands rich as lands of gold or wheat and fruit lands,
Lands of mines, lands of the manly and rugged ores,
Lands of coal, copper, lead, tin, zinc,
Lands of iron—lands of the make of the axe.

3

The log at the wood-pile, the axe supported by it,
The sylvan hut, the vine over the doorway, the space
    clear'd for a garden,
The irregular tapping of rain down on the leaves after the
    storm is lull'd,
The wailing and moaning at intervals, the thought of the
    sea,
The thought of ships struck in the storm and put on their
    beam ends, and the cutting away of masts,
The sentiment of the huge timbers of old-fashion'd houses
    and barns,
The remember'd print or narrative, the voyage at a ven-
    ture of men, families, goods,
The disembarkation, the founding of a new city,

The voyage of those who sought a New England and
    found it, the outset anywhere,
The settlements of the Arkansas, Colorado, Ottawa,
    Willamette,
The slow progress, the scant fare, the axe, rifle, saddle-
    bags;
The beauty of all adventurous and daring persons,
The beauty of wood-boys and wood-men with their clear
    untrimm'd faces,
The beauty of independence, departure, actions that rely
    on themselves,
The American contempt for statutes and ceremonies, the
    boundless impatience of restraint,
The loose drift of character, the inkling through random
    types, the solidification;
The butcher in the slaughter-house, the hands aboard
    schooners and sloops, the raftsman, the pioneer,
Lumbermen in their winter camp, daybreak in the woods,
    stripes of snow on the limbs of trees, the occasional
    snapping,
The glad clear sound of one's own voice, the merry song,
    the natural life of the woods, the strong day's work,
The blazing fire at night, the sweet taste of supper, the
    talk, the bed of hemlock-boughs and the bear-skin;
The house-builder at work in cities or anywhere,
The preparatory jointing, squaring, sawing, mortising,
The hoist-up of beams, the push of them in their places,
    laying them regular,
Setting the studs by their tenons in the mortises according
    as they were prepared,
The blows of mallets and hammers, the attitudes of the
    men, their curv'd limbs,

Bending, standing, astride the beams, driving in pins,
    holding on by posts and braces,
The hook'd arm over the plate, the other arm wielding the
    axe,
The floor-men forcing the planks close to be nail'd,
Their postures bringing their weapons downward on the
    bearers,
The echoes resounding through the vacant building;
The huge storehouse carried up in the city well under
    way,
The six framing-men, two in the middle and two at each
    end, carefully bearing on their shoulders a heavy
    stick for a cross-beam,
The crowded line of masons with trowels in their right
    hands rapidly laying the long side-wall, two hundred
    feet from front to rear,
The flexible rise and fall of backs, the continual click of the
    trowels striking the bricks,
The bricks one after another each laid so workmanlike in
    its place, and set with a knock of the trowel-handle,
The piles of materials, the mortar on the mortar-boards,
    and the steady replenishing by the hod-men;
Spar-makers in the spar-yard, the swarming row of well-
    grown apprentices,
The swing of their axes on the square-hew'd log shaping
    it toward the shape of a mast,
The brisk short crackle of the steel driven slantingly into
    the pine,
The butter-color'd chips flying off in great flakes and sliv-
    ers,
The limber motion of brawny young arms and hips in
    easy costumes,

The constructor of wharves, bridges, piers, bulk-heads,
    floats, stays against the sea;
The city fireman, the fire that suddenly bursts forth in the
    close-pack'd square,
The arriving engines, the hoarse shouts, the nimble step-
    ping and daring,
The strong command through the fire trumpets, the
    falling in line, the rise and fall of the arms forcing the
    water,
The slender, spasmic, blue-white jets, the bringing to bear
    of the hooks and ladders and their execution,
The crash and cut away of connecting wood-work, or
    through floors if the fire smoulders under them,
The crowd with their lit faces watching, the glare and
    dense shadows;
The forger at his forge-furnace and the user of iron after
    him,
The maker of the axe large and small, and the welder and
    temperer,
The chooser breathing his breath on the cold steel and try-
    ing the edge with his thumb,
The one who clean-shapes the handle and sets it firmly in
    the socket;
The shadowy processions of the portraits of the past users
    also,
The primal patient mechanics, the architects and engi-
    neers,
The far-off Assyrian edifice and Mizra edifice,
The Roman lictors preceding the consuls,
The antique European warrior with his axe in combat,
The uplifted arm, the clatter of blows on the helmeted
    head,

The death-howl, the limpsy tumbling body, the rush of
    friend and foe thither,
The siege of revolted lieges determin'd for liberty,
The summons to surrender, the battering at castle gates,
    the truce and parley,
The sack of an old city in its time,
The bursting in of mercenaries and bigots tumultuously
    and disorderly,
Roar, flames, blood, drunkenness, madness,
Goods freely rifled from houses and temples, screams of
    women in the gripe of brigands,
Craft and thievery of camp-followers, men running, old
    persons despairing,
The hell of war, the cruelties of creeds,
The list of all executive deeds and words just or unjust,
The power of personality just or unjust.

4

Muscle and pluck forever!
What invigorates life invigorates death,
And the dead advance as much as the living advance,
And the future is no more uncertain than the present,
For the roughness of the earth and of man encloses as
    much as the delicatesse of the earth and of man,
And nothing endures but personal qualities.

What do you think endures?
Do you think a great city endures?
Or a teeming manufacturing state? or a prepared consti-
    tution? or the best built steamships?

Or hotels of granite and iron? or any chef-d'œuvres of
    engineering, forts, armaments?

Away! these are not to be cherish'd for themselves,
They fill their hour, the dancers dance, the musicians play
    for them,
The show passes, all does well enough of course,
All does very well till one flash of defiance.

A great city is that which has the greatest men and
    women,
If it be a few ragged huts it is still the greatest city in the
    whole world.

5

The place where a great city stands is not the place of
    stretch'd wharves, docks, manufactures, deposits of
    produce merely,
Nor the place of ceaseless salutes of new-comers or the
    anchor-lifters of the departing,
Nor the place of the tallest and costliest buildings or
    shops selling goods from the rest of the earth,
Nor the place of the best libraries and schools, nor the
    place where money is plentiest,
Nor the place of the most numerous population.

Where the city stands with the brawniest breed of orators
    and bards,
Where the city stands that is belov'd by these, and loves
    them in return and understands them,

Where no monuments exist to heroes but in the common
    words and deeds,
Where thrift is in its place, and prudence is in its place,
Where the men and women think lightly of the laws,
Where the slave ceases, and the master of slaves ceases,
Where the populace rise at once against the never-ending
    audacity of elected persons,
Where fierce men and women pour forth as the sea to the
    whistle of death pours its sweeping and unript
    waves,
Where outside authority enters always after the prece-
    dence of inside authority,
Where the citizen is always the head and ideal, and Pres-
    ident, Mayor, Governor and what not, are agents for
    pay,
Where children are taught to be laws to themselves, and
    to depend on themselves,
Where equanimity is illustrated in affairs,
Where speculations on the soul are encouraged,
Where women walk in public processions in the streets
    the same as the men,
Where they enter the public assembly and take places the
    same as the men;
Where the city of the faithfulest friends stands,
Where the city of the cleanliness of the sexes stands,
Where the city of the healthiest fathers stands,
Where the city of the best-bodied mothers stands,
There the great city stands.

6

How beggarly appear arguments before a defiant deed!
How the floridness of the materials of cities shrivels
    before a man's or woman's look!

All waits or goes by default till a strong being appears;
A strong being is the proof of the race and of the ability
    of the universe,
When he or she appears materials are overaw'd,
The dispute on the soul stops,
The old customs and phrases are confronted, turn'd back,
    or laid away.

What is your money-making now? what can it do now?
What is your respectability now?
What are your theology, tuition, society, traditions,
    statute-books, now?
Where are your jibes of being now?
Where are your cavils about the soul now?

7

A sterile landscape covers the ore, there is as good as the
    best for all the forbidding appearance,
There is the mine, there are the miners,
The forge-furnace is there, the melt is accomplish'd, the
    hammers-men are at hand with their tongs and ham-
    mers,
What always served and always serves is at hand.

Than this nothing has better served, it has served all,
Served the fluent-tongued and subtle-sensed Greek, and
    long ere the Greek,
Served in building the buildings that last longer than any,
Served the Hebrew, the Persian, the most ancient Hin-
    dustanee,
Served the mound-raiser on the Mississippi, served those
    whose relics remain in Central America,
Served Albic temples in woods or on plains, with unhewn
    pillars and the druids,
Served the artificial clefts, vast, high, silent, on the snow-
    cover'd hills of Scandinavia,
Served those who time out of mind made on the granite
    walls rough sketches of the sun, moon, stars, ships,
    ocean waves,
Served the paths of the irruptions of the Goths, served the
    pastoral tribes and nomads,
Served the long distant Kelt, served the hardy pirates of
    the Baltic,
Served before any of those the venerable and harmless
    men of Ethiopia,
Served the making of helms for the galleys of pleasure
    and the making of those for war,
Served all great works on land and all great works on the
    sea,
For the mediæval ages and before the mediæval ages,
Served not the living only then as now, but served the
    dead.

8

I see the European headsman,
He stands mask'd, clothed in red, with huge legs and
    strong naked arms,
And leans on a ponderous axe.

(Whom have you slaughter'd lately European headsman?
Whose is that blood upon you so wet and sticky?)

I see the clear sunsets of the martyrs,
I see from the scaffolds the descending ghosts,
Ghosts of dead lords, uncrown'd ladies, impeach'd min-
    isters, rejected kings,
Rivals, traitors, poisoners, disgraced chieftains and the
    rest.

I see those who in any land have died for the good cause,
The seed is spare, nevertheless the crop shall never run
    out,
(Mind you O foreign kings, O priests, the crop shall never
    run out.)

I see the blood wash'd entirely away from the axe,
Both blade and helve are clean,
They spirt no more the blood of European nobles, they
    clasp no more the necks of queens.

I see the headsman withdraw and become useless,
I see the scaffold untrodden and mouldy, I see no longer
    any axe upon it,

I see the mighty and friendly emblem of the power of my
   own race, the newest, largest race.

                                9

(America! I do not vaunt my love for you,
I have what I have.)

The axe leaps!
The solid forest gives fluid utterances,
They tumble forth, they rise and form,
Hut, tent, landing, survey,
Flail, plough, pick, crowbar, spade,
Shingle, rail, prop, wainscot, jamb, lath, panel, gable,
Citadel, ceiling, saloon, academy, organ, exhibition-
   house, library,
Cornice, trellis, pilaster, balcony, window, turret, porch,
Hoe, rake, pitchfork, pencil, wagon, staff, saw, jack-plane,
   mallet, wedge, rounce,
Chair, tub, hoop, table, wicket, vane, sash, floor,
Work-box, chest, string'd instrument, boat, frame, and
   what not,
Capitols of States, and capitol of the nation of States,
Long stately rows in avenues, hospitals for orphans or for
   the poor or sick,
Manhattan steamboats and clippers taking the measure of
   all seas.

The shapes arise!
Shapes of the using of axes anyhow, and the users and all
   that neighbors them,

Cutters down of wood and haulers of it to the Penobscot
    or Kennebec,
Dwellers in cabins among the California mountains or by
    the little lakes or on the Columbia,
Dwellers south on the banks of the Gila or Rio Grande
    friendly gatherings, the characters and fun,
Dwellers along the St. Lawrence, or north in Kanada, or
    down by the Yellowstone, dwellers on coasts and off
    coasts,
Seal-fishers, whalers, arctic seamen breaking passages
    through the ice.

The shapes arise!
Shapes of factories, arsenals, foundries, markets,
Shapes of the two-threaded tracks of railroads,
Shapes of the sleepers of bridges, vast frameworks, gird-
    ers, arches,
Shapes of the fleets of barges, tows, lake and canal craft,
    river craft,
Ship-yards and dry-docks along the Eastern and Western
    seas, and in many a bay and by-place,
The live-oak kelsons, the pine planks, the spars, the hack-
    matack-roots for knees,
The ships themselves on their ways, the tiers of scaffolds,
    the workmen busy outside and inside,
The tools lying around, the great auger and little auger,
    the adze, bolt, line, square, gouge, and bead-plane.

10

The shapes arise!
The shape measur'd, saw'd, jack'd, join'd, stain'd,

The coffin-shape for the dead to lie within in his shroud,
The shape got out in posts, in the bedstead posts, in the
    posts of the bride's bed,
The shape of the little trough, the shape of the rockers
    beneath, the shape of the babe's cradle,
The shape of the floor-planks, the floor-planks for
    dancers' feet,
The shape of the planks of the family home, the home of
    the friendly parents and children,
The shape of the roof of the home of the happy young
    man and woman, the roof over the well-married
    young man and woman,
The roof over the supper joyously cook'd by the chaste
    wife, and joyously eaten by the chaste husband, con-
    tent after his day's work.

The shapes arise!
The shape of the prisoner's place in the court-room, and
    of him or her seated in the place,
The shape of the liquor-bar lean'd against by the young
    rum-drinker and the old rum-drinker,
The shape of the shamed and angry stairs trod by sneak-
    ing foot-steps,
The shape of the sly settee, and the adulterous unwhole-
    some couple,
The shape of the gambling-board with its devilish win-
    nings and losings,
The shape of the step-ladder for the convicted and sen-
    tenced murderer, the murderer with haggard face
    and pinion'd arms,
The sheriff at hand with his deputies, the silent and white-
    lipp'd crowd, the dangling of the rope.

The shapes arise!
Shapes of doors giving many exits and entrances,
The door passing the dissever'd friend flush'd and in
    haste,
The door that admits good news and bad news,
The door whence the son left home confident and puff'd
    up,
The door he enter'd again from a long and scandalous
    absence, diseas'd, broken down, without innocence,
    without means.

11

Her shape arises,
She less guarded than ever, yet more guarded than ever,
The gross and soil'd she moves among do not make her
    gross and soil'd,
She knows the thoughts as she passes, nothing is con-
    ceal'd from her,
She is none the less considerate or friendly therefor,
She is the best belov'd, it is without exception, she has no
    reason to fear and she does not fear,
Oaths, quarrels, hiccupp'd songs, smutty expressions, are
    idle to her as she passes,
She is silent, she is possess'd of herself, they do not offend
    her,
She receives them as the laws of Nature receive them, she
    is strong,
She too is a law of Nature—there is no law stronger than
    she is.

12

The main shapes arise!
Shapes of Democracy total, result of centuries,
Shapes ever projecting other shapes,
Shapes of turbulent manly cities,
Shapes of the friends and home-givers of the whole earth,
Shapes bracing the earth and braced with the whole earth.

✳

SONG OF THE EXPOSITION.

1

(Ah little recks the laborer,
How near his work is holding him to God,
The loving Laborer through space and time.)

After all not to create only, or found only,
But to bring perhaps from afar what is already founded,
To give it our own identity, average, limitless, free,
To fill the gross the torpid bulk with vital religious fire,
Not to repel or destroy so much as accept, fuse, rehabili-
    tate,
To obey as well as command, to follow more than to lead,
These also are the lessons of our New World;
While how little the New after all, how much the Old, Old
    World!

Long and long has the grass been growing,
Long and long has the rain been falling,
Long has the globe been rolling round.

2

Come Muse migrate from Greece and Ionia,
Cross out please those immensely overpaid accounts,
That matter of Troy and Achilles' wrath, and Æneas',
    Odysseus' wanderings,
Placard "Removed" and "To Let" on the rocks of your
    snowy Parnassus,
Repeat at Jerusalem, place the notice high on Jaffa's gate
    and on Mount Moriah,
The same on the walls of your German, French and Span-
    ish castles and Italian collections,
For know a better, fresher, busier sphere, a wide, untried
    domain awaits, demands you.

3

Responsive to our summons,
Or rather to her long-nurs'd inclination,
Join'd with an irresistible, natural gravitation,
She comes! I hear the rustling of her gown,
I scent the odor of her breath's delicious fragrance,
I mark her step divine, her curious eyes a-turning, rolling,
Upon this very scene.

The dame of dames! can I believe then
Those ancient temples, sculptures classic, could none of
    them retain her?

Nor shades of Virgil and Dante, nor myriad memories,
    poems, old associations, magnetize and hold on to
    her?
But that she's left them all—and here?

Yes, if you will allow me to say so,
I, my friends, if you do not, can plainly see her,
The same undying soul of earth's, activity's, beauty's,
    heroism's expression,
Out from her evolutions hither come, ended the strata of
    her former themes,
Hidden and cover'd by to-day's, foundation of to-day's
Ended, deceas'd through time, her voice by Castaly's
    fountain,
Silent the broken-lipp'd Sphynx in Egypt, silent all those
    century-baffling tombs,
Ended for aye the epics of Asia's, Europe's helmeted war-
    riors, ended the primitive call of the muses
Calliope's call forever closed, Clio, Melpomene, Thalia
    dead,
Ended the stately rhythmus of Una and Oriana, ended the
    quest of the holy Graal,
Jerusalem a handful of ashes blown by the wind, extinct,
The Crusaders' streams of shadowy midnight troops sped
    with the sunrise,
Amadis, Tancred, utterly gone, Charlemagne, Roland,
    Oliver gone,
Palmerin, ogre, departed, vanish'd the turrets that Usk
    from its waters reflected,
Arthur vanish'd with all his knights, Merlin and Lancelot
    and Galahad, all gone, dissolv'd utterly like an exha-
    lation;

Pass'd! pass'd! for us, forever pass'd, that once so mighty
    world, now void, inanimate, phantom world,
Embroider'd, dazzling, foreign world, with all its gor-
    geous legends, myths,
Its kings and castles proud, its priests and warlike lords
    and courtly dames,
Pass'd to its charnel vault, coffin'd with crown and armor
    on,
Blazon'd with Shakspere's purple page,
And dirged by Tennyson's sweet sad rhyme.

I say I see, my friends, if you do not, the illustrious emi-
    gré, (having it is true in her day, although the same,
    changed, journey'd considerable,)
Making directly for this rendezvous, vigorously clearing
    a path for herself, striding through the confusion,
By thud of machinery and shrill steam-whistle undis-
    may'd,
Bluff'd not a bit by drain-pipe, gasometers, artificial fer-
    tilizers,
Smiling and pleas'd with palpable intent to stay,
She's here, install'd amid the kitchen ware!

4

But hold—don't I forget my manners?
To introduce the stranger, (what else indeed do I live to
    chant for?) to thee Columbia;
In liberty's name welcome immortal! clasp hands,
And ever henceforth sisters dear be both.

Fear not O Muse! truly new ways and days receive, sur-
    round you,
I candidly confess a queer, queer race, of novel fashion,
And yet the same old human race, the same within, with-
    out,
Faces and hearts the same, feelings the same, yearnings
    the same,
The same old love, beauty and use the same.

5

We do not blame thee elder World, nor really separate
    ourselves from thee,
(Would the son separate himself from the father?)
Looking back on thee, seeing thee to thy duties,
    grandeurs, through past ages bending, building,
We build to ours to-day.

Mightier than Egypt's tombs,
Fairer than Grecia's, Roma's temples,
Prouder than Milan's statued, spired cathedral,
More picturesque than Rhenish castle-keeps,
We plan even now to raise, beyond them all,
Thy great cathedral sacred industry, no tomb,
A keep for life for practical invention.

As in a waking vision,
E'en while I chant I see it rise, I scan and prophesy outside
    and in,
Its manifold ensemble.

Around a palace, loftier, fairer, ampler than any yet,
Earth's modern wonder, history's seven outstripping,
High rising tier on tier with glass and iron façades,
Gladdening the sun and sky, enhued in cheerfulest hues,
Bronze, lilac, robin's-egg, marine and crimson,
Over whose golden roof shall flaunt, beneath thy banner
    Freedom,
The banners of the States and flags of every land,
A brood of lofty, fair, but lesser palaces shall cluster.

Somewhere within their walls shall all that forwards per-
    fect human life be started,
Tried, taught, advanced, visibly exhibited.

Not only all the world of works, trade, products,
But all the workmen of the world here to be represented.

Here shall you trace in flowing operation,
In every state of practical, busy movement, the rills of civ-
    ilization,
Materials here under your eye shall change their shape as
    if by magic,
The cotton shall be pick'd almost in the very field,
Shall be dried, clean'd, ginn'd, baled, spun into thread
    and cloth before you,
You shall see hands at work at all the old processes and all
    the new ones,
You shall see the various grains and how flour is made
    and then bread baked by the bakers,
You shall see the crude ores of California and Nevada
    passing on and on till they become bullion,

You shall watch how the printer sets type, and learn what
    a composing-stick is,
You shall mark in amazement the Hoe press whirling its
    cylinders, shedding the printed leaves steady and
    fast,
The photograph, model, watch, pin, nail, shall be created
    before you.

In large calm halls, a stately museum shall teach you the
    infinite lessons of minerals,
In another, woods, plants, vegetation shall be illus-
    trated— in another animals, animal life and develop-
    ment.

One stately house shall be the music house,
Others for other arts—learning, the sciences, shall all be
    here,
None shall be slighted, none but shall here be honor'd,
    help'd, exampled.

6

(This, this and these, America, shall be *your* pyramids and
    obelisks,
Your Alexandrian Pharos, gardens of Babylon,
Your temple at Olympia.)

The male and female many laboring not,
Shall ever here confront the laboring many,
With precious benefits to both, glory to all,
To thee America, and thee eternal Muse.

And here shall ye inhabit powerful Matrons!
In your vast state vaster than all the old,
Echoed through long, long centuries to come,
To sound of different, prouder songs, with stronger
 themes,
Practical, peaceful life, the people's life, the People them-
 selves,
Lifted, illumin'd, bathed in peace—elate, secure in peace.

7

Away with themes of war! away with war itself!
Hence from my shuddering sight to never more return
 that show of blacken'd, mutilated corpses!
That hell unpent and raid of blood, fit for wild tigers or
 for lop-tongued wolves, not reasoning men,
And in its stead speed industry's campaigns,
With thy undaunted armies, engineering,
Thy pennants labor, loosen'd to the breeze,
Thy bugles sounding loud and clear.

Away with old romance!
Away with novels, plots and plays of foreign courts,
Away with love-verses sugar'd in rhyme, the intrigues,
 amours of idlers,
Fitted for only banquets of the night where dancers to late
 music slide,
The unhealthy pleasures, extravagant dissipations of the
 few,
With perfumes, heat and wine, beneath the dazzling
 chandeliers.

To you ye reverent sane sisters,
I raise a voice for far superber themes for poets and for
    art,
To exalt the present and the real,
To teach the average man the glory of his daily walk and
    trade,
To sing in songs how exercise and chemical life are never
    to be baffled,
To manual work for each and all, to plough, hoe, dig,
To plant and tend the tree, the berry, vegetables, flowers,
For every man to see to it that he really do something, for
    every woman too;
To use the hammer and the saw, (rip, or cross-cut,)
To cultivate a turn for carpentering, plastering, painting,
To work as tailor, tailoress, nurse, hostler, porter,
To invent a little, something ingenious, to aid the wash-
    ing, cooking, cleaning,
And hold it no disgrace to take a hand at them them-
    selves.

I say I bring thee Muse to-day and here,
All occupations, duties broad and close,
Toil, healthy toil and sweat, endless, without cessation,
The old, old practical burdens, interests, joys,
The family, parentage, childhood, husband and wife,
The house-comforts, the house itself and all its belong-
    ings,
Food and its preservation, chemistry applied to it,
Whatever forms the average, strong, complete, sweet-
    blooded man or woman, the perfect longeve person-
    ality,

And helps its present life to health and happiness, and
    shapes its soul,
For the eternal real life to come.

With latest connections, works, the inter-transportation of
    the world,
Steam-power, the great express lines, gas, petroleum,
These triumphs of our time, the Atlantic's delicate cable,
The Pacific railroad, the Suez canal, the Mont Cenis and
    Gothard and Hoosac tunnels, the Brooklyn bridge,
This earth all spann'd with iron rails, with lines of
    steamships threading every sea,
Our own rondure, the current globe I bring.

8

And thou America,
Thy offspring towering e'er so high, yet higher, Thee
    above all towering,
With Victory on thy left, and at thy right hand Law;
Thou Union holding all, fusing, absorbing, tolerating all,
Thee, ever thee, I sing.

Thou, also thou, a World,
With all thy wide geographies, manifold, different, dis-
    tant,
Rounded by thee in one—one common orbic language,
One common indivisible destiny for All.

And by the spells which ye vouchsafe to those your min-
    isters in earnest,

I here personify and call my themes, to make them pass
    before ye.

Behold, America! (and thou, ineffable guest and sister!)
For thee come trooping up thy waters and thy lands;
Behold! thy fields and farms, thy far-off woods and
    mountains,
As in procession coming.

Behold, the sea itself,
And on its limitless, heaving breast, the ships;
See, where their white sails, bellying in the wind, speckle
    the green and blue,
See, the steamers coming and going, steaming in or out
    of port,
See, dusky and undulating, the long pennants of smoke.

Behold, in Oregon, far in the north and west,
Or in Maine, far in the north and east, thy cheerful axe-
    men,
Wielding all day their axes.

Behold, on the lakes, thy pilots at their wheels, thy oars-
    men,
How the ash writhes under those muscular arms!

There by the furnace, and there by the anvil,
Behold thy sturdy blacksmiths swinging their sledges,
Overhand so steady, overhand they turn and fall with
    joyous clank,
Like a tumult of laughter.

Mark the spirit of invention everywhere, thy rapid
    patents,
Thy continual workshops, foundries, risen or rising,
See, from their chimneys how the tall flame-fires stream.

Mark, thy interminable farms, North, South,
Thy wealthy daughter-states, Eastern and Western,
The varied products of Ohio, Pennsylvania, Missouri,
    Georgia, Texas, and the rest,
Thy limitless crops, grass, wheat, sugar, oil, corn, rice,
    hemp, hops,
Thy barns all fill'd, the endless freight-train and the
    bulging storehouse,
The grapes that ripen on thy vines, the apples in thy
    orchards,
Thy incalculable lumber, beef, pork, potatoes, thy coal,
    thy gold and silver,
The inexhaustible iron in thy mines.

All thine O sacred Union!
Ships, farms, shops, barns, factories, mines,
City and State, North, South, item and aggregate,
We dedicate, dread Mother, all to thee!

Protectress absolute, thou! bulwark of all!
For well we know that while thou givest each and all,
    (generous as God,)
Without thee neither all nor each, nor land, home,
Nor ship, nor mine, nor any here this day secure,
Nor aught, nor any day secure.

9

And thou, the Emblem waving over all!
Delicate beauty, a word to thee, (it may be salutary,)
Remember thou hast not always been as here to-day so
      comfortably ensovereign'd,
In other scenes than these have I observ'd thee flag,
Not quite so trim and whole and freshly blooming in
      folds of stainless silk,
But I have seen thee bunting, to tatters torn upon thy
      splinter'd staff,
Or clutch'd to some young color-bearer's breast with des-
      perate hands,
Savagely struggled for, for life or death, fought over long,
'Mid cannons' thunder-crash and many a curse and groan
      and yell, and rifle-volleys cracking sharp,
And moving masses as wild demons surging, and lives as
      nothing risk'd,
For thy mere remnant grimed with dirt and smoke and
      sopp'd in blood,
For sake of that, my beauty, and that thou might'st dally
      as now secure up there,
Many a good man have I seen go under.

Now here and these and hence in peace, all thine O Flag!
And here and hence for thee, O universal Muse! and thou
      for them!
And here and hence O Union, all the work and workmen
      thine!
None separate from thee—henceforth One only, we and
      thou,

(For the blood of the children, what is it, only the blood
  maternal?
And lives and works, what are they all at last, except the
  roads to faith and death?)

While we rehearse our measureless wealth, it is for thee,
  dear Mother,
We own it all and several to-day indissoluble in thee;
Think not our chant, our show, merely for products gross
  or lucre— it is for thee, the soul in thee, electric, spir-
  itual!
Our farms, inventions, crops, we own in thee! cities and
  States in thee!
Our freedom all in thee! our very lives in thee!

*

SONG OF THE REDWOOD-TREE.

1

A California song,
A prophecy and indirection, a thought impalpable to
  breathe as air,
A chorus of dryads, fading, departing, or hamadryads
  departing,
A murmuring, fateful, giant voice, out of the earth and
  sky,
Voice of a mighty dying tree in the redwood forest dense.

Farewell my brethren,
Farewell O earth and sky, farewell ye neighboring waters,
My time has ended, my term has come.

Along the northern coast,
Just back from the rock-bound shore and the caves,
In the saline air from the sea in the Mendocino country,
With the surge for base and accompaniment low and
     hoarse,
With crackling blows of axes sounding musically driven
     by strong arms,
Riven deep by the sharp tongues of the axes, there in the
     redwood forest dense,
I heard the mighty tree its death-chant chanting.

The choppers heard not, the camp shanties echoed not,
The quick-ear'd teamsters and chain and jack-screw men
     heard not,
As the wood-spirits came from their haunts of a thousand
     years to join the refrain,
But in my soul I plainly heard.

Murmuring out of its myriad leaves,
Down from its lofty top rising two hundred feet high,
Out of its stalwart trunk and limbs, out of its foot-thick
     bark,
That chant of the seasons and time, chant not of the past
     only but the future.

You untold life of me,
And all you venerable and innocent joys,

Perennial hardy life of me with joys 'mid rain and many a sum-
*   mer sun,*
And the white snows and night and the wild winds;
O the great patient rugged joys, my soul's strong joys unreck'd
*   by man,*
(For know I bear the soul befitting me, I too have consciousness,
*   identity,*
And all the rocks and mountains have, and all the earth,)
Joys of the life befitting me and brothers mine,
Our time, our term has come.

Nor yield we mournfully majestic brothers,
We who have grandly fill'd our time;
With Nature's calm content, with tacit huge delight,
We welcome what we wrought for through the past,
And leave the field for them.

For them predicted long,
For a superber race, they too to grandly fill their time,
For them we abdicate, in them ourselves ye forest kings!
In them these skies and airs, these mountain peaks, Shasta,
*   Nevadas,*
These huge precipitous cliffs, this amplitude, these valleys, far
*   Yosemite,*
To be in them absorb'd, assimilated.

Then to a loftier strain,
Still prouder, more ecstatic rose the chant,
As if the heirs, the deities of the West,
Joining with master-tongue bore part.

Not wan from Asia's fetiches,
Nor red from Europe's old dynastic slaughter-house,
(Area of murder-plots of thrones, with scent left yet of wars and
    scaffolds everywhere,)
But come from Nature's long and harmless throes, peacefully
    builded thence,
These virgin lands, lands of the Western shore,
To the new culminating man, to you, the empire new,
You promis'd long, we pledge, we dedicate.

You occult deep volitions,
You average spiritual manhood, purpose of all, pois'd on your-
    self, giving not taking law,
You womanhood divine, mistress and source of all, whence life
    and love and aught that comes from life and love,
You unseen moral essence of all the vast materials of America,
    (age upon age working in death the same as life,)
You that, sometimes known, oftener unknown, really shape and
    mould the New World, adjusting it to Time and Space,
You hidden national will lying in your abysms, conceal'd but
    ever alert,
You past and present purposes tenaciously pursued, may be
    unconscious of yourselves,
Unswerv'd by all the passing errors, perturbations of the sur-
    face;
You vital, universal, deathless germs, beneath all creeds, arts,
    statutes, literatures,
Here build your homes for good, establish here, these areas
    entire, lands of the Western shore,
We pledge, we dedicate to you.

For man of you, your characteristic race,
Here may he hardy, sweet, gigantic grow, here tower propor-
*   tionate to Nature,*
Here climb the vast pure spaces unconfined, uncheck'd by wall
*   or roof,*
Here laugh with storm or sun, here joy, here patiently inure,
Here heed himself, unfold himself, (not others' formulas heed,)
*   here fill his time,*
To duly fall, to aid, unreck'd at last,
To disappear, to serve.

Thus on the northern coast,
In the echo of teamsters' calls and the clinking chains, and
    the music of choppers' axes,
The falling trunk and limbs, the crash, the muffled shriek,
    the groan,
Such words combined from the redwood tree, as of voices
    ecstatic, ancient and rustling,
The century-lasting, unseen dryads, singing, withdraw-
    ing,
All their recesses of forests and mountains leaving,
From the Cascade range to the Wahsatch, or Idaho far, or
    Utah,
To the deities of the modern henceforth yielding,
The chorus and indications, the vistas of coming human-
    ity, the settlements, features all,
In the Mendocino woods I caught.

2

The flashing and golden pageant of California,
The sudden and gorgeous drama, the sunny and ample
    lands,
The long and varied stretch from Puget sound to Col-
    orado south,
Lands bathed in sweeter, rarer, healthier air, valleys and
    mountain cliffs,
The fields of Nature long prepared and fallow, the silent,
    cyclic chemistry,
The slow and steady ages plodding, the unoccupied sur-
    face ripening, the rich ores forming beneath;
At last the New arriving, assuming, taking possession,
A swarming and busy race settling and organizing every-
    where,
Ships coming in from the whole round world, and going
    out to the whole world,
To India and China and Australia and the thousand
    island paradises of the Pacific,
Populous cities, the latest inventions, the steamers on the
    rivers, the railroads, with many a thrifty farm, with
    machinery,
And wool and wheat and the grape, and diggings of yel-
    low gold.

3

But more in you than these, lands of the Western shore,
(These but the means, the implements, the standing-
    ground,)

I see in you, certain to come, the promise of thousands of
    years, till now deferr'd,
Promis'd to be fulfill'd, our common kind, the race.

The new society at last, proportionate to Nature,
In man of you, more than your mountain peaks or stal-
    wart trees imperial,
In woman more, far more, than all your gold or vines, or
    even vital air.

Fresh come, to a new world indeed, yet long prepared,
I see the genius of the modern, child of the real and ideal,
Clearing the ground for broad humanity, the true Amer-
    ica, heir of the past so grand,
To build a grander future.

*

A SONG FOR OCCUPATIONS.

1

A song for occupations!
In the labor of engines and trades and the labor of fields I
    find the developments,
And find the eternal meanings.

Workmen and Workwomen!
Were all educations practical and ornamental well dis-
    play'd out of me, what would it amount to?

Were I as the head teacher, charitable proprietor, wise
    statesman, what would it amount to?
Were I to you as the boss employing and paying you,
    would that satisfy you?

The learn'd, virtuous, benevolent, and the usual terms,
A man like me and never the usual terms.

Neither a servant nor a master I,
I take no sooner a large price than a small price, I will
    have my own whoever enjoys me,
I will be even with you and you shall be even with me.

If you stand at work in a shop I stand as nigh as the nigh-
    est in the same shop,
If you bestow gifts on your brother or dearest friend I
    demand as good as your brother or dearest friend,
If your lover, husband, wife, is welcome by day or night,
    I must be personally as welcome,
If you become degraded, criminal, ill, then I become so for
    your sake,
If you remember your foolish and outlaw'd deeds, do you
    think I cannot remember my own foolish and out-
    law'd deeds?
If you carouse at the table I carouse at the opposite side
    of the table,
If you meet some stranger in the streets and love him or
    her, why I often meet strangers in the street and love
    them.

Why what have you thought of yourself?
Is it you then that thought yourself less?

Is it you that thought the President greater than you?
Or the rich better off than you? or the educated wiser than
    you?

(Because you are greasy or pimpled, or were once drunk,
    or a thief,
Or that you are diseas'd, or rheumatic, or a prostitute,
Or from frivolity or impotence, or that you are no scholar
    and never saw your name in print,
Do you give in that you are any less immortal?)

2

Souls of men and women! it is not you I call unseen,
    unheard, untouchable and untouching,
It is not you I go argue pro and con about, and to settle
    whether you are alive or no,
I own publicly who you are, if nobody else owns.

Grown, half-grown and babe, of this country and every
    country, in-doors and out-doors, one just as much as
    the other, I see,
And all else behind or through them.

The wife, and she is not one jot less than the husband,
The daughter, and she is just as good as the son,
The mother, and she is every bit as much as the father.

Offspring of ignorant and poor, boys apprenticed to
    trades,

Young fellows working on farms and old fellows working
    on farms,
Sailor-men, merchant-men, coasters, immigrants,
All these I see, but nigher and farther the same I see,
None shall escape me and none shall wish to escape me.

I bring what you much need yet always have,
Not money, amours, dress, eating, erudition, but as good,
I send no agent or medium, offer no representative of
    value, but offer the value itself.

There is something that comes to one now and perpetu-
    ally,
It is not what is printed, preach'd, discussed, it eludes dis-
    cussion and print,
It is not to be put in a book, it is not in this book,
It is for you whoever you are, it is no farther from you
    than your hearing and sight are from you,
It is hinted by nearest, commonest, readiest, it is ever pro-
    voked by them.

You may read in many languages, yet read nothing about
    it,
You may read the President's message and read nothing
    about it there,
Nothing in the reports from the State department or Trea-
    sury department, or in the daily papers or weekly
    papers,
Or in the census or revenue returns, prices current, or any
    accounts of stock.

3

The sun and stars that float in the open air,
The apple-shaped earth and we upon it, surely the drift of
    them is something grand,
I do not know what it is except that it is grand, and that
    it is happiness,
And that the enclosing purport of us here is not a specu-
    lation or bon-mot or reconnoissance,
And that it is not something which by luck may turn out
    well for us, and without luck must be a failure for us,
And not something which may yet be retracted in a cer-
    tain contingency.

The light and shade, the curious sense of body and iden-
    tity, the greed that with perfect complaisance devours
    all things,
The endless pride and outstretching of man, unspeakable
    joys and sorrows,
The wonder every one sees in every one else he sees, and
    the wonders that fill each minute of time forever,
What have you reckon'd them for, camerado?
Have you reckon'd them for your trade or farm-work? or
    for the profits of your store?
Or to achieve yourself a position? or to fill a gentleman's
    leisure, or a lady's leisure?

Have you reckon'd that the landscape took substance and
    form that it might be painted in a picture?
Or men and women that they might be written of, and
    songs sung?

Or the attraction of gravity, and the great laws and har-
monious combinations and the fluids of the air, as
subjects for the savans?
Or the brown land and the blue sea for maps and charts?
Or the stars to be put in constellations and named fancy
names?
Or that the growth of seeds is for agricultural tables, or
agriculture itself?

Old institutions, these arts, libraries, legends, collections,
and the practice handed along in manufactures, will
we rate them so high?
Will we rate our cash and business high? I have no objec-
tion,
I rate them as high as the highest—then a child born of a
woman and man I rate beyond all rate.

We thought our Union grand, and our Constitution grand,
I do not say they are not grand and good, for they are,
I am this day just as much in love with them as you,
Then I am in love with You, and with all my fellows upon
the earth.

We consider bibles and religions divine—I do not say
they are not divine,
I say they have all grown out of you, and may grow out of
you still,
It is not they who give the life, it is you who give the life,
Leaves are not more shed from the trees, or trees from the
earth, than they are shed out of you.

4

The sum of all known reverence I add up in you whoever
    you are,
The President is there in the White House for you, it is not
    you who are here for him,
The Secretaries act in their bureaus for you, not you here
    for them,
The Congress convenes every Twelfth-month for you,
Laws, courts, the forming of States, the charters of cities,
    the going and coming of commerce and mails, are all
    for you.

List close my scholars dear,
Doctrines, politics and civilization exurge from you,
Sculpture and monuments and any thing inscribed any-
    where are tallied in you,
The gist of histories and statistics as far back as the
    records reach is in you this hour, and myths and tales
    the same,
If you were not breathing and walking here, where would
    they all be?
The most renown'd poems would be ashes, orations and
    plays would be vacuums.

All architecture is what you do to it when you look upon
    it,
(Did you think it was in the white or gray stone? or the
    lines of the arches and cornices?)

All music is what awakes from you when you are
    reminded by the instruments,

It is not the violins and the cornets, it is not the oboe nor
    the beating drums, nor the score of the baritone singer
    singing his sweet romanza, nor that of the men's cho-
    rus, nor that of the women's chorus,
It is nearer and farther than they.

5

Will the whole come back then?
Can each see signs of the best by a look in the looking-
    glass? is there nothing greater or more?
Does all sit there with you, with the mystic unseen soul?

Strange and hard that paradox true I give,
Objects gross and the unseen soul are one.

House-building, measuring, sawing the boards,
Blacksmithing, glass-blowing, nail-making, coopering,
    tin-roofing, shingle-dressing,
Ship-joining, dock-building, fish-curing, flagging of side-
    walks by flaggers,
The pump, the pile-driver, the great derrick, the coal-kiln
    and brick-kiln,
Coal-mines and all that is down there, the lamps in the
    darkness, echoes, songs, what meditations, what vast
    native thoughts looking through smutch'd faces,
Iron-works, forge-fires in the mountains or by river-
    banks, men around feeling the melt with huge crow-
    bars, lumps of ore, the due combining of ore, lime-
    stone, coal,

The blast-furnace and the puddling-furnace, the loup-
    lump at the bottom of the melt at last, the rolling-mill,
    the stumpy bars of pig-iron, the strong clean-shaped
    T-rail for railroads,
Oil-works, silk-works, white-lead works, the sugar-
    house, steam-saws, the great mills and factories,
Stone-cutting, shapely trimmings for façades or window
    or door-lintels, the mallet, the tooth-chisel, the jib to
    protect the thumb,
The calking-iron, the kettle of boiling vault-cement, and
    the fire under the kettle,
The cotton-bale, the stevedore's hook, the saw and buck
    of the sawyer, the mould of the moulder, the work-
    ing-knife of the butcher, the ice-saw, and all the work
    with ice,
The work and tools of the rigger, grappler, sail-maker,
    block-maker,
Goods of gutta-percha, papier-maché, colors, brushes,
    brush-making, glazier's implements,
The veneer and glue-pot, the confectioner's ornaments,
    the decanter and glasses, the shears and flat-iron,
The awl and knee-strap, the pint measure and quart mea-
    sure, the counter and stool, the writing-pen of quill or
    metal, the making of all sorts of edged tools,
The brewery, brewing, the malt, the vats, every thing that
    is done by brewers, wine-makers, vinegar-makers,
Leather-dressing, coach-making, boiler-making, rope-
    twisting, distilling, sign-painting, lime-burning,
    cotton-picking, electro-plating, electrotyping, stereo-
    typing,

Stave-machines, planing-machines, reaping-machines,
   ploughing-machines, thrashing-machines, steamwag-
   ons,
The cart of the carman, the omnibus, the ponderous dray,
Pyrotechny, letting off color'd fireworks at night, fancy
   figures and jets;
Beef on the butcher's stall, the slaughter-house of the
   butcher, the butcher in his killing-clothes,
The pens of live pork, the killing-hammer, the hog-hook,
   the scalder's tub, gutting, the cutter's cleaver, the
   packer's maul, and the plenteous winterwork of
   pork-packing,
Flour-works, grinding of wheat, rye, maize, rice, the bar-
   rels and the half and quarter barrels, the loaded
   barges, the high piles on wharves and levees,
The men and the work of the men on ferries, railroads,
   coasters, fish-boats, canals;
The hourly routine of your own or any man's life, the
   shop, yard, store, or factory,
These shows all near you by day and night—workman!
   whoever you are, your daily life!
In that and them the heft of the heaviest—in that and
   them far more than you estimated, (and far less also,)
In them realities for you and me, in them poems for you
   and me,
In them, not yourself—you and your soul enclose all
   things, regardless of estimation,
In them the development good—in them all themes,
   hints, possibilities.

I do not affirm that what you see beyond is futile, I do not
   advise you to stop,

I do not say leadings you thought great are not great,
But I say that none lead to greater than these lead to.

6

Will you seek afar off? you surely come back at last,
In things best known to you finding the best, or as good as
     the best,
In folks nearest to you finding the sweetest, strongest,
     lovingest,
Happiness, knowledge, not in another place but this
     place, not for another hour but this hour,
Man in the first you see or touch, always in friend,
     brother, nighest neighbor—woman in mother, sister,
     wife,
The popular tastes and employments taking precedence
     in poems or anywhere,
You workwomen and workmen of these States having
     your own divine and strong life,
And all else giving place to men and women like you.

When the psalm sings instead of the singer,
When the script preaches instead of the preacher,
When the pulpit descends and goes instead of the carver
     that carved the supporting desk,
When I can touch the body of books by night or by day,
     and when they touch my body back again,
When a university course convinces like a slumbering
     woman and child convince,
When the minted gold in the vault smiles like the night-
     watchman's daughter,

When warrantee deeds loafe in chairs opposite and are
    my friendly companions,
I intend to reach them my hand, and make as much of
    them as I do of men and women like you.

＊

A SONG OF THE ROLLING EARTH.

1

A song of the rolling earth, and of words according,
Were you thinking that those were the words, those
    upright lines? those curves, angles, dots?
No, those are not the words, the substantial words are in
    the ground and sea,
They are in the air, they are in you.

Were you thinking that those were the words, those deli-
    cious sounds out of your friends' mouths?
No, the real words are more delicious than they.

Human bodies are words, myriads of words,
(In the best poems re-appears the body, man's or
    woman's, well-shaped, natural, gay,
Every part able, active, receptive, without shame or the
    need of shame.)

Air, soil, water, fire—those are words,
I myself am a word with them—my qualities interpene-
    trate with theirs—my name is nothing to them,

Though it were told in the three thousand languages,
    what would air, soil, water, fire, know of my name?

A healthy presence, a friendly or commanding gesture,
    are words, sayings, meanings,
The charms that go with the mere looks of some men and
    women, are sayings and meanings also.

The workmanship of souls is by those inaudible words of
    the earth,
The masters know the earth's words and use them more
    than audible words.

Amelioration is one of the earth's words,
The earth neither lags nor hastens,
It has all attributes, growths, effects, latent in itself from
    the jump,
It is not half beautiful only, defects and excrescences show
    just as much as perfections show.

The earth does not withhold, it is generous enough,
The truths of the earth continually wait, they are not so
    conceal'd either,
They are calm, subtle, untransmissible by print,
They are imbued through all things conveying them-
    selves willingly,
Conveying a sentiment and invitation, I utter and utter,
I speak not, yet if you hear me not of what avail am I to
    you?
To bear, to better, lacking these of what avail am I?

(Accouche! accouchez!
Will you rot your own fruit in yourself there?
Will you squat and stifle there?)

The earth does not argue,
Is not pathetic, has no arrangements,
Does not scream, haste, persuade, threaten, promise,
Makes no discriminations, has no conceivable failures,
Closes nothing, refuses nothing, shuts none out,
Of all the powers, objects, states, it notifies, shuts none
    out.

The earth does not exhibit itself nor refuse to exhibit itself,
    possesses still underneath,
Underneath the ostensible sounds, the august chorus of
    heroes, the wail of slaves,
Persuasions of lovers, curses, gasps of the dying, laugh-
    ter of young people, accents of bargainers,
Underneath these possessing words that never fail.

To her children the words of the eloquent dumb great
    mother never fail,
The true words do not fail, for motion does not fail and
    reflection does not fail,
Also the day and night do not fail, and the voyage we
    pursue does not fail.

Of the interminable sisters,
Of the ceaseless cotillons of sisters,
Of the centripetal and centrifugal sisters, the elder and
    younger sisters,
The beautiful sister we know dances on with the rest.

With her ample back towards every beholder,
With the fascinations of youth and the equal fascinations
    of age,
Sits she whom I too love like the rest, sits undisturb'd,
Holding up in her hand what has the character of a mir-
    ror, while her eyes glance back from it,
Glance as she sits, inviting none, denying none,
Holding a mirror day and night tirelessly before her own
    face.

Seen at hand or seen at a distance,
Duly the twenty-four appear in public every day,
Duly approach and pass with their companions or a com-
    panion,
Looking from no countenances of their own, but from the
    countenances of those who are with them,
From the countenances of children or women or the
    manly countenance,
From the open countenances of animals or from inani-
    mate things,
From the landscape or waters or from the exquisite
    apparition of the sky,
From our countenances, mine and yours, faithfully
    returning them,
Every day in public appearing without fail, but never
    twice with the same companions.

Embracing man, embracing all, proceed the three hun-
    dred and sixty-five resistlessly round the sun;
Embracing all, soothing, supporting, follow close three
    hundred and sixty-five offsets of the first, sure and
    necessary as they.

Tumbling on steadily, nothing dreading,
Sunshine, storm, cold, heat, forever withstanding, pass-
ing, carrying,
The soul's realization and determination still inheriting,
The fluid vacuum around and ahead still entering and
dividing,
No balk retarding, no anchor anchoring, on no rock strik-
ing,
Swift, glad, content, unbereav'd, nothing losing,
Of all able and ready at any time to give strict account,
The divine ship sails the divine sea.

2

Whoever you are! motion and reflection are especially for
you,
The divine ship sails the divine sea for you.

Whoever you are! you are he or she for whom the earth
is solid and liquid,
You are he or she for whom the sun and moon hang in the
sky,
For none more than you are the present and the past,
For none more than you is immortality.

Each man to himself and each woman to herself, is the
word of the past and present, and the true word of
immortality;
No one can acquire for another—not one,
Not one can grow for another—not one.

The song is to the singer, and comes back most to him,
The teaching is to the teacher, and comes back most to
    him,
The murder is to the murderer, and comes back most to
    him,
The theft is to the thief, and comes back most to him,
The love is to the lover, and comes back most to him,
The gift is to the giver, and comes back most to him—it
    cannot fail,
The oration is to the orator, the acting is to the actor and
    actress not to the audience,
And no man understands any greatness or goodness but
    his own, or the indication of his own.

3

I swear the earth shall surely be complete to him or her
    who shall be complete,
The earth remains jagged and broken only to him or her
    who remains jagged and broken.

I swear there is no greatness or power that does not emu-
    late those of the earth,
There can be no theory of any account unless it corrobo-
    rate the theory of the earth,
No politics, song, religion, behavior, or what not, is of
    account, unless it compare with the amplitude of the
    earth,
Unless it face the exactness, vitality, impartiality, recti-
    tude of the earth.

I swear I begin to see love with sweeter spasms than that
    which responds love,
It is that which contains itself, which never invites and
    never refuses.

I swear I begin to see little or nothing in audible words,
All merges toward the presentation of the unspoken
    meanings of the earth,
Toward him who sings the songs of the body and of the
    truths of the earth,
Toward him who makes the dictionaries of words that
    print cannot touch.

I swear I see what is better than to tell the best,
It is always to leave the best untold.

When I undertake to tell the best I find I cannot,
My tongue is ineffectual on its pivots,
My breath will not be obedient to its organs,
I become a dumb man.

The best of the earth cannot be told anyhow, all or any is
    best,
It is not what you anticipated, it is cheaper, easier, nearer,
Things are not dismiss'd from the places they held before,
The earth is just as positive and direct as it was before,
Facts, religions, improvements, politics, trades, are as real
    as before,
But the soul is also real, it too is positive and direct,
No reasoning, no proof has establish'd it,
Undeniable growth has establish'd it.

4

These to echo the tones of souls and the phrases of souls,
(If they did not echo the phrases of souls what were they
    then?
If they had not reference to you in especial what were
    they then?)

I swear I will never henceforth have to do with the faith
    that tells the best,
I will have to do only with that faith that leaves the best
    untold.

Say on, sayers! sing on, singers!
Delve! mould! pile the words of the earth!
Work on, age after age, nothing is to be lost,
It may have to wait long, but it will certainly come in use,
When the materials are all prepared and ready, the archi-
    tects shall appear.

I swear to you the architects shall appear without fail,
I swear to you they will understand you and justify you,
The greatest among them shall be he who best knows
    you, and encloses all and is faithful to all,
He and the rest shall not forget you, they shall perceive
    that you are not an iota less than they,
You shall be fully glorified in them.

*

YOUTH, DAY, OLD AGE AND NIGHT.

Youth, large, lusty, loving—youth full of grace, force, fascination,
Do you know that Old Age may come after you with equal grace, force, fascination?

Day full-blown and splendid—day of the immense sun, action, ambition, laughter,
The Night follows close with millions of suns, and sleep and restoring darkness.

*

BIRDS OF PASSAGE.

SONG OF THE UNIVERSAL.

1

Come said the Muse,
Sing me a song no poet yet has chanted,
Sing me the universal.

In this broad earth of ours,
Amid the measureless grossness and the slag,
Enclosed and safe within its central heart,
Nestles the seed perfection.

By every life a share or more or less,
None born but it is born, conceal'd or unconceal'd the
    seed is waiting.

2

Lo! keen-eyed towering science,
As from tall peaks the modern overlooking,
Successive absolute fiats issuing.

Yet again, lo! the soul, above all science,
For it has history gather'd like husks around the globe,
For it the entire star-myriads roll through the sky.

In spiral routes by long detours,
(As a much-tacking ship upon the sea,)
For it the partial to the permanent flowing,
For it the real to the ideal tends.

For it the mystic evolution,
Not the right only justified, what we call evil also justi-
fied.

Forth from their masks, no matter what,
From the huge festering trunk, from craft and guile and
tears,
Health to emerge and joy, joy universal.

Out of the bulk, the morbid and the shallow,
Out of the bad majority, the varied countless frauds of
men and states,
Electric, antiseptic yet, cleaving, suffusing all,
Only the good is universal.

3

Over the mountain-growths disease and sorrow,
An uncaught bird is ever hovering, hovering,
High in the purer, happier air.

From imperfection's murkiest cloud,
Darts always forth one ray of perfect light,
One flash of heaven's glory.

To fashion's, custom's discord,
To the mad Babel-din, the deafening orgies,
Soothing each lull a strain is heard, just heard,
From some far shore the final chorus sounding.

O the blest eyes, the happy hearts,
That see, that know the guiding thread so fine,
Along the mighty labyrinth.

4

And thou America,
For the scheme's culmination, its thought and its reality,
For these (not for thyself) thou hast arrived.

Thou too surroundest all,
Embracing carrying welcoming all, thou too by pathways
    broad and new,
To the ideal tendest.

The measur'd faiths of other lands, the grandeurs of the
    past,
Are not for thee, but grandeurs of thine own,
Deific faiths and amplitudes, absorbing, comprehending
    all,
All eligible to all.

All, all for immortality,
Love like the light silently wrapping all,
Nature's amelioration blessing all,
The blossoms, fruits of ages, orchards divine and certain,
Forms, objects, growths, humanities, to spiritual images
    ripening.

Give me O God to sing that thought,
Give me, give him or her I love this quenchless faith,
In Thy ensemble, whatever else withheld withhold not
    from us,
Belief in plan of Thee enclosed in Time and Space,
Health, peace, salvation universal.

Is it a dream?
Nay but the lack of it the dream,
And failing it life's lore and wealth a dream,
And all the world a dream.

PIONEERS! O PIONEERS!

Come my tan-faced children,
Follow well in order, get your weapons ready,
Have you your pistols? have you your sharp-edged axes?
    Pioneers! O pioneers!

For we cannot tarry here,
We must march my darlings, we must bear the brunt of
    danger,
We the youthful sinewy races, all the rest on us depend,
    Pioneers! O pioneers!

O you youths, Western youths,
So impatient, full of action, full of manly pride and friend-
　　　　ship,
Plain I see you Western youths, see you tramping with the
　　　　foremost,
　　　　　　Pioneers! O pioneers!

Have the elder races halted?
Do they droop and end their lesson, wearied over there
　　　　beyond the seas?
We take up the task eternal, and the burden and the les-
　　　　son,
　　　　　　Pioneers! O pioneers!

All the past we leave behind,
We debouch upon a newer mightier world, varied world,
Fresh and strong the world we seize, world of labor and
　　　　the march,
　　　　　　Pioneers! O pioneers!

We detachments steady throwing,
Down the edges, through the passes, up the mountains
　　　　steep,
Conquering, holding, daring, venturing as we go the
　　　　unknown ways,
　　　　　　Pioneers! O pioneers!

We primeval forests felling,
We the rivers stemming, vexing we and piercing deep the
　　　　mines within,

We the surface broad surveying, we the virgin soil
    upheaving,
        Pioneers! O pioneers!

        Colorado men are we,
From the peaks gigantic, from the great sierras and the
    high plateaus,
From the mine and from the gully, from the hunting trail
    we come,
        Pioneers! O pioneers!

        From Nebraska, from Arkansas,
Central inland race are we, from Missouri, with the con-
    tinental blood intervein'd,
All the hands of comrades clasping, all the Southern, all
    the Northern,
        Pioneers! O pioneers!

        O resistless restless race!
O beloved race in all! O my breast aches with tender love
    for all!
O I mourn and yet exult, I am rapt with love for all,
        Pioneers! O pioneers!

        Raise the mighty mother mistress,
Waving high the delicate mistress, over all the starry mis-
    tress, (bend your heads all,)
Raise the fang'd and warlike mistress, stern, impassive,
    weapon'd mistress,
        Pioneers! O pioneers!

See my children, resolute children,
By those swarms upon our rear we must never yield or
   falter,
Ages back in ghostly millions frowning there behind us
   urging,
      Pioneers! O pioneers!

On and on the compact ranks,
With accessions ever waiting, with the places of the dead
   quickly fill'd,
Through the battle, through defeat, moving yet and never
   stopping,
      Pioneers! O pioneers!

O to die advancing on!
Are there some of us to droop and die? has the hour
   come?
Then upon the march we fittest die, soon and sure the gap
   is fill'd,
      Pioneers! O pioneers!

All the pulses of the world,
Falling in they beat for us, with the Western movement
   beat,
Holding single or together, steady moving to the front, all
   for us,
      Pioneers! O pioneers!

Life's involv'd and varied pageants,
All the forms and shows, all the workmen at their work,

All the seamen and the landsmen, all the masters with
        their slaves,
        Pioneers! O pioneers!

All the hapless silent lovers,
All the prisoners in the prisons, all the righteous and the
        wicked,
All the joyous, all the sorrowing, all the living, all the
        dying,
        Pioneers! O pioneers!

I too with my soul and body,
We, a curious trio, picking, wandering on our way,
Through these shores amid the shadows, with the appari-
        tions pressing,
        Pioneers! O pioneers!

Lo, the darting bowling orb!
Lo, the brother orbs around, all the clustering suns and
        planets,
All the dazzling days, all the mystic nights with dreams,
        Pioneers! O pioneers!

These are of us, they are with us,
All for primal needed work, while the followers there in
        embryo wait behind,
We to-day's procession heading, we the route for travel
        clearing,
        Pioneers! O pioneers!

O you daughters of the West!
O you young and elder daughters! O you mothers and
　　　you wives!
Never must you be divided, in our ranks you move
　　　united,
　　　Pioneers! O pioneers!

Minstrels latent on the prairies!
(Shrouded bards of other lands, you may rest, you have
　　　done your work,)
Soon I hear you coming warbling, soon you rise and
　　　tramp amid us,
　　　Pioneers! O pioneers!

Not for delectations sweet,
Not the cushion and the slipper, not the peaceful and the
　　　studious,
Not the riches safe and palling, not for us the tame enjoy-
　　　ment,
　　　Pioneers! O pioneers!

Do the feasters gluttonous feast?
Do the corpulent sleepers sleep? have they lock'd and
　　　bolted doors?
Still be ours the diet hard, and the blanket on the ground,
　　　Pioneers! O pioneers!

Has the night descended?
Was the road of late so toilsome? did we stop discouraged
　　　nodding on our way?

Yet a passing hour I yield you in your tracks to pause
    oblivious,
        Pioneers! O pioneers!

            Till with sound of trumpet,
Far, far off the daybreak call—hark! how loud and clear I
    hear it wind,
Swift! to the head of the army!—swift! spring to your
    places,
        Pioneers! O pioneers!

TO YOU.

Whoever you are, I fear you are walking the walks of
    dreams,
I fear these supposed realities are to melt from under your
    feet and hands,
Even now your features, joys, speech, house, trade, man-
    ners, troubles, follies, costume, crimes, dissipate away
    from you,
Your true soul and body appear before me,
They stand forth out of affairs, out of commerce, shops,
    work, farms, clothes, the house, buying, selling, eat-
    ing, drinking, suffering, dying.

Whoever you are, now I place my hand upon you, that
    you be my poem,
I whisper with my lips close to your ear,
I have loved many women and men, but I love none bet-
    ter than you.

O I have been dilatory and dumb,
I should have made my way straight to you long ago,
I should have blabb'd nothing but you, I should have
     chanted nothing but you.

I will leave all and come and make the hymns of you,
None has understood you, but I understand you,
None has done justice to you, you have not done justice to
     yourself,
None but has found you imperfect, I only find no imper-
     fection in you,
None but would subordinate you, I only am he who will
     never consent to subordinate you,
I only am he who places over you no master, owner, bet-
     ter, God, beyond what waits intrinsically in yourself.

Painters have painted their swarming groups and the cen-
     tre-figure of all,
From the head of the centre-figure spreading a nimbus of
     gold-color'd light,
But I paint myriads of heads, but paint no head without
     its nimbus of gold-color'd light,
From my hand from the brain of every man and woman it
     streams, effulgently flowing forever.

O I could sing such grandeurs and glories about you!
You have not known what you are, you have slumber'd
     upon yourself all your life,
Your eyelids have been the same as closed most of the
     time,
What you have done returns already in mockeries,

(Your thrift, knowledge, prayers, if they do not return in
    mockeries, what is their return?)

The mockeries are not you,
Underneath them and within them I see you lurk,
I pursue you where none else has pursued you,
Silence, the desk, the flippant expression, the night, the
    accustom'd routine, if these conceal you from others
    or from yourself, they do not conceal you from me,
The shaved face, the unsteady eye, the impure complex-
    ion, if these balk others they do not balk me,
The pert apparel, the deform'd attitude, drunkenness,
    greed, premature death, all these I part aside.

There is no endowment in man or woman that is not tal-
    lied in you,
There is no virtue, no beauty in man or woman, but as
    good is in you,
No pluck, no endurance in others, but as good is in you,
No pleasure waiting for others, but an equal pleasure
    waits for you.

As for me, I give nothing to any one except I give the like
    carefully to you,
I sing the songs of the glory of none, not God, sooner than
    I sing the songs of the glory of you.

Whoever you are! claim your own at any hazard!
These shows of the East and West are tame compared to
    you,
These immense meadows, these interminable rivers, you
    are immense and interminable as they,

These furies, elements, storms, motions of Nature, throes
 of apparent dissolution, you are he or she who is mas-
 ter or mistress over them,
Master or mistress in your own right over Nature, ele-
 ments, pain, passion, dissolution.

The hopples fall from your ankles, you find an unfailing
 sufficiency,
Old or young, male or female, rude, low, rejected by the
 rest, whatever you are promulges itself,
Through birth, life, death, burial, the means are provided,
 nothing is scanted,
Through angers, losses, ambition, ignorance, ennui, what
 you are picks its way.

FRANCE,

The 18th Year of these States.

A great year and place,
A harsh discordant natal scream out-sounding, to touch
 the mother's heart closer than any yet.

I walk'd the shores of my Eastern sea,
Heard over the waves the little voice,
Saw the divine infant where she woke mournfully wail-
 ing, amid the roar of cannon, curses, shouts, crash of
 falling buildings,
Was not so sick from the blood in the gutters running, nor
 from the single corpses, nor those in heaps, nor those
 borne away in the tumbrils,

Was not so desperate at the battues of death— was not so
　　shock'd at the repeated fusillades of the guns.

Pale, silent, stern, what could I say to that long-accrued
　　retribution?
Could I wish humanity different?
Could I wish the people made of wood and stone?
Or that there be no justice in destiny or time?

O Liberty! O mate for me!
Here too the blaze, the grape-shot and the axe, in reserve,
　　to fetch them out in case of need,
Here too, though long represt, can never be destroy'd,
Here too could rise at last murdering and ecstatic,
Here too demanding full arrears of vengeance.

Hence I sign this salute over the sea,
And I do not deny that terrible red birth and baptism,
But remember the little voice that I heard wailing, and
　　wait with perfect trust, no matter how long,
And from to-day sad and cogent I maintain the
　　bequeath'd cause, as for all lands,
And I send these words to Paris with my love,
And I guess some chansonniers there will understand
　　them,
For I guess there is latent music yet in France, floods of it,
O I hear already the bustle of instruments, they will soon
　　be drowning all that would interrupt them,
O I think the east wind brings a triumphal and free
　　march,
It reaches hither, it swells me to joyful madness,

I will run transpose it in words, to justify it,
I will yet sing a song for you ma femme.

MYSELF AND MINE.

Myself and mine gymnastic ever,
To stand the cold or heat, to take good aim with a gun, to
    sail a boat, to manage horses, to beget superb chil-
    dren,
To speak readily and clearly, to feel at home among com-
    mon people,
And to hold our own in terrible positions on land and sea.

Not for an embroiderer,
(There will always be plenty of embroiderers, I welcome
    them also,)
But for the fibre of things and for inherent men and
    women.

Not to chisel ornaments,
But to chisel with free stroke the heads and limbs of plen-
    teous supreme Gods, that the States may realize them
    walking and talking.

Let me have my own way,
Let others promulge the laws, I will make no account of
    the laws,
Let others praise eminent men and hold up peace, I hold
    up agitation and conflict,
I praise no eminent man, I rebuke to his face the one that
    was thought most worthy.

(Who are you? and what are you secretly guilty of all your
 life?
Will you turn aside all your life? will you grub and chat-
 ter all your life?
And who are you, blabbing by rote, years, pages, lan-
 guages, reminiscences,
Unwitting to-day that you do not know how to speak
 properly a single word?)

Let others finish specimens, I never finish specimens,
I start them by exhaustless laws as Nature does, fresh and
 modern continually.

I give nothing as duties,
What others give as duties I give as living impulses,
(Shall I give the heart's action as a duty?)

Let others dispose of questions, I dispose of nothing, I
 arouse unanswerable questions,
Who are they I see and touch, and what about them?
What about these likes of myself that draw me so close by
 tender directions and indirections?

I call to the world to distrust the accounts of my friends,
 but listen to my enemies, as I myself do,
I charge you forever reflect those who would expound
 me, for I cannot expound myself,
I charge that there be no theory or school founded out of
 me,
I charge you to leave all free, as I have left all free.

After me, vista!
O I see life is not short, but immeasurably long,
I henceforth tread the world chaste, temperate, an early
    riser, a steady grower,
Every hour the semen of centuries, and still of centuries.

I must follow up these continual lessons of the air, water,
    earth,
I perceive I have no time to lose.

YEAR OF METEORS.
(1859-60.)

Year of meteors! brooding year!
I would bind in words retrospective some of your deeds
    and signs,
I would sing your contest for the 19th Presidentiad,
I would sing how an old man, tall, with white hair,
    mounted the scaffold in Virginia,
(I was at hand, silent I stood with teeth shut close, I
    watch'd,
I stood very near you old man when cool and indifferent,
    but trembling with age and your unheal'd wounds
    you mounted the scaffold;)
I would sing in my copious song your census returns of
    the States,
The tables of population and products, I would sing of
    your ships and their cargoes,
The proud black ships of Manhattan arriving, some fill'd
    with immigrants, some from the isthmus with car-
    goes of gold,

Songs thereof would I sing, to all that hitherward comes
     would I welcome give,
And you would I sing, fair stripling! welcome to you from
     me, young prince of England!
(Remember you surging Manhattan's crowds as you
     pass'd with your cortege of nobles?
There in the crowds stood I, and singled you out with
     attachment;)
Nor forget I to sing of the wonder, the ship as she swam
     up my bay,
Well-shaped and stately the Great Eastern swam up my
     bay, she was 600 feet long,
Her moving swiftly surrounded by myriads of small craft
     I forget not to sing;
Nor the comet that came unannounced out of the north
     flaring in heaven,
Nor the strange huge meteor-procession dazzling and
     clear shooting over our heads,
(A moment, a moment long it sail'd its balls of unearthly
     light over our heads,
Then departed, dropped in the night, and was gone;)
Of such, and fitful as they, I sing—with gleams from them
     would I gleam and patch these chants,
Your chants, O year all mottled with evil and good—year
     of forebodings!
Year of comets and meteors transient and strange—lo!
     even here one equally transient and strange!
As I flit through you hastily, soon to fall and be gone,
     what is this chant,
What am I myself but one of your meteors?

WITH ANTECEDENTS.

1

With antecedents,
With my fathers and mothers and the accumulations of
    past ages,
With all which, had it not been, I would not now be here,
    as I am,
With Egypt, India, Phenicia, Greece and Rome,
With the Kelt, the Scandinavian, the Alb and the Saxon,
With antique maritime ventures, laws, artisanship, wars
    and journeys,
With the poet, the skald, the saga, the myth, and the ora-
    cle,
With the sale of slaves, with enthusiasts, with the trouba-
    dour, the crusader, and the monk,
With those old continents whence we have come to this
    new continent,
With the fading kingdoms and kings over there,
With the fading religions and priests,
With the small shores we look back to from our own large
    and present shores,
With countless years drawing themselves onward and
    arrived at these years,
You and me arrived—America arrived and making this
    year,
This year! sending itself ahead countless years to come.

2

O but it is not the years—it is I, it is You,
We touch all laws and tally all antecedents,
We are the skald, the oracle, the monk and the knight, we
easily include them and more,
We stand amid time beginningless and endless, we stand
amid evil and good,
All swings around us, there is as much darkness as light,
The very sun swings itself and its system of planets
around us,
Its sun, and its again, all swing around us.

As for me, (torn, stormy, amid these vehement days,)
I have the idea of all, and am all and believe in all,
I believe materialism is true and spiritualism is true, I
reject no part.

(Have I forgotten any part? any thing in the past?
Come to me whoever and whatever, till I give you recog-
nition.)

I respect Assyria, China, Teutonia, and the Hebrews,
I adopt each theory, myth, god, and demi-god,
I see that the old accounts, bibles, genealogies, are true,
without exception,
I assert that all past days were what they must have been,
And that they could no-how have been better than they
were,
And that to-day is what it must be, and that America is,
And that to-day and America could no-how be better
than they are.

3

In the name of these States and in your and my name, the
    Past,
And in the name of these States and in your and my
    name, the Present time.

I know that the past was great and the future will be
    great,
And I know that both curiously conjoint in the present
    time,
(For the sake of him I typify, for the common average
    man's sake, your sake if you are he,)
And that where I am or you are this present day, there is
    the centre of all days, all races,
And there is the meaning to us of all that has ever come of
    races and days, or ever will come.

*

A BROADWAY PAGEANT.

1

Over the Western sea hither from Niphon come,
Courteous, the swart-cheek'd two-sworded envoys,
Leaning back in their open barouches, bare-headed,
    impassive,
Ride to-day through Manhattan.

Libertad! I do not know whether others behold what I
behold,
In the procession along with the nobles of Niphon, the
errand-bearers,
Bringing up the rear, hovering above, around, or in the
ranks marching,
But I will sing you a song of what I behold Libertad.

When million-footed Manhattan unpent descends to her
pavements,
When the thunder-cracking guns arouse me with the
proud roar I love,
When the round-mouth'd guns out of the smoke and
smell I love spit their salutes,
When the fire-flashing guns have fully alerted me, and
heaven-clouds canopy my city with a delicate thin
haze,
When gorgeous the countless straight stems, the forests at
the wharves, thicken with colors,
When every ship richly drest carries her flag at the peak,
When pennants trail and street-festoons hang from the
windows,
When Broadway is entirely given up to foot-passengers
and foot-standers, when the mass is densest,
When the façades of the houses are alive with people,
when eyes gaze riveted tens of thousands at a time,
When the guests from the islands advance, when the
pageant moves forward visible,
When the summons is made, when the answer that
waited thousands of years answers,
I too arising, answering, descend to the pavements, merge
with the crowd, and gaze with them.

2

Superb-faced Manhattan!
Comrade Americanos! to us, then at last the Orient comes.

To us, my city,
Where our tall-topt marble and iron beauties range on
    opposite sides, to walk in the space between,
To-day our Antipodes comes.

The Originatress comes,
The nest of languages, the bequeather of poems, the race
    of eld,
Florid with blood, pensive, rapt with musings, hot with
    passion,
Sultry with perfume, with ample and flowing garments,
With sunburnt visage, with intense soul and glittering
    eyes,
The race of Brahma comes.

See my cantabile! these and more are flashing to us from
    the procession,
As it moves changing, a kaleidoscope divine it moves
    changing before us.

For not the envoys nor the tann'd Japanee from his island
    only,
Lithe and silent the Hindoo appears, the Asiatic continent
    itself appears, the past, the dead,
The murky night-morning of wonder and fable
    inscrutable,
The envelop'd mysteries, the old and unknown hive-bees,

The north, the sweltering south, eastern Assyria, the
    Hebrews, the ancient of ancients,
Vast desolated cities, the gliding present, all of these and
    more are in the pageant-procession.

Geography, the world, is in it,
The Great Sea, the brood of islands, Polynesia, the coast
    beyond,
The coast you henceforth are facing—you Libertad! from
    your Western golden shores,
The countries there with their populations, the millions
    en-masse are curiously here,
The swarming market-places, the temples with idols
    ranged along the sides or at the end, bonze, brahmin,
    and llama,
Mandarin, farmer, merchant, mechanic, and fisherman,
The singing-girl and the dancing-girl, the ecstatic persons,
    the secluded emperors,
Confucius himself, the great poets and heroes, the war-
    riors, the castes, all,
Trooping up, crowding from all directions, from the Altay
    mountains,
From Thibet, from the four winding and far-flowing
    rivers of China,
From the southern peninsulas and the demi-continental
    islands from Malaysia,
These and whatever belongs to them palpable show forth
    to me, and are seiz'd by me,
And I am seiz'd by them, and friendlily held by them,
Till as here them all I chant, Libertad! for themselves and
    for you.

For I too raising my voice join the ranks of this pageant,
I am the chanter, I chant aloud over the pageant,
I chant the world on my Western sea,
I chant copious the islands beyond, thick as stars in the
    sky,
I chant the new empire grander than any before, as in a
    vision it comes to me,
I chant America the mistress, I chant a greater supremacy,
I chant projected a thousand blooming cities yet in time
    on those groups of sea-islands,
My sail-ships and steam-ships threading the archipela-
    goes,
My stars and stripes fluttering in the wind,
Commerce opening, the sleep of ages having done its
    work, races reborn, refresh'd,
Lives, works resumed—the object I know not—but the
    old, the Asiatic renew'd as it must be,
Commencing from this day surrounded by the world.

3

And you Libertad of the world!
You shall sit in the middle well-pois'd thousands and
    thousands of years,
As to-day from one side the nobles of Asia come to you,
As to-morrow from the other side the queen of England
    sends her eldest son to you.

The sign is reversing, the orb is enclosed,
The ring is circled, the journey is done,
The box-lid is but perceptibly open'd, nevertheless the
    perfume pours copiously out of the whole box.

Young Libertad! with the venerable Asia, the all-mother,
Be considerate with her now and ever hot Libertad, for
  you are all,
Bend your proud neck to the long-off mother now send-
  ing messages over the archipelagoes to you,
Bend your proud neck low for once, young Libertad.

Were the children straying westward so long? so wide the
  tramping?
Were the precedent dim ages debouching westward from
  Paradise so long?
Were the centuries steadily footing it that way, all the
  while unknown, for you, for reasons?

They are justified, they are accomplish'd, they shall now
  be turn'd the other way also, to travel toward you
  thence,
They shall now also march obediently eastward for your
  sake Libertad.

*

SEA-DRIFT.

OUT OF THE CRADLE ENDLESSLY ROCKING.

Out of the cradle endlessly rocking,
Out of the mocking-bird's throat, the musical shuttle,
Out of the Ninth-month midnight,
Over the sterile sands and the fields beyond, where the
  child leaving his bed wander'd alone, bareheaded,
  barefoot,
Down from the shower'd halo,
Up from the mystic play of shadows twining and twisting
  as if they were alive,
Out from the patches of briers and blackberries,
From the memories of the bird that chanted to me,
From your memories sad brother, from the fitful risings
  and fallings I heard,
From under that yellow half-moon late-risen and swollen
  as if with tears,
From those beginning notes of yearning and love there in
  the mist,
From the thousand responses of my heart never to cease,
From the myriad thence-arous'd words,
From the word stronger and more delicious than any,
From such as now they start the scene revisiting,
As a flock, twittering, rising, or overhead passing,

Borne hither, ere all eludes me, hurriedly,
A man, yet by these tears a little boy again,
Throwing myself on the sand, confronting the waves,
I, chanter of pains and joys, uniter of here and hereafter,
Taking all hints to use them, but swiftly leaping beyond
    them,
A reminiscence sing.

Once Paumanok,
When the lilac-scent was in the air and Fifth-month grass
    was growing,
Up this seashore in some briers,
Two feather'd guests from Alabama, two together,
And their nest, and four light-green eggs spotted with
    brown,
And every day the he-bird to and fro near at hand,
And every day the she-bird crouch'd on her nest, silent,
    with bright eyes,
And every day I, a curious boy, never too close, never dis-
    turbing them,
Cautiously peering, absorbing, translating.

Shine! shine! shine!
Pour down your warmth, great sun!
While we bask, we two together.

Two together!
Winds blow south, or winds blow north,
Day come white, or night come black,
Home, or rivers and mountains from home,
Singing all time, minding no time,
While we two keep together.

Till of a sudden,
May-be kill'd, unknown to her mate,
One forenoon the she-bird crouch'd not on the nest,
Nor return'd that afternoon, nor the next,
Nor ever appear'd again.

And thenceforward all summer in the sound of the sea,
And at night under the full of the moon in calmer
    weather,
Over the hoarse surging of the sea,
Or flitting from brier to brier by day,
I saw, I heard at intervals the remaining one, the he-bird,
The solitary guest from Alabama.

Blow! blow! blow!
Blow up sea-winds along Paumanok's shore;
I wait and I wait till you blow my mate to me.

Yes, when the stars glisten'd,
All night long on the prong of a moss-scallop'd stake,
Down almost amid the slapping waves,
Sat the lone singer wonderful causing tears.

He call'd on his mate,
He pour'd forth the meanings which I of all men know.

Yes my brother I know,
The rest might not, but I have treasur'd every note,
For more than once dimly down to the beach gliding,
Silent, avoiding the moonbeams, blending myself with
    the shadows,

Recalling now the obscure shapes, the echoes, the sounds
   and sights after their sorts,
The white arms out in the breakers tirelessly tossing,
I, with bare feet, a child, the wind wafting my hair,
Listen'd long and long.

Listen'd to keep, to sing, now translating the notes,
Following you my brother.

Soothe! soothe! soothe!
Close on its wave soothes the wave behind,
And again another behind embracing and lapping, every one
   close,
But my love soothes not me, not me.

Low hangs the moon, it rose late,
It is lagging—O I think it is heavy with love, with love.

O madly the sea pushes upon the land,
With love, with love.

O night! do I not see my love fluttering out among the breakers?
What is that little black thing I see there in the white?

Loud! loud! loud!
Loud I call to you, my love!

High and clear I shoot my voice over the waves,
Surely you must know who is here, is here,
You must know who I am, my love.

Low-hanging moon!
What is that dusky spot in your brown yellow?
O it is the shape, the shape of my mate!
O moon do not keep her from me any longer.

Land! land! O land!
Whichever way I turn, O I think you could give me my mate
    back again if you only would,
For I am almost sure I see her dimly whichever way I look.

O rising stars!
Perhaps the one I want so much will rise, will rise with some of
    you.

O throat! O trembling throat!
Sound clearer through the atmosphere!
Pierce the woods, the earth,
Somewhere listening to catch you must be the one I want.

Shake out carols!
Solitary here, the night's carols!
Carols of lonesome love! death's carols!
Carols under that lagging, yellow, waning moon!
O under that moon where she droops almost down into the sea!
O reckless despairing carols.

But soft! sink low!
Soft! let me just murmur,
And do you wait a moment you husky-nois'd sea,
For somewhere I believe I heard my mate responding to me,
So faint, I must be still, be still to listen,

But not altogether still, for then she might not come immedi-
      ately to me.

Hither my love!
Here I am! here!
With this just-sustain'd note I announce myself to you,
This gentle call is for you my love, for you.

Do not be decoy'd elsewhere,
That is the whistle of the wind, it is not my voice,
That is the fluttering, the fluttering of the spray,
Those are the shadows of leaves.

O darkness! O in vain!
O I am very sick and sorrowful.

O brown halo in the sky near the moon, drooping upon the sea!
O troubled reflection in the sea!
O throat! O throbbing heart!
And I singing uselessly, uselessly all the night.

O past! O happy life! O songs of joy!
In the air, in the woods, over fields,
Loved! loved! loved! loved! loved!
But my mate no more, no more with me!
We two together no more.

The aria sinking,
All else continuing, the stars shining,
The winds blowing, the notes of the bird continuous echo-
      ing,

With angry moans the fierce old mother incessantly
    moaning,
On the sands of Paumanok's shore gray and rustling,
The yellow half-moon enlarged, sagging down, drooping,
    the face of the sea almost touching,
The boy ecstatic, with his bare feet the waves, with his
    hair the atmosphere dallying,
The love in the heart long pent, now loose, now at last
    tumultuously bursting,
The aria's meaning, the ears, the soul, swiftly depositing,
The strange tears down the cheeks coursing,
The colloquy there, the trio, each uttering,
The undertone, the savage old mother incessantly crying,
To the boy's soul's questions sullenly timing, some
    drown'd secret hissing,
To the outsetting bard.

Demon or bird! (said the boy's soul,)
Is it indeed toward your mate you sing? or is it really to
    me?
For I, that was a child, my tongue's use sleeping, now I
    have heard you,
Now in a moment I know what I am for, I awake,
And already a thousand singers, a thousand songs,
    clearer, louder and more sorrowful than yours,
A thousand warbling echoes have started to life within
    me, never to die.

O you singer solitary, singing by yourself, projecting me,
O solitary me listening, never more shall I cease perpetu-
    ating you,
Never more shall I escape, never more the reverberations,

Never more the cries of unsatisfied love be absent from
    me,
Never again leave me to be the peaceful child I was before
    what there in the night,
By the sea under the yellow and sagging moon,
The messenger there arous'd, the fire, the sweet hell
    within,
The unknown want, the destiny of me.

O give me the clew! (it lurks in the night here some-
    where,)
O if I am to have so much, let me have more!

A word then, (for I will conquer it,)
The word final, superior to all,
Subtle, sent up—what is it?—I listen;
Are you whispering it, and have been all the time, you
    sea-waves?
Is that it from your liquid rims and wet sands?

Whereto answering, the sea,
Delaying not, hurrying not,
Whisper'd me through the night, and very plainly before
    daybreak,
Lisp'd to me the low and delicious word death,
And again death, death, death, death,
Hissing melodious, neither like the bird nor like my
    arous'd child's heart,
But edging near as privately for me rustling at my feet,
Creeping thence steadily up to my ears and laving me
    softly all over,
Death, death, death, death, death.

Which I do not forget,
But fuse the song of my dusky demon and brother,
That he sang to me in the moonlight on Paumanok's gray
    beach,
With the thousand responsive songs at random,
My own songs awaked from that hour,
And with them the key, the word up from the waves,
The word of the sweetest song and all songs,
That strong and delicious word which, creeping to my
    feet,
(Or like some old crone rocking the cradle, swathed in
    sweet garments, bending aside,)
The sea whisper'd me.

AS I EBB'D WITH THE OCEAN OF LIFE.

1

As I ebb'd with the ocean of life,
As I wended the shores I know,
As I walk'd where the ripples continually wash you Pau-
    manok,
Where they rustle up hoarse and sibilant,
Where the fierce old mother endlessly cries for her cast-
    aways,
I musing late in the autumn day, gazing off southward,
Held by this electric self out of the pride of which I utter
    poems,
Was seiz'd by the spirit that trails in the lines underfoot,
The rim, the sediment that stands for all the water and all
    the land of the globe.

Fascinated, my eyes reverting from the south, dropt, to
    follow those slender windrows,
Chaff, straw, splinters of wood, weeds, and the sea-
    gluten,
Scum, scales from shining rocks, leaves of salt-lettuce, left
    by the tide,
Miles walking, the sound of breaking waves the other
    side of me,
Paumanok there and then as I thought the old thought of
    likenesses,
These you presented to me you fish-shaped island,
As I wended the shores I know,
As I walk'd with that electric self seeking types.

2

As I wend to the shores I know not,
As I list to the dirge, the voices of men and women
    wreck'd,
As I inhale the impalpable breezes that set in upon me,
As the ocean so mysterious rolls toward me closer and
    closer,
I too but signify at the utmost a little wash'd up drift,
A few sands and dead leaves to gather,
Gather, and merge myself as part of the sands and drift.

O baffled, balk'd, bent to the very earth,
Oppress'd with myself that I have dared to open my
    mouth,
Aware now that amid all that blab whose echoes recoil
    upon me I have not once had the least idea who or
    what I am,

But that before all my arrogant poems the real Me stands
　　yet untouch'd, untold, altogether unreach'd,
Withdrawn far, mocking me with mock-congratulatory
　　signs and bows,
With peals of distant ironical laughter at every word I
　　have written,
Pointing in silence to these songs, and then to the sand
　　beneath.

I perceive I have not really understood any thing, not a
　　single object, and that no man ever can,
Nature here in sight of the sea taking advantage of me to
　　dart upon me and sting me,
Because I have dared to open my mouth to sing at all.

3

You oceans both, I close with you,
We murmur alike reproachfully rolling sands and drift,
　　knowing not why,
These little shreds indeed standing for you and me and
　　all.

You friable shore with trails of debris,
You fish-shaped island, I take what is underfoot,
What is yours is mine my father.

I too Paumanok,
I too have bubbled up, floated the measureless float, and
　　been wash'd on your shores,
I too am but a trail of drift and debris,
I too leave little wrecks upon you, you fish-shaped island.

I throw myself upon your breast my father,
I cling to you so that you cannot unloose me,
I hold you so firm till you answer me something.

Kiss me my father,
Touch me with your lips as I touch those I love,
Breathe to me while I hold you close the secret of the mur-
    muring I envy.

4

Ebb, ocean of life, (the flow will return,)
Cease not your moaning you fierce old mother,
Endlessly cry for your castaways, but fear not, deny not
    me,
Rustle not up so hoarse and angry against my feet as I
    touch you or gather from you.

I mean tenderly by you and all,
I gather for myself and for this phantom looking down
    where we lead, and following me and mine.

Me and mine, loose windrows, little corpses,
Froth, snowy white, and bubbles,
(See, from my dead lips the ooze exuding at last,
See, the prismatic colors glistening and rolling,)
Tufts of straw, sands, fragments,
Buoy'd hither from many moods, one contradicting
    another,
From the storm, the long calm, the darkness, the swell,
Musing, pondering, a breath, a briny tear, a dab of liquid
    or soil,

Up just as much out of fathomless workings fermented
    and thrown,
A limp blossom or two, torn, just as much over waves
    floating, drifted at random,
Just as much for us that sobbing dirge of Nature,
Just as much whence we come that blare of the cloud-
    trumpets,
We, capricious, brought hither we know not whence,
    spread out before you,
You up there walking or sitting,
Whoever you are, we too lie in drifts at your feet.

TEARS.

Tears! tears! tears!
In the night, in solitude, tears,
On the white shore dripping, dripping, suck'd in by the
    sand,
Tears, not a star shining, all dark and desolate,
Moist tears from the eyes of a muffled head;
O who is that ghost? that form in the dark, with tears?
What shapeless lump is that, bent, crouch'd there on the
    sand?
Streaming tears, sobbing tears, throes, choked with wild
    cries;
O storm, embodied, rising, careering with swift steps
    along the beach!
O wild and dismal night storm, with wind—O belching
    and desperate!
O shade so sedate and decorous by day, with calm coun-
    tenance and regulated pace,

But away at night as you fly, none looking—O then the
    unloosen'd ocean,
Of tears! tears! tears!

TO THE MAN-OF-WAR-BIRD.

Thou who hast slept all night upon the storm,
Waking renew'd on thy prodigious pinions,
(Burst the wild storm? above it thou ascended'st,
And rested on the sky, thy slave that cradled thee,)
Now a blue point, far, far in heaven floating,
As to the light emerging here on deck I watch thee,
(Myself a speck, a point on the world's floating vast.)

Far, far at sea,
After the night's fierce drifts have strewn the shore with
    wrecks,
With re-appearing day as now so happy and serene,
The rosy and elastic dawn, the flashing sun,
The limpid spread of air cerulean,
Thou also re-appearest.

Thou born to match the gale, (thou art all wings,)
To cope with heaven and earth and sea and hurricane,
Thou ship of air that never furl'st thy sails,
Days, even weeks untired and onward, through spaces,
    realms gyrating,
At dusk that look'st on Senegal, at morn America,
That sport'st amid the lightning-flash and thunder-cloud,

In them, in thy experiences, had'st thou my soul,
What joys! what joys were thine!

ABOARD AT A SHIP'S HELM.

Aboard at a ship's helm,
A young steersman steering with care.

Through fog on a sea-coast dolefully ringing,
An ocean bell—O a warning bell, rock'd by the waves.

O you give good notice indeed, you bell by the sea-reefs
    ringing,
Ringing, ringing, to warn the ship from its wreck-place.

For as on the alert O steersman, you mind the loud admo-
    nition,
The bows turn, the freighted ship tacking speeds away
    under her gray sails,
The beautiful and noble ship with all her precious wealth
    speeds away gayly and safe.

But O the ship, the immortal ship! O ship aboard the ship!
Ship of the body, ship of the soul, voyaging, voyaging,
    voyaging.

ON THE BEACH AT NIGHT.

On the beach at night,
Stands a child with her father,
Watching the east, the autumn sky.

Up through the darkness,
While ravening clouds, the burial clouds, in black masses
    spreading,
Lower sullen and fast athwart and down the sky,
Amid a transparent clear belt of ether yet left in the east,
Ascends large and calm the lord-star Jupiter,
And nigh at hand, only a very little above,
Swim the delicate sisters the Pleiades.

From the beach the child holding the hand of her father,
Those burial-clouds that lower victorious soon to devour
    all,
Watching, silently weeps.

Weep not, child,
Weep not, my darling,
With these kisses let me remove your tears,
The ravening clouds shall not long be victorious,
They shall not long possess the sky, they devour the stars
    only in apparition,
Jupiter shall emerge, be patient, watch again another
    night, the Pleiades shall emerge,
They are immortal, all those stars both silvery and golden
    shall shine out again,
The great stars and the little ones shall shine out again,
    they endure,

The vast immortal suns and the long-enduring pensive
    moons shall again shine.

Then dearest child mournest thou only for Jupiter?
Considerest thou alone the burial of the stars?

Something there is,
(With my lips soothing thee, adding I whisper,
I give thee the first suggestion, the problem and indirec-
    tion,)
Something there is more immortal even than the stars,
(Many the burials, many the days and nights, passing
    away,)
Something that shall endure longer even than lustrous
    Jupiter,
Longer than sun or any revolving satellite,
Or the radiant sisters the Pleiades.

THE WORLD BELOW THE BRINE.

The world below the brine,
Forests at the bottom of the sea, the branches and leaves,
Sea-lettuce, vast lichens, strange flowers and seeds, the
    thick tangle, openings, and pink turf,
Different colors, pale gray and green, purple, white, and
    gold, the play of light through the water,
Dumb swimmers there among the rocks, coral, gluten,
    grass, rushes, and the aliment of the swimmers,
Sluggish existences grazing there suspended, or slowly
    crawling close to the bottom,

The sperm-whale at the surface blowing air and spray, or
    disporting with his flukes,
The leaden-eyed shark, the walrus, the turtle, the hairy
    sea-leopard, and the sting-ray,
Passions there, wars, pursuits, tribes, sight in those ocean-
    depths, breathing that thick-breathing air, as so many
    do,
The change thence to the sight here, and to the subtle air
    breathed by beings like us who walk this sphere,
The change onward from ours to that of beings who walk
    other spheres.

ON THE BEACH AT NIGHT ALONE.

On the beach at night alone,
As the old mother sways her to and fro singing her husky
    song,
As I watch the bright stars shining, I think a thought of
    the clef of the universes and of the future.

A vast similitude interlocks all,
All spheres, grown, ungrown, small, large, suns, moons,
    planets,
All distances of place however wide,
All distances of time, all inanimate forms,
All souls, all living bodies though they be ever so differ-
    ent, or in different worlds,
All gaseous, watery, vegetable, mineral processes, the
    fishes, the brutes,
All nations, colors, barbarisms, civilizations, languages,

All identities that have existed or may exist on this globe,
   or any globe,
All lives and deaths, all of the past, present, future,
This vast similitude spans them, and always has spann'd,
And shall forever span them and compactly hold and
   enclose them.

SONG FOR ALL SEAS, ALL SHIPS.

1

To-day a rude brief recitative,
Of ships sailing the seas, each with its special flag or ship-
   signal,
Of unnamed heroes in the ships—of waves spreading and
   spreading far as the eye can reach,
Of dashing spray, and the winds piping and blowing,
And out of these a chant for the sailors of all nations,
Fitful, like a surge.

Of sea-captains young or old, and the mates, and of all
   intrepid sailors,
Of the few, very choice, taciturn, whom fate can never
   surprise nor death dismay,
Pick'd sparingly without noise by thee old ocean, chosen
   by thee,
Thou sea that pickest and cullest the race in time, and
   unitest nations,
Suckled by thee, old husky nurse, embodying thee,
Indomitable, untamed as thee.

(Ever the heroes on water or on land, by ones or twos
   appearing,
Ever the stock preserv'd and never lost, though rare,
   enough for seed preserv'd.)

2

Flaunt out O sea your separate flags of nations!
Flaunt out visible as ever the various ship-signals!
But do you reserve especially for yourself and for the soul
   of man one flag above all the rest,
A spiritual woven signal for all nations, emblem of man
   elate above death,
Token of all brave captains and all intrepid sailors and
   mates,
And all that went down doing their duty,
Reminiscent of them, twined from all intrepid captains
   young or old,
A pennant universal, subtly waving all time, o'er all brave
   sailors,
All seas, all ships.

PATROLING BARNEGAT.

Wild, wild the storm, and the sea high running,
Steady the roar of the gale, with incessant undertone mut-
   tering,
Shouts of demoniac laughter fitfully piercing and pealing,
Waves, air, midnight, their savagest trinity lashing,
Out in the shadows there milk-white combs careering,
On beachy slush and sand spirts of snow fierce slanting,

Where through the murk the easterly death-wind breast-
     ing,
Through cutting swirl and spray watchful and firm
     advancing,
(That in the distance! is that a wreck? is the red signal flar-
     ing?)
Slush and sand of the beach tireless till daylight wending,
Steadily, slowly, through hoarse roar never remitting,
Along the midnight edge by those milk-white combs
     careering,
A group of dim, weird forms, struggling, the night con-
     fronting,
That savage trinity warily watching.

AFTER THE SEA-SHIP.

After the sea-ship, after the whistling winds,
After the white-gray sails taut to their spars and ropes,
Below, a myriad myriad waves hastening, lifting up their
     necks,
Tending in ceaseless flow toward the track of the ship,
Waves of the ocean bubbling and gurgling, blithely pry-
     ing,
Waves, undulating waves, liquid, uneven, emulous
     waves,
Toward that whirling current, laughing and buoyant,
     with curves,
Where the great vessel sailing and tacking displaced the
     surface,
Larger and smaller waves in the spread of the ocean
     yearnfully flowing,

The wake of the sea-ship after she passes, flashing and
frolicsome under the sun,
A motley procession with many a fleck of foam and many
fragments,
Following the stately and rapid ship, in the wake follow-
ing.

*

BY THE ROADSIDE.

A BOSTON BALLAD.
(1854.)

To get betimes in Boston town I rose this morning early,
Here's a good place at the corner, I must stand and see the
    show.

Clear the way there Jonathan!
Way for the President's marshal—way for the govern-
    ment cannon!
Way for the Federal foot and dragoons, (and the appari-
    tions copiously tumbling.)

I love to look on the Stars and Stripes, I hope the fifes will
    play Yankee Doodle.
How bright shine the cutlasses of the foremost troops!
Every man holds his revolver, marching stiff through
    Boston town.

A fog follows, antiques of the same come limping,
Some appear wooden-legged, and some appear ban-
    daged and bloodless.

Why this is indeed a show—it has called the dead out of
    the earth!
The old graveyards of the hills have hurried to see!
Phantoms! phantoms countless by flank and rear!
Cock'd hats of mothy mould—crutches made of mist!
Arms in slings—old men leaning on young men's shoul-
    ders.

What troubles you Yankee phantoms? what is all this
    chattering of bare gums?
Does the ague convulse your limbs? do you mistake your
    crutches for firelocks and level them?

If you blind your eyes with tears you will not see the Pres-
    ident's marshal,
If you groan such groans you might balk the government
    cannon.

For shame old maniacs—bring down those toss'd arms,
    and let your white hair be,
Here gape your great grandsons, their wives gaze at them
    from the windows,
See how well dress'd, see how orderly they conduct
    themselves.

Worse and worse—can't you stand it? are you retreating?
Is this hour with the living too dead for you?

Retreat then—pell-mell!
To your graves—back—back to the hills old limpers!
I do not think you belong here anyhow.

But there is one thing that belongs here—shall I tell you
     what it is, gentlemen of Boston?

I will whisper it to the Mayor, he shall send a committee
     to England,
They shall get a grant from the Parliament, go with a cart
     to the royal vault,
Dig out King George's coffin, unwrap him quick from the
     grave-clothes, box up his bones for a journey,
Find a swift Yankee clipper—here is freight for you,
     black-bellied clipper,
Up with your anchor—shake out your sails—steer
     straight toward Boston bay.

Now call for the President's marshal again, bring out the
     government cannon,
Fetch home the roarers from Congress, make another pro-
     cession, guard it with foot and dragoons.

This centre-piece for them;
Look, all orderly citizens—look from the windows,
     women!

The committee open the box, set up the regal ribs, glue
     those that will not stay,
Clap the skull on top of the ribs, and clap a crown on top
     of the skull.

You have got your revenge, old buster—the crown is
     come to its own, and more than its own.

Stick your hands in your pockets, Jonathan—you are a
    made man from this day,
You are mighty cute—and here is one of your bargains.

EUROPE,

The 72d and 73d Years of These States.

Suddenly out of its stale and drowsy lair, the lair of
    slaves,
Like lightning it le'pt forth half startled at itself,
Its feet upon the ashes and the rags, its hands tight to the
    throats of kings.

O hope and faith!
O aching dose of exiled patriots' lives!
O many a sicken'd heart!
Turn back unto this day and make yourselves afresh.

And you, paid to defile the People—you liars, mark!
Not for numberless agonies, murders, lusts,
For court thieving in its manifold mean forms, worming
    from his simplicity the poor man's wages,
For many a promise sworn by royal lips and broken and
    laugh'd at in the breaking,
Then in their power not for all these did the blows strike
    revenge, or the heads of the nobles fall;
The People scorn'd the ferocity of kings.

But the sweetness of mercy brew'd bitter destruction, and
    the frighten'd monarchs come back,

Each comes in state with his train, hangman, priest, tax-
gatherer,
Soldier, lawyer, lord, jailer, and sycophant.

Yet behind all lowering stealing, lo, a shape,
Vague as the night, draped interminably, head, front and
form, in scarlet folds,
Whose face and eyes none may see,
Out of its robes only this, the red robes lifted by the arm,
One finger crook'd pointed high over the top, like the
head of a snake appears.

Meanwhile corpses lie in new-made graves, bloody
corpses of young men,
The rope of the gibbet hangs heavily, the bullets of princes
are flying, the creatures of power laugh aloud,
And all these things bear fruits, and they are good.

Those corpses of young men,
Those martyrs that hang from the gibbets, those hearts
pierc'd by the gray lead,
Cold and motionless as they seem live elsewhere with
unslaughter'd vitality.

They live in other young men O kings!
They live in brothers again ready to defy you,
They were purified by death, they were taught and
exalted.

Not a grave of the murder'd for freedom but grows seed
for freedom, in its turn to bear seed,

Which the winds carry afar and re-sow, and the rains and
the snows nourish.

Not a disembodied spirit can the weapons of tyrants let
loose,
But it stalks invisibly over the earth, whispering, counsel-
ing, cautioning.

Liberty, let others despair of you—I never despair of you.

Is the house shut? is the master away?
Nevertheless, be ready, be not weary of watching,
He will soon return, his messengers come anon.

A HAND-MIRROR.

Hold it up sternly—see this it sends back, (who is it? is it
you?)
Outside fair costume, within ashes and filth,
No more a flashing eye, no more a sonorous voice or
springy step,
Now some slave's eye, voice, hands, step,
A drunkard's breath, unwholesome eater's face, vene-
realee's flesh,
Lungs rotting away piecemeal, stomach sour and canker-
ous,
Joints rheumatic, bowels clogged with abomination,
Blood circulating dark and poisonous streams,
Words babble, hearing and touch callous,
No brain, no heart left, no magnetism of sex;

Such from one look in this looking-glass ere you go hence,
Such a result so soon—and from such a beginning!

GODS.

Lover divine and perfect Comrade,
Waiting content, invisible yet, but certain,
Be thou my God.

Thou, thou, the Ideal Man,
Fair, able, beautiful, content, and loving,
Complete in body and dilate in spirit,
Be thou my God.

O Death, (for Life has served its turn,)
Opener and usher to the heavenly mansion,
Be thou my God.

Aught, aught of mightiest, best I see, conceive, or know,
(To break the stagnant tie—thee, thee to free, O soul,)
Be thou my God.

All great ideas, the races' aspirations,
All heroisms, deeds of rapt enthusiasts,
Be ye my Gods.

Or Time and Space,
Or shape of Earth divine and wondrous,
Or some fair shape I viewing, worship,

Or lustrous orb of sun or star by night,
Be ye my Gods.

GERMS.

Forms, qualities, lives, humanity, language, thoughts,
The ones known, and the ones unknown, the ones on the
    stars,
The stars themselves, some shaped, others unshaped,
Wonders as of those countries, the soil, trees, cities, inhab-
    itants, whatever they may be,
Splendid suns, the moons and rings, the countless com-
    binations and effects,
Such-like, and as good as such-like, visible here or any-
    where, stand provided for in a handful of space,
    which I extend my arm and half enclose with my
    hand,
That containing the start of each and all, the virtue, the
    germs of all.

THOUGHTS.

Of ownership—as if one fit to own things could not at
    pleasure enter upon all, and incorporate them into
    himself or herself;
Of vista—suppose some sight in arriere through the for-
    mative chaos, presuming the growth, fulness, life,
    now attain'd on the journey,

e road continued, and the journey ever con-

Of what was once lacking on earth, and in due time has
    become supplied— and of what will yet be supplied,
Because all I see and know I believe to have its main pur-
    port in what will yet be supplied.

WHEN I HEARD THE LEARN'D ASTRONOMER.

When I heard the learn'd astronomer,
When the proofs, the figures, were ranged in columns
    before me,
When I was shown the charts and diagrams, to add,
    divide, and measure them,
When I sitting heard the astronomer where he lectured
    with much applause in the lecture-room,
How soon unaccountable I became tired and sick,
Till rising and gliding out I wander'd off by myself,
In the mystical moist night-air, and from time to time,
Look'd up in perfect silence at the stars.

PERFECTIONS.

Only themselves understand themselves and the like of
    themselves,
As souls only understand souls.

O ME! O LIFE!

O me! O life! of the questions of these recurring,
Of the endless trains of the faithless, of cities fill'd with the
    foolish,
Of myself forever reproaching myself, (for who more
    foolish than I, and who more faithless?)
Of eyes that vainly crave the light, of the objects mean, of
    the struggle ever renew'd,
Of the poor results of all, of the plodding and sordid
    crowds I see around me,
Of the empty and useless years of the rest, with the rest
    me intertwined,
The question, O me! so sad, recurring—What good amid
    these, O me, O life?

Answer.

That you are here—that life exists and identity,
That the powerful play goes on, and you may contribute a
    verse.

TO A PRESIDENT.

All you are doing and saying is to America dangled
    mirages,
You have not learn'd of Nature—of the politics of Nature
    you have not learn'd the great amplitude, rectitude,
    impartiality,
You have not seen that only such as they are for these
    States,

And that what is less than they must sooner or later lift off
    from these States.

I SIT AND LOOK OUT.

I sit and look out upon all the sorrows of the world, and
    upon all oppression and shame,
I hear secret convulsive sobs from young men at anguish
    with themselves, remorseful after deeds done,
I see in low life the mother misused by her children,
    dying, neglected, gaunt, desperate,
I see the wife misused by her husband, I see the treacher-
    ous seducer of young women,
I mark the ranklings of jealousy and unrequited love
    attempted to be hid, I see these sights on the earth,
I see the workings of battle, pestilence, tyranny, I see mar-
    tyrs and prisoners,
I observe a famine at sea, I observe the sailors casting lots
    who shall be kill'd to preserve the lives of the rest,
I observe the slights and degradations cast by arrogant
    persons upon laborers, the poor, and upon negroes,
    and the like;
All these—all the meanness and agony without end I sit-
    ting look out upon,
See, hear, and am silent.

TO RICH GIVERS.

What you give me I cheerfully accept,
A little sustenance, a hut and garden, a little money, as I

rendezvous with my poems,
A traveler's lodging and breakfast as I journey through
the States,— why should I be ashamed to own such
gifts? why to advertise for them?
For I myself am not one who bestows nothing upon man
and woman,
For I bestow upon any man or woman the entrance to all
the gifts of the universe.

THE DALLIANCE OF THE EAGLES.

Skirting the river road, (my forenoon walk, my rest,)
Skyward in air a sudden muffled sound, the dalliance of
the eagles,
The rushing amorous contact high in space together,
The clinching interlocking claws, a living, fierce, gyrating
wheel,
Four beating wings, two beaks, a swirling mass tight
grappling,
In tumbling turning clustering loops, straight downward
falling,
Till o'er the river pois'd, the twain yet one, a moment's
lull,
A motionless still balance in the air, then parting, talons
loosing,
Upward again on slow-firm pinions slanting, their sepa-
rate diverse flight,
She hers, he his, pursuing.

ROAMING IN THOUGHT.

(After reading HEGEL.)

Roaming in thought over the Universe, I saw the little that
    is Good steadily hastening towards immortality,
And the vast all that is call'd Evil I saw hastening to
    merge itself and become lost and dead.

A FARM PICTURE.

Through the ample open door of the peaceful country
    barn,
A sunlit pasture field with cattle and horses feeding,
And haze and vista, and the far horizon fading away.

A CHILD'S AMAZE.

Silent and amazed even when a little boy,
I remember I heard the preacher every Sunday put God in
    his statements,
As contending against some being or influence.

THE RUNNER.

On a flat road runs the well-train'd runner,
He is lean and sinewy with muscular legs,
He is thinly clothed, he leans forward as he runs,
With lightly closed fists and arms partially rais'd.

BEAUTIFUL WOMEN.

Women sit or move to and fro, some old, some young,
The young are beautiful—but the old are more beautiful
    than the young.

MOTHER AND BABE.

I see the sleeping babe nestling the breast of its mother,
The sleeping mother and babe—hush'd, I study them
    long and long.

THOUGHT.

Of obedience, faith, adhesiveness;
As I stand aloof and look there is to me something pro-
    foundly affecting in large masses of men following
    the lead of those who do not believe in men.

VISOR'D.

A mask, a perpetual natural disguiser of herself,
Concealing her face, concealing her form,
Changes and transformations every hour, every moment,
Falling upon her even when she sleeps.

THOUGHT.

Of Justice—as if Justice could be any thing but the same
   ample law, expounded by natural judges and saviors,
As if it might be this thing or that thing, according to deci-
   sions.

GLIDING O'ER ALL.

Gliding o'er all, through all,
Through Nature, Time, and Space,
As a ship on the waters advancing,
The voyage of the soul—not life alone,
Death, many deaths I'll sing.

HAST NEVER COME TO THEE AN HOUR.

Hast never come to thee an hour,
A sudden gleam divine, precipitating, bursting all these
   bubbles, fashions, wealth?
These eager business aims—books, politics, art, amours,
To utter nothingness?

THOUGHT.

Of Equality—as if it harm'd me, giving others the same
   chances and rights as myself—as if it were not indis-
   pensable to my own rights that others possess the
   same.

TO OLD AGE.

I see in you the estuary that enlarges and spreads itself
    grandly as it pours in the great sea.

LOCATIONS AND TIMES.

Locations and times—what is it in me that meets them all,
    whenever and wherever, and makes me at home?
Forms, colors, densities, odors—what is it in me that cor-
    responds with them?

OFFERINGS.

A thousand perfect men and women appear,
Around each gathers a cluster of friends, and gay children
    and youths, with offerings.

TO THE STATES,
To Identify the 16th, 17th, or 18th Presidentiad.

Why reclining, interrogating? why myself and all drows-
    ing?
What deepening twilight—scum floating atop of the
    waters,
Who are they as bats and night-dogs askant in the capitol?
What a filthy Presidentiad! (O South, your torrid suns! O
    North, your arctic freezings!)

Are those really Congressmen? are those the great
    Judges? is that the President?
Then I will sleep awhile yet, for I see that these States
    sleep, for reasons;
(With gathering murk, with muttering thunder and lam-
    bent shoots we all duly awake,
South, North, East, West, inland and seaboard, we will
    surely awake.)

*

DRUM-TAPS.

FIRST O SONGS FOR A PRELUDE.

First O songs for a prelude,
Lightly strike on the stretch'd tympanum pride and joy
    in my city,
How she led the rest to arms, how she gave the cue,
How at once with lithe limbs unwaiting a moment she
    sprang,
(O superb! O Manhattan, my own, my peerless!
O strongest you in the hour of danger, in crisis! O truer
    than steel!)
How you sprang—how you threw off the costumes of
    peace with indifferent hand,
How your soft opera-music changed, and the drum and
    fife were heard in their stead,
How you led to the war, (that shall serve for our prelude,
    songs of soldiers,)
How Manhattan drum-taps led.

Forty years had I in my city seen soldiers parading,
Forty years as a pageant, till unawares the lady of this
    teeming and turbulent city,
Sleepless amid her ships, her houses, her incalculable
    wealth,

With her million children around her, suddenly,
At dead of night, at news from the south,
Incens'd struck with clinch'd hand the pavement.

A shock electric, the night sustain'd it,
Till with ominous hum our hive at daybreak pour'd out
    its myriads.

From the houses then and the workshops, and through all
    the doorways,
Leapt they tumultuous, and lo! Manhattan arming.

To the drum-taps prompt,
The young men falling in and arming,
The mechanics arming, (the trowel, the jack-plane, the
    black-smith's hammer, tost aside with precipitation,)
The lawyer leaving his office and arming, the judge leav-
    ing the court,
The driver deserting his wagon in the street, jumping
    down, throwing the reins abruptly down on the
    horses' backs,
The salesman leaving the store, the boss, book-keeper,
    porter, all leaving;
Squads gather everywhere by common consent and arm,
The new recruits, even boys, the old men show them how
    to wear their accoutrements, they buckle the straps
    carefully,
Outdoors arming, indoors arming, the flash of the mus-
    ket-barrels,
The white tents cluster in camps, the arm'd sentries
    around, the sunrise cannon and again at sunset,

Arm'd regiments arrive every day, pass through the city,
    and embark from the wharves,
(How good they look as they tramp down to the river,
    sweaty, with their guns on their shoulders!
How I love them! how I could hug them, with their brown
    faces and their clothes and knapsacks cover'd with
    dust!)
The blood of the city up—arm'd! arm'd! the cry every-
    where,
The flags flung out from the steeples of churches and
    from all the public buildings and stores,
The tearful parting, the mother kisses her son, the son
    kisses his mother,
(Loth is the mother to part, yet not a word does she speak
    to detain him,)
The tumultuous escort, the ranks of policemen preceding,
    clearing the way,
The unpent enthusiasm, the wild cheers of the crowd for
    their favorites,
The artillery, the silent cannons bright as gold, drawn
    along, rumble lightly over the stones,
(Silent cannons, soon to cease your silence,
Soon unlimber'd to begin the red business;)
All the mutter of preparation, all the determin'd arming,
The hospital service, the lint, bandages and medicines,
The women volunteering for nurses, the work begun for
    in earnest, no mere parade now;
War! an arm'd race is advancing! the welcome for battle,
    no turning away;
War! be it weeks, months, or years, an arm'd race is
    advancing to welcome it.

Mannahatta a-march—and it's O to sing it well!
It's O for a manly life in the camp.

And the sturdy artillery,
The guns bright as gold, the work for giants, to serve well
    the guns,
Unlimber them! (no more as the past forty years for
    salutes for courtesies merely,
Put in something now besides powder and wadding.)

And you lady of ships, you Mannahatta,
Old matron of this proud, friendly, turbulent city,
Often in peace and wealth you were pensive or covertly
    frown'd amid all your children,
But now you smile with joy exulting old Mannahatta.

EIGHTEEN SIXTY-ONE.

Arm'd year—year of the struggle,
No dainty rhymes or sentimental love verses for you ter-
    rible year,
Not you as some pale poetling seated at a desk lisping
    cadenzas piano,
But as a strong man erect, clothed in blue clothes, advanc-
    ing, carrying a rifle on your shoulder,
With well-gristled body and sunburnt face and hands,
    with a knife in the belt at your side,
As I heard you shouting loud, your sonorous voice ring-
    ing across the continent,
Your masculine voice O year, as rising amid the great
    cities,

Amid the men of Manhattan I saw you as one of the
    workmen, the dwellers in Manhattan,
Or with large steps crossing the prairies out of Illinois and
    Indiana,
Rapidly crossing the West with springy gait and descend-
    ing the Alleghanies,
Or down from the great lakes or in Pennsylvania, or on
    deck along the Ohio river,
Or southward along the Tennessee or Cumberland rivers,
    or at Chattanooga on the mountain top,
Saw I your gait and saw I your sinewy limbs clothed in
    blue, bearing weapons, robust year,
Heard your determin'd voice launch'd forth again and
    again,
Year that suddenly sang by the mouths of the round-
    lipp'd cannon,
I repeat you, hurrying, crashing, sad, distracted year.

BEAT! BEAT! DRUMS!

Beat! beat! drums!—blow! bugles! blow!
Through the windows—through doors—burst like a ruth-
    less force,
Into the solemn church, and scatter the congregation,
Into the school where the scholar is studying;
Leave not the bridegroom quiet—no happiness must he
    have now with his bride,
Nor the peaceful farmer any peace, ploughing his field or
    gathering his grain,
So fierce you whirr and pound you drums—so shrill you
    bugles blow.

Beat! beat! drums!—blow! bugles! blow!
Over the traffic of cities—over the rumble of wheels in the
      streets;
Are beds prepared for sleepers at night in the houses? no
      sleepers must sleep in those beds,
No bargainers' bargains by day—no brokers or specula-
      tors— would they continue?
Would the talkers be talking? would the singer attempt to
      sing?
Would the lawyer rise in the court to state his case before
      the judge?
Then rattle quicker, heavier drums—you bugles wilder
      blow.

Beat! beat! drums!—blow! bugles! blow!
Make no parley—stop for no expostulation,
Mind not the timid—mind not the weeper or prayer,
Mind not the old man beseeching the young man,
Let not the child's voice be heard, nor the mother's
      entreaties,
Make even the trestles to shake the dead where they lie
      awaiting the hearses,
So strong you thump O terrible drums—so loud you
      bugles blow.

FROM PAUMANOK STARTING I FLY LIKE A BIRD.

From Paumanok starting I fly like a bird,
Around and around to soar to sing the idea of all,
To the north betaking myself to sing there arctic songs,

To Kanada till I absorb Kanada in myself, to Michigan
then,
To Wisconsin, Iowa, Minnesota, to sing their songs, (they
are inimitable;)
Then to Ohio and Indiana to sing theirs, to Missouri and
Kansas and Arkansas to sing theirs,
To Tennessee and Kentucky, to the Carolinas and Georgia
to sing theirs,
To Texas and so along up toward California, to roam
accepted everywhere;
To sing first, (to the tap of the war-drum if need be,)
The idea of all, of the Western world one and insepara-
ble,
And then the song of each member of these States.

SONG OF THE BANNER AT DAYBREAK.

Poet.

O a new song, a free song,
Flapping, flapping, flapping, flapping, by sounds, by
voices clearer,
By the wind's voice and that of the drum,
By the banner's voice and child's voice and sea's voice
and father's voice,
Low on the ground and high in the air,
On the ground where father and child stand,
In the upward air where their eyes turn,
Where the banner at daybreak is flapping.

Words! book-words! what are you?
Words no more, for hearken and see,

My song is there in the open air, and I must sing,
With the banner and pennant a-flapping.

I'll weave the chord and twine in,
Man's desire and babe's desire, I'll twine them in, I'll put
    in life,
I'll put the bayonet's flashing point, I'll let bullets and
    slugs whizz,
(As one carrying a symbol and menace far into the future,
Crying with trumpet voice, *Arouse and beware! Beware and
    arouse!*)
I'll pour the verse with streams of blood, full of volition,
    full of joy,
Then loosen, launch forth, to go and compete,
With the banner and pennant a-flapping.

Pennant.

Come up here, bard, bard,
Come up here, soul, soul,
Come up here, dear little child,
To fly in the clouds and winds with me, and play with the
    measureless light.

Child.

Father what is that in the sky beckoning to me with long
    finger?
And what does it say to me all the while?

Father.

Nothing my babe you see in the sky,
And nothing at all to you it says—but look you my babe,
Look at these dazzling things in the houses, and see you
    the money-shops opening,
And see you the vehicles preparing to crawl along the
    streets with goods;
These, ah these, how valued and toil'd for these!
How envied by all the earth.

Poet.

Fresh and rosy red the sun is mounting high,
On floats the sea in distant blue careering through its
    channels,
On floats the wind over the breast of the sea setting in
    toward land,
The great steady wind from west or west-by-south,
Floating so buoyant with milk-white foam on the waters.

But I am not the sea nor the red sun,
I am not the wind with girlish laughter,
Not the immense wind which strengthens, not the wind
    which lashes,
Not the spirit that ever lashes its own body to terror and
    death,
But I am that which unseen comes and sings, sings, sings,
Which babbles in brooks and scoots in showers on the
    land,
Which the birds know in the woods mornings and
    evenings,

And the shore-sands know and the hissing wave, and that
    banner and pennant,
Aloft there flapping and flapping.

Child.

O father it is alive—it is full of people—it has children,
O now it seems to me it is talking to its children,
I hear it—it talks to me—O it is wonderful!
O it stretches—it spreads and runs so fast—O my father,
It is so broad it covers the whole sky.

Father.

Cease, cease, my foolish babe,
What you are saying is sorrowful to me, much it dis-
    pleases me;
Behold with the rest again I say, behold not banners and
    pennants aloft,
But the well-prepared pavements behold, and mark the
    solid-wall'd houses.

Banner and Pennant.

Speak to the child O bard out of Manhattan,
To our children all, or north or south of Manhattan,
Point this day, leaving all the rest, to us over all—and yet
    we know not why,
For what are we, mere strips of cloth profiting nothing,
Only flapping in the wind?

Poet.

I hear and see not strips of cloth alone,
I hear the tramp of armies, I hear the challenging sentry,
I hear the jubilant shouts of millions of men, I hear Lib-
    erty!
I hear the drums beat and the trumpets blowing,
I myself move abroad swift-rising flying then,
I use the wings of the land-bird and use the wings of the
    sea-bird, and look down as from a height,
I do not deny the precious results of peace, I see populous
    cities with wealth incalculable,
I see numberless farms, I see the farmers working in their
    fields or barns,
I see mechanics working, I see buildings everywhere
    founded, going up, or finish'd,
I see trains of cars swiftly speeding along railroad tracks
    drawn by the locomotives,
I see the stores, depots, of Boston, Baltimore, Charleston,
    New Orleans,
I see far in the West the immense area of grain, I dwell
    awhile hovering,
I pass to the lumber forests of the North, and again to the
    Southern plantation, and again to California;
Sweeping the whole I see the countless profit, the busy
    gatherings, earn'd wages,
See the Identity formed out of thirty-eight spacious and
    haughty States, (and many more to come,)
See forts on the shores of harbors, see ships sailing in and
    out;
Then over all, (aye! aye!) my little and lengthen'd pennant
    shaped like a sword,

Runs swiftly up indicating war and defiance— and now
    the halyards have rais'd it,
Side of my banner broad and blue, side of my starry ban-
    ner,
Discarding peace over all the sea and land.

Banner and Pennant.

Yet louder, higher, stronger, bard! yet farther, wider
    cleave!
No longer let our children deem us riches and peace
    alone,
We may be terror and carnage, and are so now,
Not now are we any one of these spacious and haughty
    States, (nor any five, nor ten,)
Nor market nor depot we, nor money-bank in the city,
But these and all, and the brown and spreading land, and
    the mines below, are ours,
And the shores of the sea are ours, and the rivers great
    and small,
And the fields they moisten, and the crops and the fruits
    are ours,
Bays and channels and ships sailing in and out are ours—
    while we over all,
Over the area spread below, the three or four millions of
    square miles, the capitals,
The forty millions of people,—O bard! in life and death
    supreme,
We, even we, henceforth flaunt out masterful, high up
    above,

Not for the present alone, for a thousand years chanting
    through you,
This song to the soul of one poor little child.

Child.

O my father I like not the houses,
They will never to me be any thing, nor do I like money,
But to mount up there I would like, O father dear, that
    banner I like,
That pennant I would be and must be.

Father.

Child of mine you fill me with anguish,
To be that pennant would be too fearful,
Little you know what it is this day, and after this day, for-
    ever,
It is to gain nothing, but risk and defy every thing,
Forward to stand in front of wars—and O, such wars!—
    what have you to do with them?
With passions of demons, slaughter, premature death?

Banner.

Demons and death then I sing,
Put in all, aye all will I, sword-shaped pennant for war,
And a pleasure new and ecstatic, and the prattled yearn-
    ing of children,
Blent with the sounds of the peaceful land and the liquid
    wash of the sea,

And the black ships fighting on the sea envelop'd in
    smoke,
And the icy cool of the far, far north, with rustling cedars
    and pines,
And the whirr of drums and the sound of soldiers march-
    ing, and the hot sun shining south,
And the beach-waves combing over the beach on my
    Eastern shore, and my Western shore the same,
And all between those shores, and my ever running Mis-
    sissippi with bends and chutes,
And my Illinois fields, and my Kansas fields, and my
    fields of Missouri,
The Continent, devoting the whole identity without
    reserving an atom,
Pour in! whelm that which asks, which sings, with all and
    the yield of all,
Fusing and holding, claiming, devouring the whole,
No more with tender lip, nor musical labial sound,
But out of the night emerging for good, our voice persua-
    sive no more,
Croaking like crows here in the wind.

Poet.

My limbs, my veins dilate, my theme is clear at last,
Banner so broad advancing out of the night, I sing you
    haughty and resolute,
I burst through where I waited long, too long, deafen'd
    and blinded,
My hearing and tongue are come to me, (a little child
    taught me,)

I hear from above O pennant of war your ironical call and
demand,

Insensate! insensate! (yet I at any rate chant you,) O ban-
ner!

Not houses of peace indeed are you, nor any nor all their
prosperity, (if need be, you shall again have every one
of those houses to destroy them,

You thought not to destroy those valuable houses, stand-
ing fast, full of comfort, built with money,

May they stand fast, then? not an hour except you above
them and all stand fast;)

O banner, not money so precious are you, not farm pro-
duce you, nor the material good nutriment,

Nor excellent stores, nor landed on wharves from the
ships,

Not the superb ships with sail-power or steam-power,
fetching and carrying cargoes,

Nor machinery, vehicles, trade, nor revenues—but you as
henceforth I see you,

Running up out of the night, bringing your cluster of
stars, (ever enlarging stars,)

Divider of daybreak you, cutting the air, touch'd by the
sun, measuring the sky,

(Passionately seen and yearn'd for by one poor little child,

While others remain busy or smartly talking, forever
teaching thrift, thrift;)

O you up there! O pennant! where you undulate like a
snake hissing so curious,

Out of reach, an idea only, yet furiously fought for, risk-
ing bloody death, loved by me,

So loved—O you banner leading the day with stars
brought from the night!

Valueless, object of eyes, over all and demanding all—
    (absolute owner of all)—O banner and pennant!
I too leave the rest—great as it is, it is nothing—houses,
    machines are nothing—I see them not,
I see but you, O warlike pennant! O banner so broad, with
    stripes, I sing you only,
Flapping up there in the wind.

RISE O DAYS FROM YOUR FATHOMLESS DEEPS.

1

Rise O days from your fathomless deeps, till you loftier,
    fiercer sweep,
Long for my soul hungering gymnastic I devour'd what
    the earth gave me,
Long I roam'd the woods of the north, long I watch'd Nia-
    gara pouring,
I travel'd the prairies over and slept on their breast, I
    cross'd the Nevadas, I cross'd the plateaus,
I ascended the towering rocks along the Pacific, I sail'd
    out to sea,
I sail'd through the storm, I was refresh'd by the storm,
I watch'd with joy the threatening maws of the waves,
I mark'd the white combs where they career'd so high,
    curling over,
I heard the wind piping, I saw the black clouds,
Saw from below what arose and mounted, (O superb! O
    wild as my heart, and powerful!)
Heard the continuous thunder as it bellow'd after the
    lightning,

Noted the slender and jagged threads of lightning as sud-
den and fast amid the din they chased each other
across the sky;
These, and such as these, I, elate, saw—saw with wonder,
yet pensive and masterful,
All the menacing might of the globe uprisen around me,
Yet there with my soul I fed, I fed content, supercilious.

2

'Twas well, O soul—'twas a good preparation you gave
me,
Now we advance our latent and ampler hunger to fill,
Now we go forth to receive what the earth and the sea
never gave us,
Not through the mighty woods we go, but through the
mightier cities,
Something for us is pouring now more than Niagara
pouring,
Torrents of men, (sources and rills of the Northwest are
you indeed inexhaustible?)
What, to pavements and homesteads here, what were
those storms of the mountains and sea?
What, to passions I witness around me to-day? was the
sea risen?
Was the wind piping the pipe of death under the black
clouds?
Lo! from deeps more unfathomable, something more
deadly and savage,
Manhattan rising, advancing with menacing front—
Cincinnati, Chicago, unchain'd;

What was that swell I saw on the ocean? behold what
    comes here,
How it climbs with daring feet and hands—how it
    dashes!
How the true thunder bellows after the lightning—how
    bright the flashes of lightning!
How Democracy with desperate vengeful port strides on,
    shown through the dark by those flashes of lightning!
(Yet a mournful wail and low sob I fancied I heard
    through the dark,
In a lull of the deafening confusion.)

3

Thunder on! stride on, Democracy! strike with vengeful
    stroke!
And do you rise higher than ever yet O days, O cities!
Crash heavier, heavier yet O storms! you have done me
    good,
My soul prepared in the mountains absorbs your immor-
    tal strong nutriment,
Long had I walk'd my cities, my country roads through
    farms, only half satisfied,
One doubt nauseous undulating like a snake, crawl'd on
    the ground before me,
Continually preceding my steps, turning upon me oft,
    ironically hissing low;
The cities I loved so well I abandon'd and left, I sped to
    the certainties suitable to me,
Hungering, hungering, hungering, for primal energies
    and Nature's dauntlessness,

I refresh'd myself with it only, I could relish it only,
I waited the bursting forth of the pent fire—on the water
    and air I waited long;
But now I no longer wait, I am fully satisfied, I am glut-
    ted,
I have witness'd the true lightning, I have witness'd my
    cities electric,
I have lived to behold man burst forth and warlike Amer-
    ica rise,
Hence I will seek no more the food of the northern soli-
    tary wilds,
No more the mountains roam or sail the stormy sea.

VIRGINIA—THE WEST.

The noble sire fallen on evil days,
I saw with hand uplifted, menacing, brandishing,
(Memories of old in abeyance, love and faith in abeyance,)
The insane knife toward the Mother of All.

The noble son on sinewy feet advancing,
I saw, out of the land of prairies, land of Ohio's waters
    and of Indiana,
To the rescue the stalwart giant hurry his plenteous off-
    spring,
Drest in blue, bearing their trusty rifles on their shoulders.

Then the Mother of All with calm voice speaking,
As to you Rebellious, (I seemed to hear her say,) why
    strive against me, and why seek my life?

When you yourself forever provide to defend me?
For you provided me Washington—and now these also.

CITY OF SHIPS.

City of ships!
(O the black ships! O the fierce ships!
O the beautiful sharp-bow'd steam-ships and sail-ships!)
City of the world! (for all races are here,
All the lands of the earth make contributions here;)
City of the sea! city of hurried and glittering tides!
City whose gleeful tides continually rush or recede,
    whirling in and out with eddies and foam!
City of wharves and stores—city of tall façades of marble
    and iron!
Proud and passionate city—mettlesome, mad, extrava-
    gant city!
Spring up O city—not for peace alone, but be indeed
    yourself, warlike!
Fear not—submit to no models but your own O city!
Behold me—incarnate me as I have incarnated you!
I have rejected nothing you offer'd me—whom you
    adopted I have adopted,
Good or bad I never question you—I love all—I do not
    condemn any thing,
I chant and celebrate all that is yours—yet peace no more,
In peace I chanted peace, but now the drum of war is
    mine,
War, red war is my song through your streets, O city!

THE CENTENARIAN'S STORY.

(Volunteer of 1861-2, at Washington Park, Brooklyn, assisting the
Centenarian.)

Give me your hand old Revolutionary,
The hill-top is nigh, but a few steps, (make room gentle-
    men,)
Up the path you have follow'd me well, spite of your hun-
    dred and extra years,
You can walk old man, though your eyes are almost done,
Your faculties serve you, and presently I must have them
    serve me.

Rest, while I tell what the crowd around us means,
On the plain below recruits are drilling and exercising,
There is the camp, one regiment departs to-morrow,
Do you hear the officers giving their orders?
Do you hear the clank of the muskets?

Why what comes over you now old man?
Why do you tremble and clutch my hand so convul-
    sively?
The troops are but drilling, they are yet surrounded with
    smiles,
Around them at hand the well-drest friends and the
    women,
While splendid and warm the afternoon sun shines down,
Green the midsummer verdure and fresh blows the dal-
    lying breeze,
O'er proud and peaceful cities and arm of the sea
    between.

But drill and parade are over, they march back to quar-
    ters,
Only hear that approval of hands! hear what a clapping!

As wending the crowds now part and disperse—but we
    old man,
Not for nothing have I brought you hither—we must
    remain,
You to speak in your turn, and I to listen and tell.

The Centenarian.

When I clutch'd your hand it was not with terror,
But suddenly pouring about me here on every side,
And below there where the boys were drilling, and up the
    slopes they ran,
And where tents are pitch'd, and wherever you see south
    and south-east and south-west,
Over hills, across lowlands, and in the skirts of woods,
And along the shores, in mire (now fill'd over) came again
    and suddenly raged,
As eighty-five years a-gone no mere parade receiv'd with
    applause of friends,
But a battle which I took part in myself—aye, long ago as
    it is, I took part in it,
Walking then this hilltop, this same ground.

Aye, this is the ground,
My blind eyes even as I speak behold it re-peopled from
    graves,
The years recede, pavements and stately houses disap-
    pear,

Rude forts appear again, the old hoop'd guns are
mounted,
I see the lines of rais'd earth stretching from river to bay,
I mark the vista of waters, I mark the uplands and slopes;
Here we lay encamp'd, it was this time in summer also.

As I talk I remember all, I remember the Declaration,
It was read here, the whole army paraded, it was read to
us here,
By his staff surrounded the General stood in the middle,
he held up his unsheath'd sword,
It glitter'd in the sun in full sight of the army.

'Twas a bold act then—the English war-ships had just
arrived,
We could watch down the lower bay where they lay at
anchor,
And the transports swarming with soldiers.

A few days more and they landed, and then the battle.

Twenty thousand were brought against us,
A veteran force furnish'd with good artillery.

I tell not now the whole of the battle,
But one brigade early in the forenoon order'd forward to
engage the red-coats,
Of that brigade I tell, and how steadily it march'd,
And how long and well it stood confronting death.

Who do you think that was marching steadily sternly con-
fronting death?

It was the brigade of the youngest men, two thousand
strong,
Rais'd in Virginia and Maryland, and most of them
known personally to the General.

Jauntily forward they went with quick step toward
Gowanus' waters,
Till of a sudden unlook'd for by defiles through the
woods, gain'd at night,
The British advancing, rounding in from the east, fiercely
playing their guns,
That brigade of the youngest was cut off and at the
enemy's mercy.

The General watch'd them from this hill,
They made repeated desperate attempts to burst their
environment,
Then drew close together, very compact, their flag flying
in the middle,
But O from the hills how the cannon were thinning and
thinning them!

It sickens me yet, that slaughter!
I saw the moisture gather in drops on the face of the Gen-
eral.
I saw how he wrung his hands in anguish.

Meanwhile the British manœuvr'd to draw us out for a
pitch'd battle,
But we dared not trust the chances of a pitch'd battle.

We fought the fight in detachments,
Sallying forth we fought at several points, but in each the
luck was against us,
Our foe advancing, steadily getting the best of it, push'd
us back to the works on this hill,
Till we turn'd menacing here, and then he left us.

That was the going out of the brigade of the youngest
men, two thousand strong,
Few return'd, nearly all remain in Brooklyn.

That and here my General's first battle,
No women looking on nor sunshine to bask in, it did not
conclude with applause,
Nobody clapp'd hands here then.

But in darkness in mist on the ground under a chill rain,
Wearied that night we lay foil'd and sullen,
While scornfully laugh'd many an arrogant lord off
against us encamp'd,
Quite within hearing, feasting, clinking wineglasses
together over their victory.

So dull and damp and another day,
But the night of that, mist lifting, rain ceasing,
Silent as a ghost while they thought they were sure of
him, my General retreated.

I saw him at the river-side,
Down by the ferry lit by torches, hastening the embarca-
tion;

My General waited till the soldiers and wounded were all
    pass'd over,
And then, (it was just ere sunrise,) these eyes rested on
    him for the last time.

Every one else seem'd fill'd with gloom,
Many no doubt thought of capitulation.

But when my General pass'd me,
As he stood in his boat and look'd toward the coming sun,
I saw something different from capitulation.

Terminus.

Enough, the Centenarian's story ends,
The two, the past and present, have interchanged,
I myself as connecter, as chansonnier of a great future, am
    now speaking.

And is this the ground Washington trod?
And these waters I listlessly daily cross, are these the
    waters he cross'd,
As resolute in defeat as other generals in their proudest
    triumphs?

I must copy the story, and send it eastward and west-
    ward,
I must preserve that look as it beam'd on you rivers of
    Brooklyn.

See—as the annual round returns the phantoms return,
It is the 27th of August and the British have landed,
The battle begins and goes against us, behold through the
smoke Washington's face,
The brigade of Virginia and Maryland have march'd forth
to intercept the enemy,
They are cut off, murderous artillery from the hills plays
upon them,
Rank after rank falls, while over them silently droops the
flag,
Baptized that day in many a young man's bloody
wounds,
In death, defeat, and sisters', mothers' tears.

Ah, hills and slopes of Brooklyn! I perceive you are more
valuable than your owners supposed;
In the midst of you stands an encampment very old,
Stands forever the camp of that dead brigade.

CAVALRY CROSSING A FORD.

A line in long array where they wind betwixt green
islands,
They take a serpentine course, their arms flash in the
sun— hark to the musical clank,
Behold the silvery river, in it the splashing horses loiter-
ing stop to drink,
Behold the brown-faced men, each group, each person a
picture, the negligent rest on the saddles,
Some emerge on the opposite bank, others are just enter-
ing the ford—while,

Scarlet and blue and snowy white,
The guidon flags flutter gayly in the wind.

BIVOUAC ON A MOUNTAIN SIDE.

I see before me now a traveling army halting,
Below a fertile valley spread, with barns and the orchards
of summer,
Behind, the terraced sides of a mountain, abrupt, in places
rising high,
Broken, with rocks, with clinging cedars, with tall shapes
dingily seen,
The numerous camp-fires scatter'd near and far, some
away up on the mountain,
The shadowy forms of men and horses, looming, large-
sized, flickering,
And over all the sky—the sky! far, far out of reach, stud-
ded, breaking out, the eternal stars.

AN ARMY CORPS ON THE MARCH.

With its cloud of skirmishers in advance,
With now the sound of a single shot snapping like a whip,
and now an irregular volley,
The swarming ranks press on and on, the dense brigades
press on,
Glittering dimly, toiling under the sun—the dust-cover'd
men,
In columns rise and fall to the undulations of the ground,

With artillery interspers'd—the wheels rumble, the horses
    sweat,
As the army corps advances.

BY THE BIVOUAC'S FITFUL FLAME.

By the bivouac's fitful flame,
A procession winding around me, solemn and sweet and
    slow— but first I note,
The tents of the sleeping army, the fields' and woods' dim
    outline,
The darkness lit by spots of kindled fire, the silence,
Like a phantom far or near an occasional figure moving,
The shrubs and trees, (as I lift my eyes they seem to be
    stealthily watching me,)
While wind in procession thoughts, O tender and won-
    drous thoughts,
Of life and death, of home and the past and loved, and of
    those that are far away;
A solemn and slow procession there as I sit on the
    ground,
By the bivouac's fitful flame.

COME UP FROM THE FIELDS FATHER.

Come up from the fields father, here's a letter from our
    Pete,
And come to the front door mother, here's a letter from
    thy dear son.

Lo, 'tis autumn,

Lo, where the trees, deeper green, yellower and redder,

Cool and sweeten Ohio's villages with leaves fluttering in
the moderate wind,

Where apples ripe in the orchards hang and grapes on the
trellis'd vines,

(Smell you the smell of the grapes on the vines?

Smell you the buckwheat where the bees were lately
buzzing?)

Above all, lo, the sky so calm, so transparent after the rain,
and with wondrous clouds,

Below too, all calm, all vital and beautiful, and the farm
prospers well.

Down in the fields all prospers well,

But now from the fields come father, come at the daugh-
ter's call,

And come to the entry mother, to the front door come
right away.

Fast as she can she hurries, something ominous, her steps
trembling,

She does not tarry to smooth her hair nor adjust her cap.

Open the envelope quickly,

O this is not our son's writing, yet his name is sign'd,

O a strange hand writes for our dear son, O stricken
mother's soul!

All swims before her eyes, flashes with black, she catches
the main words only,

Sentences broken, *gunshot wound in the breast, cavalry skir-*
    mish, taken to hospital,
At present low, but will soon be better.

Ah now the single figure to me,
Amid all teeming and wealthy Ohio with all its cities and
    farms,
Sickly white in the face and dull in the head, very faint,
By the jamb of a door leans.

Grieve not so, dear mother, (the just-grown daughter speaks
    through her sobs,
The little sisters huddle around speechless and dismay'd,)
See, dearest mother, the letter says Pete will soon be better.

Alas poor boy, he will never be better, (nor may-be needs
    to be better, that brave and simple soul,)
While they stand at home at the door he is dead already,
The only son is dead.

But the mother needs to be better,
She with thin form presently drest in black,
By day her meals untouch'd, then at night fitfully sleep-
    ing, often waking,
In the midnight waking, weeping, longing with one deep
    longing,
O that she might withdraw unnoticed, silent from life
    escape and withdraw,
To follow, to seek, to be with her dear dead son.

VIGIL STRANGE I KEPT ON THE FIELD ONE NIGHT.

Vigil strange I kept on the field one night;
When you my son and my comrade dropt at my side that
    day,
One look I but gave which your dear eyes return'd with
    a look I shall never forget,
One touch of your hand to mine O boy, reach'd up as you
    lay on the ground,
Then onward I sped in the battle, the even-contested bat-
    tle,
Till late in the night reliev'd to the place at last again I
    made my way,
Found you in death so cold dear comrade, found your
    body son of responding kisses, (never again on earth
    responding,)
Bared your face in the starlight, curious the scene, cool
    blew the moderate night-wind,
Long there and then in vigil I stood, dimly around me the
    battle-field spreading,
Vigil wondrous and vigil sweet there in the fragrant silent
    night,
But not a tear fell, not even a long-drawn sigh, long, long
    I gazed,
Then on the earth partially reclining sat by your side lean-
    ing my chin in my hands,
Passing sweet hours, immortal and mystic hours with
    you dearest comrade— not a tear, not a word,
Vigil of silence, love and death, vigil for you my son and
    my soldier,
As onward silently stars aloft, eastward new ones
    upward stole,

Vigil final for you brave boy, (I could not save you, swift
    was your death,
I faithfully loved you and cared for you living, I think we
    shall surely meet again,)
Till at latest lingering of the night, indeed just as the dawn
    appear'd,
My comrade I wrapt in his blanket, envelop'd well his
    form,
Folded the blanket well, tucking it carefully over head
    and carefully under feet,
And there and then and bathed by the rising sun, my son
    in his grave, in his rude-dug grave I deposited,
Ending my vigil strange with that, vigil of night and bat-
    tle-field dim,
Vigil for boy of responding kisses, (never again on earth
    responding,)
Vigil for comrade swiftly slain, vigil I never forget, how as
    day brighten'd,
I rose from the chill ground and folded my soldier well
    in his blanket,
And buried him where he fell.

A MARCH IN THE RANKS HARD-PREST,
AND THE ROAD UNKNOWN.

A march in the ranks hard-prest, and the road unknown,
A route through a heavy wood with muffled steps in the
    darkness,
Our army foil'd with loss severe, and the sullen remnant
    retreating,

Till after midnight glimmer upon us the lights of a dim-
lighted building,
We come to an open space in the woods, and halt by the
dim-lighted building,
'Tis a large old church at the crossing roads, now an
impromptu hospital,
Entering but for a minute I see a sight beyond all the pic-
tures and poems ever made,
Shadows of deepest, deepest black, just lit by moving can-
dles and lamps,
And by one great pitchy torch stationary with wild red
flame and clouds of smoke,
By these, crowds, groups of forms vaguely I see on the
floor, some in the pews laid down,
At my feet more distinctly a soldier, a mere lad, in dan-
ger of bleeding to death, (he is shot in the abdomen,)
I stanch the blood temporarily, (the youngster's face is
white as a lily,)
Then before I depart I sweep my eyes o'er the scene fain
to absorb it all,
Faces, varieties, postures beyond description, most in
obscurity, some of them dead,
Surgeons operating, attendants holding lights, the smell
of ether, the odor of blood,
The crowd, O the crowd of the bloody forms, the yard
outside also fill'd,
Some on the bare ground, some on planks or stretchers,
some in the death-spasm sweating,
An occasional scream or cry, the doctor's shouted orders
or calls,
The glisten of the little steel instruments catching the glint
of the torches,

These I resume as I chant, I see again the forms, I smell the
    odor,
Then hear outside the orders given, *Fall in, my men, fall in;*
But first I bend to the dying lad, his eyes open, a half-
    smile gives he me,
Then the eyes close, calmly close, and I speed forth to the
    darkness,
Resuming, marching, ever in darkness marching, on in
    the ranks,
The unknown road still marching.

A SIGHT IN CAMP IN THE DAYBREAK
GRAY AND DIM.

A sight in camp in the daybreak gray and dim,
As from my tent I emerge so early sleepless,
As slow I walk in the cool fresh air the path near by the
    hospital tent,
Three forms I see on stretchers lying, brought out there
    untended lying,
Over each the blanket spread, ample brownish woolen
    blanket,
Gray and heavy blanket, folding, covering all.

Curious I halt and silent stand,
Then with light fingers I from the face of the nearest the
    first just lift the blanket;
Who are you elderly man so gaunt and grim, with well-
    gray'd hair, and flesh all sunken about the eyes?
Who are you my dear comrade?

Then to the second I step—and who are you my child and
    darling?
Who are you sweet boy with cheeks yet blooming?

Then to the third—a face nor child nor old, very calm, as
    of beautiful yellow-white ivory;
Young man I think I know you—I think this face is the
    face of the Christ himself,
Dead and divine and brother of all, and here again he lies.

AS TOILSOME I WANDER'D VIRGINIA'S WOODS.

As toilsome I wander'd Virginia's woods,
To the music of rustling leaves kick'd by my feet, (for
    'twas autumn,)
I mark'd at the foot of a tree the grave of a soldier;
Mortally wounded he and buried on the retreat, (easily all
    could I understand,)
The halt of a mid-day hour, when up! no time to lose—yet
    this sign left,
On a tablet scrawl'd and nail'd on the tree by the grave,
Bold, cautious, true, and my loving comrade.

Long, long I muse, then on my way go wandering,
Many a changeful season to follow, and many a scene of
    life,
Yet at times through changeful season and scene, abrupt,
    alone, or in the crowded street,
Comes before me the unknown soldier's grave, comes the
    inscription rude in Virginia's woods,
Bold, cautious, true, and my loving comrade.

NOT THE PILOT.

Not the pilot has charged himself to bring his ship into
  port, though beaten back and many times baffled;
Not the pathfinder penetrating inland weary and long,
By deserts parch'd, snows chill'd, rivers wet, perseveres
  till he reaches his destination,
More than I have charged myself, heeded or unheeded, to
  compose a march for these States,
For a battle-call, rousing to arms if need be, years, cen-
  turies hence.

YEAR THAT TREMBLED AND REEL'D BENEATH ME.

Year that trembled and reel'd beneath me!
Your summer wind was warm enough, yet the air I
  breathed froze me,
A thick gloom fell through the sunshine and darken'd me,
Must I change my triumphant songs? said I to myself,
Must I indeed learn to chant the cold dirges of the baffled?
And sullen hymns of defeat?

THE WOUND-DRESSER.

1

An old man bending I come among new faces,
Years looking backward resuming in answer to children,
Come tell us old man, as from young men and maidens
  that love me,

(Arous'd and angry, I'd thought to beat the alarum, and
    urge relentless war,
But soon my fingers fail'd me, my face droop'd and I
    resign'd myself,
To sit by the wounded and soothe them, or silently watch
    the dead;)
Years hence of these scenes, of these furious passions,
    these chances,
Of unsurpass'd heroes, (was one side so brave? the other
    was equally brave;)
Now be witness again, paint the mightiest armies of earth,
Of those armies so rapid so wondrous what saw you to
    tell us?
What stays with you latest and deepest? of curious pan-
    ics,
Of hard-fought engagements or sieges tremendous what
    deepest remains?

2

O maidens and young men I love and that love me,
What you ask of my days those the strangest and sudden
    your talking recalls,
Soldier alert I arrive after a long march cover'd with sweat
    and dust,
In the nick of time I come, plunge in the fight, loudly
    shout in the rush of successful charge,
Enter the captur'd works—yet lo, like a swift-running
    river they fade,
Pass and are gone they fade—I dwell not on soldiers' per-
    ils or soldiers' joys,

(Both I remember well—many the hardships, few the
  joys, yet I was content.)

But in silence, in dreams' projections,
While the world of gain and appearance and mirth goes
  on,
So soon what is over forgotten, and waves wash the
  imprints off the sand,
With hinged knees returning I enter the doors, (while for
  you up there,
Whoever you are, follow without noise and be of strong
  heart.)

Bearing the bandages, water and sponge,
Straight and swift to my wounded I go,
Where they lie on the ground after the battle brought in,
Where their priceless blood reddens the grass the ground,
Or to the rows of the hospital tent, or under the roof'd
  hospital,
To the long rows of cots up and down each side I return,
To each and all one after another I draw near, not one do
  I miss,
An attendant follows holding a tray, he carries a refuse
  pail,
Soon to be fill'd with clotted rags and blood, emptied, and
  fill'd again.

I onward go, I stop,
With hinged knees and steady hand to dress wounds,
I am firm with each, the pangs are sharp yet unavoidable,
One turns to me his appealing eyes—poor boy! I never
  knew you,

Yet I think I could not refuse this moment to die for you,
    if that would save you.

3

On, on I go, (open doors of time! open hospital doors!)
The crush'd head I dress, (poor crazed hand tear not the
    bandage away,)
The neck of the cavalry-man with the bullet through and
    through I examine,
Hard the breathing rattles, quite glazed already the eye,
    yet life struggles hard,
(Come sweet death! be persuaded O beautiful death!
In mercy come quickly.)

From the stump of the arm, the amputated hand,
I undo the clotted lint, remove the slough, wash off the
    matter and blood,
Back on his pillow the soldier bends with curv'd neck and
    side-falling head,
His eyes are closed, his face is pale, he dares not look on
    the bloody stump,
And has not yet look'd on it.

I dress a wound in the side, deep, deep,
But a day or two more, for see the frame all wasted and
    sinking,
And the yellow-blue countenance see.

I dress the perforated shoulder, the foot with the bullet-
    wound,

Cleanse the one with a gnawing and putrid gangrene, so
  sickening, so offensive,
While the attendant stands behind aside me holding the
  tray and pail.

I am faithful, I do not give out,
The fractur'd thigh, the knee, the wound in the abdomen,
These and more I dress with impassive hand, (yet deep
  in my breast a fire, a burning flame.)

4

Thus in silence in dreams' projections,
Returning, resuming, I thread my way through the hospi-
  tals,
The hurt and wounded I pacify with soothing hand,
I sit by the restless all the dark night, some are so young,
Some suffer so much, I recall the experience sweet and
  sad,
(Many a soldier's loving arms about this neck have
  cross'd and rested,
Many a soldier's kiss dwells on these bearded lips.)

LONG, TOO LONG AMERICA.

Long, too long America,
Traveling roads all even and peaceful you learn'd from
  joys and prosperity only,
But now, ah now, to learn from crises of anguish, advanc-
  ing, grappling with direst fate and recoiling not,

And now to conceive and show to the world what your
    children en-masse really are,
(For who except myself has yet conceiv'd what your chil-
    dren en-masse really are?)

GIVE ME THE SPLENDID SILENT SUN.

1

Give me the splendid silent sun with all his beams full-
    dazzling,
Give me juicy autumnal fruit ripe and red from the
    orchard,
Give me a field where the unmow'd grass grows,
Give me an arbor, give me the trellis'd grape,
Give me fresh corn and wheat, give me serene-moving
    animals teaching content,
Give me nights perfectly quiet as on high plateaus west of
    the Mississippi, and I looking up at the stars,
Give me odorous at sunrise a garden of beautiful flowers
    where I can walk undisturb'd,
Give me for marriage a sweet-breath'd woman of whom
    I should never tire,
Give me a perfect child, give me away aside from the
    noise of the world a rural domestic life,
Give me to warble spontaneous songs recluse by myself,
    for my own ears only,
Give me solitude, give me Nature, give me again O
    Nature your primal sanities!

These demanding to have them, (tired with ceaseless
    excitement, and rack'd by the war-strife,)
These to procure incessantly asking, rising in cries from
    my heart,
While yet incessantly asking still I adhere to my city,
Day upon day and year upon year O city, walking your
    streets,
Where you hold me enchain'd a certain time refusing to
    give me up,
Yet giving to make me glutted, enrich'd of soul, you give
    me forever faces;
(O I see what I sought to escape, confronting, reversing
    my cries,
I see my own soul trampling down what it ask'd for.)

2

Keep your splendid silent sun,
Keep your woods O Nature, and the quiet places by the
    woods,
Keep your fields of clover and timothy, and your corn-
    fields and orchards,
Keep the blossoming buckwheat fields where the Ninth-
    month bees hum;
Give me faces and streets—give me these phantoms inces-
    sant and endless along the trottoirs!
Give me interminable eyes—give me women—give me
    comrades and lovers by the thousand!
Let me see new ones every day—let me hold new ones by
    the hand every day!
Give me such shows—give me the streets of Manhattan!

Give me Broadway, with the soldiers marching—give me
    the sound of the trumpets and drums!
(The soldiers in companies or regiments—some starting
    away, flush'd and reckless,
Some, their time up, returning with thinn'd ranks, young,
    yet very old, worn, marching, noticing nothing;)
Give me the shores and wharves heavy-fringed with
    black ships!
O such for me! O an intense life, full to repletion and var-
    ied!
The life of the theatre, bar-room, huge hotel, for me!
The saloon of the steamer! the crowded excursion for me!
    the torchlight procession!
The dense brigade bound for the war, with high piled mil-
    itary wagons following;
People, endless, streaming, with strong voices, passions,
    pageants,
Manhattan streets with their powerful throbs, with beat-
    ing drums as now,
The endless and noisy chorus, the rustle and clank of
    muskets, (even the sight of the wounded,)
Manhattan crowds, with their turbulent musical chorus,
Manhattan faces and eyes forever for me.

DIRGE FOR TWO VETERANS.

        The last sunbeam
Lightly falls from the finish'd Sabbath,
On the pavement here, and there beyond it is looking,
        Down a new-made double grave.

Lo, the moon ascending,
Up from the east the silvery round moon,
Beautiful over the house-tops, ghastly, phantom moon,
    Immense and silent moon.

I see a sad procession,
And I hear the sound of coming full-key'd bugles,
All the channels of the city streets they're flooding,
    As with voices and with tears.

I hear the great drums pounding,
And the small drums steady whirring,
And every blow of the great convulsive drums,
    Strikes me through and through.

For the son is brought with the father,
(In the foremost ranks of the fierce assault they fell,
Two veterans son and father dropt together,
    And the double grave awaits them.)

Now nearer blow the bugles,
And the drums strike more convulsive,
And the daylight o'er the pavement quite has faded,
    And the strong dead-march enwraps me.

In the eastern sky up-buoying,
The sorrowful vast phantom moves illumin'd,
('Tis some mother's large transparent face,
    In heaven brighter growing.)

O strong dead-march you please me!
O moon immense with your silvery face you soothe me!
O my soldiers twain! O my veterans passing to burial!
    What I have I also give you.

    The moon gives you light,
And the bugles and the drums give you music,
And my heart, O my soldiers, my veterans,
    My heart gives you love.

OVER THE CARNAGE ROSE PROPHETIC A VOICE.

Over the carnage rose prophetic a voice,
Be not dishearten'd, affection shall solve the problems of
    freedom yet,
Those who love each other shall become invincible,
They shall yet make Columbia victorious.

Sons of the Mother of All, you shall yet be victorious,
You shall yet laugh to scorn the attacks of all the remain-
    der of the earth.

No danger shall balk Columbia's lovers,
If need be a thousand shall sternly immolate themselves
    for one.

One from Massachusetts shall be a Missourian's comrade,
From Maine and from hot Carolina, and another an Ore-
    gonese, shall be friends triune,
More precious to each other than all the riches of the
    earth.

To Michigan, Florida perfumes shall tenderly come,
Not the perfumes of flowers, but sweeter, and wafted
    beyond death.

It shall be customary in the houses and streets to see
    manly affection,
The most dauntless and rude shall touch face to face
    lightly,
The dependence of Liberty shall be lovers,
The continuance of Equality shall be comrades.

These shall tie you and band you stronger than hoops of
    iron,
I, ecstatic, O partners! O lands! with the love of lovers tie
    you.

(Were you looking to be held together by lawyers?
Or by an agreement on a paper? or by arms?
Nay, nor the world, nor any living thing, will so cohere.)

I SAW OLD GENERAL AT BAY.

I saw old General at bay,
(Old as he was, his gray eyes yet shone out in battle like
    stars,)
His small force was now completely hemm'd in, in his
    works,
He call'd for volunteers to run the enemy's lines, a des-
    perate emergency,
I saw a hundred and more step forth from the ranks, but
    two or three were selected,

I saw them receive their orders aside, they listen'd with
    care, the adjutant was very grave,
I saw them depart with cheerfulness, freely risking their
    lives.

THE ARTILLERYMAN'S VISION.

While my wife at my side lies slumbering, and the wars
    are over long,
And my head on the pillow rests at home, and the vacant
    midnight passes,
And through the stillness, through the dark, I hear, just
    hear, the breath of my infant,
There in the room as I wake from sleep this vision presses
    upon me;
The engagement opens there and then in fantasy unreal,
The skirmishers begin, they crawl cautiously ahead, I hear
    the irregular snap! snap!
I hear the sounds of the different missiles, the short *t-h-t!*
    t-h-t! of the rifle balls,
I see the shells exploding leaving small white clouds, I
    hear the great shells shrieking as they pass,
The grape like the hum and whirr of wind through the
    trees, (tumultuous now the contest rages,)
All the scenes at the batteries rise in detail before me
    again,
The crashing and smoking, the pride of the men in their
    pieces,
The chief-gunner ranges and sights his piece and selects
    a fuse of the right time,

After firing I see him lean aside and look eagerly off to
 note the effect;

Elsewhere I hear the cry of a regiment charging, (the
 young colonel leads himself this time with brandish'd
 sword,)

I see the gaps cut by the enemy's volleys, (quickly fill'd
 up, no delay,)

I breathe the suffocating smoke, then the flat clouds hover
 low concealing all;

Now a strange lull for a few seconds, not a shot fired on
 either side,

Then resumed the chaos louder than ever, with eager calls
 and orders of officers,

While from some distant part of the field the wind wafts
 to my ears a shout of applause, (some special suc-
 cess,)

And ever the sound of the cannon far or near, (rousing
 even in dreams a devilish exultation and all the old
 mad joy in the depths of my soul,)

And ever the hastening of infantry shifting positions, bat-
 teries, cavalry, moving hither and thither,

(The falling, dying, I heed not, the wounded dripping and
 red I heed not, some to the rear are hobbling,)

Grime, heat, rush, aide-de-camps galloping by or on a full
 run,

With the patter of small arms, the warning s-s-t of the
 rifles, (these in my vision I hear or see,)

And bombs bursting in air, and at night the vari-color'd
 rockets.

ETHIOPIA SALUTING THE COLORS.

Who are you dusky woman, so ancient hardly human,
With your woolly-white and turban'd head, and bare
bony feet?
Why rising by the roadside here, do you the colors greet?

('Tis while our army lines Carolina's sands and pines,
Forth from thy hovel door thou Ethiopia com'st to me,
As under doughty Sherman I march toward the sea.)

Me master years a hundred since from my parents sunder'd,
A little child, they caught me as the savage beast is caught,
Then hither me across the sea the cruel slaver brought.

No further does she say, but lingering all the day,
Her high-borne turban'd head she wags, and rolls her
darkling eye,
And courtesies to the regiments, the guidons moving by.

What is it fateful woman, so blear, hardly human?
Why wag your head with turban bound, yellow, red and
green?
Are the things so strange and marvelous you see or have
seen?

NOT YOUTH PERTAINS TO ME.

Not youth pertains to me,
Nor delicatesse, I cannot beguile the time with talk,
Awkward in the parlor, neither a dancer nor elegant,

In the learn'd coterie sitting constrain'd and still, for
    learning inures not to me,
Beauty, knowledge, inure not to me— yet there are two or
    three things inure to me,
I have nourish'd the wounded and sooth'd many a dying
    soldier,
And at intervals waiting or in the midst of camp,
Composed these songs.

RACE OF VETERANS.

Race of veterans—race of victors!
Race of the soil, ready for conflict—race of the conquering
    march!
(No more credulity's race, abiding-temper'd race,)
Race henceforth owning no law but the law of itself,
Race of passion and the storm.

WORLD TAKE GOOD NOTICE.

World take good notice, silver stars fading,
Milky hue ript, weft of white detaching,
Coals thirty-eight, baleful and burning,
Scarlet, significant, hands off warning,
Now and henceforth flaunt from these shores.

O TAN-FACED PRAIRIE-BOY.

O tan-faced prairie-boy,
Before you came to camp came many a welcome gift,
Praises and presents came and nourishing food, till at last
    among the recruits,
You came, taciturn, with nothing to give—we but look'd
    on each other,
When lo! more than all the gifts of the world you gave me.

LOOK DOWN FAIR MOON.

Look down fair moon and bathe this scene,
Pour softly down night's nimbus floods on faces ghastly,
    swollen, purple,
On the dead on their backs with arms toss'd wide,
Pour down your unstinted nimbus sacred moon.

RECONCILIATION.

Word over all, beautiful as the sky,
Beautiful that war and all its deeds of carnage must in
    time be utterly lost,
That the hands of the sisters Death and Night incessantly
    softly wash again, and ever again, this soil'd world;
For my enemy is dead, a man divine as myself is dead,
I look where he lies white-faced and still in the coffin—I
    draw near,
Bend down and touch lightly with my lips the white face
    in the coffin.

HOW SOLEMN AS ONE BY ONE.

(*Washington City, 1865.*)

How solemn as one by one,
As the ranks returning worn and sweaty, as the men file
    by where I stand,
As the faces the masks appear, as I glance at the faces
    studying the masks,
(As I glance upward out of this page studying you, dear
    friend, whoever you are,)
How solemn the thought of my whispering soul to each in
    the ranks, and to you,
I see behind each mask that wonder a kindred soul,
O the bullet could never kill what you really are, dear
    friend,
Nor the bayonet stab what you really are;
The soul! yourself I see, great as any, good as the best,
Waiting secure and content, which the bullet could never
    kill,
Nor the bayonet stab O friend.

AS I LAY WITH MY HEAD IN YOUR LAP CAMERADO.

As I lay with my head in your lap camerado,
The confession I made I resume, what I said to you and
    the open air I resume,
I know I am restless and make others so,
I know my words are weapons full of danger, full of
    death,
For I confront peace, security, and all the settled laws, to
    unsettle them,

I am more resolute because all have denied me than I
    could ever have been had all accepted me,
I heed not and have never heeded either experience, cau-
    tions, majorities, nor ridicule,
And the threat of what is call'd hell is little or nothing to
    me,
And the lure of what is call'd heaven is little or nothing
    to me;
Dear camerado! I confess I have urged you onward with
    me, and still urge you, without the least idea what is
    our destination,
Or whether we shall be victorious, or utterly quell'd and
    defeated.

DELICATE CLUSTER.

Delicate cluster! flag of teeming life!
Covering all my lands—all my seashores lining!
Flag of death! (how I watch'd you through the smoke of
    battle pressing!
How I heard you flap and rustle, cloth defiant!)
Flag cerulean—sunny flag, with the orbs of night dap-
    pled!
Ah my silvery beauty—ah my wooly white and crimson!
Ah to sing the song of you, my matron mighty!
My sacred one, my mother.

TO A CERTAIN CIVILIAN.

Did you ask dulcet rhymes from me?
Did you seek the civilian's peaceful and languishing
    rhymes?
Did you find what I sang erewhile so hard to follow?
Why I was not singing erewhile for you to follow, to
    understand—nor am I now;
(I have been born of the same as the war was born,
The drum-corps' rattle is ever to me sweet music, I love
    well the martial dirge,
With slow wail and convulsive throb leading the officer's
    funeral;)
What to such as you anyhow such a poet as I? therefore
    leave my works,
And go lull yourself with what you can understand, and
    with piano-tunes,
For I lull nobody, and you will never understand me.

LO, VICTRESS ON THE PEAKS.

Lo, Victress on the peaks,
Where thou with mighty brow regarding the world,
(The world O Libertad, that vainly conspired against
    thee,)
Out of its countless beleaguering toils, after thwarting
    them all,
Dominant, with the dazzling sun around thee,
Flauntest now unharm'd in immortal soundness and
    bloom— lo, in these hours supreme,

No poem proud, I chanting bring to thee, nor mastery's
      rapturous verse,
But a cluster containing night's darkness and blood-drip-
      ping wounds,
And psalms of the dead.

SPIRIT WHOSE WORK IS DONE.
(Washington City, 1865.)

Spirit whose work is done—spirit of dreadful hours!
Ere departing fade from my eyes your forests of bayonets;
Spirit of gloomiest fears and doubts, (yet onward ever
      unfaltering pressing,)
Spirit of many a solemn day and many a savage scene—
      electric spirit,
That with muttering voice through the war now closed,
      like a tireless phantom flitted,
Rousing the land with breath of flame, while you beat and
      beat the drum,
Now as the sound of the drum, hollow and harsh to the
      last, reverberates round me,
As your ranks, your immortal ranks, return, return from
      the battles,
As the muskets of the young men yet lean over their
      shoulders,
As I look on the bayonets bristling over their shoulders,
As those slanted bayonets, whole forests of them appear-
      ing in the distance, approach and pass on, returning
      homeward,
Moving with steady motion, swaying to and fro to the
      right and left,

Evenly lightly rising and falling while the steps keep time;
Spirit of hours I knew, all hectic red one day, but pale as
    death next day,
Touch my mouth ere you depart, press my lips close,
Leave me your pulses of rage—bequeath them to me—fill
    me with currents convulsive,
Let them scorch and blister out of my chants when you
    are gone,
Let them identify you to the future in these songs.

ADIEU TO A SOLDIER.

Adieu O soldier,
You of the rude campaigning, (which we shared,)
The rapid march, the life of the camp,
The hot contention of opposing fronts, the long manœu-
    vre,
Red battles with their slaughter, the stimulus, the strong
    terrific game,
Spell of all brave and manly hearts, the trains of time
    through you and like of you all fill'd,
With war and war's expression.

Adieu dear comrade,
Your mission is fulfill'd—but I, more warlike,
Myself and this contentious soul of mine,
Still on our own campaigning bound,
Through untried roads with ambushes opponents lined,
Through many a sharp defeat and many a crisis, often
    baffled,

Here marching, ever marching on, a war fight out—aye
    here,
To fiercer, weightier battles give expression.

TURN O LIBERTAD.

Turn O Libertad, for the war is over,
From it and all henceforth expanding, doubting no more,
    resolute, sweeping the world,
Turn from lands retrospective recording proofs of the
    past,
From the singers that sing the trailing glories of the past,
From the chants of the feudal world, the triumphs of
    kings, slavery, caste,
Turn to the world, the triumphs reserv'd and to come—
    give up that backward world,
Leave to the singers of hitherto, give them the trailing
    past,
But what remains remains for singers for you—wars to
    come are for you,
(Lo, how the wars of the past have duly inured to you,
    and the wars of the present also inure;)
Then turn, and be not alarm'd O Libertad—turn your
    undying face,
To where the future, greater than all the past,
Is swiftly, surely preparing for you.

TO THE LEAVEN'D SOIL THEY TROD.

To the leaven'd soil they trod calling I sing for the last,
(Forth from my tent emerging for good, loosing, untying
the tent-ropes,)
In the freshness the forenoon air, in the far-stretching cir-
cuits and vistas again to peace restored,
To the fiery fields emanative and the endless vistas
beyond, to the South and the North,
To the leaven'd soil of the general Western world to attest
my songs,
To the Alleghanian hills and the tireless Mississippi,
To the rocks I calling sing, and all the trees in the woods,
To the plains of the poems of heroes, to the prairies
spreading wide,
To the far-off sea and the unseen winds, and the sane
impalpable air;
And responding they answer all, (but not in words,)
The average earth, the witness of war and peace,
acknowledges mutely,
The prairie draws me close, as the father to bosom broad
the son,
The Northern ice and rain that began me nourish me to
the end,
But the hot sun of the South is to fully ripen my songs.

*

MEMORIES OF PRESIDENT LINCOLN.

WHEN LILACS LAST IN THE DOORYARD BLOOM'D.

1

When lilacs last in the dooryard bloom'd,
And the great star early droop'd in the western sky in the
 night,
I mourn'd, and yet shall mourn with ever-returning
 spring.

Ever-returning spring, trinity sure to me you bring,
Lilac blooming perennial and drooping star in the west,
And thought of him I love.

2

O powerful western fallen star!
O shades of night—O moody, tearful night!
O great star disappear'd—O the black murk that hides the
 star!

O cruel hands that hold me powerless—O helpless soul of
    me!
O harsh surrounding cloud that will not free my soul.

3

In the dooryard fronting an old farm-house near the
    white-wash'd palings,
Stands the lilac-bush tall-growing with heart-shaped
    leaves of rich green,
With many a pointed blossom rising delicate, with the
    perfume strong I love,
With every leaf a miracle—and from this bush in the
    dooryard,
With delicate-color'd blossoms and heart-shaped leaves
    of rich green,
A sprig with its flower I break.

4

In the swamp in secluded recesses,
A shy and hidden bird is warbling a song.

Solitary the thrush,
The hermit withdrawn to himself, avoiding the settle-
    ments,
Sings by himself a song.

Song of the bleeding throat,
Death's outlet song of life, (for well dear brother I know,
If thou wast not granted to sing thou would'st surely die.)

5

Over the breast of the spring, the land, amid cities,
Amid lanes and through old woods, where lately the vio-
    lets peep'd from the ground, spotting the gray debris,
Amid the grass in the fields each side of the lanes, passing
    the endless grass,
Passing the yellow-spear'd wheat, every grain from its
    shroud in the dark-brown fields uprisen,
Passing the apple-tree blows of white and pink in the
    orchards,
Carrying a corpse to where it shall rest in the grave,
Night and day journeys a coffin.

6

Coffin that passes through lanes and streets,
Through day and night with the great cloud darkening
    the land,
With the pomp of the inloop'd flags with the cities draped
    in black,
With the show of the States themselves as of crape-veil'd
    women standing,
With processions long and winding and the flambeaus of
    the night,
With the countless torches lit, with the silent sea of faces
    and the unbared heads,
With the waiting depot, the arriving coffin, and the som-
    bre faces,
With dirges through the night, with the thousand voices
    rising strong and solemn,

With all the mournful voices of the dirges pour'd around
    the coffin,
The dim-lit churches and the shuddering organs—where
    amid these you journey,
With the tolling tolling bells' perpetual clang,
Here, coffin that slowly passes,
I give you my sprig of lilac.

7

(Nor for you, for one alone,
Blossoms and branches green to coffins all I bring,
For fresh as the morning, thus would I chant a song for
    you O sane and sacred death.

All over bouquets of roses,
O death, I cover you over with roses and early lilies,
But mostly and now the lilac that blooms the first,
Copious I break, I break the sprigs from the bushes,
With loaded arms I come, pouring for you,
For you and the coffins all of you O death.)

8

O western orb sailing the heaven,
Now I know what you must have meant as a month since
    I walk'd,
As I walk'd in silence the transparent shadowy night,
As I saw you had something to tell as you bent to me
    night after night,

As you droop'd from the sky low down as if to my side,
  (while the other stars all look'd on,)
As we wander'd together the solemn night, (for some-
  thing I know not what kept me from sleep,)
As the night advanced, and I saw on the rim of the west
  how full you were of woe,
As I stood on the rising ground in the breeze in the cool
  transparent night,
As I watch'd where you pass'd and was lost in the nether-
  ward black of the night,
As my soul in its trouble dissatisfied sank, as where you
  sad orb,
Concluded, dropt in the night, and was gone.

9

Sing on there in the swamp,
O singer bashful and tender, I hear your notes, I hear your
  call,
I hear, I come presently, I understand you,
But a moment I linger, for the lustrous star has detain'd
  me,
The star my departing comrade holds and detains me.

10

O how shall I warble myself for the dead one there I
  loved?
And how shall I deck my song for the large sweet soul
  that has gone?

And what shall my perfume be for the grave of him I
    love?

Sea-winds blown from east and west,
Blown from the Eastern sea and blown from the Western
    sea, till there on the prairies meeting,
These and with these and the breath of my chant,
I'll perfume the grave of him I love.

11

O what shall I hang on the chamber walls?
And what shall the pictures be that I hang on the walls,
To adorn the burial-house of him I love?

Pictures of growing spring and farms and homes,
With the Fourth-month eve at sundown, and the gray
    smoke lucid and bright,
With floods of the yellow gold of the gorgeous, indolent,
    sinking sun, burning, expanding the air,
With the fresh sweet herbage under foot, and the pale
    green leaves of the trees prolific,
In the distance the flowing glaze, the breast of the river,
    with a wind-dapple here and there,
With ranging hills on the banks, with many a line against
    the sky, and shadows,
And the city at hand with dwellings so dense, and stacks
    of chimneys,
And all the scenes of life and the workshops, and the
    workmen homeward returning.

12

Lo, body and soul—this land,
My own Manhattan with spires, and the sparkling and
    hurrying tides, and the ships,
The varied and ample land, the South and the North in
    the light, Ohio's shores and flashing Missouri,
And ever the far-spreading prairies cover'd with grass
    and corn.

Lo, the most excellent sun so calm and haughty,
The violet and purple morn with just-felt breezes,
The gentle soft-born measureless light,
The miracle spreading bathing all, the fulfill'd noon,
The coming eve delicious, the welcome night and the
    stars,
Over my cities shining all, enveloping man and land.

13

Sing on, sing on you gray-brown bird,
Sing from the swamps, the recesses, pour your chant from
    the bushes,
Limitless out of the dusk, out of the cedars and pines.

Sing on dearest brother, warble your reedy song,
Loud human song, with voice of uttermost woe.

O liquid and free and tender!
O wild and loose to my soul—O wondrous singer!

You only I hear—yet the star holds me, (but will soon
    depart,)
Yet the lilac with mastering odor holds me.

14

Now while I sat in the day and look'd forth,
In the close of the day with its light and the fields of
    spring, and the farmers preparing their crops,
In the large unconscious scenery of my land with its lakes
    and forests,
In the heavenly aerial beauty, (after the perturb'd winds
    and the storms,)
Under the arching heavens of the afternoon swift passing,
    and the voices of children and women,
The many-moving sea-tides, and I saw the ships how they
    sail'd,
And the summer approaching with richness, and the
    fields all busy with labor,
And the infinite separate houses, how they all went on,
    each with its meals and minutia of daily usages,
And the streets how their throbbings throbb'd, and the
    cities pent—lo, then and there,
Falling upon them all and among them all, enveloping me
    with the rest,
Appear'd the cloud, appear'd the long black trail,
And I knew death, its thought, and the sacred knowledge
    of death.

Then with the knowledge of death as walking one side of
    me,

And the thought of death close-walking the other side of
    me,
And I in the middle as with companions, and as holding
    the hands of companions,
I fled forth to the hiding receiving night that talks not,
Down to the shores of the water, the path by the swamp
    in the dimness,
To the solemn shadowy cedars and ghostly pines so still.

And the singer so shy to the rest receiv'd me,
The gray-brown bird I know receiv'd us comrades three,
And he sang the carol of death, and a verse for him I love.

From deep secluded recesses,
From the fragrant cedars and the ghostly pines so still,
Came the carol of the bird.

And the charm of the carol rapt me,
As I held as if by their hands my comrades in the night,
And the voice of my spirit tallied the song of the bird.

Come lovely and soothing death,
Undulate round the world, serenely arriving, arriving,
In the day, in the night, to all, to each,
Sooner or later delicate death.

Prais'd be the fathomless universe,
For life and joy, and for objects and knowledge curious,
And for love, sweet love—but praise! praise! praise!
For the sure-enwinding arms of cool-enfolding death.

Dark mother always gliding near with soft feet,
Have none chanted for thee a chant of fullest welcome?
Then I chant it for thee, I glorify thee above all,
I bring thee a song that when thou must indeed come, come
  unfalteringly.

Approach strong deliveress,
When it is so, when thou hast taken them I joyously sing the
  dead,
Lost in the loving floating ocean of thee,
Laved in the flood of thy bliss O death.

From me to thee glad serenades,
Dances for thee I propose saluting thee, adornments and feast-
  ings for thee,
And the sights of the open landscape and the high-spread sky
  are fitting,
And life and the fields, and the huge and thoughtful night.

The night in silence under many a star,
The ocean shore and the husky whispering wave whose voice I
  know,
And the soul turning to thee O vast and well-veil'd death,
And the body gratefully nestling close to thee.

Over the tree-tops I float thee a song,
Over the rising and sinking waves, over the myriad fields and
  the prairies wide,
Over the dense-pack'd cities all and the teeming wharves and
  ways,
I float this carol with joy, with joy to thee O death.

15

To the tally of my soul,
Loud and strong kept up the gray-brown bird,
With pure deliberate notes spreading filling the night.

Loud in the pines and cedars dim,
Clear in the freshness moist and the swamp-perfume,
And I with my comrades there in the night.

While my sight that was bound in my eyes unclosed,
As to long panoramas of visions.

And I saw askant the armies,
I saw as in noiseless dreams hundreds of battle-flags,
Borne through the smoke of the battles and pierc'd with
    missiles I saw them,
And carried hither and yon through the smoke, and torn
    and bloody,
And at last but a few shreds left on the staffs, (and all in
    silence,)
And the staffs all splinter'd and broken.

I saw battle-corpses, myriads of them,
And the white skeletons of young men, I saw them,
I saw the debris and debris of all the slain soldiers of the
    war,
But I saw they were not as was thought,
They themselves were fully at rest, they suffer'd not,
The living remain'd and suffer'd, the mother suffer'd,

And the wife and the child and the musing comrade suf-
fer'd,
And the armies that remain'd suffer'd.

16

Passing the visions, passing the night,
Passing, unloosing the hold of my comrades' hands,
Passing the song of the hermit bird and the tallying song
of my soul,
Victorious song, death's outlet song, yet varying ever-
altering song,
As low and wailing, yet clear the notes, rising and falling,
flooding the night,
Sadly sinking and fainting, as warning and warning, and
yet again bursting with joy,
Covering the earth and filling the spread of the heaven,
As that powerful psalm in the night I heard from recesses,
Passing, I leave thee lilac with heart-shaped leaves,
I leave thee there in the door-yard, blooming, returning
with spring.

I cease from my song for thee,
From my gaze on thee in the west, fronting the west,
communing with thee,
O comrade lustrous with silver face in the night.

Yet each to keep and all, retrievements out of the night,
The song, the wondrous chant of the gray-brown bird,
And the tallying chant, the echo arous'd in my soul,
With the lustrous and drooping star with the countenance
full of woe,

With the holders holding my hand nearing the call of the
    bird,
Comrades mine and I in the midst, and their memory ever
    to keep, for the dead I loved so well,
For the sweetest, wisest soul of all my days and lands—
    and this for his dear sake,
Lilac and star and bird twined with the chant of my soul,
There in the fragrant pines and the cedars dusk and dim.

O CAPTAIN! MY CAPTAIN!

O Captain! my Captain! our fearful trip is done,
The ship has weather'd every rack, the prize we sought
    is won,
The port is near, the bells I hear, the people all exulting,
While follow eyes the steady keel, the vessel grim and
    daring;
            But O heart! heart! heart!
                O the bleeding drops of red,
                    Where on the deck my Captain lies,
                    Fallen cold and dead.

O Captain! my Captain! rise up and hear the bells;
Rise up—for you the flag is flung—for you the bugle trills,
For you bouquets and ribbon'd wreaths—for you the
    shores a-crowding,

For you they call, the swaying mass, their eager faces
    turning;
            Here Captain! dear father!
            This arm beneath your head!
                It is some dream that on the deck,
                    You've fallen cold and dead.

My Captain does not answer, his lips are pale and still,
My father does not feel my arm, he has no pulse nor will,
The ship is anchor'd safe and sound, its voyage closed
    and done,
From fearful trip the victor ship comes in with object won;
            Exult O shores, and ring O bells!
                But I with mournful tread,
                Walk the deck my Captain lies,
                    Fallen cold and dead.

HUSH'D BE THE CAMPS TO-DAY.
(May 4, 1865.)

Hush'd be the camps to-day,
And soldiers let us drape our war-worn weapons,
And each with musing soul retire to celebrate,
Our dear commander's death.

No more for him life's stormy conflicts,
Nor victory, nor defeat—no more time's dark events,
Charging like ceaseless clouds across the sky.

But sing poet in our name,
Sing of the love we bore him—because you, dweller in
  camps, know it truly.

As they invault the coffin there,
Sing—as they close the doors of earth upon him—one
  verse,
For the heavy hearts of soldiers.

THIS DUST WAS ONCE THE MAN.

This dust was once the man,
Gentle, plain, just and resolute, under whose cautious
  hand,
Against the foulest crime in history known in any land or
  age,
Was saved the Union of these States.

*

BY BLUE ONTARIO'S SHORE.

1

By blue Ontario's shore,
As I mused of these warlike days and of peace return'd,
  and the dead that return no more,
A Phantom gigantic superb, with stern visage accosted
  me,

Chant me the poem, it said, *that comes from the soul of Amer-
     ica, chant me the carol of victory,*
*And strike up the marches of Libertad, marches more powerful
     yet,*
And sing me before you go the song of the throes of Democracy.

(Democracy, the destin'd conqueror, yet treacherous lip-
     smiles everywhere,
And death and infidelity at every step.)

2

A Nation announcing itself,
I myself make the only growth by which I can be appre-
     ciated,
I reject none, accept all, then reproduce all in my own
     forms.

A breed whose proof is in time and deeds,
What we are we are, nativity is answer enough to objec-
     tions,
We wield ourselves as a weapon is wielded,
We are powerful and tremendous in ourselves,
We are executive in ourselves, we are sufficient in the
     variety of ourselves,
We are the most beautiful to ourselves and in ourselves,
We stand self-pois'd in the middle, branching thence over
     the world,
From Missouri, Nebraska, or Kansas, laughing attacks to
     scorn.

Nothing is sinful to us outside of ourselves,
Whatever appears, whatever does not appear, we are
    beautiful or sinful in ourselves only.

(O Mother—O Sisters dear!
If we are lost, no victor else has destroy'd us,
It is by ourselves we go down to eternal night.)

3

Have you thought there could be but a single supreme?
There can be any number of supremes—one does not
    countervail another any more than one eyesight
    countervails another, or one life countervails another.

All is eligible to all,
All is for individuals, all is for you,
No condition is prohibited, not God's or any.

All comes by the body, only health puts you rapport with
    the universe.

Produce great Persons, the rest follows.

4

Piety and conformity to them that like,
Peace, obesity, allegiance, to them that like,
I am he who tauntingly compels men, women, nations,
Crying, Leap from your seats and contend for your lives!

I am he who walks the States with a barb'd tongue, ques-
tioning every one I meet,
Who are you that wanted only to be told what you knew
before?
Who are you that wanted only a book to join you in your
nonsense?

(With pangs and cries as thine own O bearer of many chil-
dren,
These clamors wild to a race of pride I give.)

O lands, would you be freer than all that has ever been
before?
If you would be freer than all that has been before, come
listen to me.

Fear grace, elegance, civilization, delicatesse,
Fear the mellow sweet, the sucking of honey-juice,
Beware the advancing mortal ripening of Nature,
Beware what precedes the decay of the ruggedness of
states and men.

5

Ages, precedents, have long been accumulating undi-
rected materials,
America brings builders, and brings its own styles.

The immortal poets of Asia and Europe have done their
work and pass'd to other spheres,
A work remains, the work of surpassing all they have
done.

America, curious toward foreign characters, stands by its
    own at all hazards,
Stands removed, spacious, composite, sound, initiates the
    true use of precedents,
Does not repel them or the past or what they have pro-
    duced under their forms,
Takes the lesson with calmness, perceives the corpse
    slowly borne from the house,
Perceives that it waits a little while in the door, that it was
    fittest for its days,
That its life has descended to the stalwart and well-
    shaped heir who approaches,
And that he shall be fittest for his days.

Any period one nation must lead,
One land must be the promise and reliance of the future.

These States are the amplest poem,
Here is not merely a nation but a teeming Nation of
    nations,
Here the doings of men correspond with the broadcast
    doings of the day and night,
Here is what moves in magnificent masses careless of par-
    ticulars,
Here are the roughs, beards, friendliness, combativeness,
    the soul loves,
Here the flowing trains, here the crowds, equality, diver-
    sity, the soul loves.

6

Land of lands and bards to corroborate!
Of them standing among them, one lifts to the light a
    west-bred face,
To him the hereditary countenance bequeath'd both
    mother's and father's,
His first parts substances, earth, water, animals, trees,
Built of the common stock, having room for far and near,
Used to dispense with other lands, incarnating this land,
Attracting it body and soul to himself, hanging on its neck
    with incomparable love,
Plunging his seminal muscle into its merits and demer-
    its,
Making its cities, beginnings, events, diversities, wars,
    vocal in him,
Making its rivers, lakes, bays, embouchure in him,
Mississippi with yearly freshets and changing chutes,
    Columbia, Niagara, Hudson, spending themselves
    lovingly in him,
If the Atlantic coast stretch or the Pacific coast stretch, he
    stretching with them North or South,
Spanning between them East and West, and touching
    whatever is between them,
Growths growing from him to offset the growths of pine,
    cedar, hemlock, live oak, locust, chestnut, hickory,
    cottonwood, orange, magnolia,
Tangles as tangled in him as any canebrake or swamp,
He likening sides and peaks of mountains, forests coated
    with northern transparent ice,
Off him pasturage sweet and natural as savanna, upland,
    prairie,

Through him flights, whirls, screams, answering those of
    the fish-hawk, mocking-bird, night-heron, and eagle,
His spirit surrounding his country's spirit, unclosed to
    good and evil,
Surrounding the essences of real things, old times and
    present times,
Surrounding just found shores, islands, tribes of red ab-
    origines,
Weather-beaten vessels, landings, settlements, embryo
    stature and muscle,
The haughty defiance of the Year One, war, peace, the for-
    mation of the Constitution,
The separate States, the simple elastic scheme, the immi-
    grants,
The Union always swarming with blatherers and always
    sure and impregnable,
The unsurvey'd interior, log-houses, clearings, wild ani-
    mals, hunters, trappers,
Surrounding the multiform agriculture, mines, tempera-
    ture, the gestation of new States,
Congress convening every Twelfth-month, the members
    duly coming up from the uttermost parts,
Surrounding the noble character of mechanics and farm-
    ers, especially the young men,
Responding their manners, speech, dress, friendships, the
    gait they have of persons who never knew how it felt
    to stand in the presence of superiors,
The freshness and candor of their physiognomy, the copi-
    ousness and decision of their phrenology,
The picturesque looseness of their carriage, their fierce-
    ness when wrong'd,

The fluency of their speech, their delight in music, their
curiosity, good temper and open-handedness, the
whole composite make,
The prevailing ardor and enterprise, the large amative-
ness,
The perfect equality of the female with the male, the fluid
movement of the population,
The superior marine, free commerce, fisheries, whaling,
gold-digging,
Wharf-hemm'd cities, railroad and steamboat lines inter-
secting all points,
Factories, mercantile life, labor-saving machinery, the
Northeast, Northwest, Southwest,
Manhattan firemen, the Yankee swap, southern planta-
tion life,
Slavery—the murderous, treacherous conspiracy to raise
it upon the ruins of all the rest,
On and on to the grapple with it—Assassin! then your life
or ours be the stake, and respite no more.

7

(Lo, high toward heaven, this day,
Libertad, from the conqueress' field return'd,
I mark the new aureola around your head,
No more of soft astral, but dazzling and fierce,
With war's flames and the lambent lightnings playing,
And your port immovable where you stand,
With still the inextinguishable glance and the clinch'd and
lifted fist,
And your foot on the neck of the menacing one, the
scorner utterly crush'd beneath you,

The menacing arrogant one that strode and advanced
    with his senseless scorn, bearing the murderous knife,
The wide-swelling one, the braggart that would yesterday
    do so much,
To-day a carrion dead and damn'd, the despised of all the
    earth,
An offal rank, to the dunghill maggots spurn'd.)

8

Others take finish, but the Republic is ever constructive
    and ever keeps vista,
Others adorn the past, but you O days of the present, I
    adorn you,
O days of the future I believe in you—I isolate myself for
    your sake,
O America because you build for mankind I build for you,
O well-beloved stone-cutters, I lead them who plan with
    decision and science,
Lead the present with friendly hand toward the future.

(Bravas to all impulses sending sane children to the next
    age!
But damn that which spends itself with no thought of the
    stain, pains, dismay, feebleness, it is bequeathing.)

9

I listened to the Phantom by Ontario's shore,
I heard the voice arising demanding bards,

By them all native and grand, by them alone can these
States be fused into the compact organism of a
Nation.

To hold men together by paper and seal or by compulsion
is no account,
That only holds men together which aggregates all in a
living principle, as the hold of the limbs of the body
or the fibres of plants.

Of all races and eras these States with veins full of poeti-
cal stuff most need poets, and are to have the greatest,
and use them the greatest,
Their Presidents shall not be their common referee so
much as their poets shall.

(Soul of love and tongue of fire!
Eye to pierce the deepest deeps and sweep the world!
Ah Mother, prolific and full in all besides, yet how long
barren, barren?)

10

Of these States the poet is the equable man,
Not in him but off from him things are grotesque, eccen-
tric, fail of their full returns,
Nothing out of its place is good, nothing in its place is
bad,
He bestows on every object or quality its fit proportion,
neither more nor less,
He is the arbiter of the diverse, he is the key,
He is the equalizer of his age and land,

He supplies what wants supplying, he checks what wants
    checking,
In peace out of him speaks the spirit of peace, large, rich,
    thrifty, building populous towns, encouraging agri-
    culture, arts, commerce, lighting the study of man,
    the soul, health, immortality, government,
In war he is the best backer of the war, he fetches artillery
    as good as the engineer's, he can make every word he
    speaks draw blood,
The years straying toward infidelity he withholds by his
    steady faith,
He is no arguer, he is judgment, (Nature accepts him
    absolutely,)
He judges not as the judge judges but as the sun falling
    round a helpless thing,
As he sees the farthest he has the most faith,
His thoughts are the hymns of the praise of things,
In the dispute on God and eternity he is silent,
He sees eternity less like a play with a prologue and
    denouement,
He sees eternity in men and women, he does not see men
    and women as dreams or dots.

For the great Idea, the idea of perfect and free individuals,
For that, the bard walks in advance, leader of leaders,
The attitude of him cheers up slaves and horrifies foreign
    despots.

Without extinction is Liberty, without retrograde is
    Equality,

They live in the feelings of young men and the best
   women,
(Not for nothing have the indomitable heads of the earth
   been always ready to fall for Liberty.)

11

For the great Idea,
That, O my brethren, that is the mission of poets.

Songs of stern defiance ever ready,
Songs of the rapid arming and the march,
The flag of peace quick-folded, and instead the flag we
   know,
Warlike flag of the great Idea.

(Angry cloth I saw there leaping!
I stand again in leaden rain your flapping folds saluting,
I sing you over all, flying beckoning through the fight—
   O the hard-contested fight!
The cannons ope their rosy-flashing muzzles—the hur-
   tled balls scream,
The battle-front forms amid the smoke—the volleys pour
   incessant from the line,
Hark, the ringing word *Charge!*—now the tussle and the
   furious maddening yells,
Now the corpses tumble curl'd upon the ground,
Cold, cold in death, for precious life of you,
Angry cloth I saw there leaping.)

12

Are you he who would assume a place to teach or be a
    poet here in the States?
The place is august, the terms obdurate.

Who would assume to teach here may well prepare him-
    self body and mind,
He may well survey, ponder, arm, fortify, harden, make
    lithe himself,
He shall surely be question'd beforehand by me with
    many and stern questions.
Who are you indeed who would talk or sing to America?
Have you studied out the land, its idioms and men?
Have you learn'd the physiology, phrenology, politics,
    geography, pride, freedom, friendship of the land? its
    substratums and objects?
Have you consider'd the organic compact of the first day
    of the first year of Independence, sign'd by the Com-
    missioners, ratified by the States, and read by Wash-
    ington at the head of the army?
Have you possess'd yourself of the Federal Constitution?
Do you see who have left all feudal processes and poems
    behind them, and assumed the poems and processes
    of Democracy?
Are you faithful to things? do you teach what the land
    and sea, the bodies of men, womanhood, amative-
    ness, heroic angers, teach?
Have you sped through fleeting customs, popularities?
Can you hold your hand against all seductions, follies,
    whirls, fierce contentions? are you very strong? are
    you really of the whole People?

Are you not of some coterie? some school or mere reli-
gion?

Are you done with reviews and criticisms of life? animat-
ing now to life itself?

Have you vivified yourself from the maternity of these
States?

Have you too the old ever-fresh forbearance and impar-
tiality?

Do you hold the like love for those hardening to matu-
rity? for the last born? little and big? and for the
errant?

What is this you bring my America?

Is it uniform with my country?

Is it not something that has been better told or done
before?

Have you not imported this or the spirit of it in some
ship?

Is it not a mere tale? a rhyme? a prettiness?—is the good
old cause in it?

Has it not dangled long at the heels of the poets, politi-
cians, literats, of enemies' lands?

Does it not assume that what is notoriously gone is still
here?

Does it answer universal needs? will it improve manners?

Does it sound with trumpet-voice the proud victory of the
Union in that secession war?

Can your performance face the open fields and the sea-
side?

Will it absorb into me as I absorb food, air, to appear
again in my strength, gait, face?

Have real employments contributed to it? original mak-
    ers, not mere amanuenses?
Does it meet modern discoveries, calibres, facts, face to
    face?
What does it mean to American persons, progresses,
    cities? Chicago, Kanada, Arkansas?
Does it see behind the apparent custodians the real cus-
    todians standing, menacing, silent, the mechanics,
    Manhattanese, Western men, Southerners, significant
    alike in their apathy, and in the promptness of their
    love?
Does it see what finally befalls, and has always finally
    befallen, each temporizer, patcher, outsider, partial-
    ist, alarmist, infidel, who has ever ask'd any thing of
    America?
What mocking and scornful negligence?
The track strew'd with the dust of skeletons,
By the roadside others disdainfully toss'd.

                              13

Rhymes and rhymers pass away, poems distill'd from
    poems pass away,
The swarms of reflectors and the polite pass, and leave
    ashes,
Admirers, importers, obedient persons, make but the soil
    of literature,
America justifies itself, give it time, no disguise can
    deceive it or conceal from it, it is impassive enough,
Only toward the likes of itself will it advance to meet
    them,

If its poets appear it will in due time advance to meet
    them, there is no fear of mistake,
(The proof of a poet shall be sternly deferr'd till his coun-
    try absorbs him as affectionately as he has absorb'd
    it.)

He masters whose spirit masters, he tastes sweetest who
    results sweetest in the long run,
The blood of the brawn beloved of time is unconstraint;
In the need of songs, philosophy, an appropriate native
    grand-opera, shipcraft, any craft,
He or she is greatest who contributes the greatest origi-
    nal practical example.

Already a nonchalant breed, silently emerging, appears
    on the streets,
People's lips salute only doers, lovers, satisfiers, positive
    knowers,
There will shortly be no more priests, I say their work is
    done,
Death is without emergencies here, but life is perpetual
    emergencies here,
Are your body, days, manners, superb? after death you
    shall be superb,
Justice, health, self-esteem, clear the way with irresistible
    power;
How dare you place any thing before a man?

14

Fall behind me States!
A man before all—myself, typical, before all.

Give me the pay I have served for,

Give me to sing the songs of the great Idea, take all the
rest,

I have loved the earth, sun, animals, I have despised
riches,

I have given alms to every one that ask'd, stood up for the
stupid and crazy, devoted my income and labor to
others,

Hated tyrants, argued not concerning God, had patience
and indulgence toward the people, taken off my hat
to nothing known or unknown,

Gone freely with powerful uneducated persons and with
the young, and with the mothers of families,

Read these leaves to myself in the open air, tried them by
trees, stars, rivers,

Dismiss'd whatever insulted my own soul or defiled my
body,

Claim'd nothing to myself which I have not carefully
claim'd for others on the same terms,

Sped to the camps, and comrades found and accepted
from every State,

(Upon this breast has many a dying soldier lean'd to
breathe his last,

This arm, this hand, this voice, have nourish'd, rais'd,
restored,

To life recalling many a prostrate form;)

I am willing to wait to be understood by the growth of the
taste of myself,

Rejecting none, permitting all.

(Say O Mother, have I not to your thought been faithful?
Have I not through life kept you and yours before me?)

15

I swear I begin to see the meaning of these things,
It is not the earth, it is not America who is so great,
It is I who am great or to be great, it is You up there, or
    any one,
It is to walk rapidly through civilizations, governments,
    theories,
Through poems, pageants, shows, to form individuals.

Underneath all, individuals,
I swear nothing is good to me now that ignores individu-
    als,
The American compact is altogether with individuals,
The only government is that which makes minute of indi-
    viduals,
The whole theory of the universe is directed unerringly to
    one single individual—namely to You.

(Mother! with subtle sense severe, with the naked sword
    in your hand,
I saw you at last refuse to treat but directly with individ-
    uals.)

16

Underneath all, Nativity,
I swear I will stand by my own nativity, pious or impious
    so be it;
I swear I am charm'd with nothing except nativity,
Men, women, cities, nations, are only beautiful from
    nativity.

Underneath all is the Expression of love for men and
    women,
(I swear I have seen enough of mean and impotent modes
    of expressing love for men and women,
After this day I take my own modes of expressing love for
    men and women.)

I swear I will have each quality of my race in myself,
(Talk as you like, he only suits these States whose man-
    ners favor the audacity and sublime turbulence of the
    States.)

Underneath the lessons of things, spirits, Nature, govern-
    ments, ownerships, I swear I perceive other lessons,
Underneath all to me is myself, to you yourself, (the same
    monotonous old song.)

17

O I see flashing that this America is only you and me,
Its power, weapons, testimony, are you and me,
Its crimes, lies, thefts, defections, are you and me,
Its Congress is you and me, the officers, capitols, armies,
    ships, are you and me,
Its endless gestations of new States are you and me,
The war, (that war so bloody and grim, the war I will
    henceforth forget), was you and me,
Natural and artificial are you and me,
Freedom, language, poems, employments, are you and
    me,
Past, present, future, are you and me.

I dare not shirk any part of myself,
Not any part of America good or bad,
Not to build for that which builds for mankind,
Not to balance ranks, complexions, creeds, and the sexes,
Not to justify science nor the march of equality,
Nor to feed the arrogant blood of the brawn belov'd of
    time.

I am for those that have never been master'd,
For men and women whose tempers have never been
    master'd,
For those whom laws, theories, conventions, can never
    master.

I am for those who walk abreast with the whole earth,
Who inaugurate one to inaugurate all.

I will not be outfaced by irrational things,
I will penetrate what it is in them that is sarcastic upon
    me,
I will make cities and civilizations defer to me,
This is what I have learnt from America—it is the amount,
    and it I teach again.

(Democracy, while weapons were everywhere aim'd at
    your breast,
I saw you serenely give birth to immortal children, saw
    in dreams your dilating form,
Saw you with spreading mantle covering the world.)

18

I will confront these shows of the day and night,
I will know if I am to be less than they,
I will see if I am not as majestic as they,
I will see if I am not as subtle and real as they,
I will see if I am to be less generous than they,
I will see if I have no meaning, while the houses and ships
    have meaning,
I will see if the fishes and birds are to be enough for them-
    selves, and I am not to be enough for myself.

I match my spirit against yours you orbs, growths, moun-
    tains, brutes,
Copious as you are I absorb you all in myself, and become
    the master myself,
America isolated yet embodying all, what is it finally
    except myself?
These States, what are they except myself?

I know now why the earth is gross, tantalizing, wicked,
    it is for my sake,
I take you specially to be mine, you terrible, rude forms.

(Mother, bend down, bend close to me your face,
I know not what these plots and wars and deferments are
    for,
I know not fruition's success, but I know that through war
    and crime your work goes on, and must yet go on.)

19

Thus by blue Ontario's shore,
While the winds fann'd me and the waves came trooping
    toward me,
I thrill'd with the power's pulsations, and the charm of
    my theme was upon me,
Till the tissues that held me parted their ties upon me.

And I saw the free souls of poets,
The loftiest bards of past ages strode before me,
Strange large men, long unwaked, undisclosed, were dis-
    closed to me.

20

O my rapt verse, my call, mock me not!
Not for the bards of the past, not to invoke them have I
    launch'd you forth,
Not to call even those lofty bards here by Ontario's
    shores,
Have I sung so capricious and loud my savage song.

Bards for my own land only I invoke,
(For the war the war is over, the field is clear'd,)
Till they strike up marches henceforth triumphant and
    onward,
To cheer O Mother your boundless expectant soul.

Bards of the great Idea! bards of the peaceful inventions!
    (for the war, the war is over!)

Yet bards of latent armies, a million soldiers waiting ever-
  ready,
Bards with songs as from burning coals or the lightning's
  fork'd stripes!
Ample Ohio's, Kanada's bards—bards of California!
  inland bards—bards of the war!
You by my charm I invoke.

*

REVERSALS.

Let that which stood in front go behind,
Let that which was behind advance to the front,
Let bigots, fools, unclean persons, offer new propositions,
Let the old propositions be postponed,
Let a man seek pleasure everywhere except in himself,
Let a woman seek happiness everywhere except in her-
  self.

AUTUMN RIVULETS.

AS CONSEQUENT, *ETC.*

As consequent from store of summer rains,
Or wayward rivulets in autumn flowing,
Or many a herb-lined brook's reticulations,
Or subterranean sea-rills making for the sea,
Songs of continued years I sing.

Life's ever-modern rapids first, (soon, soon to blend,
With the old streams of death.)

Some threading Ohio's farm-fields or the woods,
Some down Colorado's cañons from sources of perpetual
    snow,
Some half-hid in Oregon, or away southward in Texas,
Some in the north finding their way to Erie, Niagara,
    Ottawa,
Some to Atlantica's bays, and so to the great salt brine.

In you whoe'er you are my book perusing,
In I myself, in all the world, these currents flowing,
All, all toward the mystic ocean tending.

Currents for starting a continent new,
Overtures sent to the solid out of the liquid,
Fusion of ocean and land, tender and pensive waves,
(Not safe and peaceful only, waves rous'd and ominous
    too,
Out of the depths the storm's abysmic waves, who knows
    whence?
Raging over the vast, with many a broken spar and tat-
    ter'd sail.)

Or from the sea of Time, collecting vasting all, I bring,
A windrow-drift of weeds and shells.

O little shells, so curious-convolute, so limpid-cold and
    voiceless,
Will you not little shells to the tympans of temples held,
Murmurs and echoes still call up, eternity's music faint
    and far,
Wafted inland, sent from Atlantica's rim, strains for the
    soul of the prairies,
Whisper'd reverberations, chords for the ear of the West
    joyously sounding,
Your tidings old, yet ever new and untranslatable,
Infinitesimals out of my life, and many a life,
(For not my life and years alone I give—all, all I give,)
These waifs from the deep, cast high and dry,
Wash'd on America's shores?

THE RETURN OF THE HEROES.

1

For the lands and for these passionate days and for
    myself,
Now I awhile retire to thee O soil of autumn fields,
Reclining on thy breast, giving myself to thee,
Answering the pulses of thy sane and equable heart,
Tuning a verse for thee.

O earth that hast no voice, confide to me a voice,
O harvest of my lands—O boundless summer growths,
O lavish brown parturient earth—O infinite teeming
    womb,
A song to narrate thee.

2

Ever upon this stage,
Is acted God's calm annual drama,
Gorgeous processions, songs of birds,
Sunrise that fullest feeds and freshens most the soul,
The heaving sea, the waves upon the shore, the musical,
    strong waves,
The woods, the stalwart trees, the slender, tapering trees,
The liliput countless armies of the grass,
The heat, the showers, the measureless pasturages,
The scenery of the snows, the winds' free orchestra,
The stretching light-hung roof of clouds, the clear
    cerulean and the silvery fringes,

The high dilating stars, the placid beckoning stars,
The moving flocks and herds, the plains and emerald
    meadows,
The shows of all the varied lands and all the growths and
    products.

3

Fecund America—to-day,
Thou art all over set in births and joys!
Thou groan'st with riches, thy wealth clothes thee as a
    swathing-garment,
Thou laughest loud with ache of great possessions,
A myriad twining life like interlacing vines binds all thy
    vast demesne,
As some huge ship freighted to water's edge thou ridest
    into port,
As rain falls from the heaven and vapors rise from earth,
    so have the precious values fallen upon thee and risen
    out of thee;
Thou envy of the globe! thou miracle!
Thou, bathed, choked, swimming in plenty,
Thou lucky Mistress of the tranquil barns,
Thou Prairie Dame that sittest in the middle and lookest
    out upon thy world, and lookest East and lookest
    West,
Dispensatress, that by a word givest a thousand miles, a
    million farms, and missest nothing,
Thou all-acceptress—thou hospitable, (thou only art hos-
    pitable as God is hospitable.)

4

When late I sang sad was my voice,
Sad were the shows around me with deafening noises of
    hatred and smoke of war;
In the midst of the conflict, the heroes, I stood,
Or pass'd with slow step through the wounded and
    dying.

But now I sing not war,
Nor the measur'd march of soldiers, nor the tents of
    camps,
Nor the regiments hastily coming up deploying in line of
    battle;
No more the sad, unnatural shows of war.

Ask'd room those flush'd immortal ranks, the first forth-
    stepping armies?
Ask room alas the ghastly ranks, the armies dread that
    follow'd.

(Pass, pass, ye proud brigades, with your tramping
    sinewy legs,
With your shoulders young and strong, with your knap-
    sacks and your muskets;
How elate I stood and watch'd you, where starting off
    you march'd.

Pass—then rattle drums again,
For an army heaves in sight, O another gathering army,

Swarming, trailing on the rear, O you dread accruing
    army,
O you regiments so piteous, with your mortal diarrhœa,
    with your fever,
O my land's maim'd darlings, with the plenteous bloody
    bandage and the crutch,
Lo, your pallid army follows.)

5

But on these days of brightness,
On the far-stretching beauteous landscape, the roads and
    lanes, the high-piled farm-wagons, and the fruits and
    barns,
Should the dead intrude?

Ah the dead to me mar not, they fit well in Nature,
They fit very well in the landscape under the trees and
    grass,
And along the edge of the sky in the horizon's far mar-
    gin.

Nor do I forget you Departed,
Nor in winter or summer my lost ones,
But most in the open air as now when my soul is rapt and
    at peace, like pleasing phantoms,
Your memories rising glide silently by me.

6

I saw the day the return of the heroes,
(Yet the heroes never surpass'd shall never return,
Them that day I saw not.)

I saw the interminable corps, I saw the processions of
    armies,
I saw them approaching, defiling by with divisions,
Streaming northward, their work done, camping awhile
    in clusters of mighty camps.

No holiday soldiers—youthful, yet veterans,
Worn, swart, handsome, strong, of the stock of homestead
    and workshop,
Harden'd of many a long campaign and sweaty march,
Inured on many a hard-fought bloody field.

A pause—the armies wait,
A million flush'd embattled conquerors wait,
The world too waits, then soft as breaking night and sure
    as dawn,
They melt, they disappear.

Exult O lands! victorious lands!
Not there your victory on those red shuddering fields,
But here and hence your victory.

Melt, melt away ye armies—disperse ye blue-clad sol-
    diers,
Resolve ye back again, give up for good your deadly
    arms,

Other the arms the fields henceforth for you, or South or
    North,
With saner wars, sweet wars, life-giving wars.

7

Loud O my throat, and clear O soul!
The season of thanks and the voice of full-yielding,
The chant of joy and power for boundless fertility.

All till'd and untill'd fields expand before me,
I see the true arenas of my race, or first or last,
Man's innocent and strong arenas.

I see the heroes at other toils,
I see well-wielded in their hands the better weapons.

I see where the Mother of All,
With full-spanning eye gazes forth, dwells long,
And counts the varied gathering of the products.

Busy the far, the sunlit panorama,
Prairie, orchard, and yellow grain of the North,
Cotton and rice of the South and Louisianian cane,
Open unseeded fallows, rich fields of clover and timothy,
Kine and horses feeding, and droves of sheep and swine,
And many a stately river flowing and many a jocund
    brook,
And healthy uplands with herby-perfumed breezes,
And the good green grass, that delicate miracle the ever-
    recurring grass.

8

Toil on heroes! harvest the products!
Not alone on those warlike fields the Mother of All,
With dilated form and lambent eyes watch'd you.

Toil on heroes! toil well! handle the weapons well!
The Mother of All, yet here as ever she watches you.

Well-pleased America thou beholdest,
Over the fields of the West those crawling monsters,
The human-divine inventions, the labor-saving imple-
    ments;
Beholdest moving in every direction imbued as with life
    the revolving hay-rakes,
The steam-power reaping-machines and the horse-power
    machines,
The engines, thrashers of grain and cleaners of grain, well
    separating the straw, the nimble work of the patent
    pitchfork,
Beholdest the newer saw-mill, the southern cotton-gin,
    and the rice-cleanser.
Beneath thy look O Maternal,
With these and else and with their own strong hands the
    heroes harvest.

All gather and all harvest,
Yet but for thee O Powerful, not a scythe might swing as
    now in security,
Not a maize-stalk dangle as now its silken tassels in
    peace.

Under thee only they harvest, even but a wisp of hay
    under thy great face only,
Harvest the wheat of Ohio, Illinois, Wisconsin, every
    barbed spear under thee,
Harvest the maize of Missouri, Kentucky, Tennessee, each
    ear in its light-green sheath,
Gather the hay to its myriad mows in the odorous tran-
    quil barns,
Oats to their bins, the white potato, the buckwheat of
    Michigan, to theirs;
Gather the cotton in Mississippi or Alabama, dig and
    hoard the golden the sweet potato of Georgia and the
    Carolinas,
Clip the wool of California or Pennsylvania,
Cut the flax in the Middle States, or hemp or tobacco in
    the Borders,
Pick the pea and the bean, or pull apples from the trees
    or bunches of grapes from the vines,
Or aught that ripens in all these States or North or South,
Under the beaming sun and under thee.

THERE WAS A CHILD WENT FORTH.

There was a child went forth every day,
And the first object he look'd upon, that object he became,
And that object became part of him for the day or a certain
    part of the day,
Or for many years or stretching cycles of years.

The early lilacs became part of this child,
And grass and white and red morning-glories, and white
and red clover, and the song of the phœbe-bird,
And the Third-month lambs and the sow's pink-faint lit-
ter, and the mare's foal and the cow's calf,
And the noisy brood of the barnyard or by the mire of the
pond-side,
And the fish suspending themselves so curiously below
there, and the beautiful curious liquid,
And the water-plants with their graceful flat heads, all
became part of him.

The field-sprouts of Fourth-month and Fifth-month
became part of him,
Winter-grain sprouts and those of the light-yellow corn,
and the esculent roots of the garden,
And the apple-trees cover'd with blossoms and the fruit
afterward, and wood-berries, and the commonest
weeds by the road,
And the old drunkard staggering home from the out-
house of the tavern whence he had lately risen,
And the schoolmistress that pass'd on her way to the
school,
And the friendly boys that pass'd, and the quarrelsome
boys,
And the tidy and fresh-cheek'd girls, and the barefoot
negro boy and girl,
And all the changes of city and country wherever he
went.

His own parents, he that had father'd him and she that
had conceiv'd him in her womb and birth'd him,

They give this child more of themselves than that,
They gave him afterward every day, they became part of
    him.

The mother at home quietly placing the dishes on the sup-
    per-table,
The mother with mild words, clean her cap and gown, a
    wholesome odor falling off her person and clothes as
    she walks by,
The father, strong, self-sufficient, manly, mean, anger'd,
    unjust,
The blow, the quick loud word, the tight bargain, the
    crafty lure,
The family usages, the language, the company, the furni-
    ture, the yearning and swelling heart,
Affection that will not be gainsay'd, the sense of what is
    real, the thought if after all it should prove unreal,
The doubts of day-time and the doubts of night-time, the
    curious whether and how,
Whether that which appears so is so, or is it all flashes and
    specks?
Men and women crowding fast in the streets, if they are
    not flashes and specks what are they?
The streets themselves and the façades of houses, and
    goods in the windows,
Vehicles, teams, the heavy-plank'd wharves, the huge
    crossing at the ferries,
The village on the highland seen from afar at sunset, the
    river between,
Shadows, aureola and mist, the light falling on roofs and
    gables of white or brown two miles off,

The schooner near by sleepily dropping down the tide,
   the little boat slack-tow'd astern,
The hurrying tumbling waves, quick-broken crests, slap-
   ping,
The strata of color'd clouds, the long bar of maroon-tint
   away solitary by itself, the spread of purity it lies
   motionless in,
The horizon's edge, the flying sea-crow, the fragrance of
   salt marsh and shore mud,
These became part of that child who went forth every
   day, and who now goes, and will always go forth
   every day.

OLD IRELAND.

Far hence amid an isle of wondrous beauty,
Crouching over a grave an ancient sorrowful mother,
Once a queen, now lean and tatter'd seated on the
   ground,
Her old white hair drooping dishevel'd round her shoul-
   ders,
At her feet fallen an unused royal harp,
Long silent, she too long silent, mourning her shrouded
   hope and heir,
Of all the earth her heart most full of sorrow because most
   full of love.

Yet a word ancient mother,
You need crouch there no longer on the cold ground with
   forehead between your knees,

O you need not sit there veil'd in your old white hair so
    dishevel'd,
For know you the one you mourn is not in that grave,
It was an illusion, the son you love was not really dead,
The Lord is not dead, he is risen again young and strong
    in another country,
Even while you wept there by your fallen harp by the
    grave,
What you wept for was translated, pass'd from the grave,
The winds favor'd and the sea sail'd it,
And now with rosy and new blood,
Moves to-day in a new country.

THE CITY DEAD-HOUSE.

By the city dead-house by the gate,
As idly sauntering wending my way from the clangor,
I curious pause, for lo, an outcast form, a poor dead pros-
    titute brought,
Her corpse they deposit unclaim'd, it lies on the damp
    brick pavement,
The divine woman, her body, I see the body, I look on it
    alone,
That house once full of passion and beauty, all else I
    notice not,
Nor stillness so cold, nor running water from faucet, nor
    odors morbific impress me,
But the house alone—that wondrous house—that delicate
    fair house—that ruin!
That immortal house more than all the rows of dwellings
    ever built!

Or white-domed capitol with majestic figure surmounted,
or all the old high-spired cathedrals,
That little house alone more than them all—poor, desper-
ate house!
Fair, fearful wreck—tenement of a soul—itself a soul,
Unclaim'd, avoided house—take one breath from my
tremulous lips,
Take one tear dropt aside as I go for thought of you,
Dead house of love—house of madness and sin, crum-
bled, crush'd,
House of life, erewhile talking and laughing—but ah,
poor house, dead even then,
Months, years, an echoing, garnish'd house—but dead,
dead, dead.

THIS COMPOST.

1

Something startles me where I thought I was safest,
I withdraw from the still woods I loved,
I will not go now on the pastures to walk,
I will not strip the clothes from my body to meet my lover
the sea,
I will not touch my flesh to the earth as to other flesh to
renew me.

O how can it be that the ground itself does not sicken?
How can you be alive you growths of spring?
How can you furnish health you blood of herbs, roots,
orchards, grain?

Are they not continually putting distemper'd corpses
  within you?
Is not every continent work'd over and over with sour
  dead?

Where have you disposed of their carcasses?
Those drunkards and gluttons of so many generations?
Where have you drawn off all the foul liquid and meat?
I do not see any of it upon you to-day, or perhaps I am
  deceiv'd,
I will run a furrow with my plough, I will press my spade
  through the sod and turn it up underneath,
I am sure I shall expose some of the foul meat.

2

Behold this compost! behold it well!
Perhaps every mite has once form'd part of a sick per-
  son—yet behold!
The grass of spring covers the prairies,
The bean bursts noiselessly through the mould in the gar-
  den,
The delicate spear of the onion pierces upward,
The apple-buds cluster together on the apple-branches,
The resurrection of the wheat appears with pale visage
  out of its graves,
The tinge awakes over the willow-tree and the mulberry-
  tree,
The he-birds carol mornings and evenings while the she-
  birds sit on their nests,
The young of poultry break through the hatch'd eggs,

The new-born of animals appear, the calf is dropt from
    the cow, the colt from the mare,
Out of its little hill faithfully rise the potato's dark green
    leaves,
Out of its hill rises the yellow maize-stalk, the lilacs bloom
    in the dooryards,
The summer growth is innocent and disdainful above all
    those strata of sour dead.

What chemistry!
That the winds are really not infectious,
That this is no cheat, this transparent green-wash of the
    sea which is so amorous after me,
That it is safe to allow it to lick my naked body all over
    with its tongues,
That it will not endanger me with the fevers that have
    deposited themselves in it,
That all is clean forever and forever,
That the cool drink from the well tastes so good,
That blackberries are so flavorous and juicy,
That the fruits of the apple-orchard and the orange-
    orchard, that melons, grapes, peaches, plums, will
    none of them poison me,
That when I recline on the grass I do not catch any dis-
    ease,
Though probably every spear of grass rises out of what
    was once a catching disease.

Now I am terrified at the Earth, it is that calm and patient,
It grows such sweet things out of such corruptions,
It turns harmless and stainless on its axis, with such end-
    less successions of diseas'd corpses,

It distills such exquisite winds out of such infused fetor,
It renews with such unwitting looks its prodigal, annual,
	sumptuous crops,
It gives such divine materials to men, and accepts such
	leavings from them at last.

TO A FOIL'D EUROPEAN REVOLUTIONAIRE.

Courage yet, my brother or my sister!
Keep on—Liberty is to be subserv'd whatever occurs;
That is nothing that is quell'd by one or two failures, or
	any number of failures,
Or by the indifference or ingratitude of the people, or by
	any unfaithfulness,
Or the show of the tushes of power, soldiers, cannon,
	penal statutes.

What we believe in waits latent forever through all the
	continents,
Invites no one, promises nothing, sits in calmness and
	light, is positive and composed, knows no discour-
	agement,
Waiting patiently, waiting its time.

(Not songs of loyalty alone are these,
But songs of insurrection also,
For I am the sworn poet of every dauntless rebel the
	world over,
And he going with me leaves peace and routine behind
	him,
And stakes his life to be lost at any moment.)

The battle rages with many a loud alarm and frequent
    advance and retreat,
The infidel triumphs, or supposes he triumphs,
The prison, scaffold, garroté, handcuffs, iron necklace and
    lead-balls do their work,
The named and unnamed heroes pass to other spheres,
The great speakers and writers are exiled, they lie sick in
    distant lands,
The cause is asleep, the strongest throats are choked with
    their own blood,
The young men droop their eyelashes toward the ground
    when they meet;
But for all this Liberty has not gone out of the place, nor
    the infidel enter'd into full possession.
When liberty goes out of a place it is not the first to go, nor
    the second or third to go,
It waits for all the rest to go, it is the last.

When there are no more memories of heroes and martyrs,
And when all life and all the souls of men and women are
    discharged from any part of the earth,
Then only shall liberty or the idea of liberty be discharged
    from that part of the earth,
And the infidel come into full possession.

Then courage European revolter, revoltress!
For till all ceases neither must you cease.

I do not know what you are for, (I do not know what I am
    for myself, nor what any thing is for,)

But I will search carefully for it even in being foil'd,
In defeat, poverty, misconception, imprisonment—for
    they too are great.

Did we think victory great?
So it is—but now it seems to me, when it cannot be help'd,
    that defeat is great,
And that death and dismay are great.

UNNAMED LANDS.

Nations ten thousand years before these States, and many
    times ten thousand years before these States,
Garner'd clusters of ages that men and women like us
    grew up and travel'd their course and pass'd on,
What vast-built cities, what orderly republics, what pas-
    toral tribes and nomads,
What histories, rulers, heroes, perhaps transcending all
    others,
What laws, customs, wealth, arts, traditions,
What sort of marriage, what costumes, what physiology
    and phrenology,
What of liberty and slavery among them, what they
    thought of death and the soul,
Who were witty and wise, who beautiful and poetic, who
    brutish and undevelop'd,
Not a mark, not a record remains—and yet all remains.

O I know that those men and women were not for noth-
    ing, any more than we are for nothing,

I know that they belong to the scheme of the world every
    bit as much as we now belong to it.

Afar they stand, yet near to me they stand,
Some with oval countenances learn'd and calm,
Some naked and savage, some like huge collections of
    insects,
Some in tents, herdsmen, patriarchs, tribes, horsemen,
Some prowling through woods, some living peaceably on
    farms, laboring, reaping, filling barns,
Some traversing paved avenues, amid temples, palaces,
    factories, libraries, shows, courts, theatres, wonder-
    ful monuments.

Are those billions of men really gone?
Are those women of the old experience of the earth gone?
Do their lives, cities, arts, rest only with us?
Did they achieve nothing for good for themselves?

I believe of all those men and women that fill'd the
    unnamed lands, every one exists this hour here or
    elsewhere, invisible to us,
In exact proportion to what he or she grew from in life,
    and out of what he or she did, felt, became, loved,
    sinn'd, in life.

I believe that was not the end of those nations or any per-
    son of them, any more than this shall be the end of my
    nation, or of me;
Of their languages, governments, marriage, literature,
    products, games, wars, manners, crimes, prisons,
    slaves, heroes, poets,

I suspect their results curiously await in the yet unseen
    world, counterparts of what accrued to them in the
    seen world,
I suspect I shall meet them there,
I suspect I shall there find each old particular of those
    unnamed lands.

SONG OF PRUDENCE.

Manhattan's streets I saunter'd pondering,
On Time, Space, Reality—on such as these, and abreast
    with them Prudence.

The last explanation always remains to be made about
    prudence,
Little and large alike drop quietly aside from the pru-
    dence that suits immortality.

The soul is of itself,
All verges to it, all has reference to what ensues,
All that a person does, says, thinks, is of consequence,
Not a move can a man or woman make, that affects him
    or her in a day, month, any part of the direct lifetime,
    or the hour of death,
But the same affects him or her onward afterward
    through the indirect lifetime.

The indirect is just as much as the direct,
The spirit receives from the body just as much as it gives
    to the body, if not more.

Not one word or deed, not venereal sore, discoloration,
    privacy of the onanist,
Putridity of gluttons or rum-drinkers, peculation, cun-
    ning, betrayal, murder, seduction, prostitution,
But has results beyond death as really as before death.

Charity and personal force are the only investments
    worth any thing.

No specification is necessary, all that a male or female
    does, that is vigorous, benevolent, clean, is so much
    profit to him or her,
In the unshakable order of the universe and through the
    whole scope of it forever.

Who has been wise receives interest,
Savage, felon, President, judge, farmer, sailor, mechanic,
    literat, young, old, it is the same,
The interest will come round—all will come round.

Singly, wholly, to affect now, affected their time, will for-
    ever affect, all of the past and all of the present and all
    of the future,
All the brave actions of war and peace,
All help given to relatives, strangers, the poor, old, sor-
    rowful, young children, widows, the sick, and to
    shunn'd persons,
All self-denial that stood steady and aloof on wrecks, and
    saw others fill the seats of the boats,
All offering of substance or life for the good old cause, or
    for a friend's sake, or opinion's sake,

All pains of enthusiasts scoff'd at by their neighbors,
All the limitless sweet love and precious suffering of
    mothers,
All honest men baffled in strifes recorded or unrecorded,
All the grandeur and good of ancient nations whose frag-
    ments we inherit,
All the good of the dozens of ancient nations unknown to
    us by name, date, location,
All that was ever manfully begun, whether it succeeded
    or no,
All suggestions of the divine mind of man or the divinity
    of his mouth, or the shaping of his great hands,
All that is well thought or said this day on any part of the
    globe, or on any of the wandering stars, or on any of
    the fix'd stars, by those there as we are here,
All that is henceforth to be thought or done by you who-
    ever you are, or by any one,
These inure, have inured, shall inure, to the identities
    from which they sprang, or shall spring.

Did you guess any thing lived only its moment?
The world does not so exist, no parts palpable or impal-
    pable so exist,
No consummation exists without being from some long
    previous consummation, and that from some other,
Without the farthest conceivable one coming a bit nearer
    the beginning than any.

Whatever satisfies souls is true;
Prudence entirely satisfies the craving and glut of souls,

Itself only finally satisfies the soul,
The soul has that measureless pride which revolts from
    every lesson but its own.

Now I breathe the word of the prudence that walks
    abreast with time, space, reality,
That answers the pride which refuses every lesson but its
    own.

What is prudence is indivisible,
Declines to separate one part of life from every part,
Divides not the righteous from the unrighteous or the liv-
    ing from the dead,
Matches every thought or act by its correlative,
Knows no possible forgiveness or deputed atonement,
Knows that the young man who composedly peril'd his
    life and lost it has done exceedingly well for himself
    without doubt,
That he who never peril'd his life, but retains it to old age
    in riches and ease, has probably achiev'd nothing for
    himself worth mentioning,
Knows that only that person has really learn'd who has
    learn'd to prefer results,
Who favors body and soul the same,
Who perceives the indirect assuredly following the direct,
Who in his spirit in any emergency whatever neither hur-
    ries nor avoids death.

THE SINGER IN THE PRISON.

1

O sight of pity, shame and dole!
O fearful thought—a convict soul.

Rang the refrain along the hall, the prison,
Rose to the roof, the vaults of heaven above,
Pouring in floods of melody in tones so pensive sweet and
    strong the like whereof was never heard,
Reaching the far-off sentry and the armed guards, who
    ceas'd their pacing,
Making the hearer's pulses stop for ecstasy and awe.

2

The sun was low in the west one winter day,
When down a narrow aisle amid the thieves and outlaws
    of the land,
(There by the hundreds seated, sear-faced murderers,
    wily counterfeiters,
Gather'd to Sunday church in prison walls, the keepers
    round,
Plenteous, well-armed, watching with vigilant eyes,)
Calmly a lady walk'd holding a little innocent child by
    either hand,
Whom seating on their stools beside her on the platform,
She, first preluding with the instrument a low and musi-
    cal prelude,
In voice surpassing all, sang forth a quaint old hymn.

A soul confined by bars and bands,
Cries, help! O help! and wrings her hands,
Blinded her eyes, bleeding her breast,
Nor pardon finds, nor balm of rest.

Ceaseless she paces to and fro,
O heart-sick days! O nights of woe!
Nor hand of friend, nor loving face,
Nor favor comes, nor word of grace.

It was not I that sinn'd the sin,
The ruthless body dragg'd me in;
Though long I strove courageously,
The body was too much for me.

Dear prison'd soul bear up a space,
For soon or late the certain grace;
To set thee free and bear thee home,
The heavenly pardoner death shall come.

    Convict no more, nor shame, nor dole!
    Depart—a God enfranchis'd soul!

3

The singer ceas'd,
One glance swept from her clear calm eyes o'er all those
    upturn'd faces,
Strange sea of prison faces, a thousand varied, crafty, bru-
    tal, seam'd and beauteous faces,
Then rising, passing back along the narrow aisle between
    them,

While her gown touch'd them rustling in the silence,
She vanish'd with her children in the dusk.

While upon all, convicts and armed keepers ere they
    stirr'd,
(Convict forgetting prison, keeper his loaded pistol,)
A hush and pause fell down a wondrous minute,
With deep half-stifled sobs and sound of bad men bow'd
    and moved to weeping,
And youth's convulsive breathings, memories of home,
The mother's voice in lullaby, the sister's care, the happy
    childhood,
The long-pent spirit rous'd to reminiscence;
A wondrous minute then—but after in the solitary night,
    to many, many there,
Years after, even in the hour of death, the sad refrain, the
    tune, the voice, the words,
Resumed, the large calm lady walks the narrow aisle,
The wailing melody again, the singer in the prison sings,

> O sight of pity, shame and dole!
> O fearful thought—a convict soul.

WARBLE FOR LILAC-TIME.

Warble me now for joy of lilac-time, (returning in remi-
    niscence,)
Sort me O tongue and lips for Nature's sake, souvenirs of
    earliest summer,
Gather the welcome signs, (as children with pebbles or
    stringing shells,)

Put in April and May, the hylas croaking in the ponds, the
elastic air,
Bees, butterflies, the sparrow with its simple notes,
Blue-bird and darting swallow, nor forget the high-hole
flashing his golden wings,
The tranquil sunny haze, the clinging smoke, the vapor,
Shimmer of waters with fish in them, the cerulean above,
All that is jocund and sparkling, the brooks running,
The maple woods, the crisp February days and the sugar-
making,
The robin where he hops, bright-eyed, brown-breasted,
With musical clear call at sunrise, and again at sunset,
Or flitting among the trees of the apple-orchard, building
the nest of his mate,
The melted snow of March, the willow sending forth its
yellow-green sprouts,
For spring-time is here! the summer is here! and what is
this in it and from it?
Thou, soul, unloosen'd—the restlessness after I know not
what;
Come, let us lag here no longer, let us be up and away!
O if one could but fly like a bird!
O to escape, to sail forth as in a ship!
To glide with thee O soul, o'er all, in all, as a ship o'er the
waters;
Gathering these hints, the preludes, the blue sky, the
grass, the morning drops of dew,
The lilac-scent, the bushes with dark green heart-shaped
leaves,
Wood-violets, the little delicate pale blossoms called inno-
cence,

Samples and sorts not for themselves alone, but for their
  atmosphere,
To grace the bush I love—to sing with the birds,
A warble for joy of lilac-time, returning in reminiscence.

OUTLINES FOR A TOMB.
(G.P., Buried 1870.)

1

What may we chant, O thou within this tomb?
What tablets, outlines, hang for thee, O millionaire?
The life thou lived'st we know not,
But that thou walk'dst thy years in barter, 'mid the haunts
  of brokers,
Nor heroism thine, nor war, nor glory.

2

Silent, my soul,
With drooping lids, as waiting, ponder'd,
Turning from all the samples, monuments of heroes.

While through the interior vistas,
Noiseless uprose, phantasmic, (as by night Auroras of the
  north,)
Lambent tableaus, prophetic, bodiless scenes,
Spiritual projections.

In one, among the city streets a laborer's home appear'd,
After his day's work done, cleanly, sweet-air'd, the
    gaslight burning,
The carpet swept and a fire in the cheerful stove.

In one, the sacred parturition scene,
A happy painless mother birth'd a perfect child.

In one, at a bounteous morning meal,
Sat peaceful parents with contented sons.

In one, by twos and threes, young people,
Hundreds concentring, walk'd the paths and streets and
    roads,
Toward a tall-domed school.

In one a trio beautiful,
Grandmother, loving daughter, loving daughter's daugh-
    ter, sat,
Chatting and sewing.

In one, along a suite of noble rooms,
'Mid plenteous books and journals, paintings on the
    walls, fine statuettes,
Were groups of friendly journeymen, mechanics young
    and old,
Reading, conversing.

All, all the shows of laboring life,
City and country, women's, men's and children's,

Their wants provided for, hued in the sun and tinged for
    once with joy,
Marriage, the street, the factory, farm, the house-room,
    lodging-room,
Labor and toil, the bath, gymnasium, playground, library,
    college,
The student, boy or girl, led forward to be taught,
The sick cared for, the shoeless shod, the orphan father'd
    and mother'd,
The hungry fed, the houseless housed;
(The intentions perfect and divine,
The workings, details, haply human.)

3

O thou within this tomb,
From thee such scenes, thou stintless, lavish giver,
Tallying the gifts of earth, large as the earth,
Thy name an earth, with mountains, fields and tides.

Nor by your streams alone, you rivers,
By you, your banks Connecticut,
By you and all your teeming life old Thames,
By you Potomac laving the ground Washington trod, by
    you Patapsco,
You Hudson, you endless Mississippi—nor you alone,
But to the high seas launch, my thought, his memory.

OUT FROM BEHIND THIS MASK.
(To Confront a Portrait.)

1

Out from behind this bending rough-cut mask,
These lights and shades, this drama of the whole,
This common curtain of the face contain'd in me for me,
    in you for you, in each for each,
(Tragedies, sorrows, laughter, tears—O heaven!
The passionate teeming plays this curtain hid!)
This glaze of God's serenest purest sky,
This film of Satan's seething pit,
This heart's geography's map, this limitless small conti-
    nent, this soundless sea;
Out from the convolutions of this globe,
This subtler astronomic orb than sun or moon, than
    Jupiter, Venus, Mars,
This condensation of the universe, (nay here the only uni-
    verse,
Here the idea, all in this mystic handful wrapt;)
These burin'd eyes, flashing to you to pass to future time,
To launch and spin through space revolving sideling,
    from these to emanate,
To you whoe'er you are—a look.

2

A traveler of thoughts and years, of peace and war,
Of youth long sped and middle age declining,
(As the first volume of a tale perused and laid away, and
    this the second,

Songs, ventures, speculations, presently to close,)
Lingering a moment here and now, to you I opposite turn,
As on the road or at some crevice door by chance, or
    open'd window,
Pausing, inclining, baring my head, you specially I greet,
To draw and clinch your soul for once inseparably with
    mine,
Then travel travel on.

VOCALISM.

1

Vocalism, measure, concentration, determination, and the
    divine power to speak words;
Are you full-lung'd and limber-lipp'd from long trial?
    from vigorous practice? from physique?
Do you move in these broad lands as broad as they?
Come duly to the divine power to speak words?
For only at last after many years, after chastity, friend-
    ship, procreation, prudence, and nakedness,
After treading ground and breasting river and lake,
After a loosen'd throat, after absorbing eras, tempera-
    ments, races, after knowledge, freedom, crimes,
After complete faith, after clarifyings, elevations, and
    removing obstructions,
After these and more, it is just possible there comes to a
    man, a woman, the divine power to speak words;

Then toward that man or that woman swiftly hasten all—
    none refuse, all attend,
Armies, ships, antiquities, libraries, paintings, machines,
    cities, hate, despair, amity, pain, theft, murder, aspi-
    ration, form in close ranks,
They debouch as they are wanted to march obediently
    through the mouth of that man or that woman.

2

O what is it in me that makes me tremble so at voices?
Surely whoever speaks to me in the right voice, him or her
    I shall follow,
As the water follows the moon, silently, with fluid steps,
    anywhere around the globe.

All waits for the right voices;
Where is the practis'd and perfect organ? where is the
    develop'd soul?
For I see every word utter'd thence has deeper, sweeter,
    new sounds, impossible on less terms.

I see brains and lips closed, tympans and temples
    unstruck,
Until that comes which has the quality to strike and to
    unclose,
Until that comes which has the quality to bring forth what
    lies slumbering forever ready in all words.

TO HIM THAT WAS CRUCIFIED.

My spirit to yours dear brother,
Do not mind because many sounding your name do not
    understand you,
I do not sound your name, but I understand you,
I specify you with joy O my comrade to salute you, and
    to salute those who are with you, before and since,
    and those to come also,
That we all labor together transmitting the same charge
    and succession,
We few equals indifferent of lands, indifferent of times,
We, enclosers of all continents, all castes, allowers of all
    theologies,
Compassionaters, perceivers, rapport of men,
We walk silent among disputes and assertions, but reject
    not the disputers nor any thing that is asserted,
We hear the bawling and din, we are reach'd at by divi-
    sions, jealousies, recriminations on every side,
They close peremptorily upon us to surround us, my
    comrade,
Yet we walk unheld, free, the whole earth over, journey-
    ing up and down till we make our ineffaceable mark
    upon time and the diverse eras,
Till we saturate time and eras, that the men and women of
    races, ages to come, may prove brethren and lovers as
    we are.

YOU FELONS ON TRIAL IN COURTS.

You felons on trial in courts,
You convicts in prison-cells, you sentenced assassins
    chain'd and handcuffed with iron,
Who am I too that I am not on trial or in prison?
Me ruthless and devilish as any, that my wrists are not
    chain'd with iron, or my ankles with iron?

You prostitutes flaunting over the trottoirs or obscene in
    your rooms,
Who am I that I should call you more obscene than
    myself?

O culpable! I acknowledge—I exposé!
(O admirers, praise not me—compliment not me—you
    make me wince,
I see what you do not—I know what you do not.)

Inside these breast-bones I lie smutch'd and choked,
Beneath this face that appears so impassive hell's tides
    continually run,
Lusts and wickedness are acceptable to me,
I walk with delinquents with passionate love,
I feel I am of them—I belong to those convicts and prosti-
    tutes myself,
And henceforth I will not deny them—for how can I deny
    myself?

LAWS FOR CREATIONS.

Laws for creations,
For strong artists and leaders, for fresh broods of teach-
ers and perfect literats for America,
For noble savans and coming musicians.

All must have reference to the ensemble of the world, and
the compact truth of the world,
There shall be no subject too pronounced—all works shall
illustrate the divine law of indirections.

What do you suppose creation is?
What do you suppose will satisfy the soul, except to walk
free and own no superior?
What do you suppose I would intimate to you in a hun-
dred ways, but that man or woman is as good as
God?
And that there is no God any more divine than Yourself?
And that that is what the oldest and newest myths finally
mean?
And that you or any one must approach creations
through such laws?

TO A COMMON PROSTITUTE.

Be composed—be at ease with me—I am Walt Whitman,
liberal and lusty as Nature,
Not till the sun excludes you do I exclude you,

Not till the waters refuse to glisten for you and the leaves
    to rustle for you, do my words refuse to glisten and
    rustle for you.

My girl I appoint with you an appointment, and I charge
    you that you make preparation to be worthy to meet
    me,
And I charge you that you be patient and perfect till I
    come.

Till then I salute you with a significant look that you do
    not forget me.

I WAS LOOKING A LONG WHILE.

I was looking a long while for Intentions,
For a clew to the history of the past for myself, and for
    these chants—and now I have found it,
It is not in those paged fables in the libraries, (them I nei-
    ther accept nor reject,)
It is no more in the legends than in all else,
It is in the present—it is this earth to-day,
It is in Democracy—(the purport and aim of all the past,)
It is the life of one man or one woman to-day—the aver-
    age man of to-day,
It is in languages, social customs, literatures, arts,
It is in the broad show of artificial things, ships, machin-
    ery, politics, creeds, modern improvements, and the
    interchange of nations,
All for the modern—all for the average man of to-day.

THOUGHT.

Of persons arrived at high positions, ceremonies, wealth,
    scholarships, and the like;
(To me all that those persons have arrived at sinks away
    from them, except as it results to their bodies and
    souls,
So that often to me they appear gaunt and naked,
And often to me each one mocks the others, and mocks
    himself or herself,
And of each one the core of life, namely happiness, is full
    of the rotten excrement of maggots,
And often to me those men and women pass unwittingly
    the true realities of life, and go toward false realities,
And often to me they are alive after what custom has
    served them, but nothing more,
And often to me they are sad, hasty, unwaked sonnam-
    bules walking the dusk.)

MIRACLES.

Why, who makes much of a miracle?
As to me I know of nothing else but miracles,
Whether I walk the streets of Manhattan,
Or dart my sight over the roofs of houses toward the sky,
Or wade with naked feet along the beach just in the edge
    of the water,
Or stand under trees in the woods,
Or talk by day with any one I love, or sleep in the bed at
    night with any one I love,

Or sit at table at dinner with the rest,
Or look at strangers opposite me riding in the car,
Or watch honey-bees busy around the hive of a summer
    forenoon,
Or animals feeding in the fields,
Or birds, or the wonderfulness of insects in the air,
Or the wonderfulness of the sundown, or of stars shining
    so quiet and bright,
Or the exquisite delicate thin curve of the new moon in
    spring;
These with the rest, one and all, are to me miracles,
The whole referring, yet each distinct and in its place.

To me every hour of the light and dark is a miracle,
Every cubic inch of space is a miracle,
Every square yard of the surface of the earth is spread
    with the same,
Every foot of the interior swarms with the same.

To me the sea is a continual miracle,
The fishes that swim—the rocks—the motion of the
    waves—the ships with men in them,
What stranger miracles are there?

SPARKLES FROM THE WHEEL.

Where the city's ceaseless crowd moves on the livelong
    day,
Withdrawn I join a group of children watching, I pause
    aside with them.

By the curb toward the edge of the flagging,
A knife-grinder works at his wheel sharpening a great
    knife,
Bending over he carefully holds it to the stone, by foot
    and knee,
With measur'd tread he turns rapidly, as he presses with
    light but firm hand,
Forth issue then in copious golden jets,
Sparkles from the wheel.

The scene and all its belongings, how they seize and affect
    me,
The sad sharp-chinn'd old man with worn clothes and
    broad shoulder-band of leather,
Myself effusing and fluid, a phantom curiously floating,
    now here absorb'd and arrested,
The group, (an unminded point set in a vast surround-
    ing,)
The attentive, quiet children, the loud, proud, restive base
    of the streets,
The low hoarse purr of the whirling stone, the light-
    press'd blade,
Diffusing, dropping, sideways-darting, in tiny showers of
    gold,
Sparkles from the wheel.

TO A PUPIL.

Is reform needed? is it through you?
The greater the reform needed, the greater the Personality
    you need to accomplish it.

You! do you not see how it would serve to have eyes,
    blood, complexion, clean and sweet?
Do you not see how it would serve to have such a body
    and soul that when you enter the crowd an atmos-
    phere of desire and command enters with you, and
    every one is impress'd with your Personality?

O the magnet! the flesh over and over!
Go, dear friend, if need be give up all else, and commence
    to-day to inure yourself to pluck, reality, self-esteem,
    definiteness, elevatedness,
Rest not till you rivet and publish yourself of your own
    Personality.

UNFOLDED OUT OF THE FOLDS.

Unfolded out of the folds of the woman man comes
    unfolded, and is always to come unfolded,
Unfolded only out of the superbest woman of the earth is
    to come the superbest man of the earth,
Unfolded out of the friendliest woman is to come the
    friendliest man,
Unfolded only out of the perfect body of a woman can a
    man be form'd of perfect body,
Unfolded only out of the inimitable poems of woman can
    come the poems of man, (only thence have my poems
    come;)
Unfolded out of the strong and arrogant woman I love,
    only thence can appear the strong and arrogant man
    I love,

Unfolded by brawny embraces from the well-muscled
    woman I love, only thence come the brawny
    embraces of the man,
Unfolded out of the folds of the woman's brain come all
    the folds of the man's brain, duly obedient,
Unfolded out of the justice of the woman all justice is
    unfolded,
Unfolded out of the sympathy of the woman is all sym-
    pathy;
A man is a great thing upon the earth and through eter-
    nity, but every jot of the greatness of man is unfolded
    out of woman;
First the man is shaped in the woman, he can then be
    shaped in himself.

WHAT AM I AFTER ALL.

What am I after all but a child, pleas'd with the sound of
    my own name? repeating it over and over;
I stand apart to hear—it never tires me.

To you your name also;
Did you think there was nothing but two or three pro-
    nunciations in the sound of your name?

KOSMOS.

Who includes diversity and is Nature,

Who is the amplitude of the earth, and the coarseness and
sexuality of the earth, and the great charity of the
earth, and the equilibrium also,

Who has not look'd forth from the windows the eyes for
nothing, or whose brain held audience with messen-
gers for nothing,

Who contains believers and disbelievers, who is the most
majestic lover,

Who holds duly his or her triune proportion of realism,
spiritualism, and of the æsthetic or intellectual,

Who having consider'd the body finds all its organs and
parts good,

Who, out of the theory of the earth and of his or her body
understands by subtle analogies all other theories,

The theory of a city, a poem, and of the large politics of
these States;

Who believes not only in our globe with its sun and
moon, but in other globes with their suns and moons,

Who, constructing the house of himself or herself, not for
a day but for all time, sees races, eras, dates, genera-
tions,

The past, the future, dwelling there, like space, insepara-
ble together.

OTHERS MAY PRAISE WHAT THEY LIKE.

Others may praise what they like;
But I, from the banks of the running Missouri, praise
    nothing in art or aught else,
Till it has well inhaled the atmosphere of this river, also
    the western prairie-scent,
And exudes it all again.

WHO LEARNS MY LESSON COMPLETE?

Who learns my lesson complete?
Boss, journeyman, apprentice, churchman and atheist,
The stupid and the wise thinker, parents and offspring,
    merchant, clerk, porter and customer,
Editor, author, artist, and schoolboy—draw nigh and
    commence;
It is no lesson—it lets down the bars to a good lesson,
And that to another, and every one to another still.

The great laws take and effuse without argument,
I am of the same style, for I am their friend,
I love them quits and quits, I do not halt and make
    salaams.

I lie abstracted and hear beautiful tales of things and the
    reasons of things,
They are so beautiful I nudge myself to listen.

I cannot say to any person what I hear—I cannot say it to
    myself—it is very wonderful.

It is no small matter, this round and delicious globe mov-
    ing so exactly in its orbit for ever and ever, without
    one jolt or the untruth of a single second,
I do not think it was made in six days, nor in ten thousand
    years, nor ten billions of years,
Nor plann'd and built one thing after another as an archi-
    tect plans and builds a house.

I do not think seventy years is the time of a man or
    woman,
Nor that seventy millions of years is the time of a man or
    woman,
Nor that years will ever stop the existence of me, or any
    one else.

Is it wonderful that I should be immortal? as every one is
    immortal;
I know it is wonderful, but my eyesight is equally won-
    derful, and how I was conceived in my mother's
    womb is equally wonderful,
And pass'd from a babe in the creeping trance of a cou-
    ple of summers and winters to articulate and walk—
    all this is equally wonderful.

And that my soul embraces you this hour, and we affect
    each other without ever seeing each other, and never
    perhaps to see each other, is every bit as wonderful.

And that I can think such thoughts as these is just as won-
    derful,
And that I can remind you, and you think them and know
    them to be true, is just as wonderful.

And that the moon spins round the earth and on with the
    earth, is equally wonderful,
And that they balance themselves with the sun and stars
    is equally wonderful.

TESTS.

All submit to them where they sit, inner, secure, unap-
    proachable to analysis in the soul,
Not traditions, not the outer authorities are the judges,
They are the judges of outer authorities and of all tradi-
    tions,
They corroborate as they go only whatever corroborates
    themselves, and touches themselves;
For all that, they have it forever in themselves to corrob-
    orate far and near without one exception.

THE TORCH.

On my Northwest coast in the midst of the night a fisher-
    men's group stands watching,
Out on the lake that expands before them, others are
    spearing salmon,
The canoe, a dim shadowy thing, moves across the black
    water,
Bearing a torch ablaze at the prow.

O STAR OF FRANCE.
1870-71.

O star of France,
The brightness of thy hope and strength and fame,
Like some proud ship that led the fleet so long,
Beseems to-day a wreck driven by the gale, a mastless
        hulk,
And 'mid its teeming madden'd half-drown'd crowds,
Nor helm nor helmsman.

Dim smitten star,
Orb not of France alone, pale symbol of my soul, its dear-
        est hopes,
The struggle and the daring, rage divine for liberty,
Of aspirations toward the far ideal, enthusiast's dreams of
        brotherhood,
Of terror to the tyrant and the priest.

Star crucified—by traitors sold,
Star panting o'er a land of death, heroic land,
Strange, passionate, mocking, frivolous land.

Miserable! yet for thy errors, vanities, sins, I will not now
        rebuke thee,
Thy unexampled woes and pangs have quell'd them all,
And left thee sacred.

In that amid thy many faults thou ever aimedst highly,
In that thou wouldst not really sell thyself however great
        the price,

In that thou surely wakedst weeping from thy drugg'd
    sleep,
In that alone among thy sisters thou, giantess, didst rend
    the ones that shamed thee,
In that thou couldst not, wouldst not, wear the usual
    chains,
This cross, thy livid face, thy pierced hands and feet,
The spear thrust in thy side.

O star! O ship of France, beat back and baffled long!
Bear up O smitten orb! O ship continue on!

Sure as the ship of all, the Earth itself,
Product of deathly fire and turbulent chaos,
Forth from its spasms of fury and its poisons,
Issuing at last in perfect power and beauty,
Onward beneath the sun following its course,
So thee O ship of France!

Finish'd the days, the clouds dispel'd,
The travail o'er, the long-sought extrication,
When lo! reborn, high o'er the European world,
(In gladness answering thence, as face afar to face, reflect-
    ing ours Columbia,)
Again thy star O France, fair lustrous star,
In heavenly peace, clearer, more bright than ever,
Shall beam immortal.

THE OX-TAMER.

In a far-away northern county in the placid pastoral
    region,
Lives my farmer friend, the theme of my recitative, a
    famous tamer of oxen,
There they bring him the three-year-olds and the four-
    year-olds to break them,
He will take the wildest steer in the world and break him
    and tame him,
He will go fearless without any whip where the young
    bullock chafes up and down the yard,
The bullock's head tosses restless high in the air with rag-
    ing eyes,
Yet see you! how soon his rage subsides—how soon this
    tamer tames him;
See you! on the farms hereabout a hundred oxen young
    and old, and he is the man who has tamed them,
They all know him, all are affectionate to him;
See you! some are such beautiful animals, so lofty look-
    ing;
Some are buff-color'd, some mottled, one has a white line
    running along his back, some are brindled,
Some have wide flaring horns (a good sign)—see you! the
    bright hides,
See, the two with stars on their foreheads—see, the round
    bodies and broad backs,
How straight and square they stand on their legs—what
    fine sagacious eyes!
How they watch their tamer—they wish him near them—
    how they turn to look after him!

What yearning expression! how uneasy they are when he
    moves away from them;
Now I marvel what it can be he appears to them, (books,
    politics, poems, depart—all else departs,)
I confess I envy only his fascination—my silent, illiterate
    friend,
Whom a hundred oxen love there in his life on farms,
In the northern county far, in the placid pastoral region.

AN OLD MAN'S THOUGHT OF SCHOOL.

For the Inauguration of a Public School, Camden, New Jersey,
1874.

An old man's thought of school,
An old man gathering youthful memories and blooms
    that youth itself cannot.

Now only do I know you,
O fair auroral skies—O morning dew upon the grass!

And these I see, these sparkling eyes,
These stores of mystic meaning, these young lives,
Building, equipping like a fleet of ships, immortal ships,
Soon to sail out over the measureless seas,
On the soul's voyage.

Only a lot of boys and girls?
Only the tiresome spelling, writing, ciphering classes?
Only a public school?

Ah more, infinitely more;
(As George Fox rais'd his warning cry, "Is it this pile of
    brick and mortar, these dead floors, windows, rails,
    you call the church?
Why this is not the church at all—the church is living,
    ever living souls.")

And you America,
Cast you the real reckoning for your present?
The lights and shadows of your future, good or evil?
To girlhood, boyhood look, the teacher and the school.

WANDERING AT MORN.

Wandering at morn,
Emerging from the night from gloomy thoughts, thee in
    my thoughts,
Yearning for thee harmonious Union! thee, singing bird
    divine!
Thee coil'd in evil times my country, with craft and black
    dismay, with every meanness, treason thrust upon
    thee,
This common marvel I beheld—the parent thrush I
    watch'd feeding its young,
The singing thrush whose tones of joy and faith ecstatic,
Fail not to certify and cheer my soul.

There ponder'd, felt I,
If worms, snakes, loathsome grubs, may to sweet spiritual
    songs be turn'd,

If vermin so transposed, so used and bless'd may be,
Then may I trust in you, your fortunes, days, my country;
Who knows but these may be the lessons fit for you?
From these your future song may rise with joyous trills,
Destin'd to fill the world.

ITALIAN MUSIC IN DAKOTA.

["*The Seventeenth—the finest Regimental Band I ever heard.*"]

Through the soft evening air enwinding all,
Rocks, woods, fort, cannon, pacing sentries, endless
    wilds,
In dulcet streams, in flutes' and cornets' notes,
Electric, pensive, turbulent, artificial,
(Yet strangely fitting even here, meanings unknown
    before,
Subtler than ever, more harmony, as if born here, related
    here,
Not to the city's fresco'd rooms, not to the audience of the
    opera house,
Sounds, echoes, wandering strains, as really here at home,
Sonnambula's innocent love, trios with *Norma's* anguish,
And thy ecstatic chorus *Poliuto*;)
Ray'd in the limpid yellow slanting sundown,
Music, Italian music in Dakota.

While Nature, sovereign of this gnarl'd realm,
Lurking in hidden barbaric grim recesses,
Acknowledging rapport however far remov'd,

(As some old root or soil of earth its last-born flower or
   fruit,)
Listens well pleas'd.

WITH ALL THY GIFTS.

With all thy gifts America,
Standing secure, rapidly tending, overlooking the world,
Power, wealth, extent, vouchsafed to thee—with these
   and like of these vouchsafed to thee,
What if one gift thou lackest? (the ultimate human prob-
   lem never solving,)
The gift of perfect women fit for thee—what if that gift of
   gifts thou lackest?
The towering feminine of thee? the beauty, health, com-
   pletion, fit for thee?
The mothers fit for thee?

MY PICTURE-GALLERY.

In a little house keep I pictures suspended, it is not a fix'd
   house,
It is round, it is only a few inches from one side to the
   other;
Yet behold, it has room for all the shows of the world, all
   memories!
Here the tableaus of life, and here the groupings of death;
Here, do you know this? this is cicerone himself,
With finger rais'd he points to the prodigal pictures.

THE PRAIRIE STATES.

A newer garden of creation, no primal solitude,
Dense, joyous, modern, populous millions, cities and
     farms,
With iron interlaced, composite, tied, many in one,
By all the world contributed—freedom's and law's and
     thrift's society,
The crown and teeming paradise, so far, of time's accu-
     mulations,
To justify the past.

*

PROUD MUSIC OF THE STORM.

1

Proud music of the storm,
Blast that careers so free, whistling across the prairies,
Strong hum of forest tree-tops—wind of the mountains,
Personified dim shapes—you hidden orchestras,
You serenades of phantoms with instruments alert,
Blending with Nature's rhythmus all the tongues of
     nations;
You chords left as by vast composers—you choruses,
You formless, free, religious dances—you from the Ori-
     ent,
You undertone of rivers, roar of pouring cataracts,
You sounds from distant guns with galloping cavalry,
Echoes of camps with all the different bugle-calls,

Trooping tumultuous, filling the midnight late, bending
    me powerless,
Entering my lonesome slumber-chamber, why have you
    seiz'd me?

2

Come forward O my soul, and let the rest retire,
Listen, lose not, it is toward thee they tend,
Parting the midnight, entering my slumber-chamber,
For thee they sing and dance O soul.

A festival song,
The duet of the bridegroom and the bride, a marriage-
    march,
With lips of love, and hearts of lovers fill'd to the brim
    with love,
The red-flush'd cheeks and perfumes, the cortege swarm-
    ing full of friendly faces young and old,
To flutes' clear notes and sounding harps' cantabile.

Now loud approaching drums,
Victoria! see'st thou in powder-smoke the banners torn
    but flying? the rout of the baffled?
Hearest those shouts of a conquering army?

(Ah soul, the sobs of women, the wounded groaning in
    agony,
The hiss and crackle of flames, the blacken'd ruins, the
    embers of cities,
The dirge and desolation of mankind.)

Now airs antique and mediæval fill me,
I see and hear old harpers with their harps at Welsh festi-
    vals,
I hear the minnesingers singing their lays of love,
I hear the minstrels, gleemen, troubadours, of the middle
    ages.

Now the great organ sounds,
Tremulous, while underneath, (as the hid footholds of the
    earth,
On which arising rest, and leaping forth depend,
All shapes of beauty, grace and strength, all hues we
    know,
Green blades of grass and warbling birds, children that
    gambol and play, the clouds of heaven above,)
The strong base stands, and its pulsations intermits not,
Bathing, supporting, merging all the rest, maternity of all
    the rest,
And with it every instrument in multitudes,
The players playing, all the world's musicians,
The solemn hymns and masses rousing adoration,
All passionate heart-chants, sorrowful appeals,
The measureless sweet vocalists of ages,
And for their solvent setting earth's own diapason,
Of winds and woods and mighty ocean waves,
A new composite orchestra, binder of years and climes,
    ten-fold renewer,
As of the far-back days the poets tell, the Paradiso,
The straying thence, the separation long, but now the
    wandering done,
The journey done, the journeyman come home,
And man and art with Nature fused again.

Tutti! for earth and heaven;
(The Almighty leader now for once has signal'd with his
    wand.)

The manly strophe of the husbands of the world,
And all the wives responding.

The tongues of violins,
(I think O tongues ye tell this heart, that cannot tell itself,
This brooding yearning heart, that cannot tell itself.)

3

Ah from a little child,
Thou knowest soul how to me all sounds became music,
My mother's voice in lullaby or hymn,
(The voice, O tender voices, memory's loving voices,
Last miracle of all, O dearest mother's, sister's, voices;)
The rain, the growing corn, the breeze among the long-
    leav'd corn,
The measur'd sea-surf beating on the sand,
The twittering bird, the hawk's sharp scream,
The wild-fowl's notes at night as flying low migrating
    north or south,
The psalm in the country church or mid the clustering
    trees, the open air camp-meeting,
The fiddler in the tavern, the glee, the long-strung sailor-
    song,
The lowing cattle, bleating sheep, the crowing cock at
    dawn.

All songs of current lands come sounding round me,
The German airs of friendship, wine and love,
Irish ballads, merry jigs and dances, English warbles,
Chansons of France, Scotch tunes, and o'er the rest,
Italia's peerless compositions.

Across the stage with pallor on her face, yet lurid passion,
Stalks Norma brandishing the dagger in her hand.

I see poor crazed Lucia's eyes' unnatural gleam,
Her hair down her back falls loose and dishevel'd.

I see where Ernani walking the bridal garden,
Amid the scent of night-roses, radiant, holding his bride
      by the hand,
Hears the infernal call, the death-pledge of the horn.

To crossing swords and gray hairs bared to heaven,
The clear electric base and baritone of the world,
The trombone duo, Libertad forever!

From Spanish chestnut trees' dense shade,
By old and heavy convent walls a wailing song,
Song of lost love, the torch of youth and life quench'd in
      despair,
Song of the dying swan, Fernando's heart is breaking.

Awaking from her woes at last retriev'd Amina sings,
Copious as stars and glad as morning light the torrents of
      her joy.

(The teeming lady comes,
The lustrious orb, Venus contralto, the blooming mother,
Sister of loftiest gods, Alboni's self I hear.)

4

I hear those odes, symphonies, operas,
I hear in the *William Tell* the music of an arous'd and
    angry people,
I hear Meyerbeer's *Huguenots*, the *Prophet*, or *Robert*,
Gounod's *Faust*, or Mozart's *Don Juan*.

I hear the dance-music of all nations,
The waltz, some delicious measure, lapsing, bathing me
    in bliss,
The bolero to tinkling guitars and clattering castanets.

I see religious dances old and new,
I hear the sound of the Hebrew lyre,
I see the crusaders marching bearing the cross on high, to
    the martial clang of cymbals,
I hear dervishes monotonously chanting, interspers'd
    with frantic shouts, as they spin around turning
    always towards Mecca,
I see the rapt religious dances of the Persians and the
    Arabs,
Again, at Eleusis, home of Ceres, I see the modern Greeks
    dancing,
I hear them clapping their hands as they bend their bod-
    ies,
I hear the metrical shuffling of their feet.

I see again the wild old Corybantian dance, the perform-
    ers wounding each other,
I see the Roman youth to the shrill sound of flageolets
    throwing and catching their weapons,
As they fall on their knees and rise again.

I hear from the Mussulman mosque the muezzin calling,
I see the worshippers within, nor form nor sermon, argu-
    ment nor word,
But silent, strange, devout, rais'd, glowing heads, ecstat-
    ic faces.

I hear the Egyptian harps of many strings,
The primitive chants of the Nile boatmen,
The sacred imperial hymns of China,
To the delicate sounds of the king, (the stricken wood and
    stone,)
Or to Hindu flutes and the fretting twang of the vina,
A band of bayaderes.

5

Now Asia, Africa leave me, Europe seizing inflates me,
To organs huge and bands I hear as from vast concourses
    of voices,
Luther's strong hymn *Eine feste Burg ist unser Gott*,
Rossini's *Stabat Mater dolorosa*,
Or floating in some high cathedral dim with gorgeous
    color'd windows,
The passionate *Agnus Dei* or *Gloria in Excelsis*.

Composers! mighty maestros!
And you, sweet singers of old lands, soprani, tenori, bassi!
To you a new bard caroling in the West,
Obeisant sends his love.

(Such led to thee O soul,
All senses, shows and objects, lead to thee,
But now it seems to me sound leads o'er all the rest.)

I hear the annual singing of the children in St. Paul's
    cathedral,
Or, under the high roof of some colossal hall, the sym-
    phonies, oratorios of Beethoven, Handel, or Haydn,
The *Creation* in billows of godhood laves me.

Give me to hold all sounds, (I madly struggling cry,)
Fill me with all the voices of the universe,
Endow me with their throbbings, Nature's also,
The tempests, waters, winds, operas and chants, marches
    and dances,
Utter, pour in, for I would take them all!

6

Then I woke softly,
And pausing, questioning awhile the music of my dream,
And questioning all those reminiscences, the tempest in
    its fury,
And all the songs of sopranos and tenors,
And those rapt oriental dances of religious fervor,

And the sweet varied instruments, and the diapason of
    organs,
And all the artless plaints of love and grief and death,
I said to my silent curious soul out of the bed of the slum-
    ber-chamber,
Come, for I have found the clue I sought so long,
Let us go forth refresh'd amid the day,
Cheerfully tallying life, walking the world, the real,
Nourish'd henceforth by our celestial dream.

And I said, moreover,
Haply what thou hast heard O soul was not the sound of
    winds,
Nor dream of raging storm, nor sea-hawk's flapping
    wings nor harsh scream,
Nor vocalism of sun-bright Italy,
Nor German organ majestic, nor vast concourse of voices,
    nor layers of harmonies,
Nor strophes of husbands and wives, nor sound of
    marching soldiers,
Nor flutes, nor harps, nor the bugle-calls of camps,
But to a new rhythmus fitted for thee,
Poems bridging the way from Life to Death, vaguely
    wafted in night air, uncaught, unwritten,
Which let us go forth in the bold day and write.

PASSAGE TO INDIA.

1

Singing my days,
Singing the great achievements of the present,
Singing the strong light works of engineers,
Our modern wonders, (the antique ponderous Seven out-
    vied,)
In the Old World the east the Suez canal,
The New by its mighty railroad spann'd,
The seas inlaid with eloquent gentle wires;
Yet first to sound, and ever sound, the cry with thee O
    soul,
The Past! the Past! the Past!

The Past—the dark unfathom'd retrospect!
The teeming gulf—the sleepers and the shadows!
The past—the infinite greatness of the past!
For what is the present after all but a growth out of the
    past?
(As a projectile form'd, impell'd, passing a certain line,
    still keeps on,
So the present, utterly form'd, impell'd by the past.)

2

Passage O soul to India!
Eclaircise the myths Asiatic, the primitive fables.

Not you alone proud truths of the world,
Nor you alone ye facts of modern science,
But myths and fables of eld, Asia's, Africa's fables,
The far-darting beams of the spirit, the unloos'd dreams,
The deep diving bibles and legends,
The daring plots of the poets, the elder religions;
O you temples fairer than lilies pour'd over by the rising
    sun!
O you fables spurning the known, eluding the hold of the
    known, mounting to heaven!
You lofty and dazzling towers, pinnacled, red as roses,
    burnish'd with gold!
Towers of fables immortal fashion'd from mortal dreams!
You too I welcome and fully the same as the rest!
You too with joy I sing.

Passage to India!
Lo, soul, seest thou not God's purpose from the first?
The earth to be spann'd, connected by network,
The races, neighbors, to marry and be given in marriage,
The oceans to be cross'd, the distant brought near,
The lands to be welded together.

A worship new I sing,
You captains, voyagers, explorers, yours,
You engineers, you architects, machinists, yours,
You, not for trade or transportation only,
But in God's name, and for thy sake O soul.

3

Passage to India!
Lo soul for thee of tableaus twain,
I see in one the Suez canal initiated, open'd,
I see the procession of steamships, the Empress Eugenie's
    leading the van,
I mark from on deck the strange landscape, the pure sky,
    the level sand in the distance,
I pass swiftly the picturesque groups, the workmen
    gather'd,
The gigantic dredging machines.

In one again, different, (yet thine, all thine, O soul, the
    same,)
I see over my own continent the Pacific railroad sur-
    mounting every barrier,
I see continual trains of cars winding along the Platte car-
    rying freight and passengers,
I hear the locomotives rushing and roaring, and the shrill
    steam-whistle,
I hear the echoes reverberate through the grandest
    scenery in the world,
I cross the Laramie plains, I note the rocks in grotesque
    shapes, the buttes,
I see the plentiful larkspur and wild onions, the barren,
    colorless, sage-deserts,
I see in glimpses afar or towering immediately above me
    the great mountains, I see the Wind river and the
    Wahsatch mountains,
I see the Monument mountain and the Eagle's Nest, I pass
    the Promontory, I ascend the Nevadas,

I scan the noble Elk mountain and wind around its base,
I see the Humboldt range, I thread the valley and cross
     the river,
I see the clear waters of lake Tahoe, I see forests of majes-
     tic pines,
Or crossing the great desert, the alkaline plains, I behold
     enchanting mirages of waters and meadows,
Marking through these and after all, in duplicate slender
     lines,
Bridging the three or four thousand miles of land travel,
Tying the Eastern to the Western sea,
The road between Europe and Asia.

(Ah Genoese thy dream! thy dream!
Centuries after thou art laid in thy grave,
The shore thou foundest verifies thy dream.)

4

Passage to India!
Struggles of many a captain, tales of many a sailor dead,
Over my mood stealing and spreading they come,
Like clouds and cloudlets in the unreach'd sky.

Along all history, down the slopes,
As a rivulet running, sinking now, and now again to the
     surface rising,
A ceaseless thought, a varied train—lo, soul, to thee, thy
     sight, they rise,
The plans, the voyages again, the expeditions;
Again Vasco de Gama sails forth,
Again the knowledge gain'd, the mariner's compass,

Lands found and nations born, thou born America,
For purpose vast, man's long probation fill'd,
Thou rondure of the world at last accomplish'd.

5

O vast Rondure, swimming in space,
Cover'd all over with visible power and beauty,
Alternate light and day and the teeming spiritual dark-
      ness,
Unspeakable high processions of sun and moon and
      countless stars above,
Below, the manifold grass and waters, animals, moun-
      tains, trees,
With inscrutable purpose, some hidden prophetic inten-
      tion,
Now first it seems my thought begins to span thee.

Down from the gardens of Asia descending radiating,
Adam and Eve appear, then their myriad progeny after
      them,
Wandering, yearning, curious, with restless explorations,
With questionings, baffled, formless, feverish, with never-
      happy hearts,
With that sad incessant refrain, *Wherefore unsatisfied soul?*
      and *Whither O mocking life?*

Ah who shall soothe these feverish children?
Who justify these restless explorations?
Who speak the secret of impassive earth?
Who bind it to us? what is this separate Nature so unnat-
      ural?

What is this earth to our affections? (unloving earth, with-
    out a throb to answer ours,
Cold earth, the place of graves.)

Yet soul be sure the first intent remains, and shall be car-
    ried out,
Perhaps even now the time has arrived.

After the seas are all cross'd, (as they seem already
    cross'd,)
After the great captains and engineers have accomplish'd
    their work,
After the noble inventors, after the scientists, the chemist,
    the geologist, ethnologist,
Finally shall come the poet worthy that name,
The true son of God shall come singing his songs.

Then not your deeds only O voyagers, O scientists and
    inventors, shall be justified,
All these hearts as of fretted children shall be sooth'd,
All affection shall be fully responded to, the secret shall be
    told,
All these separations and gaps shall be taken up and
    hook'd and link'd together,
The whole earth, this cold, impassive, voiceless earth,
    shall be completely justified,
Trinitas divine shall be gloriously accomplish'd and com-
    pacted by the true son of God, the poet,
(He shall indeed pass the straits and conquer the moun-
    tains,
He shall double the cape of Good Hope to some purpose,)

Nature and Man shall be disjoin'd and diffused no more,
The true son of God shall absolutely fuse them.

6

Year at whose wide-flung door I sing!
Year of the purpose accomplish'd!
Year of the marriage of continents, climates and oceans!
(No mere doge of Venice now wedding the Adriatic,)
I see O year in you the vast terraqueous globe given and
    giving all,
Europe to Asia, Africa join'd, and they to the New World,
The lands, geographies, dancing before you, holding a
    festival garland,
As brides and bridegrooms hand in hand.

Passage to India!
Cooling airs from Caucasus far, soothing cradle of man,
The river Euphrates flowing, the past lit up again.

Lo soul, the retrospect brought forward,
The old, most populous, wealthiest of earth's lands,
The streams of the Indus and the Ganges and their many
    affluents,
(I my shores of America walking to-day behold, resuming
    all,)
The tale of Alexander on his warlike marches suddenly
    dying,
On one side China and on the other side Persia and Ara-
    bia,
To the south the great seas and the bay of Bengal,

The flowing literatures, tremendous epics, religions,
    castes,
Old occult Brahma interminably far back, the tender and
    junior Buddha,
Central and southern empires and all their belongings,
    possessors,
The wars of Tamerlane, the reign of Aurungzebe,
The traders, rulers, explorers, Moslems, Venetians,
    Byzantium, the Arabs, Portuguese,
The first travelers famous yet, Marco Polo, Batouta the
    Moor,
Doubts to be solv'd, the map incognita, blanks to be fill'd,
The foot of man unstay'd, the hands never at rest,
Thyself O soul that will not brook a challenge.

The mediæval navigators rise before me,
The world of 1492, with its awaken'd enterprise,
Something swelling in humanity now like the sap of the
    earth in spring,
The sunset splendor of chivalry declining.

And who art thou sad shade?
Gigantic, visionary, thyself a visionary,
With majestic limbs and pious beaming eyes,
Spreading around with every look of thine a golden
    world,
Enhuing it with gorgeous hues.

As the chief histrion,
Down to the footlights walks in some great scena,
Dominating the rest I see the Admiral himself,
(History's type of courage, action, faith,)

Behold him sail from Palos leading his little fleet,
His voyage behold, his return, his great fame,
His misfortunes, calumniators, behold him a prisoner,
    chain'd,
Behold his dejection, poverty, death.

(Curious in time I stand, noting the efforts of heroes,
Is the deferment long? bitter the slander, poverty, death?
Lies the seed unreck'd for centuries in the ground? lo, to
    God's due occasion,
Uprising in the night, it sprouts, blooms,
And fills the earth with use and beauty.)

7

Passage indeed O soul to primal thought,
Not lands and seas alone, thy own clear freshness,
The young maturity of brood and bloom,
To realms of budding bibles.

O soul, repressless, I with thee and thou with me,
Thy circumnavigation of the world begin,
Of man, the voyage of his mind's return,
To reason's early paradise,
Back, back to wisdom's birth, to innocent intuitions,
Again with fair creation.

8

O we can wait no longer,
We too take ship O soul,
Joyous we too launch out on trackless seas,

Fearless for unknown shores on waves of ecstasy to sail,
Amid the wafting winds, (thou pressing me to thee, I thee
to me, O soul,)
Caroling free, singing our song of God,
Chanting our chant of pleasant exploration.

With laugh and many a kiss,
(Let others deprecate, let others weep for sin, remorse,
humiliation,)
O soul thou pleasest me, I thee.

Ah more than any priest O soul we too believe in God,
But with the mystery of God we dare not dally.

O soul thou pleasest me, I thee,
Sailing these seas or on the hills, or waking in the night,
Thoughts, silent thoughts, of Time and Space and Death,
like waters flowing,
Bear me indeed as through the regions infinite,
Whose air I breathe, whose ripples hear, lave me all over,
Bathe me O God in thee, mounting to thee,
I and my soul to range in range of thee.

O Thou transcendent,
Nameless, the fibre and the breath,
Light of the light, shedding forth universes, thou centre of
them,
Thou mightier centre of the true, the good, the loving,
Thou moral, spiritual fountain—affection's source—thou
reservoir,
(O pensive soul of me—O thirst unsatisfied—waitest not
there?

Waitest not haply for us somewhere there the Comrade
    perfect?)
Thou pulse—thou motive of the stars, suns, systems,
That, circling, move in order, safe, harmonious,
Athwart the shapeless vastnesses of space,
How should I think, how breathe a single breath, how
    speak, if, out of myself,
I could not launch, to those, superior universes?

Swiftly I shrivel at the thought of God,
At Nature and its wonders, Time and Space and Death,
But that I, turning, call to thee O soul, thou actual Me,
And lo, thou gently masterest the orbs,
Thou matest Time, smilest content at Death,
And fillest, swellest full the vastnesses of Space.

Greater than stars or suns,
Bounding O soul thou journeyest forth;
What love than thine and ours could wider amplify?
What aspirations, wishes, outvie thine and ours O soul?
What dreams of the ideal? what plans of purity, perfec-
    tion, strength?
What cheerful willingness for others' sake to give up all?
For others' sake to suffer all?

Reckoning ahead O soul when thou, the time achiev'd,
The seas all cross'd, weather'd the capes, the voyage
    done,
Surrounded, copest, frontest God, yieldest, the aim
    attain'd,

As fill'd with friendship, love complete, the Elder Brother
    found,
The Younger melts in fondness in his arms.

9

Passage to more than India!
Are thy wings plumed indeed for such far flights?
O soul, voyagest thou indeed on voyages like those?
Disportest thou on waters such as those?
Soundest below the Sanscrit and the Vedas?
Then have thy bent unleash'd.

Passage to you, your shores, ye aged fierce enigmas!
Passage to you, to mastership of you, ye strangling prob-
    lems!
You, strew'd with the wrecks of skeletons, that, living,
    never reach'd you.

Passage to more than India!
O secret of the earth and sky!
Of you O waters of the sea! O winding creeks and rivers!
Of you O woods and fields! of you strong mountains of
    my land!
Of you O prairies! of you gray rocks!
O morning red! O clouds! O rain and snows!
O day and night, passage to you!

O sun and moon and all you stars! Sirius and Jupiter!
Passage to you!

Passage, immediate passage! the blood burns in my veins!
Away O soul! hoist instantly the anchor!
Cut the hawsers—haul out—shake out every sail!
Have we not stood here like trees in the ground long
    enough?
Have we not grovel'd here long enough, eating and
    drinking like mere brutes?
Have we not darken'd and dazed ourselves with books
    long enough?

Sail forth—steer for the deep waters only,
Reckless O soul, exploring, I with thee, and thou with me,
For we are bound where mariner has not yet dared to go,
And we will risk the ship, ourselves and all.

O my brave soul!
O farther farther sail!
O daring joy, but safe! are they not all the seas of God?
O farther, farther, farther sail!

*

PRAYER OF COLUMBUS.

A batter'd, wreck'd old man,
Thrown on this savage shore, far, far from home,
Pent by the sea and dark rebellious brows, twelve dreary
    months,
Sore, stiff with many toils, sicken'd and nigh to death,
I take my way along the island's edge,
Venting a heavy heart.

I am too full of woe!
Haply I may not live another day;
I cannot rest O God, I cannot eat or drink or sleep,
Till I put forth myself, my prayer, once more to Thee,
Breathe, bathe myself once more in Thee, commune with
    Thee,
Report myself once more to Thee.

Thou knowest my years entire, my life,
My long and crowded life of active work, not adoration
    merely;
Thou knowest the prayers and vigils of my youth,
Thou knowest my manhood's solemn and visionary med-
    itations,
Thou knowest how before I commenced I devoted all to
    come to Thee,
Thou knowest I have in age ratified all those vows and
    strictly kept them,
Thou knowest I have not once lost nor faith nor ecstasy
    in Thee,
In shackles, prison'd, in disgrace, repining not,
Accepting all from Thee, as duly come from Thee.

All my emprises have been fill'd with Thee,
My speculations, plans, begun and carried on in thoughts
    of Thee,
Sailing the deep or journeying the land for Thee;
Intentions, purports, aspirations mine, leaving results to
    Thee.

O I am sure they really came from Thee,
The urge, the ardor, the unconquerable will,

The potent, felt, interior command, stronger than words,
A message from the Heavens whispering to me even in
    sleep,
These sped me on.

By me and these the work so far accomplish'd,
By me earth's elder cloy'd and stifled lands uncloy'd,
    unloos'd,
By me the hemispheres rounded and tied, the unknown
    to the known.

The end I know not, it is all in Thee,
Or small or great I know not—haply what broad fields,
    what lands,
Haply the brutish measureless human undergrowth I
    know,
Transplanted there may rise to stature, knowledge wor-
    thy Thee,
Haply the swords I know may there indeed be turn'd to
    reaping-tools,
Haply the lifeless cross I know, Europe's dead cross, may
    bud and blossom there.

One effort more, my altar this bleak sand;
That Thou O God my life hast lighted,
With ray of light, steady, ineffable, vouchsafed of Thee,
Light rare untellable, lighting the very light,
Beyond all signs, descriptions, languages;
For that O God, be it my latest word, here on my knees,
Old, poor, and paralyzed, I thank Thee.

My terminus near,
The clouds already closing in upon me,
The voyage balk'd, the course disputed, lost,
I yield my ships to Thee.

My hands, my limbs grow nerveless,
My brain feels rack'd, bewilder'd,
Let the old timbers part, I will not part,
I will cling fast to Thee, O God, though the waves buffet
    me,
Thee, Thee at least I know.

Is it the prophet's thought I speak, or am I raving?
What do I know of life? what of myself?
I know not even my own work past or present,
Dim ever-shifting guesses of it spread before me,
Of newer better worlds, their mighty parturition,
Mocking, perplexing me.

And these things I see suddenly, what mean they?
As if some miracle, some hand divine unseal'd my eyes,
Shadowy vast shapes smile through the air and sky,
And on the distant waves sail countless ships,
And anthems in new tongues I hear saluting me.

THE SLEEPERS.

1

I wander all night in my vision,
Stepping with light feet, swiftly and noiselessly stepping
    and stopping,
Bending with open eyes over the shut eyes of sleepers,
Wandering and confused, lost to myself, ill-assorted, con-
    tradictory,
Pausing, gazing, bending, and stopping.

How solemn they look there, stretch'd and still,
How quiet they breathe, the little children in their cradles.

The wretched features of ennuyés, the white features of
    corpses, the livid faces of drunkards, the sick-gray
    faces of onanists,
The gash'd bodies on battle-fields, the insane in their
    strong-door'd rooms, the sacred idiots, the new-born
    emerging from gates, and the dying emerging from
    gates,
The night pervades them and infolds them.

The married couple sleep calmly in their bed, he with his
    palm on the hip of the wife, and she with her palm on
    the hip of the husband,
The sisters sleep lovingly side by side in their bed,
The men sleep lovingly side by side in theirs,

And the mother sleeps with her little child carefully
   wrapt.

The blind sleep, and the deaf and dumb sleep,
The prisoner sleeps well in the prison, the runaway son
   sleeps,
The murderer that is to be hung next day, how does he
   sleep?
And the murder'd person, how does he sleep?

The female that loves unrequited sleeps,
And the male that loves unrequited sleeps,
The head of the money-maker that plotted all day sleeps,
And the enraged and treacherous dispositions, all, all
   sleep.

I stand in the dark with drooping eyes by the worst-suf-
   fering and the most restless,
I pass my hands soothingly to and fro a few inches from
   them,
The restless sink in their beds, they fitfully sleep.

Now I pierce the darkness, new beings appear,
The earth recedes from me into the night,
I saw that it was beautiful, and I see that what is not the
   earth is beautiful.

I go from bedside to bedside, I sleep close with the other
   sleepers each in turn,

I dream in my dream all the dreams of the other dream-
    ers,
And I become the other dreamers.

I am a dance—play up there! the fit is whirling me fast!

I am the ever-laughing—it is new moon and twilight,
I see the hiding of douceurs, I see nimble ghosts
    whichever way I look,
Cache and cache again deep in the ground and sea, and
    where it is neither ground nor sea.

Well do they do their jobs those journeymen divine,
Only from me can they hide nothing, and would not if
    they could,
I reckon I am their boss and they make me a pet besides,
And surround me and lead me and run ahead when I
    walk,
To lift their cunning covers to signify me with stretch'd
    arms, and resume the way;
Onward we move, a gay gang of blackguards! with mirth-
    shouting music and wild-flapping pennants of joy!

I am the actor, the actress, the voter, the politician,
The emigrant and the exile, the criminal that stood in the
    box,
He who has been famous and he who shall be famous
    after to-day,
The stammerer, the well-form'd person, the wasted or
    feeble person.

I am she who adorn'd herself and folded her hair expec-
    tantly,
My truant lover has come, and it is dark.

Double yourself and receive me darkness,
Receive me and my lover too, he will not let me go with-
    out him.

I roll myself upon you as upon a bed, I resign myself to
    the dusk.

He whom I call answers me and takes the place of my
    lover,
He rises with me silently from the bed.

Darkness, you are gentler than my lover, his flesh was
    sweaty and panting,
I feel the hot moisture yet that he left me.

My hands are spread forth, I pass them in all directions,
I would sound up the shadowy shore to which you are
    journeying.

Be careful darkness! already what was it touch'd me?
I thought my lover had gone, else darkness and he are
    one,
I hear the heart-beat, I follow, I fade away.

2

I descend my western course, my sinews are flaccid,
Perfume and youth course through me and I am their
wake.

It is my face yellow and wrinkled instead of the old
woman's,
I sit low in a straw-bottom chair and carefully darn my
grandson's stockings.

It is I too, the sleepless widow looking out on the winter
midnight,
I see the sparkles of starshine on the icy and pallid earth.

A shroud I see and I am the shroud, I wrap a body and lie
in the coffin,
It is dark here under ground, it is not evil or pain here, it
is blank here, for reasons.

(It seems to me that every thing in the light and air ought
to be happy,
Whoever is not in his coffin and the dark grave let him
know he has enough.)

3

I see a beautiful gigantic swimmer swimming naked
through the eddies of the sea,
His brown hair lies close and even to his head, he strikes
out with courageous arms, he urges himself with his
legs,

I see his white body, I see his undaunted eyes,
I hate the swift-running eddies that would dash him
    head-foremost on the rocks.

What are you doing you ruffianly red-trickled waves?
Will you kill the courageous giant? will you kill him in the
    prime of his middle age?

Steady and long he struggles,
He is baffled, bang'd, bruis'd, he holds out while his
    strength holds out,
The slapping eddies are spotted with his blood, they bear
    him away, they roll him, swing him, turn him,
His beautiful body is borne in the circling eddies, it is con-
    tinually bruis'd on rocks,
Swiftly and out of sight is borne the brave corpse.

4

I turn but do not extricate myself,
Confused, a past-reading, another, but with darkness yet.

The beach is cut by the razory ice-wind, the wreck-guns
    sound,
The tempest lulls, the moon comes floundering through
    the drifts.

I look where the ship helplessly heads end on, I hear the
    burst as she strikes, I hear the howls of dismay, they
    grow fainter and fainter.

I cannot aid with my wringing fingers,
I can but rush to the surf and let it drench me and freeze
    upon me.

I search with the crowd, not one of the company is wash'd
    to us alive,
In the morning I help pick up the dead and lay them in
    rows in a barn.

5

Now of the older war-days, the defeat at Brooklyn,
Washington stands inside the lines, he stands on the
    intrench'd hills amid a crowd of officers,
His face is cold and damp, he cannot repress the weeping
    drops,
He lifts the glass perpetually to his eyes, the color is
    blanch'd from his cheeks,
He sees the slaughter of the southern braves confided to
    him by their parents.

The same at last and at last when peace is declared,
He stands in the room of the old tavern, the well-belov'd
    soldiers all pass through,
The officers speechless and slow draw near in their turns,
The chief encircles their necks with his arm and kisses
    them on the cheek,
He kisses lightly the wet cheeks one after another, he
    shakes hands and bids good-by to the army.

6

Now what my mother told me one day as we sat at dinner
    together,
Of when she was a nearly grown girl living home with
    her parents on the old homestead.

A red squaw came one breakfast-time to the old home-
    stead,
On her back she carried a bundle of rushes for rush-bot-
    toming chairs,
Her hair, straight, shiny, coarse, black, profuse, half-
    envelop'd her face,
Her step was free and elastic, and her voice sounded
    exquisitely as she spoke.

My mother look'd in delight and amazement at the
    stranger,
She look'd at the freshness of her tall-borne face and full
    and pliant limbs,
The more she look'd upon her she loved her,
Never before had she seen such wonderful beauty and
    purity,
She made her sit on a bench by the jamb of the fireplace,
    she cook'd food for her,
She had no work to give her, but she gave her remem-
    brance and fondness.

The red squaw staid all the forenoon, and toward the
    middle of the afternoon she went away,
O my mother was loth to have her go away,

All the week she thought of her, she watch'd for her many
    a month,
She remember'd her many a winter and many a summer,
But the red squaw never came nor was heard of there
    again.

7

A show of the summer softness—a contact of something
    unseen—an amour of the light and air,
I am jealous and overwhelm'd with friendliness,
And will go gallivant with the light and air myself.

O love and summer, you are in the dreams and in me,
Autumn and winter are in the dreams, the farmer goes
    with his thrift,
The droves and crops increase, the barns are well-fill'd.

Elements merge in the night, ships make tacks in the
    dreams,
The sailor sails, the exile returns home,
The fugitive returns unharm'd, the immigrant is back
    beyond months and years,
The poor Irishman lives in the simple house of his child-
    hood with the well-known neighbors and faces,
They warmly welcome him, he is barefoot again, he for-
    gets he is well off,
The Dutchman voyages home, and the Scotchman and
    Welshman voyage home, and the native of the
    Mediterranean voyages home,

To every port of England, France, Spain, enter well-fill'd
    ships,
The Swiss foots it toward his hills, the Prussian goes his
    way, the Hungarian his way, and the Pole his way,
The Swede returns, and the Dane and Norwegian return.

The homeward bound and the outward bound,
The beautiful lost swimmer, the ennuyé, the onanist, the
    female that loves unrequited, the money-maker,
The actor and actress, those through with their parts and
    those waiting to commence,
The affectionate boy, the husband and wife, the voter, the
    nominee that is chosen and the nominee that has
    fail'd,
The great already known and the great any time after to-
    day,
The stammerer, the sick, the perfect-form'd, the homely,
The criminal that stood in the box, the judge that sat and
    sentenced him, the fluent lawyers, the jury, the audi-
    ence,
The laugher and weeper, the dancer, the midnight
    widow, the red squaw,
The consumptive, the erysipalite, the idiot, he that is
    wrong'd,
The antipodes, and every one between this and them in
    the dark,
I swear they are averaged now—one is no better than the
    other,
The night and sleep have liken'd them and restored them.

I swear they are all beautiful,
Every one that sleeps is beautiful, every thing in the dim
    light is beautiful,
The wildest and bloodiest is over, and all is peace.

Peace is always beautiful,
The myth of heaven indicates peace and night.

The myth of heaven indicates the soul,
The soul is always beautiful, it appears more or it appears
    less, it comes or it lags behind,
It comes from its embower'd garden and looks pleasantly
    on itself and encloses the world,
Perfect and clean the genitals previously jetting, and per-
    fect and clean the womb cohering,
The head well-grown proportion'd and plumb, and the
    bowels and joints proportion'd and plumb.

The soul is always beautiful,
The universe is duly in order, every thing is in its place,
What has arrived is in its place and what waits shall be in
    its place,
The twisted skull waits, the watery or rotten blood waits,
The child of the glutton or venerealee waits long, and the
    child of the drunkard waits long, and the drunkard
    himself waits long,
The sleepers that lived and died wait, the far advanced
    are to go on in their turns, and the far behind are to
    come on in their turns,
The diverse shall be no less diverse, but they shall flow
    and unite—they unite now.

8

The sleepers are very beautiful as they lie unclothed,
They flow hand in hand over the whole earth from east
    to west as they lie unclothed,
The Asiatic and African are hand in hand, the European
    and American are hand in hand,
Learn'd and unlearn'd are hand in hand, and male and
    female are hand in hand,
The bare arm of the girl crosses the bare breast of her
    lover, they press close without lust, his lips press her
    neck,
The father holds his grown or ungrown son in his arms
    with measureless love, and the son holds the father in
    his arms with measureless love,
The white hair of the mother shines on the white wrist of
    the daughter,
The breath of the boy goes with the breath of the man,
    friend is inarm'd by friend,
The scholar kisses the teacher and the teacher kisses the
    scholar, the wrong'd is made right,
The call of the slave is one with the master's call, and the
    master salutes the slave,
The felon steps forth from the prison, the insane becomes
    sane, the suffering of sick persons is reliev'd,
The sweatings and fevers stop, the throat that was
    unsound is sound, the lungs of the consumptive are
    resumed, the poor distress'd head is free,
The joints of the rheumatic move as smoothly as ever, and
    smoother than ever,
Stiflings and passages open, the paralyzed become sup-
    ple,

The swell'd and convuls'd and congested awake to them-
  selves in condition,
They pass the invigoration of the night and the chemistry
  of the night, and awake.

I too pass from the night,
I stay a while away O night, but I return to you again and
  love you.

Why should I be afraid to trust myself to you?
I am not afraid, I have been well brought forward by you,
I love the rich running day, but I do not desert her in
  whom I lay so long,
I know not how I came of you and I know not where I go
  with you, but I know I came well and shall go well.

I will stop only a time with the night, and rise betimes,
I will duly pass the day O my mother, and duly return to
  you.

❇

TRANSPOSITIONS.

Let the reformers descend from the stands where they are
  forever bawling—let an idiot or insane person appear
  on each of the stands;

Let judges and criminals be transposed—let the prison-
      keepers be put in prison—let those that were prison-
      ers take the keys;
Let them that distrust birth and death lead the rest.

*

TO THINK OF TIME.

1

To think of time—of all that retrospection,
To think of to-day, and the ages continued henceforward.

Have you guess'd you yourself would not continue?
Have you dreaded these earth-beetles?
Have you fear'd the future would be nothing to you?

Is to-day nothing? is the beginningless past nothing?
If the future is nothing they are just as surely nothing.

To think that the sun rose in the east—that men and
      women were flexible, real, alive—that every thing
      was alive,
To think that you and I did not see, feel, think, nor bear
      our part,
To think that we are now here and bear our part.

2

Not a day passes, not a minute or second without an
    accouchement,
Not a day passes, not a minute or second without a
    corpse.

The dull nights go over and the dull days also,
The soreness of lying so much in bed goes over,
The physician after long putting off gives the silent and
    terrible look for an answer,
The children come hurried and weeping, and the brothers
    and sisters are sent for,
Medicines stand unused on the shelf, (the camphor-smell
    has long pervaded the rooms,)
The faithful hand of the living does not desert the hand
    of the dying,
The twitching lips press lightly on the forehead of the
    dying,
The breath ceases and the pulse of the heart ceases,
The corpse stretches on the bed and the living look upon
    it,
It is palpable as the living are palpable.

The living look upon the corpse with their eyesight,
But without eyesight lingers a different living and looks
    curiously on the corpse.

3

To think the thought of death merged in the thought of
materials,
To think of all these wonders of city and country, and oth-
ers taking great interest in them, and we taking no
interest in them.

To think how eager we are in building our houses,
To think others shall be just as eager, and we quite indif-
ferent.

(I see one building the house that serves him a few years,
or seventy or eighty years at most,
I see one building the house that serves him longer than
that.)

Slow-moving and black lines creep over the whole
earth—they never cease—they are the burial lines,
He that was President was buried, and he that is now
President shall surely be buried.

4

A reminiscence of the vulgar fate,
A frequent sample of the life and death of workmen,
Each after his kind.

Cold dash of waves at the ferry-wharf, posh and ice in the
river, half-frozen mud in the streets,
A gray discouraged sky overhead, the short last daylight
of December,

A hearse and stages, the funeral of an old Broadway
    stage-driver, the cortege mostly drivers.

Steady the trot to the cemetery, duly rattles the death-bell,
The gate is pass'd, the new-dug grave is halted at, the liv-
    ing alight, the hearse uncloses,
The coffin is pass'd out, lower'd and settled, the whip is
    laid on the coffin, the earth is swiftly shovel'd in,
The mound above is flatted with the spades—silence,
A minute—no one moves or speaks—it is done,
He is decently put away—is there any thing more?

He was a good fellow, free-mouth'd, quick-temper'd, not
    bad-looking,
Ready with life or death for a friend, fond of women,
    gambled, ate hearty, drank hearty,
Had known what it was to be flush, grew low-spirited
    toward the last, sicken'd, was help'd by a contribu-
    tion,
Died, aged forty-one years—and that was his funeral.

Thumb extended, finger uplifted, apron, cape, gloves,
    strap, wet-weather clothes, whip carefully chosen,
Boss, spotter, starter, hostler, somebody loafing on you,
    you loafing on somebody, headway, man before and
    man behind,
Good day's work, bad day's work, pet stock, mean stock,
    first out, last out, turning-in at night,
To think that these are so much and so nigh to other dri-
    vers, and he there takes no interest in them.

5

The markets, the government, the working-man's wages,
    to think what account they are through our nights
    and days,
To think that other working-men will make just as great
    account of them, yet we make little or no account.

The vulgar and the refined, what you call sin and what
    you call goodness, to think how wide a difference,
To think the difference will still continue to others, yet we
    lie beyond the difference.

To think how much pleasure there is,
Do you enjoy yourself in the city? or engaged in business?
    or planning a nomination and election? or with your
    wife and family?
Or with your mother and sisters? or in womanly house-
    work? or the beautiful maternal cares?
These also flow onward to others, you and I flow onward,
But in due time you and I shall take less interest in them.

Your farm, profits, crops—to think how engross'd you
    are,
To think there will still be farms, profits, crops, yet for you
    of what avail?

6

What will be will be well, for what is is well,
To take interest is well, and not to take interest shall be
    well.

The domestic joys, the daily housework or business, the
    building of houses are not phantasms, they have
    weight, form, location,
Farms, profits, crops, markets, wages, government, are
    none of them phantasms,
The difference between sin and goodness is no delusion,
The earth is not an echo, man and his life and all the
    things of his life are well-consider'd.

You are not thrown to the winds, you gather certainly and
    safely around yourself,
Yourself! yourself! yourself, for ever and ever!

7

It is not to diffuse you that you were born of your mother
    and father, it is to identify you,
It is not that you should be undecided, but that you
    should be decided,
Something long preparing and formless is arrived and
    form'd in you,
You are henceforth secure, whatever comes or goes.

The threads that were spun are gather'd, the weft crosses
    the warp, the pattern is systematic.

The preparations have every one been justified,
The orchestra have sufficiently tuned their instruments,
    the baton has given the signal.

The guest that was coming, he waited long, he is now
    housed,

He is one of those who are beautiful and happy, he is one
of those that to look upon and be with is enough.

The law of the past cannot be eluded,
The law of the present and future cannot be eluded,
The law of the living cannot be eluded, it is eternal,
The law of promotion and transformation cannot be
eluded,
The law of heroes and good-doers cannot be eluded,
The law of drunkards, informers, mean persons, not one
iota thereof can be eluded.

8

Slow moving and black lines go ceaselessly over the earth,
Northerner goes carried and Southerner goes carried, and
they on the Atlantic side and they on the Pacific,
And they between, and all through the Mississippi coun-
try, and all over the earth.

The great masters and kosmos are well as they go, the
heroes and good-doers are well,
The known leaders and inventors and the rich owners
and pious and distinguish'd may be well,
But there is more account than that, there is strict account
of all.

The interminable hordes of the ignorant and wicked are
not nothing,
The barbarians of Africa and Asia are not nothing,
The perpetual successions of shallow people are not noth-
ing as they go.

Of and in all these things,
I have dream'd that we are not to be changed so much,
    nor the law of us changed,
I have dream'd that heroes and good-doers shall be under
    the present and past law,
And that murderers, drunkards, liars, shall be under the
    present and past law,
For I have dream'd that the law they are under now is
    enough.

And I have dream'd that the purpose and essence of the
    known life, the transient,
Is to form and decide identity for the unknown life, the
    permanent.

If all came but to ashes of dung,
If maggots and rats ended us, then Alarum! for we are
    betray'd,
Then indeed suspicion of death.

Do you suspect death? if I were to suspect death I should
    die now,
Do you think I could walk pleasantly and well-suited
    toward annihilation?

Pleasantly and well-suited I walk,
Whither I walk I cannot define, but I know it is good,
The whole universe indicates that it is good,
The past and the present indicate that it is good.

How beautiful and perfect are the animals!
How perfect the earth, and the minutest thing upon it!

What is called good is perfect, and what is called bad is
    just as perfect,
The vegetables and minerals are all perfect, and the
    imponderable fluids perfect;
Slowly and surely they have pass'd on to this, and slowly
    and surely they yet pass on.

9

I swear I think now that every thing without exception
    has an eternal soul!
The trees have, rooted in the ground! the weeds of the sea
    have! the animals!

I swear I think there is nothing but immortality!
That the exquisite scheme is for it, and the nebulous float
    is for it, and the cohering is for it!
And all preparation is for it—and identity is for it—and
    life and materials are altogether for it!

WHISPERS OF HEAVENLY DEATH.

DAREST THOU NOW O SOUL.

Darest thou now O soul,
Walk out with me toward the unknown region,
Where neither ground is for the feet nor any path to fol-
low?

No map there, nor guide,
Nor voice sounding, nor touch of human hand,
Nor face with blooming flesh, nor lips, nor eyes, are in
that land.

I know it not O soul,
Nor dost thou, all is a blank before us,
All waits undream'd of in that region, that inaccessible
land.

Till when the ties loosen,
All but the ties eternal, Time and Space,
Nor darkness, gravitation, sense, nor any bounds bound-
ing us.

Then we burst forth, we float,
In Time and Space O soul, prepared for them,
Equal, equipt at last, (O joy! O fruit of all!) them to fulfil
      O soul.

WHISPERS OF HEAVENLY DEATH.

Whispers of heavenly death murmur'd I hear,
Labial gossip of night, sibilant chorals,
Footsteps gently ascending, mystical breezes wafted soft
      and low,
Ripples of unseen rivers, tides of a current flowing, for-
      ever flowing,
(Or is it the plashing of tears? the measureless waters of
      human tears?)

I see, just see skyward, great cloud masses,
Mournfully slowly they roll, silently swelling and mixing,
With at times a half-dimm'd sadden'd far-off star,
Appearing and disappearing.

(Some parturition rather, some solemn immortal birth;
On the frontiers to eyes impenetrable,
Some soul is passing over.)

CHANTING THE SQUARE DEIFIC.

1

Chanting the square deific, out of the One advancing, out
of the sides,
Out of the old and new, out of the square entirely divine,
Solid, four-sided, (all the sides needed,) from this side
Jehovah am I,
Old Brahm I, and I Saturnius am;
Not Time affects me—I am Time, old, modern as any,
Unpersuadable, relentless, executing righteous judg-
ments,
As the Earth, the Father, the brown old Kronos, with laws,
Aged beyond computation, yet ever new, ever with those
mighty laws rolling,
Relentless I forgive no man—whoever sins dies—I will
have that man's life;
Therefore let none expect mercy—have the seasons, grav-
itation, the appointed days, mercy? no more have I,
But as the seasons and gravitation, and as all the
appointed days that forgive not,
I dispense from this side judgments inexorable without
the least remorse.

2

Consolator most mild, the promis'd one advancing,
With gentle hand extended, the mightier God am I,
Foretold by prophets and poets in their most rapt prophe-
cies and poems,

From this side, lo! the Lord Christ gazes—lo! Hermes I—
lo! mine is Hercules' face,
All sorrow, labor, suffering, I, tallying it, absorb in myself,
Many times have I been rejected, taunted, put in prison,
and crucified, and many times shall be again,
All the world have I given up for my dear brothers' and
sisters' sake, for the soul's sake,
Wending my way through the homes of men, rich or
poor, with the kiss of affection,
For I am affection, I am the cheer-bringing God, with
hope and all-enclosing charity,
With indulgent words as to children, with fresh and sane
words, mine only,
Young and strong I pass knowing well I am destin'd
myself to an early death;
But my charity has no death—my wisdom dies not, nei-
ther early nor late,
And my sweet love bequeath'd here and elsewhere never
dies.

3

Aloof, dissatisfied, plotting revolt,
Comrade of criminals, brother of slaves,
Crafty, despised, a drudge, ignorant,
With sudra face and worn brow, black, but in the depths
of my heart, proud as any,
Lifted now and always against whoever scorning
assumes to rule me,
Morose, full of guile, full of reminiscences, brooding, with
many wiles,

(Though it was thought I was baffled and dispel'd, and
        my wiles done, but that will never be,)
Defiant, I, Satan, still live, still utter words, in new lands
        duly appearing, (and old ones also,)
Permanent here from my side, warlike, equal with any,
        real as any,
Nor time nor change shall ever change me or my words.

4

Santa Spirita, breather, life,
Beyond the light, lighter than light,
Beyond the flames of hell, joyous, leaping easily above
        hell,
Beyond Paradise, perfumed solely with mine own per-
        fume,
Including all life on earth, touching, including God,
        including Saviour and Satan,
Ethereal, pervading all, (for without me what were all?
        what were God?)
Essence of forms, life of the real identities, permanent,
        positive, (namely the unseen,)
Life of the great round world, the sun and stars, and of
        man, I, the general soul,
Here the square finishing, the solid, I the most solid,
Breathe my breath also through these songs.

OF HIM I LOVE DAY AND NIGHT.

Of him I love day and night I dream'd I heard he was
   dead,
And I dream'd I went where they had buried him I love,
   but he was not in that place,
And I dream'd I wander'd searching among burial-places
   to find him,
And I found that every place was a burial-place;
The houses full of life were equally full of death, (this
   house is now,)
The streets, the shipping, the places of amusement, the
   Chicago, Boston, Philadelphia, the Mannahatta, were
   as full of the dead as of the living,
And fuller, O vastly fuller of the dead than of the living;
And what I dream'd I will henceforth tell to every person
   and age,
And I stand henceforth bound to what I dream'd,
And now I am willing to disregard burial-places and dis-
   pense with them,
And if the memorials of the dead were put up indiffer-
   ently everywhere, even in the room where I eat or
   sleep, I should be satisfied,
And if the corpse of any one I love, or if my own corpse,
   be duly render'd to powder and pour'd in the sea, I
   shall be satisfied,
Or if it be distributed to the winds I shall be satisfied.

YET, YET, YE DOWNCAST HOURS.

Yet, yet, ye downcast hours, I know ye also,
Weights of lead, how ye clog and cling at my ankles,
Earth to a chamber of mourning turns—I hear the
    o'erweening, mocking voice,
Matter is conqueror—matter, triumphant only, continues
    onward.

Despairing cries float ceaselessly toward me,
The call of my nearest lover, putting forth, alarm'd, uncer-
    tain,
The sea I am quickly to sail, come tell me,
Come tell me where I am speeding, tell me my destination.

I understand your anguish, but I cannot help you,
I approach, hear, behold, the sad mouth, the look out of
    the eyes, your mute inquiry,
Whither I go from the bed I recline on, come tell me;
Old age, alarm'd, uncertain—a young woman's voice,
    appealing to me for comfort;
A young man's voice, *Shall I not escape?*

AS IF A PHANTOM CARESS'D ME.

As if a phantom caress'd me,
I thought I was not alone walking here by the shore;
But the one I thought was with me as now I walk by the
    shore, the one I loved that caress'd me,

As I lean and look through the glimmering light, that one
has utterly disappear'd,
And those appear that are hateful to me and mock me.

ASSURANCES.

I need no assurances, I am a man who is pre-occupied of
his own soul;
I do not doubt that from under the feet and beside the
hands and face I am cognizant of, are now looking
faces I am not cognizant of, calm and actual faces,
I do not doubt but the majesty and beauty of the world
are latent in any iota of the world,
I do not doubt I am limitless, and that the universes are
limitless, in vain I try to think how limitless,
I do not doubt that the orbs and the systems of orbs play
their swift sports through the air on purpose, and that
I shall one day be eligible to do as much as they, and
more than they,
I do not doubt that temporary affairs keep on and on mil-
lions of years,
I do not doubt interiors have their interiors, and exteriors
have their exteriors, and that the eyesight has another
eyesight, and the hearing another hearing, and the
voice another voice,
I do not doubt that the passionately-wept deaths of young
men are provided for, and that the deaths of young
women and the deaths of little children are provided
for,
(Did you think Life was so well provided for, and Death,
the purport of all Life, is not well provided for?)

I do not doubt that wrecks at sea, no matter what the hor-
    rors of them, no matter whose wife, child, husband,
    father, lover, has gone down, are provided for, to the
    minutest points,
I do not doubt that whatever can possibly happen any-
    where at any time, is provided for in the inherences of
    things,
I do not think Life provides for all and for Time and
    Space, but I believe Heavenly Death provides for all.

QUICKSAND YEARS.

Quicksand years that whirl me I know not whither,
Your schemes, politics, fail, lines give way, substances
    mock and elude me,
Only the theme I sing, the great and strong possess'd soul,
    eludes not,
One's-self must never give way—that is the final sub-
    stance— that out of all is sure,
Out of politics, triumphs, battles, life, what at last finally
    remains?
When shows break up what but One's-Self is sure?

THAT MUSIC ALWAYS ROUND ME.

That music always round me, unceasing, unbeginning,
    yet long untaught I did not hear,
But now the chorus I hear and am elated,
A tenor, strong, ascending with power and health, with
    glad notes of daybreak I hear,

A soprano at intervals sailing buoyantly over the tops of
    immense waves,
A transparent base shuddering lusciously under and
    through the universe,
The triumphant tutti, the funeral wailings with sweet
    flutes and violins, all these I fill myself with,
I hear not the volumes of sound merely, I am moved by
    the exquisite meanings,
I listen to the different voices winding in and out, striving,
    contending with fiery vehemence to excel each other
    in emotion;
I do not think the performers know themselves—but now
    I think I begin to know them.

WHAT SHIP PUZZLED AT SEA.

What ship puzzled at sea, cons for the true reckoning?
Or coming in, to avoid the bars and follow the channel a
    perfect pilot needs?
Here, sailor! here, ship! take aboard the most perfect pilot,
Whom, in a little boat, putting off and rowing, I hailing
    you offer.

A NOISELESS PATIENT SPIDER.

A noiseless patient spider,
I mark'd where on a little promontory it stood isolated,
Mark'd how to explore the vacant vast surrounding,
It launch'd forth filament, filament, filament, out of itself,
Ever unreeling them, ever tirelessly speeding them.

And you O my soul where you stand,
Surrounded, detached, in measureless oceans of space,
Ceaselessly musing, venturing, throwing, seeking the
    spheres to connect them,
Till the bridge you will need be form'd, till the ductile
    anchor hold,
Till the gossamer thread you fling catch somewhere, O
    my soul.

O LIVING ALWAYS, ALWAYS DYING.

O living always, always dying!
O the burials of me past and present,
O me while I stride ahead, material, visible, imperious as
    ever;
O me, what I was for years, now dead, (I lament not, I am
    content;)
O to disengage myself from those corpses of me, which I
    turn and look at where I cast them,
To pass on, (O living! always living!) and leave the
    corpses behind.

TO ONE SHORTLY TO DIE.

From all the rest I single out you, having a message for
    you,
You are to die—let others tell you what they please, I can-
    not prevaricate,
I am exact and merciless, but I love you—there is no
    escape for you.

Softly I lay my right hand upon you, you just feel it,
I do not argue, I bend my head close and half envelop it,
I sit quietly by, I remain faithful,
I am more than nurse, more than parent or neighbor,
I absolve you from all except yourself spiritual bodily,
    that is eternal, you yourself will surely escape,
The corpse you leave will be but excrementitious.

The sun bursts through in unlooked-for directions,
Strong thoughts fill you and confidence, you smile,
You forget you are sick, as I forget you are sick,
You do not see the medicines, you do not mind the weep-
    ing friends, I am with you,
I exclude others from you, there is nothing to be commis-
    erated,
I do not commiserate, I congratulate you.

NIGHT ON THE PRAIRIES.

Night on the prairies,
The supper is over, the fire on the ground burns low,
The wearied emigrants sleep, wrapt in their blankets;
I walk by myself—I stand and look at the stars, which I
    think now I never realized before.

Now I absorb immortality and peace,
I admire death and test propositions.

How plenteous! how spiritual! how resumé!
The same old man and soul—the same old aspirations,
    and the same content.

I was thinking the day most splendid till I saw what the
    not-day exhibited,
I was thinking this globe enough till there sprang out so
    noiseless around me myriads of other globes.

Now while the great thoughts of space and eternity fill me
    I will measure myself by them,
And now touch'd with the lives of other globes arrived
    as far along as those of the earth,
Or waiting to arrive, or pass'd on farther than those of the
    earth,
I henceforth no more ignore them than I ignore my own
    life,
Or the lives of the earth arrived as far as mine, or waiting
    to arrive.

O I see now that life cannot exhibit all to me, as the day
    cannot,
I see that I am to wait for what will be exhibited by death.

THOUGHT.

As I sit with others at a great feast, suddenly while the
    music is playing,
To my mind, (whence it comes I know not,) spectral in
    mist of a wreck at sea,
Of certain ships, how they sail from port with flying
    streamers and wafted kisses, and that is the last of
    them,
Of the solemn and murky mystery about the fate of the
    President,

Of the flower of the marine science of fifty generations
    founder'd off the Northeast coast and going down—
    of the steamship Arctic going down,
Of the veil'd tableau—women gather'd together on deck,
    pale, heroic, waiting the moment that draws so
    close—O the moment!
A huge sob—a few bubbles—the white foam spirting
    up—and then the women gone,
Sinking there while the passionless wet flows on—and I
    now pondering, Are those women indeed gone?
Are souls drown'd and destroy'd so?
Is only matter triumphant?

THE LAST INVOCATION.

At the last, tenderly,
From the walls of the powerful fortress'd house,
From the clasp of the knitted locks, from the keep of the
    well-closed doors,
Let me be wafted.

Let me glide noiselessly forth;
With the key of softness unlock the locks—with a whis-
    per,
Set ope the doors O soul.

Tenderly—be not impatient,
(Strong is your hold O mortal flesh,
Strong is your hold O love.)

AS I WATCH'D THE PLOUGHMAN PLOUGHING.

As I watch'd the ploughman ploughing,
Or the sower sowing in the fields, or the harvester har-
    vesting,
I saw there too, O life and death, your analogies;
(Life, life is the tillage, and Death is the harvest accord-
    ing.)

PENSIVE AND FALTERING.

Pensive and faltering,
The words *the Dead* I write,
For living are the Dead,
(Haply the only living, only real,
And I the apparition, I the spectre.)

*

THOU MOTHER WITH
THY EQUAL BROOD.

1

Thou Mother with thy equal brood,
Thou varied chain of different States, yet one identity
    only,
A special song before I go I'd sing o'er all the rest,
For thee, the future.

I'd sow a seed for thee of endless Nationality,
I'd fashion thy ensemble including body and soul,
I'd show away ahead thy real Union, and how it may be
 accomplish'd.

The paths to the house I seek to make,
But leave to those to come the house itself.

Belief I sing, and preparation;
As Life and Nature are not great with reference to the pre-
 sent only,
But greater still from what is yet to come,
Out of that formula for thee I sing.

2

As a strong bird on pinions free,
Joyous, the amplest spaces heavenward cleaving,
Such be the thought I'd think of thee America,
Such be the recitative I'd bring for thee.

The conceits of the poets of other lands I'd bring thee not,
Nor the compliments that have served their turn so long,
Nor rhyme, nor the classics, nor perfume of foreign court
 or indoor library;
But an odor I'd bring as from forests of pine in Maine, or
 breath of an Illinois prairie,
With open airs of Virginia or Georgia or Tennessee, or
 from Texas uplands, or Florida's glades,
Or the Saguenay's black stream, or the wide blue spread
 of Huron,

With presentment of Yellowstone's scenes, or Yosemite,
And murmuring under, pervading all, I'd bring the
rustling sea-sound,
That endlessly sounds from the two Great Seas of the
world.

And for thy subtler sense subtler refrains dread Mother,
Preludes of intellect tallying these and thee, mind-formu-
las fitted for thee, real and sane and large as these and
thee,
Thou! mounting higher, diving deeper than we knew,
thou transcendental Union!
By thee fact to be justified, blended with thought,
Thought of man justified, blended with God,
Through thy idea, lo, the immortal reality!
Through thy reality, lo, the immortal idea!

3

Brain of the New World, what a task is thine,
To formulate the Modern—out of the peerless grandeur
of the modern,
Out of thyself, comprising science, to recast poems,
churches, art,
(Recast, may-be discard them, end them—may-be their
work is done, who knows?)
By vision, hand, conception, on the background of the
mighty past, the dead,
To limn with absolute faith the mighty living present.

And yet thou living present brain, heir of the dead, the
    Old World brain,
Thou that lay folded like an unborn babe within its folds
    so long,
Thou carefully prepared by it so long—haply thou but
    unfoldest it, only maturest it,
It to eventuate in thee—the essence of the by-gone time
    contain'd in thee,
Its poems, churches, arts, unwitting to themselves, des-
    tined with reference to thee;
Thou but the apples, long, long, long a-growing,
The fruit of all the Old ripening to-day in thee.

4

Sail, sail thy best, ship of Democracy,
Of value is thy freight, 'tis not the Present only,
The Past is also stored in thee,
Thou holdest not the venture of thyself alone, not of the
    Western continent alone,
Earth's *résumé* entire floats on thy keel O ship, is steadied
    by thy spars,
With thee Time voyages in trust, the antecedent nations
    sink or swim with thee,
With all their ancient struggles, martyrs, heroes, epics,
    wars, thou bear'st the other continents,
Theirs, theirs as much as thine, the destination-port tri-
    umphant;
Steer then with good strong hand and wary eye O helms-
    man, thou carriest great companions,
Venerable priestly Asia sails this day with thee,
And royal feudal Europe sails with thee.

5

Beautiful world of new superber birth that rises to my
    eyes,
Like a limitless golden cloud filling the western sky,
Emblem of general maternity lifted above all,
Sacred shape of the bearer of daughters and sons,
Out of thy teeming womb thy giant babes in ceaseless
    procession issuing,
Acceding from such gestation, taking and giving contin-
    ual strength and life,
World of the real—world of the twain in one,
World of the soul, born by the world of the real alone, led
    to identity, body, by it alone,
Yet in beginning only, incalculable masses of composite
    precious materials,
By history's cycles forwarded, by every nation, language,
    hither sent,
Ready, collected here, a freer, vast, electric world, to be
    constructed here,
(The true New World, the world of orbic science, morals,
    literatures to come,)
Thou wonder world yet undefined, unform'd, neither do
    I define thee,
How can I pierce the impenetrable blank of the future?
I feel thy ominous greatness evil as well as good,
I watch thee advancing, absorbing the present, transcend-
    ing the past,
I see thy light lighting, and thy shadow shadowing, as if
    the entire globe,
But I do not undertake to define thee, hardly to compre-
    hend thee,

I but thee name, thee prophesy, as now,
I merely thee ejaculate!

Thee in thy future,
Thee in thy only permanent life, career, thy own
    unloosen'd mind, thy soaring spirit,
Thee as another equally needed sun, radiant, ablaze,
    swift-moving, fructifying all,
Thee risen in potent cheerfulness and joy, in endless great
    hilarity,
Scattering for good the cloud that hung so long, that
    weigh'd so long upon the mind of man,
The doubt, suspicion, dread, of gradual, certain deca-
    dence of man;
Thee in thy larger, saner brood of female, male—thee in
    thy athletes, moral, spiritual, South, North, West,
    East,
(To thy immortal breasts, Mother of All, thy every daugh-
    ter, son, endear'd alike, forever equal,)
Thee in thy own musicians, singers, artists, unborn yet,
    but certain,
Thee in thy moral wealth and civilization, (until which
    thy proudest material civilization must remain in
    vain,)
Thee in thy all-supplying, all-enclosing worship—thee in
    no single bible, saviour, merely,
Thy saviours countless, latent within thyself, thy bibles
    incessant within thyself, equal to any, divine as any,
(Thy soaring course thee formulating, not in thy two great
    wars, nor in thy century's visible growth,
But far more in these leaves and chants, thy chants, great
    Mother!)

Thee in an education grown of thee, in teachers, studies,
    students, born of thee,
Thee in thy democratic fêtes en-masse, thy high original
    festivals, operas, lecturers, preachers,
Thee in thy ultimata, (the preparations only now com-
    pleted, the edifice on sure foundations tied,)
Thee in thy pinnacles, intellect, thought, thy topmost
    rational joys, thy love and godlike aspiration,
In thy resplendent coming literati, thy full-lung'd orators,
    thy sacerdotal bards, kosmic savans,
These! these in thee, (certain to come,) to-day I prophesy.

6

Land tolerating all, accepting all, not for the good alone,
    all good for thee,
Land in the realms of God to be a realm unto thyself,
Under the rule of God to be a rule unto thyself.

(Lo, where arise three peerless stars,
To be thy natal stars my country, Ensemble, Evolution,
    Freedom,
Set in the sky of Law.)

Land of unprecedented faith, God's faith,
Thy soil, thy very subsoil, all upheav'd,
The general inner earth so long so sedulously draped
    over, now hence for what it is boldly laid bare,
Open'd by thee to heaven's light for benefit or bale.

Not for success alone,
Not to fair-sail unintermitted always,

The storm shall dash thy face, the murk of war and worse
    than war shall cover thee all over,
(Wert capable of war, its tug and trials? be capable of
    peace, its trials,
For the tug and mortal strain of nations come at last in
    prosperous peace, not war;)
In many a smiling mask death shall approach beguiling
    thee, thou in disease shalt swelter,
The livid cancer spread its hideous claws, clinging upon
    thy breasts, seeking to strike thee deep within,
Consumption of the worst, moral consumption, shall
    rouge thy face with hectic,
But thou shalt face thy fortunes, thy diseases, and sur-
    mount them all,
Whatever they are to-day and whatever through time
    they may be,
They each and all shall lift and pass away and cease from
    thee,
While thou, Time's spirals rounding, out of thyself, thy-
    self still extricating, fusing,
Equable, natural, mystical Union thou, (the mortal with
    immortal blent,)
Shalt soar toward the fulfilment of the future, the spirit
    of the body and the mind,
The soul, its destinies.

The soul, its destinies, the real real,
(Purport of all these apparitions of the real;)
In thee America, the soul, its destinies,
Thou globe of globes! thou wonder nebulous!

By many a throe of heat and cold convuls'd, (by these thy-
    self solidifying,)
Thou mental, moral orb—thou New, indeed new, Spiri-
    tual World!
The Present holds thee not—for such vast growth as
    thine,
For such unparallel'd flight as thine, such brood as thine,
The FUTURE only holds thee and can hold thee.

＊

A PAUMANOK PICTURE.

Two boats with nets lying off the sea-beach, quite still,
Ten fishermen waiting—they discover a thick school of
    mossbonkers—they drop the join'd seine-ends in the
    water,
The boats separate and row off, each on its rounding
    course to the beach, enclosing the mossbonkers,
The net is drawn in by a windlass by those who stop
    ashore,
Some of the fishermen lounge in their boats, others stand
    ankle-deep in the water, pois'd on strong legs,
The boats partly drawn up, the water slapping against
    them,
Strew'd on the sand in heaps and windrows, well out
    from the water, the green-back'd spotted moss-
    bonkers.

*

FROM NOON TO STARRY NIGHT.

THOU ORB ALOFT FULL-DAZZLING.

Thou orb aloft full-dazzling! thou hot October noon!
Flooding with sheeny light the gray beach sand,
The sibilant near sea with vistas far and foam,
And tawny streaks and shades and spreading blue;
O sun of noon refulgent! my special word to thee.

Hear me illustrious!
Thy lover me, for always I have loved thee,
Even as basking babe, then happy boy alone by some
    wood edge, thy touching-distant beams enough,
Or man matured, or young or old, as now to thee I launch
    my invocation.

(Thou canst not with thy dumbness me deceive,
I know before the fitting man all Nature yields,
Though answering not in words, the skies, trees, hear his
    voice—and thou O sun,
As for thy throes, thy perturbations, sudden breaks and
    shafts of flame gigantic,

I understand them, I know those flames, those perturba-
tions well.)

Thou that with fructifying heat and light,
O'er myriad farms, o'er lands and waters North and
South,
O'er Mississippi's endless course, o'er Texas' grassy
plains, Kanada's woods,
O'er all the globe that turns its face to thee shining in
space,
Thou that impartially infoldest all, not only continents,
seas,
Thou that to grapes and weeds and little wild flowers
givest so liberally,
Shed, shed thyself on mine and me, with but a fleeting ray
out of thy million millions,
Strike through these chants.

Nor only launch thy subtle dazzle and thy strength for
these,
Prepare the later afternoon of me myself—prepare my
lengthening shadows,
Prepare my starry nights.

FACES.

1

Sauntering the pavement or riding the country by-road,
lo, such faces!
Faces of friendship, precision, caution, suavity, ideality,

The spiritual-prescient face, the always welcome common
    benevolent face.
The face of the singing of music, the grand faces of natural
    lawyers and judges broad at the back-top,
The faces of hunters and fishers bulged at the brows, the
    shaved blanch'd faces of orthodox citizens,
The pure, extravagant, yearning, questioning artist's face,
The ugly face of some beautiful soul, the handsome
    detested or despised face,
The sacred faces of infants, the illuminated face of the
    mother of many children,
The face of an amour, the face of veneration,
The face as of a dream, the face of an immobile rock,
The face withdrawn of its good and bad, a castrated face,
A wild hawk, his wings clipp'd by the clipper,
A stallion that yielded at last to the thongs and knife of
    the gelder.

Sauntering the pavement thus, or crossing the ceaseless
    ferry, faces and faces and faces,
I see them and complain not, and am content with all.

2

Do you suppose I could be content with all if I thought
    them their own finalè?

This now is too lamentable a face for a man,
Some abject louse asking leave to be, cringing for it,
Some milk-nosed maggot blessing what lets it wrig to its
    hole.

This face is a dog's snout sniffing for garbage,
Snakes nest in that mouth, I hear the sibilant threat.

This face is a haze more chill than the arctic sea,
Its sleepy and wabbling icebergs crunch as they go.

This is a face of bitter herbs, this an emetic, they need no
    label,
And more of the drug-shelf, laudanum, caoutchouc, or
    hog's-lard.

This face is an epilepsy, its wordless tongue gives out the
    unearthly cry,
Its veins down the neck distend, its eyes roll till they show
    nothing but their whites,
Its teeth grit, the palms of the hands are cut by the turn'd-
    in nails,
The man falls struggling and foaming to the ground,
    while he speculates well.

This face is bitten by vermin and worms,
And this is some murderer's knife with a half-pull'd scab-
    bard.

This face owes to the sexton his dismalest fee,
An unceasing death-bell tolls there.

3

Features of my equals would you trick me with your
    creas'd and cadaverous march?
Well you cannot trick me.

I see your rounded never-erased flow,
I see 'neath the rims of your haggard and mean disguises.

Splay and twist as you like, poke with the tangling fores
　　　of fishes or rats,
You'll be unmuzzled, you certainly will.

I saw the face of the most smear'd and slobbering idiot
　　　they had at the asylum,
And I knew for my consolation what they knew not,
I knew of the agents that emptied and broke my brother,
The same wait to clear the rubbish from the fallen tene-
　　　ment,
And I shall look again in a score or two of ages,
And I shall meet the real landlord perfect and unharm'd,
　　　every inch as good as myself.

4

The Lord advances, and yet advances,
Always the shadow in front, always the reach'd hand
　　　bringing up the laggards.

Out of this face emerge banners and horses—O superb! I
　　　see what is coming,
I see the high pioneer-caps, see staves of runners clearing
　　　the way,
I hear victorious drums.

This face is a life-boat,
This is the face commanding and bearded, it asks no odds
　　　of the rest,

This face is flavor'd fruit ready for eating,
This face of a healthy honest boy is the programme of all
good.

These faces bear testimony slumbering or awake,
They show their descent from the Master himself.

Off the word I have spoken I except not one—red, white,
black, are all deific,
In each house is the ovum, it comes forth after a thousand
years.

Spots or cracks at the windows do not disturb me,
Tall and sufficient stand behind and make signs to me,
I read the promise and patiently wait.

This is a full-grown lily's face,
She speaks to the limber-hipp'd man near the garden
pickets,
Come here she blushingly cries, *Come nigh to me limber-
hipp'd man,*
Stand at my side till I lean as high as I can upon you,
Fill me with albescent honey, bend down to me,
*Rub to me with your chafing beard, rub to my breast and shoul-
ders.*

5

The old face of the mother of many children,
Whist! I am fully content.

Lull'd and late is the smoke of the First-day morning,
It hangs low over the rows of trees by the fences,
It hangs thin by the sassafras and wild-cherry and cat-
    brier under them.

I saw the rich ladies in full dress at the soiree,
I heard what the singers were singing so long,
Heard who sprang in crimson youth from the white froth
    and the water-blue.

Behold a woman!
She looks out from her quaker cap, her face is clearer and
    more beautiful than the sky.

She sits in an armchair under the shaded porch of the
    farmhouse,
The sun just shines on her old white head.

Her ample gown is of cream-hued linen,
Her grandsons raised the flax, and her grand-daughters
    spun it with the distaff and the wheel.

The melodious character of the earth,
The finish beyond which philosophy cannot go and does
    not wish to go,
The justified mother of men.

THE MYSTIC TRUMPETER.

1

Hark, some wild trumpeter, some strange musician,
Hovering unseen in air, vibrates capricious tunes to-
    night.

I hear thee trumpeter, listening alert I catch thy notes,
Now pouring, whirling like a tempest round me,
Now low, subdued, now in the distance lost.

2

Come nearer bodiless one, haply in thee resounds
Some dead composer, haply thy pensive life
Was fill'd with aspirations high, unform'd ideals,
Waves, oceans musical, chaotically surging,
That now ecstatic ghost, close to me bending, thy cornet
    echoing, pealing,
Gives out to no one's ears but mine, but freely gives to
    mine,
That I may thee translate.

3

Blow trumpeter free and clear, I follow thee,
While at thy liquid prelude, glad, serene,
The fretting world, the streets, the noisy hours of day
    withdraw,
A holy calm descends like dew upon me,
I walk in cool refreshing night the walks of Paradise,

I scent the grass, the moist air and the roses;
Thy song expands my numb'd imbonded spirit, thou
      freest, launchest me,
Floating and basking upon heaven's lake.

4

Blow again trumpeter! and for my sensuous eyes,
Bring the old pageants, show the feudal world.

What charm thy music works! thou makest pass before
      me,
Ladies and cavaliers long dead, barons are in their castle
      halls, the troubadours are singing,
Arm'd knights go forth to redress wrongs, some in quest
      of the holy Graal;
I see the tournament, I see the contestants incased in
      heavy armor seated on stately champing horses,
I hear the shouts, the sounds of blows and smiting steel;
I see the Crusaders' tumultuous armies—hark, how the
      cymbals clang,
Lo, where the monks walk in advance, bearing the cross
      on high.

5

Blow again trumpeter! and for thy theme,
Take now the enclosing theme of all, the solvent and the
      setting,
Love, that is pulse of all, the sustenance and the pang,
The heart of man and woman all for love,

No other theme but love—knitting, enclosing, all-diffusing love.

O how the immortal phantoms crowd around me!
I see the vast alembic ever working, I see and know the flames that heat the world,
The glow, the blush, the beating hearts of lovers,
So blissful happy some, and some so silent, dark, and nigh to death;
Love, that is all the earth to lovers—love, that mocks time and space,
Love, that is day and night—love, that is sun and moon and stars,
Love, that is crimson, sumptuous, sick with perfume,
No other words but words of love, no other thought but love.

6

Blow again trumpeter—conjure war's alarums.

Swift to thy spell a shuddering hum like distant thunder rolls,
Lo, where the arm'd men hasten—lo, mid the clouds of dust the glint of bayonets,
I see the grime-faced cannoneers, I mark the rosy flash amid the smoke, I hear the cracking of the guns;
Not war alone—thy fearful music-song, wild player, brings every sight of fear,
The deeds of ruthless brigands, rapine, murder—I hear the cries for help!

I see ships foundering at sea, I behold on deck and below
　　deck the terrible tableaus.

7

O trumpeter, methinks I am myself the instrument thou
　　playest,
Thou melt'st my heart, my brain—thou movest, drawest,
　　changest them at will;
And now thy sullen notes send darkness through me,
Thou takest away all cheering light, all hope,
I see the enslaved, the overthrown, the hurt, the opprest
　　of the whole earth,
I feel the measureless shame and humiliation of my race,
　　it becomes all mine,
Mine too the revenges of humanity, the wrongs of ages,
　　baffled feuds and hatreds,
Utter defeat upon me weighs—all lost—the foe victori-
　　ous,
(Yet 'mid the ruins Pride colossal stands unshaken to the
　　last,
Endurance, resolution to the last.)

8

Now trumpeter for thy close,
Vouchsafe a higher strain than any yet,
Sing to my soul, renew its languishing faith and hope,
Rouse up my slow belief, give me some vision of the
　　future,
Give me for once its prophecy and joy.

O glad, exulting, culminating song!
A vigor more than earth's is in thy notes,
.Marches of victory—man disenthral'd—the conqueror at
   last,
Hymns to the universal God from universal man—all joy!
A reborn race appears—a perfect world, all joy!
Women and men in wisdom innocence and health—all
   joy!
Riotous laughing bacchanals fill'd with joy!
War, sorrow, suffering gone—the rank earth purged—
   nothing but joy left!
The ocean fill'd with joy—the atmosphere all joy!
Joy! joy! in freedom, worship, love! joy in the ecstasy of
   life!
Enough to merely be! enough to breathe!
Joy! joy! all over joy!

TO A LOCOMOTIVE IN WINTER.

Thee for my recitative,
Thee in the driving storm even as now, the snow, the win-
   ter-day declining,
Thee in thy panoply, thy measur'd dual throbbing and
   thy beat convulsive,
Thy black cylindric body, golden brass and silvery steel,
Thy ponderous side-bars, parallel and connecting rods,
   gyrating, shuttling at thy sides,
Thy metrical, now swelling pant and roar, now tapering
   in the distance,
Thy great protruding head-light fix'd in front,

Thy long, pale, floating vapor-pennants, tinged with del-
    icate purple,
The dense and murky clouds out-belching from thy
    smoke-stack,
Thy knitted frame, thy springs and valves, the tremulous
    twinkle of thy wheels,
Thy train of cars behind, obedient, merrily following,
Through gale or calm, now swift, now slack, yet steadily
    careering;
Type of the modern—emblem of motion and power—
    pulse of the continent,
For once come serve the Muse and merge in verse, even as
    here I see thee,
With storm and buffeting gusts of wind and falling snow,
By day thy warning ringing bell to sound its notes,
By night thy silent signal lamps to swing.

Fierce-throated beauty!
Roll through my chant with all thy lawless music, thy
    swinging lamps at night,
Thy madly-whistled laughter, echoing, rumbling like an
    earthquake, rousing all,
Law of thyself complete, thine own track firmly holding,
(No sweetness debonair of tearful harp or glib piano
    thine,)
Thy trills of shrieks by rocks and hills return'd,
Launch'd o'er the prairies wide, across the lakes,
To the free skies unpent and glad and strong.

O MAGNET-SOUTH.

O magnet-South! O glistening perfumed South! my South!
O quick mettle, rich blood, impulse and love! good and
    evil! O all dear to me!
O dear to me my birth-things—all moving things and the
    trees where I was born—the grains, plants, rivers,
Dear to me my own slow sluggish rivers where they flow,
    distant, over flats of silvery sands or through
    swamps,
Dear to me the Roanoke, the Savannah, the Altamahaw,
    the Pedee, the Tombigbee, the Santee, the Coosa and
    the Sabine,
O pensive, far away wandering, I return with my soul to
    haunt their banks again,
Again in Florida I float on transparent lakes, I float on the
    Okeechobee, I cross the hummock-land or through
    pleasant openings or dense forests,
I see the parrots in the woods, I see the papaw-tree and
    the blossoming titi;
Again, sailing in my coaster on deck, I coast off Georgia,
    I coast up the Carolinas,
I see where the live-oak is growing, I see where the yel-
    low-pine, the scented bay-tree, the lemon and orange,
    the cypress, the graceful palmetto,
I pass rude sea-headlands and enter Pamlico sound
    through an inlet, and dart my vision inland;
O the cotton plant! the growing fields of rice, sugar,
    hemp!
The cactus guarded with thorns, the laurel-tree with large
    white flowers,

The range afar, the richness and barrenness, the old
    woods charged with mistletoe and trailing moss,
The piney odor and the gloom, the awful natural stillness,
    (here in these dense swamps the freebooter carries his
    gun, and the fugitive has his conceal'd hut;)
O the strange fascination of these half-known half-
    impassable swamps, infested by reptiles, resounding
    with the bellow of the alligator, the sad noises of the
    night-owl and the wild-cat, and the whirr of the rat-
    tlesnake,
The mocking-bird, the American mimic, singing all the
    forenoon, singing through the moon-lit night,
The humming-bird, the wild turkey, the raccoon, the
    opossum;
A Kentucky corn-field, the tall, graceful, long-leav'd corn,
    slender, flapping, bright green, with tassels, with
    beautiful ears each well-sheath'd in its husk;
O my heart! O tender and fierce pangs, I can stand them
    not, I will depart;
O to be a Virginian where I grew up! O to be a Carolin-
    ian!
O longings irrepressible! O I will go back to old Tennessee
    and never wander more.

MANNAHATTA.

I was asking for something specific and perfect for my
    city,
Whereupon lo! upsprang the aboriginal name.

Now I see what there is in a name, a word, liquid, sane,
 unruly, musical, self-sufficient,
I see that the word of my city is that word from of old,
Because I see that word nested in nests of water-bays,
 superb,
Rich, hemm'd thick all around with sailships and
 steamships, an island sixteen miles long, solid-
 founded,
Numberless crowded streets, high growths of iron, slen-
 der, strong, light, splendidly uprising toward clear
 skies,
Tides swift and ample, well-loved by me, toward sun-
 down,
The flowing sea-currents, the little islands, larger adjoin-
 ing islands, the heights, the villas,
The countless masts, the white shore-steamers, the
 lighters, the ferry-boats, the black sea-steamers well-
 model'd,
The down-town streets, the jobbers' houses of business,
 the houses of business of the ship-merchants and
 money-brokers, the river-streets,
Immigrants arriving, fifteen or twenty thousand in a
 week,
The carts hauling goods, the manly race of drivers of
 horses, the brown-faced sailors,
The summer air, the bright sun shining, and the sailing
 clouds aloft,
The winter snows, the sleigh-bells, the broken ice in the
 river, passing along up or down with the flood-tide or
 ebb-tide,
The mechanics of the city, the masters, well-form'd, beau-
 tiful-faced, looking you straight in the eyes,

Trottoirs throng'd, vehicles, Broadway, the women, the
   shops and shows,
A million people—manners free and superb—open
   voices—hospitality—the most courageous and
   friendly young men,
City of hurried and sparkling waters! city of spires and
   masts!
City nested in bays! my city!

ALL IS TRUTH.

O me, man of slack faith so long,
Standing aloof, denying portions so long,
Only aware to-day of compact all-diffused truth,
Discovering to-day there is no lie or form of lie, and can
   be none, but grows as inevitably upon itself as the
   truth does upon itself,
Or as any law of the earth or any natural production of
   the earth does.

(This is curious and may not be realized immediately, but
   it must be realized,
I feel in myself that I represent falsehoods equally with
   the rest,
And that the universe does.)

Where has fail'd a perfect return indifferent of lies or the
   truth?
Is it upon the ground, or in water or fire? or in the spirit of
   man? or in the meat and blood?

Meditating among liars and retreating sternly into myself,
    I see that there are really no liars or lies after all,
And that nothing fails its perfect return, and that what are
    called lies are perfect returns,
And that each thing exactly represents itself and what has
    preceded it,
And that the truth includes all, and is compact just as
    much as space is compact,
And that there is no flaw or vacuum in the amount of the
    truth—but that all is truth without exception;
And henceforth I will go celebrate any thing I see or am,
And sing and laugh and deny nothing.

A RIDDLE SONG.

That which eludes this verse and any verse,
Unheard by sharpest ear, unform'd in clearest eye or cun-
    ningest mind,
Nor lore nor fame, nor happiness nor wealth,
And yet the pulse of every heart and life throughout the
    world incessantly,
Which you and I and all pursuing ever ever miss,
Open but still a secret, the real of the real, an illusion,
Costless, vouchsafed to each, yet never man the owner,
Which poets vainly seek to put in rhyme, historians in
    prose,
Which sculptor never chisel'd yet, nor painter painted,
Which vocalist never sung, nor orator nor actor ever
    utter'd,
Invoking here and now I challenge for my song.

Indifferently, 'mid public, private haunts, in solitude,
Behind the mountain and the wood,
Companion of the city's busiest streets, through the
    assemblage,
It and its radiations constantly glide.

In looks of fair unconscious babes,
Or strangely in the coffin'd dead,
Or show of breaking dawn or stars by night,
As some dissolving delicate film of dreams,
Hiding yet lingering.

Two little breaths of words comprising it,
Two words, yet all from first to last comprised in it.

How ardently for it!
How many ships have sail'd and sunk for it!
How many travelers started from their homes and ne'er
    return'd!
How much of genius boldly staked and lost for it!
What countless stores of beauty, love, ventur'd for it!
How all superbest deeds since Time began are traceable
    to it—and shall be to the end!
How all heroic martyrdoms to it!
How, justified by it, the horrors, evils, battles of the earth!
How the bright fascinating lambent flames of it, in every
    age and land, have drawn men's eyes,
Rich as a sunset on the Norway coast, the sky, the islands,
    and the cliffs,
Or midnight's silent glowing northern lights unreachable.

Haply God's riddle it, so vague and yet so certain,
The soul for it, and all the visible universe for it,
And heaven at last for it.

EXCELSIOR.

Who has gone farthest? for I would go farther,
And who has been just? for I would be the most just per-
son of the earth,
And who most cautious? for I would be more cautious,
And who has been happiest? O I think it is I—I think no
one was ever happier than I,
And who has lavish'd all? for I lavish constantly the best
I have,
And who proudest? for I think I have reason to be the
proudest son alive—for I am the son of the brawny
and tall-topt city,
And who has been bold and true? for I would be the bold-
est and truest being of the universe,
And who benevolent? for I would show more benevo-
lence than all the rest,
And who has receiv'd the love of the most friends? for I
know what it is to receive the passionate love of many
friends,
And who possesses a perfect and enamour'd body? for I
do not believe any one possesses a more perfect or
enamour'd body than mine,
And who thinks the amplest thoughts? for I would sur-
round those thoughts,

And who has made hymns fit for the earth? for I am mad
     with devouring ecstasy to make joyous hymns for the
     whole earth.

AH POVERTIES, WINCINGS, AND SULKY RETREATS.

Ah poverties, wincings, and sulky retreats,
Ah you foes that in conflict have overcome me,
(For what is my life or any man's life but a conflict with
     foes, the old, the incessant war?)
You degradations, you tussle with passions and appetites,
You smarts from dissatisfied friendships, (ah wounds the
     sharpest of all!)
You toil of painful and choked articulations, you mean-
     nesses,
You shallow tongue-talks at tables, (my tongue the shal-
     lowest of any;)
You broken resolutions, you racking angers, you
     smother'd ennuis!
Ah think not you finally triumph, my real self has yet to
     come forth,
It shall yet march forth o'ermastering, till all lies beneath
     me,
It shall yet stand up the soldier of ultimate victory.

THOUGHTS.

Of public opinion,
Of a calm and cool fiat sooner or later, (how impassive!
     how certain and final!)

Of the President with pale face asking secretly to himself,
    What will the people say at last?
Of the frivolous Judge—of the corrupt Congressman,
    Governor, Mayor—of such as these standing helpless
    and exposed,
Of the mumbling and screaming priest, (soon, soon
    deserted,)
Of the lessening year by year of venerableness, and of the
    dicta of officers, statutes, pulpits, schools,
Of the rising forever taller and stronger and broader of
    the intuitions of men and women, and of Self-esteem
    and Personality;
Of the true New World—of the Democracies resplendent
    en-masse,
Of the conformity of politics, armies, navies, to them,
Of the shining sun by them—of the inherent light, greater
    than the rest,
Of the envelopment of all by them, and the effusion of all
    from them.

MEDIUMS.

They shall arise in the States,
They shall report Nature, laws, physiology, and happi-
    ness,
They shall illustrate Democracy and the kosmos,
They shall be alimentive, amative, perceptive,
They shall be complete women and men, their pose
    brawny and supple, their drink water, their blood
    clean and clear,

They shall fully enjoy materialism and the sight of prod-
ucts, they shall enjoy the sight of the beef, lumber,
bread-stuffs, of Chicago the great city,
They shall train themselves to go in public to become ora-
tors and oratresses,
Strong and sweet shall their tongues be, poems and mate-
rials of poems shall come from their lives, they shall
be makers and finders,
Of them and of their works shall emerge divine convey-
ers, to convey gospels,
Characters, events, retrospections, shall be convey'd in
gospels, trees, animals, waters, shall be convey'd,
Death, the future, the invisible faith, shall all be convey'd.

WEAVE IN, MY HARDY LIFE.

Weave in, weave in, my hardy life,
Weave yet a soldier strong and full for great campaigns to
come,
Weave in red blood, weave sinews in like ropes, the
senses, sight weave in,
Weave lasting sure, weave day and night the weft, the
warp, incessant weave, tire not,
(We know not what the use O life, nor know the aim, the
end, nor really aught we know,
But know the work, the need goes on and shall go on, the
death-envelop'd march of peace as well as war goes
on,)
For great campaigns of peace the same the wiry threads to
weave,
We know not why or what, yet weave, forever weave.

SPAIN, 1873-74.

Out of the murk of heaviest clouds,
Out of the feudal wrecks and heap'd-up skeletons of
   kings,
Out of that old entire European debris, the shatter'd
   mummeries,
Ruin'd cathedrals, crumble of palaces, tombs of priests,
Lo, Freedom's features fresh undimm'd look forth—the
   same immortal face looks forth;
(A glimpse as of thy Mother's face Columbia,
A flash significant as of a sword,
Beaming towards thee.)

Nor think we forget thee maternal;
Lag'd'st thou so long? shall the clouds close again upon
   thee?
Ah, but thou hast thyself now appear'd to us—we know
   thee,
Thou hast given us a sure proof, the glimpse of thyself,
Thou waitest there as everywhere thy time.

BY BROAD POTOMAC'S SHORE.

By broad Potomac's shore, again old tongue,
(Still uttering, still ejaculating, canst never cease this bab-
   ble?)
Again old heart so gay, again to you, your sense, the full
   flush spring returning,
Again the freshness and the odors, again Virginia's sum-
   mer sky, pellucid blue and silver,

Again the forenoon purple of the hills,
Again the deathless grass, so noiseless soft and green,
Again the blood-red roses blooming.

Perfume this book of mine O blood-red roses!
Lave subtly with your waters every line Potomac!
Give me of you O spring, before I close, to put between its
     pages!
O forenoon purple of the hills, before I close, of you!
O deathless grass, of you!

FROM FAR DAKOTA'S CAÑONS.

June 25, 1876

From far Dakota's cañons,
Lands of the wild ravine, the dusky Sioux, the lonesome
     stretch, the silence,
Haply to-day a mournful wail, haply a trumpet-note for
     heroes.

The battle-bulletin,
The Indian ambuscade, the craft, the fatal environment,
The cavalry companies fighting to the last in sternest
     heroism,
In the midst of their little circle, with their slaughter'd
     horses for breastworks,
The fall of Custer and all his officers and men.

Continues yet the old, old legend of our race,
The loftiest of life upheld by death,

The ancient banner perfectly maintain'd,
O lesson opportune, O how I welcome thee!

As sitting in dark days,
Lone, sulky, through the time's thick murk looking in
    vain for light, for hope,
From unsuspected parts a fierce and momentary proof,
(The sun there at the centre though conceal'd,
Electric life forever at the centre,)
Breaks forth a lightning flash.

Thou of the tawny flowing hair in battle,
I erewhile saw, with erect head, pressing ever in front,
    bearing a bright sword in thy hand,
Now ending well in death the splendid fever of thy deeds,
(I bring no dirge for it or thee, I bring a glad triumphal
    sonnet,)
Desperate and glorious, aye in defeat most desperate,
    most glorious,
After thy many battles in which never yielding up a gun
    or a color,
Leaving behind thee a memory sweet to soldiers,
Thou yieldest up thyself.

OLD WAR-DREAMS.

In midnight sleep of many a face of anguish,
Of the look at first of the mortally wounded, (of that inde-
    scribable look,)
Of the dead on their backs with arms extended wide,
        I dream, I dream, I dream.

Of scenes of Nature, fields and mountains,
Of skies so beauteous after a storm, and at night the moon
 so unearthly bright,
Shining sweetly, shining down, where we dig the
 trenches and gather the heaps,
   I dream, I dream, I dream.

Long have they pass'd, faces and trenches and fields,
Where through the carnage I moved with a callous com-
 posure, or away from the fallen,
Onward I sped at the time—but now of their forms at
 night,
   I dream, I dream, I dream.

THICK-SPRINKLED BUNTING.

Thick sprinkled bunting! flag of stars!
Long yet your road, fateful flag—long yet your road, and
 lined with bloody death,
For the prize I see at issue at last is the world,
All its ships and shores I see interwoven with your
 threads greedy banner;
Dream'd again the flags of kings, highest borne, to flaunt
 unrival'd?
O hasten flag of man—O with sure and steady step, pass-
 ing highest flags of kings,
Walk supreme to the heavens mighty symbol—run up
 above them all,
Flag of stars! thick sprinkled bunting!

WHAT BEST I SEE IN THEE.

To U. S. G. return'd from his World's Tour.

What best I see in thee,
Is not that where thou mov'st down history's great high-
　　ways,
Ever undimm'd by time shoots warlike victory's dazzle,
Or that thou sat'st where Washington sat, ruling the land
　　in peace,
Or thou the man whom feudal Europe feted, venerable
　　Asia swarm'd upon,
Who walk'd with kings with even pace the round world's
　　promenade;
But that in foreign lands, in all thy walks with kings,
Those prairie sovereigns of the West, Kansas, Missouri,
　　Illinois,
Ohio's, Indiana's millions, comrades, farmers, soldiers, all
　　to the front,
Invisibly with thee walking with kings with even pace the
　　round world's promenade,
Were all so justified.

SPIRIT THAT FORM'D THIS SCENE.

Written in Platte Cañon, Colorado.

Spirit that form'd this scene,
These tumbled rock-piles grim and red,
These reckless heaven-ambitious peaks,
These gorges, turbulent-clear streams, this naked fresh-
　　ness,

These formless wild arrays, for reasons of their own,
I know thee, savage spirit—we have communed together,
Mine too such wild arrays, for reasons of their own;
Was't charged against my chants they had forgotten art?
To fuse within themselves its rules precise and deli-
catesse?
The lyrist's measur'd beat, the wrought-out temple's
grace—column and polish'd arch forgot?
But thou that revelest here—spirit that form'd this scene,
They have remember'd thee.

AS I WALK THESE BROAD MAJESTIC DAYS.

As I walk these broad majestic days of peace,
(For the war, the struggle of blood finish'd, wherein, O
terrific Ideal,
Against vast odds erewhile having gloriously won,
Now thou stridest on, yet perhaps in time toward denser
wars,
Perhaps to engage in time in still more dreadful contests,
dangers,
Longer campaigns and crises, labors beyond all others,)
Around me I hear that eclat of the world, politics, pro-
duce,
The announcements of recognized things, science,
The approved growth of cities and the spread of inven-
tions.

I see the ships, (they will last a few years,)
The vast factories with their foremen and workmen,
And hear the indorsement of all, and do not object to it.

But I too announce solid things,
Science, ships, politics, cities, factories, are not nothing,
Like a grand procession to music of distant bugles pour-
    ing, triumphantly moving, and grander heaving in
    sight,
They stand for realities—all is as it should be.

Then my realities;
What else is so real as mine?
Libertad and the divine average, freedom to every slave
    on the face of the earth,
The rapt promises and luminè of seers, the spiritual
    world, these centuries-lasting songs,
And our visions, the visions of poets, the most solid
    announcements of any.

A CLEAR MIDNIGHT.

This is thy hour O Soul, thy free flight into the wordless,
Away from books, away from art, the day erased, the les-
    son done,
Thee fully forth emerging, silent, gazing, pondering the
    themes thou lovest best,
Night, sleep, death and the stars.

*

SONGS OF PARTING.

AS THE TIME DRAWS NIGH.

As the time draws nigh glooming a cloud,
A dread beyond of I know not what darkens me.

I shall go forth,
I shall traverse the States awhile, but I cannot tell whither
or how long,
Perhaps soon some day or night while I am singing my
voice will suddenly cease.

O book, O chants! must all then amount to but this?
Must we barely arrive at this beginning of us?—and yet
it is enough, O soul;
O soul, we have positively appear'd—that is enough.

YEARS OF THE MODERN.

Years of the modern! years of the unperform'd!
Your horizon rises, I see it parting away for more august
dramas,
I see not America only, not only Liberty's nation but other
nations preparing,

I see tremendous entrances and exits, new combinations,
    the solidarity of races,
I see that force advancing with irresistible power on the
    world's stage,
(Have the old forces, the old wars, played their parts? are
    the acts suitable to them closed?)
I see Freedom, completely arm'd and victorious and very
    haughty, with Law on one side and Peace on the
    other,
A stupendous trio all issuing forth against the idea of
    caste;
What historic denouements are these we so rapidly
    approach?
I see men marching and countermarching by swift mil-
    lions,
I see the frontiers and boundaries of the old aristocracies
    broken,
I see the landmarks of European kings removed,
I see this day the People beginning their landmarks, (all
    others give way;)
Never were such sharp questions ask'd as this day,
Never was average man, his soul, more energetic, more
    like a God,
Lo, how he urges and urges, leaving the masses no rest!
His daring foot is on land and sea everywhere, he colo-
    nizes the Pacific, the archipelagoes,
With the steamship, the electric telegraph, the newspaper,
    the wholesale engines of war,
With these and the world-spreading factories he inter-
    links all geography, all lands;
What whispers are these O lands, running ahead of you,
    passing under the seas?

Are all nations communing? is there going to be but one
    heart to the globe?
Is humanity forming en-masse? for lo, tyrants tremble,
    crowns grow dim,
The earth, restive, confronts a new era, perhaps a general
    divine war,
No one knows what will happen next, such portents fill
    the days and nights;
Years prophetical! the space ahead as I walk, as I vainly
    try to pierce it, is full of phantoms,
Unborn deeds, things soon to be, project their shapes
    around me,
This incredible rush and heat, this strange ecstatic fever of
    dreams O years!
Your dreams O years, how they penetrate through me! (I
    know not whether I sleep or wake;)
The perform'd America and Europe grow dim, retiring in
    shadow behind me,
The unperform'd, more gigantic than ever, advance,
    advance, upon me.

ASHES OF SOLDIERS.

Ashes of soldiers South or North,
As I muse retrospective murmuring a chant in thought,
The war resumes, again to my sense your shapes,
And again the advance of the armies.

Noiseless as mists and vapors,
From their graves in the trenches ascending,
From cemeteries all through Virginia and Tennessee,

From every point of the compass out of the countless
    graves,
In wafted clouds, in myriads large, or squads of twos or
    threes or single ones they come,
And silently gather round me.

Now sound no note O trumpeters,
Not at the head of my cavalry parading on spirited
    horses,
With sabres drawn and glistening, and carbines by their
    thighs, (ah my brave horsemen!
My handsome tan-faced horsemen! what life, what joy
    and pride,
With all the perils were yours.)

Nor you drummers, neither at reveillé at dawn,
Nor the long roll alarming the camp, nor even the muffled
    beat for a burial,
Nothing from you this time O drummers bearing my war-
    like drums.

But aside from these and the marts of wealth and the
    crowded promenade,
Admitting around me comrades close unseen by the rest
    and voiceless,
The slain elate and alive again, the dust and debris alive,
I chant this chant of my silent soul in the name of all dead
    soldiers.

Faces so pale with wondrous eyes, very dear, gather
    closer yet,
Draw close, but speak not.

Phantoms of countless lost,
Invisible to the rest henceforth become my companions,
Follow me ever—desert me not while I live.

Sweet are the blooming cheeks of the living—sweet are
     the musical voices sounding,
But sweet, ah sweet, are the dead with their silent eyes.

Dearest comrades, all is over and long gone,
But love is not over—and what love, O comrades!
Perfume from battle-fields rising, up from the fœtor aris-
     ing.

Perfume therefore my chant, O love, immortal love,
Give me to bathe the memories of all dead soldiers,
Shroud them, embalm them, cover them all over with ten-
     der pride.

Perfume all—make all wholesome,
Make these ashes to nourish and blossom,
O love, solve all, fructify all with the last chemistry.

Give me exhaustless, make me a fountain,
That I exhale love from me wherever I go like a moist
     perennial dew,
For the ashes of all dead soldiers South or North.

THOUGHTS.

1

Of these years I sing,
How they pass and have pass'd through convuls'd pains,
as through parturitions,
How America illustrates birth, muscular youth, the
promise, the sure fulfilment the absolute success,
despite of people—illustrates evil as well as good,
The vehement struggle so fierce for unity in one's-self;
How many hold despairingly yet to the models departed,
caste, myths, obedience, compulsion, and to infi-
delity,
How few see the arrived models, the athletes, the Western
States, or see freedom or spirituality, or hold any faith
in results,
(But I see the athletes, and I see the results of the war glo-
rious and inevitable and they again leading to other
results.)

How the great cities appear—how the Democratic
masses, turbulent, wilful, as I love them,
How the whirl, the contest, the wrestle of evil with good,
the sounding and resounding, keep on and on,
How society waits unform'd, and is for a while between
things ended and things begun,
How America is the continent of glories, and of the tri-
umph of freedom and of the Democracies, and of the
fruits of society, and of all that is begun,

And how the States are complete in themselves—and
how all triumphs and glories are complete in them-
selves, to lead onward,
And how these of mine and of the States will in their turn
be convuls'd, and serve other parturitions and tran-
sitions,
And how all people, sights, combinations, the democra-
tic masses too, serve—and how every fact, and war
itself, with all its horrors, serves,
And how now or at any time each serves the exquisite
transition of death.

2

Of seeds dropping into the ground, of births,
Of the steady concentration of America, inland, upward,
to impregnable and swarming places,
Of what Indiana, Kentucky, Arkansas, and the rest, are to
be,
Of what a few years will show there in Nebraska, Col-
orado, Nevada, and the rest,
(Or afar, mounting the Northern Pacific to Sitka or
Aliaska,)
Of what the feuillage of America is the preparation for—
and of what all sights, North, South, East and West,
are,
Of this Union welded in blood, of the solemn price paid,
of the unnamed lost ever present in my mind;
Of the temporary use of materials for identity's sake,
Of the present, passing, departing—of the growth of com-
pleter men than any yet,

Of all sloping down there where the fresh free giver the
    mother, the Mississippi flows,
Of mighty inland cities yet unsurvey'd and unsuspected,
Of the new and good names, of the modern develop-
    ments, of inalienable homesteads,
Of a free and original life there, of simple diet and clean
    and sweet blood,
Of litheness, majestic faces, clear eyes, and perfect
    physique there,
Of immense spiritual results future years far West, each
    side of the Anahuacs,
Of these songs, well understood there, (being made for
    that area,)
Of the native scorn of grossness and gain there,
(O it lurks in me night and day—what is gain after all to
    savageness and freedom?)

SONG AT SUNSET.

Splendor of ended day floating and filling me,
Hour prophetic, hour resuming the past,
Inflating my throat, you divine average,
You earth and life till the last ray gleams I sing.

Open mouth of my soul uttering gladness,
Eyes of my soul seeing perfection,
Natural life of me faithfully praising things,
Corroborating forever the triumph of things.

Illustrious every one!

Illustrious what we name space, sphere of unnumber'd
spirits,

Illustrious the mystery of motion in all beings, even the
tiniest insect,

Illustrious the attribute of speech, the senses, the body,

Illustrious the passing light—illustrious the pale reflec-
tion on the new moon in the western sky,

Illustrious whatever I see or hear or touch, to the last.

Good in all,

In the satisfaction and aplomb of animals,

In the annual return of the seasons,

In the hilarity of youth,

In the strength and flush of manhood,

In the grandeur and exquisiteness of old age,

In the superb vistas of death.

Wonderful to depart!

Wonderful to be here!

The heart, to jet the all-alike and innocent blood!

To breathe the air, how delicious!

To speak—to walk—to seize something by the hand!

To prepare for sleep, for bed, to look on my rose-color'd
flesh!

To be conscious of my body, so satisfied, so large!

To be this incredible God I am!

To have gone forth among other Gods, these men and
women I love.

Wonderful how I celebrate you and myself!

How my thoughts play subtly at the spectacles around!

How the clouds pass silently overhead!
How the earth darts on and on! and how the sun, moon,
     stars, dart on and on!
How the water sports and sings! (surely it is alive!)
How the trees rise and stand up, with strong trunks, with
     branches and leaves!
(Surely there is something more in each of the trees, some
     living soul.)

O amazement of things—even the least particle!
O spirituality of things!
O strain musical flowing through ages and continents,
     now reaching me and America!
I take your strong chords, intersperse them, and cheer-
     fully pass them forward.

I too carol the sun, usher'd or at noon, or as now, setting,
I too throb to the brain and beauty of the earth and of all
     the growths of the earth,
I too have felt the resistless call of myself.

As I steam'd down the Mississippi,
As I wander'd over the prairies,
As I have lived, as I have look'd through my windows my
     eyes,
As I went forth in the morning, as I beheld the light break-
     ing in the east,
As I bathed on the beach of the Eastern Sea, and again on
     the beach of the Western Sea,
As I roam'd the streets of inland Chicago, whatever
     streets I have roam'd,
Or cities or silent woods, or even amid the sights of war,

Wherever I have been I have charged myself with con-
    tentment and triumph.

I sing to the last the equalities modern or old,
I sing the endless finalés of things,
I say Nature continues, glory continues,
I praise with electric voice,
For I do not see one imperfection in the universe,
And I do not see one cause or result lamentable at last in
    the universe.

O setting sun! though the time has come,
I still warble under you, if none else does, unmitigated
    adoration.

AS AT THY PORTALS ALSO DEATH.

As at thy portals also death,
Entering thy sovereign, dim, illimitable grounds,
To memories of my mother, to the divine blending, mater-
    nity,
To her, buried and gone, yet buried not, gone not from
    me,
(I see again the calm benignant face fresh and beautiful
    still,
I sit by the form in the coffin,
I kiss and kiss convulsively again the sweet old lips, the
    cheeks, the closed eyes in the coffin;)
To her, the ideal woman, practical, spiritual, of all of
    earth, life, love, to me the best,

I grave a monumental line, before I go, amid these songs,
And set a tombstone here.

MY LEGACY.

The business man the acquirer vast,
After assiduous years surveying results, preparing for
    departure,
Devises houses and lands to his children, bequeaths
    stocks, goods, funds for a school or hospital,
Leaves money to certain companions to buy tokens, sou-
    venirs of gems and gold.

But I, my life surveying, closing,
With nothing to show to devise from its idle years,
Nor houses nor lands, nor tokens of gems or gold for my
    friends,
Yet certain remembrances of the war for you, and after
    you,
And little souvenirs of camps and soldiers, with my love,
I bind together and bequeath in this bundle of songs.

PENSIVE ON HER DEAD GAZING.

Pensive on her dead gazing I heard the Mother of All,
Desperate on the torn bodies, on the forms covering the
    battlefields gazing,
(As the last gun ceased, but the scent of the powder-
    smoke linger'd,)

As she call'd to her earth with mournful voice while she
    stalk'd,
Absorb them well O my earth, she cried, I charge you lose
    not my sons, lose not an atom,
And you streams absorb them well, taking their dear
    blood,
And you local spots, and you airs that swim above lightly
    impalpable,
And all you essences of soil and growth, and you my
    rivers' depths,
And you mountain sides, and the woods where my dear
    children's blood trickling redden'd,
And you trees down in your roots to bequeath to all
    future trees,
My dead absorb or South or North—my young men's
    bodies absorb, and their precious precious blood,
Which holding in trust for me faithfully back again give
    me many a year hence,
In unseen essence and odor of surface and grass, centuries
    hence,
In blowing airs from the fields back again give me my
    darlings, give my immortal heroes,
Exhale me them centuries hence, breathe me their breath,
    let not an atom be lost,
O years and graves! O air and soil! O my dead, an aroma
    sweet!
Exhale them perennial sweet death, years, centuries
    hence.

CAMPS OF GREEN.

Not alone those camps of white, old comrades of the
  wars,
When as order'd forward, after a long march,
Footsore and weary, soon as the light lessens we halt for
  the night,
Some of us so fatigued carrying the gun and knapsack,
  dropping asleep in our tracks,
Others pitching the little tents, and the fires lit up begin to
  sparkle,
Outposts of pickets posted surrounding alert through the
  dark,
And a word provided for countersign, careful for safety,
Till to the call of the drummers at daybreak loudly beat-
  ing the drums,
We rise up refresh'd, the night and sleep pass'd over, and
  resume our journey,
Or proceed to battle.

Lo, the camps of the tents of green,
Which the days of peace keep filling, and the days of war
  keep filling,
With a mystic army, (is it too order'd forward? is it too
  only halting awhile,
Till night and sleep pass over?)

Now in those camps of green, in their tents dotting the
  world,
In the parents, children, husbands, wives, in them, in the
  old and young,

Sleeping under the sunlight, sleeping under the moon-
    light, content and silent there at last,
Behold the mighty bivouac-field and waiting-camp of all,
Of the corps and generals all, and the President over the
    corps and generals all,
And of each of us O soldiers, and of each and all in the
    ranks we fought,
(There without hatred we all, all meet.)

For presently O soldiers, we too camp in our place in the
    bivouac-camps of green,
But we need not provide for outposts, nor word for the
    countersign,
Nor drummer to beat the morning drum.

THE SOBBING OF THE BELLS.
(*Midnight, Sept. 19-20, 1881.*)

The sobbing of the bells, the sudden death-news every-
    where,
The slumberers rouse, the rapport of the People,
(Full well they know that message in the darkness,
Full well return, respond within their breasts, their brains,
    the sad reverberations,)
The passionate toll and clang—city to city, joining, sound-
    ing, passing,
Those heart-beats of a Nation in the night.

AS THEY DRAW TO A CLOSE.

As they draw to a close,
Of what underlies the precedent songs—of my aims in
　　them,
Of the seed I have sought to plant in them,
Of joy, sweet joy, through many a year, in them,
(For them, for them have I lived, in them my work is
　　done,)
Of many an aspiration fond, of many a dream and plan;
Through Space and Time fused in a chant, and the flow-
　　ing eternal identity,
To Nature encompassing these, encompassing God—to
　　the joyous, electric all,
To the sense of Death, and accepting exulting in Death in
　　its turn the same as life,
The entrance of man to sing;
To compact you, ye parted, diverse lives,
To put rapport the mountains and rocks and streams,
And the winds of the north, and the forests of oak and
　　pine,
With you O soul.

JOY, SHIPMATE, JOY!

Joy, shipmate, joy!
(Pleas'd to my soul at death I cry,)
Our life is closed, our life begins,
The long, long anchorage we leave,
The ship is clear at last, she leaps!

She swiftly courses from the shore,
Joy, shipmate, joy.

THE UNTOLD WANT.

The untold want by life and land ne'er granted,
Now voyager sail thou forth to seek and find.

PORTALS.

What are those of the known but to ascend and enter the
    Unknown?
And what are those of life but for Death?

THESE CAROLS.

These carols sung to cheer my passage through the world
    I see,
For completion I dedicate to the Invisible World.

NOW FINALÉ TO THE SHORE.

Now finalé to the shore,
Now land and life finalé and farewell,
Now Voyager depart, (much, much for thee is yet in
    store,)
Often enough hast thou adventur'd o'er the seas,
Cautiously cruising, studying the charts,

Duly again to port and hawser's tie returning;
But now obey thy cherish'd secret wish,
Embrace thy friends, leave all in order,
To port and hawser's tie no more returning,
Depart upon thy endless cruise old Sailor.

SO LONG!

To conclude, I announce what comes after me.

I remember I said before my leaves sprang at all,
I would raise my voice jocund and strong with reference
   to consummations.

When America does what was promis'd,
When through these States walk a hundred millions of
   superb persons,
When the rest part away for superb persons and con-
   tribute to them,
When breeds of the most perfect mothers denote Amer-
   ica,
Then to me and mine our due fruition.

I have press'd through in my own right,
I have sung the body and the soul, war and peace have I
   sung, and the songs of life and death,
And the songs of birth, and shown that there are many
   births.

I have offer'd my style to every one, I have journey'd with
   confident step;

While my pleasure is yet at the full I whisper *So long!*
And take the young woman's hand and the young man's
    hand for the last time.

I announce natural persons to arise,
I announce justice triumphant,
I announce uncompromising liberty and equality,
I announce the justification of candor and the justification
    of pride.

I announce that the identity of these States is a single
    identity only,
I announce the Union more and more compact, indissolu-
    ble,
I announce splendors and majesties to make all the pre-
    vious politics of the earth insignificant.

I announce adhesiveness, I say it shall be limitless, un-
    loosen'd,
I say you shall yet find the friend you were looking for.

I announce a man or woman coming, perhaps you are the
    one, (*So long!*)
I announce the great individual, fluid as Nature, chaste,
    affectionate, compassionate, fully arm'd.

I announce a life that shall be copious, vehement, spiri-
    tual, bold,
I announce an end that shall lightly and joyfully meet its
    translation.

I announce myriads of youths, beautiful, gigantic, sweet-
blooded,
I announce a race of splendid and savage old men.

O thicker and faster—(*So long!*)
O crowding too close upon me,
I foresee too much, it means more than I thought,
It appears to me I am dying.

Hasten throat and sound your last,
Salute me—salute the days once more. Peal the old cry
once more.

Screaming electric, the atmosphere using,
At random glancing, each as I notice absorbing,
Swiftly on, but a little while alighting,
Curious envelop'd messages delivering,
Sparkles hot, seed ethereal down in the dirt dropping,
Myself unknowing, my commission obeying, to question
it never daring,
To ages and ages yet the growth of the seed leaving,
To troops out of the war arising, they the tasks I have set
promulging,
To women certain whispers of myself bequeathing, their
affection me more clearly explaining,
To young men my problems offering—no dallier I—I the
muscle of their brains trying,
So I pass, a little time vocal, visible, contrary,
Afterward a melodious echo, passionately bent for, (death
making me really undying,)

The best of me then when no longer visible, for toward
    that I have been incessantly preparing.

What is there more, that I lag and pause and crouch
    extended with unshut mouth?
Is there a single final farewell?

My songs cease, I abandon them,
From behind the screen where I hid I advance personally
    solely to you.

Camerado, this is no book,
Who touches this touches a man,
(Is it night? are we here together alone?)
It is I you hold and who holds you,
I spring from the pages into your arms—decease calls me
    forth.

O how your fingers drowse me,
Your breath falls around me like dew, your pulse lulls the
    tympans of my ears,
I feel immerged from head to foot,
Delicious, enough.

Enough O deed impromptu and secret,
Enough O gliding present—enough O summ'd-up past.

Dear friend whoever you are take this kiss,
I give it especially to you, do not forget me,
I feel like one who has done work for the day to retire
    awhile,

I receive now again of my many translations, from my
   avataras ascending, while others doubtless await me,
An unknown sphere more real than I dream'd, more
   direct, darts awakening rays about me, *So long!*
Remember my words, I may again return,
I love you, I depart from materials,
I am as one disembodied, triumphant, dead.

SANDS AT SEVENTY.

MANNAHATTA.

My city's fit and noble name resumed,
Choice aboriginal name, with marvellous beauty, mean-
　　ing,
A rocky founded island—shores where ever gayly dash the com-
　　ing, going, hurrying sea waves.

PAUMANOK.

Sea beauty! stretch'd and basking!
One side thy inland ocean laving, broad, with copious
　　commerce, steamers, sails,
And one the Atlantic's wind caressing, fierce or gentle—
　　mighty hulls dark-gliding in the distance.
Isle of sweet brooks of drinking-water—healthy air and
　　soil!
Isle of the salty shore and breeze and brine!

FROM MONTAUK POINT.

I stand as on some mighty eagle's beak,
Eastward the sea absorbing, viewing, (nothing but sea
    and sky,)
The tossing waves, the foam, the ships in the distance,
The wild unrest, the snowy, curling caps—that inbound
    urge and urge of waves,
Seeking the shores forever.

TO THOSE WHO'VE FAIL'D.

To those who've fail'd, in aspiration vast,
To unnam'd soldiers fallen in front on the lead,
To calm, devoted engineers—to over-ardent travelers—to
    pilots on their ships,
To many a lofty song and picture without recognition—
    I'd rear a laurel-cover'd monument,
High, high above the rest—To all cut off before their time,
Possess'd by some strange spirit of fire,
Quench'd by an early death.

A CAROL CLOSING SIXTY-NINE.

A carol closing sixty-nine—a *résumé*—a repetition,
My lines in joy and hope continuing on the same,
Of ye, O God, Life, Nature, Freedom, Poetry;
Of you, my Land—your rivers, prairies, States—you,
    mottled Flag I love,

Your aggregate retain'd entire—Of north, south, east and
    west, your items all;
Of me myself—the jocund heart yet beating in my breast,
The body wreck'd, old, poor and paralyzed—the strange
    inertia falling pall-like round me,
The burning fires down in my sluggish blood not yet
    extinct,
The undiminish'd faith—the groups of loving friends.

THE BRAVEST SOLDIERS.

Brave, brave were the soldiers (high named to-day) who
    lived through the fight;
But the bravest press'd to the front and fell unnamed,
    unknown.

A FONT OF TYPE.

This latent mine—these unlaunch'd voices—passionate
    powers,
Wrath, argument, or praise, or comic leer, or prayer
    devout,
(Not nonpareil, brevier, bourgeois, long primer merely,)
These ocean waves arousable to fury and to death,
Or sooth'd to ease and sheeny sun and sleep,
Within the pallid slivers slumbering.

AS I SIT WRITING HERE.

As I sit writing here, sick and grown old,
Not my least burden is that dulness of the years, querilities,
Ungracious glooms, aches, lethargy, constipation, whimpering *ennui*,
May filter in my daily songs.

MY CANARY BIRD.

Did we count great, O soul, to penetrate the themes of mighty books,
Absorbing deep and full from thoughts, plays, speculations?
But now from thee to me, caged bird, to feel thy joyous warble,
Filling the air, the lonesome room, the long forenoon,
Is it not just as great, O soul?

QUERIES TO MY SEVENTIETH YEAR.

Approaching, nearing, curious,
Thou dim, uncertain spectre—bringest thou life or death?
Strength, weakness, blindness, more paralysis and heavier?
Or placid skies and sun? Wilt stir the waters yet?
Or haply cut me short for good? Or leave me here as now,
Dull, parrot-like and old, with crack'd voice harping, screeching?

THE WALLABOUT MARTYRS.

[In Brooklyn, in an old vault, mark'd by no special recognition, lie hud-
dled at this moment the undoubtedly authentic remains of the stanchest
and earliest revolutionary patriots from the British prison ships and
prisons of the times of 1776-83, in and around New York, and from all
over Long Island; originally buried—many thousands of them—in
trenches in the Wallabout sands.]

Greater than memory of Achilles or Ulysses,
More, more by far to thee than tomb of Alexander,
Those cart loads of old charnel ashes, scales and splints
    of mouldy bones,
Once living men—once resolute courage, aspiration,
    strength,
The stepping stones to thee to-day and here, America.

THE FIRST DANDELION.

Simple and fresh and fair from winter's close emerging,
As if no artifice of fashion, business, politics, had ever
    been,
Forth from its sunny nook of shelter'd grass—innocent,
    golden, calm as the dawn,
The spring's first dandelion shows its trustful face.

AMERICA.

Centre of equal daughters, equal sons,
All, all alike endear'd, grown, ungrown, young or old,
Strong, ample, fair, enduring, capable, rich,
Perennial with the Earth, with Freedom, Law and Love,

A grand, sane, towering, seated Mother,
Chair'd in the adamant of Time.

MEMORIES.

How sweet the silent backward tracings!
The wanderings as in dreams—the meditation of old
    times resumed—their loves, joys, persons, voyages.

TO-DAY AND THEE.

The appointed winners in a long-stretch'd game;
The course of Time and nations—Egypt, India, Greece
    and Rome;
The past entire, with all its heroes, histories, arts, experi-
    ments,
Its store of songs, inventions, voyages, teachers, books,
Garner'd for now and thee—To think of it!
The heirdom all converged in thee!

AFTER THE DAZZLE OF DAY.

After the dazzle of day is gone,
Only the dark, dark night shows to my eyes the stars;
After the clangor of organ majestic, or chorus, or perfect
    band,
Silent, athwart my soul, moves the symphony true.

ABRAHAM LINCOLN, BORN FEB. 12, 1809

To-day, from each and all, a breath of prayer—a pulse of
    thought,
To memory of Him—to birth of Him.

Publish'd Feb. 12, 1888.

OUT OF MAY'S SHOWS SELECTED.

Apple orchards, the trees all cover'd with blossoms;
Wheat fields carpeted far and near in vital emerald green;
The eternal, exhaustless freshness of each early morning;
The yellow, golden, transparent haze of the warm after-
    noon sun;
The aspiring lilac bushes with profuse purple or white
    flowers.

HALCYON DAYS.

Not from successful love alone,
Nor wealth, nor honor'd middle age, nor victories of pol-
    itics or war;
But as life wanes, and all the turbulent passions calm,
As gorgeous, vapory, silent hues cover the evening sky,
As softness, fulness, rest, suffuse the frame, like freshier,
    balmier air,
As the days take on a mellower light, and the apple at last
    hangs really finish'd and indolent-ripe on the tree,
Then for the teeming quietest, happiest days of all!
The brooding and blissful halcyon days!

*

FANCIES AT NAVESINK.

The Pilot in the Mist.

Steaming the northern rapids—(an old St. Lawrence rem-
    iniscence,
A sudden memory-flash comes back, I know not why,
Here waiting for the sunrise, gazing from this hill;)*
Again 'tis just at morning—a heavy haze contends with
    daybreak,
Again the trembling, laboring vessel veers me—I press
    through foam-dash'd rocks that almost touch me,
Again I mark where aft the small thin Indian helmsman
Looms in the mist, with brow elate and governing hand.

Had I the Choice.

Had I the choice to tally greatest bards,
To limn their portraits, stately, beautiful, and emulate at
    will,
Homer with all his wars and warriors—Hector, Achilles,
    Ajax,
Or Shakspere's woe-entangled Hamlet, Lear, Othello—
    Tennyson's fair ladies,
Metre or wit the best, or choice conceit to wield in perfect
    rhyme, delight of singers;
These, these, O sea, all these I'd gladly barter,

*Navesink—a sea-side mountain, lower entrance of New York Bay.

Would you the undulation of one wave, its trick to me
    transfer,
Or breathe one breath of yours upon my verse,
And leave its odor there.

You Tides with Ceaseless Swell.

You tides with ceaseless swell! you power that does this
    work!
You unseen force, centripetal, centrifugal, through space's
    spread,
Rapport of sun, moon, earth, and all the constellations,
What are the messages by you from distant stars to us?
    what Sirius'? what Capella's?
What central heart—and you the pulse—vivifies all? what
    boundless aggregate of all?
What subtle indirection and significance in you? what
    clue to all in you? what fluid, vast identity,
Holding the universe with all its parts as one—as sailing
    in a ship?

Last of Ebb, and Daylight Waning.

Last of ebb, and daylight waning,
Scented sea-cool landward making, smells of sedge and
    salt incoming,
With many a half-caught voice sent up from the eddies,
Many a muffled confession—many a sob and whisper'd
    word,
As of speakers far or hid.

How they sweep down and out! how they mutter!
Poets unnamed—artists greatest of any, with cherish'd
    lost designs,
Love's unresponse—a chorus of age's complaints—
    hope's last words,
Some suicide's despairing cry, *Away to the boundless waste,*
    and never again return.

On to oblivion then!
On, on, and do your part, ye burying, ebbing tide!
On for your time, ye furious debouché!

And Yet Not You Alone.

And yet not you alone, twilight and burying ebb,
Nor you, ye lost designs alone—nor failures, aspirations;
I know, divine deceitful ones, your glamour's seeming;
Duly by you, from you, the tide and light again—duly the
    hinges turning,
Duly the needed discord-parts offsetting, blending,
Weaving from you, from Sleep, Night, Death itself,
The rhythmus of Birth eternal.

Proudly the Flood Comes In.

Proudly the flood comes in, shouting, foaming, advanc-
    ing,
Long it holds at the high, with bosom broad outswelling,

All throbs, dilates—the farms, woods, streets of cities—
    workmen at work,
Mainsails, topsails, jibs, appear in the offing—steamers'
    pennants of smoke—and under the forenoon sun,
Freighted with human lives, gaily the outward bound,
    gaily the inward bound,
Flaunting from many a spar the flag I love.

By That Long Scan of Waves.

By that long scan of waves, myself call'd back, resumed
    upon myself,
In every crest some undulating light or shade—some ret-
    rospect,
Joys, travels, studies, silent panoramas—scenes
    ephemeral,
The long past war, the battles, hospital sights, the
    wounded and the dead,
Myself through every by-gone phase—my idle youth—
    old age at hand,
My three-score years of life summ'd up, and more, and
    past,
By any grand ideal tried, intentionless, the whole a noth-
    ing,
And haply yet some drop within God's scheme's ensem-
    ble—some wave, or part of wave,
Like one of yours, ye multitudinous ocean.

Then Last of All.

Then last of all, caught from these shores, this hill,
Of you O tides, the mystic human meaning:
Only by law of you, your swell and ebb, enclosing me the
same,
The brain that shapes, the voice that chants this song.

ELECTION DAY, NOVEMBER, 1884.

If I should need to name, O Western World, your power-
fulest scene and show,
'Twould not be you, Niagara—nor you, ye limitless
prairies—nor your huge rifts of canyons, Colorado,
Nor you, Yosemite—nor Yellowstone, with all its spasmic
geyser-loops ascending to the skies, appearing and
disappearing,
Nor Oregon's white cones—nor Huron's belt of mighty
lakes—nor Mississippi's stream:
—This seething hemisphere's humanity, as now, I'd
name—*the still small voice* vibrating—America's
choosing day,
(The heart of it not in the chosen—the act itself the main,
the quadriennial choosing,)
The stretch of North and South arous'd—sea-board and
inland—Texas to Maine—the Prairie States—Ver-
mont, Virginia, California,
The final ballot-shower from East to West—the paradox
and conflict,
The countless snow-flakes falling—(a swordless conflict,

Yet more than all Rome's wars of old, or modern
    Napoleon's:) the peaceful choice of all,
Or good or ill humanity—welcoming the darker odds, the
    dross:
—Foams and ferments the wine? it serves to purify—
    while the heart pants, life glows:
These stormy gusts and winds waft precious ships,
Swell'd Washington's, Jefferson's, Lincoln's sails.

WITH HUSKY-HAUGHTY LIPS, O SEA!

With husky-haughty lips, O sea!
Where day and night I wend thy surf-beat shore,
Imaging to my sense thy varied strange suggestions,
(I see and plainly list thy talk and conference here,)
Thy troops of white-maned racers racing to the goal,
Thy ample, smiling face, dash'd with the sparkling dim-
    ples of the sun,
Thy brooding scowl and murk—thy unloos'd hurricanes,
Thy unsubduedness, caprices, wilfulness;
Great as thou art above the rest, thy many tears—a lack
    from all eternity in thy content,
(Naught but the greatest struggles, wrongs, defeats, could
    make thee greatest—no less could make thee,)
Thy lonely state—something thou ever seek'st and
    seek'st, yet never gain'st,
Surely some right withheld—some voice, in huge monot-
    onous rage, of freedom-lover pent,
Some vast heart, like a planet's, chain'd and chafing in
    those breakers,

By lengthen'd swell, and spasm, and panting breath,
And rhythmic rasping of thy sands and waves,
And serpent hiss, and savage peals of laughter,
And undertones of distant lion roar,
(Sounding, appealing to the sky's deaf ear—but now, rap-
    port for once,
A phantom in the night thy confidant for once,)
The first and last confession of the globe,
Outsurging, muttering from thy soul's abysms,
The tale of cosmic elemental passion,
Thou tellest to a kindred soul.

DEATH OF GENERAL GRANT.

As one by one withdraw the lofty actors,
From that great play on history's stage eterne,
That lurid, partial act of war and peace—of old and new
    contending,
Fought out through wrath, fears, dark dismays, and many
    a long suspense;
All past—and since, in countless graves receding, mel-
    lowing,
Victor's and vanquish'd—Lincoln's and Lee's—now thou
    with them,
Man of the mighty days—and equal to the days!
Thou from the prairies!—tangled and many-vein'd and
    hard has been thy part,
To admiration has it been enacted!

RED JACKET (FROM ALOFT.)

[*Impromptu on Buffalo City's monument to, and re-burial of the old Iroquois orator, October 9, 1884.*]

Upon this scene, this show,
Yielded to-day by fashion, learning, wealth,
(Nor in caprice alone—some grains of deepest meaning,)
Haply, aloft, (who knows?) from distant sky-clouds'
    blended shapes,
As some old tree, or rock or cliff, thrill'd with its soul,
Product of Nature's sun, stars, earth direct—a towering
    human form,
In hunting-shirt of film, arm'd with the rifle, a half-ironi-
    cal smile curving its phantom lips,
Like one of Ossian's ghosts looks down.

WASHINGTON'S MONUMENT, FEBRUARY, 1885.

Ah, not this marble, dead and cold:
Far from its base and shaft expanding—the round zones
    circling, comprehending,
Thou, Washington, art all the world's, the continents'
    entire—not yours alone, America,
Europe's as well, in every part, castle of lord or laborer's
    cot,
Or frozen North, or sultry South—the African's—the
    Arab's in his tent,
Old Asia's there with venerable smile, seated amid her
    ruins;
(Greets the antique the hero new? 'tis but the same—the
    heir legitimate, continued ever,

The indomitable heart and arm—proofs of the never-bro-
    ken line,
Courage, alertness, patience, faith, the same—e'en in
    defeat defeated not, the same:)
Wherever sails a ship, or house is built on land, or day or
    night,
Through teeming cities' streets, indoors or out, factories
    or farms,
Now, or to come, or past—where patriot wills existed or
    exist,
Wherever Freedom, pois'd by Toleration, sway'd by Law,
Stands or is rising thy true monument.

OF THAT BLITHE THROAT OF THINE.

[*More than eighty-three degrees north—about a good day's steaming
distance to the Pole by one of our fast oceaners in clear water—Greely
the explorer heard the song of a single snow-bird merrily sounding over
the desolation.*]

Of that blithe throat of thine from arctic bleak and blank,
I'll mind the lesson, solitary bird—let me too welcome
    chilling drifts,
E'en the profoundest chill, as now—a torpid pulse, a
    brain unnerv'd,
Old age land-lock'd within its winter bay—(cold, cold, O
    cold!)
These snowy hairs, my feeble arm, my frozen feet,
For them thy faith, thy rule I take, and grave it to the last;
Not summer's zones alone—not chants of youth, or
    south's warm tides alone,

But held by sluggish floes, pack'd in the northern ice, the
    cumulus of years,
These with gay heart I also sing.

BROADWAY.

What hurrying human tides, or day or night!
What passions, winnings, losses, ardors, swim thy waters!
What whirls of evil, bliss and sorrow, stem thee!
What curious questioning glances—glints of love!
Leer, envy, scorn, contempt, hope, aspiration!
Thou portal—thou arena—thou of the myriad long-
    drawn lines and groups!
(Could but thy flagstones, curbs, façades, tell their inim-
    itable tales;
Thy windows rich, and huge hotels—thy side-walks
    wide;)
Thou of the endless sliding, mincing, shuffling feet!
Thou, like the parti-colored world itself—like infinite,
    teeming, mocking life!
Thou visor'd, vast, unspeakable show and lesson!

TO GET THE FINAL LILT OF SONGS.

To get the final lilt of songs,
To penetrate the inmost lore of poets—to know the
    mighty ones,
Job, Homer, Eschylus, Dante, Shakspere, Tennyson,
    Emerson;

To diagnose the shifting-delicate tints of love and pride
and doubt—to truly understand,
To encompass these, the last keen faculty and entrance-
price,
Old age, and what it brings from all its past experiences.

OLD SALT KOSSABONE.

Far back, related on my mother's side,
Old Salt Kossabone, I'll tell you how he died:
(Had been a sailor all his life—was nearly 90—lived with
his married grandchild, Jenny;
House on a hill, with view of bay at hand, and distant
cape, and stretch to open sea;)
The last of afternoons, the evening hours, for many a year
his regular custom,
In his great arm chair by the window seated,
(Sometimes, indeed, through half the day,)
Watching the coming, going of the vessels, he mutters to
himself—And now the close of all:
One struggling outbound brig, one day, baffled for long—
cross-tides and much wrong going,
At last at nightfall strikes the breeze aright, her whole
luck veering,
And swiftly bending round the cape, the darkness
proudly entering, cleaving, as he watches,
"She's free—she's on her destination"—these the last
words—when Jenny came, he sat there dead,
Dutch Kossabone, Old Salt, related on my mother's side,
far back.

THE DEAD TENOR.

As down the stage again,
With Spanish hat and plumes, and gait inimitable,
Back from the fading lessons of the past, I'd call, I'd tell
      and own,
How much from thee! the revelation of the singing voice
      from thee!
(So firm—so liquid-soft—again that tremulous, manly
      timbre!
The perfect singing voice—deepest of all to me the les-
      son—trial and test of all:)
How through those strains distill'd—how the rapt ears,
      the soul of me, absorbing
Fernando's heart, *Manrico's* passionate call, *Ernani's*, sweet
      Gennaro's,
I fold thenceforth, or seek to fold, within my chants trans-
      muting,
Freedom's and Love's and Faith's unloos'd cantabile,
(As perfume's, color's, sunlight's correlation:)
From these, for these, with these, a hurried line, dead
      tenor,
A wafted autumn leaf, dropt in the closing grave, the
      shovel'd earth,
To memory of thee.

CONTINUITIES.

[From a talk I had lately with a German spiritualist.]

Nothing is ever really lost, or can be lost,
No birth, identity, form—no object of the world.

Nor life, nor force, nor any visible thing;
Appearance must not foil, nor shifted sphere confuse thy
   brain.
Ample are time and space—ample the fields of Nature.
The body, sluggish, aged, cold—the embers left from ear-
   lier fires,
The light in the eye grown dim, shall duly flame again;
The sun now low in the west rises for mornings and for
   noons continual;
To frozen clods ever the spring's invisible law returns,
With grass and flowers and summer fruits and corn.

YONNONDIO.

[The sense of the word is *lament for the aborigines*. It is an Iroquois
term; and has been used for a personal name.]

A song, a poem of itself—the word itself a dirge,
Amid the wilds, the rocks, the storm and wintry night,
To me such misty, strange tableaux the syllables calling
   up;
Yonnondio—I see, far in the west or north, a limitless
   ravine, with plains and mountains dark,
I see swarms of stalwart chieftains, medicine-men, and
   warriors,
As flitting by like clouds of ghosts, they pass and are gone
   in the twilight,
(Race of the woods, the landscapes free, and the falls!
No picture, poem, statement, passing them to the future :)
Yonnondio! Yonnondio!—unlimn'd they disappear;
To-day gives place, and fades—the cities, farms, factories
   fade;

A muffled sonorous sound, a wailing word is borne
    through the air for a moment,
Then blank and gone and still, and utterly lost.

LIFE.

Ever the undiscouraged, resolute, struggling soul of man;
(Have former armies fail'd? then we send fresh armies—
    and fresh again;)
Ever the grappled mystery of all earth's ages old or new;
Ever the eager eyes, hurrahs, the welcome-clapping
    hands, the loud applause;
Ever the soul dissatisfied, curious, unconvinced at last;
Struggling to-day the same—battling the same.

"GOING SOMEWHERE."

My science-friend, my noblest woman-friend,
(Now buried in an English grave—and this a memory-
    leaf for her dear sake,)
Ended our talk—"The sum, concluding all we know of
    old or modern learning, intuitions deep,
"Of all Geologies—Histories—of all Astronomy—of Evo-
    lution, Metaphysics all,
"Is, that we all are onward, onward, speeding slowly,
    surely bettering,
"Life, life an endless march, an endless army, (no halt, but
    it is duly over,)

"The world, the race, the soul—in space and time the uni-
     verses,
"All bound as is befitting each—all surely going some-
     where."
From the 1867 edition L. of G.

SMALL THE THEME OF MY CHANT.

Small the theme of my Chant, yet the greatest—namely,
     One's-Self—a simple, separate person. That, for the
     use of the New World, I sing.
Man's physiology complete, from top to toe, I sing. Not
     physiognomy alone, nor brain alone, is worthy for the
     Muse;—I say the Form complete is worthier far. The
     Female equally with the Male, I sing.
Nor cease at the theme of One's-Self. I speak the word of
     the modern, the word En-Masse.
My Days I sing, and the Lands—with interstice I knew of
     hapless War.
(O friend, whoe'er you are, at last arriving hither to com-
     mence, I feel through every leaf the pressure of your
     hand, which I return.
And thus upon our journey, footing the road, and more
     than once, and link'd together let us go.)

TRUE CONQUERORS.

Old farmers, travelers, workmen (no matter how crippled
     or bent,)

Old sailors, out of many a perilous voyage, storm and
    wreck,
Old soldiers from campaigns, with all their wounds,
    defeats and scars;
Enough that they've survived at all—long life's unflinch-
    ing ones!
Forth from their struggles, trials, fights, to have emerged
    at all—in that alone,
True conquerors o'er all the rest.

THE UNITED STATES TO OLD WORLD CRITICS.

Here first the duties of to-day, the lessons of the concrete,
Wealth, order, travel, shelter, products, plenty;
As of the building of some varied, vast, perpetual edifice,
Whence to arise inevitable in time, the towering roofs, the
    lamps,
The solid-planted spires tall shooting to the stars.

THE CALMING THOUGHT OF ALL.

That coursing on, whate'er men's speculations,
Amid the changing schools, theologies, philosophies,
Amid the bawling presentations new and old,
The round earth's silent vital laws, facts, modes continue.

THANKS IN OLD AGE.

Thanks in old age—thanks ere I go,
For health, the midday sun, the impalpable air—for life,
    mere life,
For precious ever-lingering memories, (of you my mother
    dear—you, father—you, brothers, sisters, friends,)
For all my days—not those of peace alone—the days of
    war the same,
For gentle words, caresses, gifts from foreign lands,
For shelter, wine and meat—for sweet appreciation,
(You distant, dim unknown—or young or old—countless,
    unspecified, readers belov'd,
We never met, and ne'er shall meet—and yet our souls
    embrace, long, close and long;)
For beings, groups, love, deeds, words, books—for colors,
    forms,
For all the brave strong men—devoted, hardy men—
    who've forward sprung in freedom's help, all years,
    all lands,
For braver, stronger, more devoted men—(a special laurel
    ere I go, to life's war's chosen ones.
The cannoneers of song and thought—the great
    artillerists—the foremost leaders, captains of the
    soul:)
As soldier from an ended war return'd—As traveler out
    of myriads, to the long procession retrospective,
Thanks—joyful thanks!—a soldier's, traveler's thanks.

LIFE AND DEATH.

The two old, simple problems ever intertwined,
Close home, elusive, present, baffled, grappled.
By each successive age insoluble, pass'd on,
To ours to-day—and we pass on the same.

THE VOICE OF THE RAIN.

And who art thou? said I to the soft-falling shower,
Which, strange to tell, gave me an answer, as here trans-
      lated:
I am the Poem of Earth, said the voice of the rain,
Eternal I rise impalpable out of the land and the bottom-
      less sea,
Upward to heaven, whence, vaguely form'd, altogether
      changed, and yet the same,
I descend to lave the drouths, atomies, dust-layers of the
      globe,
And all that in them without me were seeds only, latent,
      unborn;
And forever, by day and night, I give back life to my own
      origin, and make pure and beautify it;
(For song, issuing from its birth-place, after fulfilment,
      wandering,
Reck'd or unreck'd, duly with love returns.)

SOON SHALL THE WINTER'S FOIL BE HERE.

Soon shall the winter's foil be here;
Soon shall these icy ligatures unbind and melt—A little
    while,
And air, soil, wave, suffused shall be in softness, bloom
    and growth—a thousand forms shall rise
From these dead clods and chills as from low burial
    graves.
Thine eyes, ears—all thy best attributes—all that takes
    cognizance of natural beauty,
Shall wake and fill. Thou shalt perceive the simple shows,
    the delicate miracles of earth,
Dandelions, clover, the emerald grass, the early scents
    and flowers,
The arbutus under foot, the willow's yellow-green, the
    blossoming plum and cherry;
With these the robin, lark and thrush, singing their
    songs—the flitting bluebird;
For such the scenes the annual play brings on.

WHILE NOT THE PAST FORGETTING.

While not the past forgetting,
To-day, at least, contention sunk entire—peace, brother-
    hood uprisen;
For sign reciprocal our Northern, Southern hands,
Lay on the graves of all dead soldiers, North or South,
(Nor for the past alone—for meanings to the future,)
Wreaths of roses and branches of palm.
    Publish'd May 30, 1888.

THE DYING VETERAN.

[A Long Island incident—early part of the present century.]

Amid these days of order, ease, prosperity,
Amid the current songs of beauty, peace, decorum,
I cast a reminiscence—(likely 'twill offend you,
I heard it in my boyhood;)—More than a generation
    since,
A queer old savage man, a fighter under Washington
    himself,
(Large, brave, cleanly, hot-blooded, no talker, rather spir-
    itualistic,
Had fought in the ranks—fought well—had been all
    through the Revolutionary war,)
Lay dying—sons, daughters, church-deacons, lovingly
    tending him,
Sharping their sense, their ears, towards his murmuring,
    half-caught words:
"Let me return again to my war-days,
To the sights and scenes—to forming the line of battle,
To the scouts ahead reconnoitering,
To the cannons, the grim artillery,
To the galloping aids, carrying orders,
To the wounded, the fallen, the heat, the suspense,
The perfume strong, the smoke, the deafening noise;
Away with your life of peace!—your joys of peace!
Give me my old wild battle-life again!"

STRONGER LESSONS.

Have you learn'd lessons only of those who admired you,
    and were tender with you, and stood aside for you?
Have you not learn'd great lessons from those who reject
    you, and brace themselves against you? or who treat
    you with contempt, or dispute the passage with you?

A PRAIRIE SUNSET.

Shot gold, maroon and violet, dazzling silver, emerald,
    fawn,
The earth's whole amplitude and Nature's multiform
    power consign'd for once to colors;
The light, the general air possess'd by them—colors till
    now unknown,
No limit, confine—not the Western sky alone—the high
    meridian—North, South, all,
Pure luminous color fighting the silent shadows to the
    last.

TWENTY YEARS.

Down on the ancient wharf, the sand, I sit, with a new-
    comer chatting:
He shipp'd as green-hand boy, and sail'd away, (took
    some sudden, vehement notion;)
Since, twenty years and more have circled round and
    round,

While he the globe was circling round and round,—and
    now returns:
How changed the place—all the old land-marks gone—
    the parents dead;
(Yes, he comes back *to lay in port for good—to settle*—has a
    well-fill'd purse—no spot will do but this;)
The little boat that scull'd him from the sloop, now held in
    leash I see,
I hear the slapping waves, the restless keel, the rocking in
    the sand,
I see the sailor kit, the canvas bag, the great box bound
    with brass,
I scan the face all berry-brown and bearded—the stout-
    strong frame,
Dress'd in its russet suit of good Scotch cloth:
(Then what the told-out story of those twenty years?
    What of the future?)

ORANGE BUDS BY MAIL FROM FLORIDA.

*[Voltaire closed a famous argument by claiming that a ship of war and
the grand opera were proofs enough of civilization's and France's
progress, in his day.]*

A lesser proof than old Voltaire's, yet greater,
Proof of this present time, and thee, thy broad expanse,
    America,
To my plain Northern hut, in outside clouds and snow,
Brought safely for a thousand miles o'er land and tide,
Some three days since on their own soil live-sprouting,
Now here their sweetness through my room unfolding,
A bunch of orange buds by mail from Florida.

TWILIGHT.

The soft voluptuous opiate shades,
The sun just gone, the eager light dispell'd—(I too will
    soon be gone, dispell'd,)
A haze—nirwana—rest and night—oblivion.

YOU LINGERING SPARSE LEAVES OF ME.

You lingering sparse leaves of me on winter-nearing
    boughs,
And I some well-shorn tree of field or orchard-row;
You tokens diminute and lorn—(not now the flush of
    May or July clover-bloom—no grain of August now;)
You pallid banner-staves—you pennants valueless—you
    over-stay'd of time,
Yet my soul-dearest leaves confirming all the rest,
The faithfulest—hardiest—last.

NOT MEAGRE, LATENT BOUGHS ALONE.

Not meagre, latent boughs alone, O songs! (scaly and
    bare, like eagles' talons,)
But haply for some sunny day (who knows?) some future
    spring, some summer—bursting forth,
To verdant leaves, or sheltering shade—to nourishing
    fruit,
Apples and grapes—the stalwart limbs of trees emerg-
    ing—the fresh, free, open air,
And love and faith, like scented roses blooming.

THE DEAD EMPEROR.

To-day, with bending head and eyes, thou, too, Colum-
　　bia,
Less for the mighty crown laid low in sorrow—less for the
　　Emperor,
Thy true condolence breathest, sendest out o'er many a
　　salt sea mile,
Mourning a good old man—a faithful shepherd, patriot.
　Publish'd March 10, 1888.

AS THE GREEK'S SIGNAL FLAME.
[For Whittier's eightieth birthday, December 17, 1887.]

As the Greek's signal flame, by antique records told,
Rose from the hill-top, like applause and glory,
Welcoming in fame some special veteran, hero,
With rosy tinge reddening the land he'd served,
So I aloft from Mannahatta's ship-fringed shore,
Lift high a kindled brand for thee, Old Poet.

THE DISMANTLED SHIP.

In some unused lagoon, some nameless bay,
On sluggish, lonesome waters, anchor'd near the shore,
An old, dismasted, gray and batter'd ship, disabled, done,
After free voyages to all the seas of earth, haul'd up at last
　　and hawser'd tight,
Lies rusting, mouldering.

NOW PRECEDENT SONGS, FAREWELL.

Now precedent songs, farewell—by every name farewell,
(Trains of a staggering line in many a strange procession,
    waggons,
From ups and downs—with intervals—from elder years,
    mid-age, or youth,)
"In Cabin'd Ships," or "Thee Old Cause" or "Poets to
    Come"
Or "Paumanok," "Song of Myself," "Calamus," or
    "Adam,"
Or "Beat! Beat! Drums!" or "To the Leaven'd Soil they
    Trod,"
Or "Captain! My Captain!" "Kosmos," "Quicksand
    Years," or "Thoughts,"
"Thou Mother with thy Equal Brood," and many, many
    more unspecified,
From fibre heart of mine—from throat and tongue—(My
    life's hot pulsing blood,
The personal urge and form for me—not merely paper,
    automatic type and ink,)
Each song of mine—each utterance in the past—having its
    long, long history,
Of life or death, or soldier's wound, of country's loss or
    safety,
(O heaven! what flash and started endless train of all!
    compared indeed to that!
What wretched shred e'en at the best of all!)

AN EVENING LULL.

After a week of physical anguish,
Unrest and pain, and feverish heat,
Toward the ending day a calm and lull comes on,
Three hours of peace and soothing rest of brain.[*]

OLD AGE'S LAMBENT PEAKS.

The touch of flame—the illuminating fire—the loftiest
　　look at last,
O'er city, passion, sea—o'er prairie, mountain, wood—
　　the earth itself;
The airy, different, changing hues of all, in falling twi-
　　light,
Objects and groups, bearings, faces, reminiscences;
The calmer sight—the golden setting, clear and broad:
So much i' the atmosphere, the points of view, the situa-
　　tions whence we scan,
Bro't out by them alone—so much (perhaps the best)
　　unreck'd before;
The lights indeed from them—old age's lambent peaks.

[*]The two songs on this page are eked out during an afternoon, June,
1888, in my seventieth year, at a critical spell of illness. Of course no
reader and probably no human being at any time will ever have such
phases of emotional and solemn action as these involve to me. I feel in
them an end and close of all.

AFTER THE SUPPER AND TALK.

After the supper and talk—after the day is done,
As a friend from friends his final withdrawal prolonging,
Good-bye and Good-bye with emotional lips repeating,
(So hard for his hand to release those hands—no more
    will they meet,
No more for communion of sorrow and joy, of old and
    young,
A far-stretching journey awaits him, to return no more,)
Shunning, postponing severance—seeking to ward off the
    last word ever so little,
E'en at the exit door turning—charges superfluous calling
    back—e'en as he descends the steps,
Something to eke out a minute additional—shadows of
    nightfall deepening,
Farewells, messages lessening—dimmer the forthgoer's
    visage and form,
Soon to be lost for aye in the darkness—loth, O so loth to
    depart!
Garrulous to the very last.

SECOND ANNEX

✳

GOOD-BYE MY FANCY.

PREFACE NOTE TO 2D ANNEX, CONCLUDING L. OF G.—1891.

Had I not better withhold (in this old age and paralysis of me) such little tags and fringe-dots (maybe specks, stains,) as follow a long dusty journey, and witness it afterward? I have probably not been enough afraid of careless touches, from the first—and am not now—nor of parrot-like repetitions—nor platitudes and the commonplace. Perhaps I am too democratic for such avoidances. Besides, is not the verse-field, as originally plann'd by my theory, now sufficiently illustrated—and full time for me to silently retire?—(indeed amid no loud call or market for my sort of poetic utterance.)

In answer, or rather defiance, to that kind of well-put interrogation, here comes this little cluster, and conclusion of my preceding clusters. Though not at all clear that, as here collated, it is worth printing (certainly I have nothing fresh to write)—I while away the hours of my 72d year—hours of forced confinement in my den—by putting in shape this small old age collation:

Last droplets of and after spontaneous rain,
From many limpid distillations and past showers;

(Will they germinate anything? mere exhalations as they all
    are—the land's and sea's—America's;
Will they filter to any deep emotion? any heart and brain?)

However that may be, I feel like improving to-day's
opportunity and wind up. During the last two years I
have sent out, in the lulls of illness and exhaustion, certain
chirps—lingering-dying ones probably (undoubtedly)—
which now I may as well gather and put in fair type while
able to see correctly—(for my eyes plainly warn me they
are dimming, and my brain more and more palpably
neglects or refuses, month after month, even slight tasks
or revisions.)

In fact, here I am these current years 1890 and '91,
(each successive fortnight getting stiffer and stuck deeper)
much like some hard-cased dilapidated grim ancient
shell-fish or time-bang'd conch (no legs, utterly non-loco-
motive) cast up high and dry on the shore-sands, helpless
to move anywhere—nothing left but behave myself quiet,
and while away the days yet assign'd, and discover if
there is anything for the said grim and time-bang'd conch
to be got at last out of inherited good spirits and primal
buoyant centre-pulses down there deep somewhere
within his gray-blurr'd old shell............(Reader, you must
allow a little fun here—for one reason there are too many
of the following poemets about death, &c., and for
another the passing hours (July 5, 1890) are so sunny-fine.
And old as I am I feel to-day almost a part of some frolic-
some wave, or for sporting yet like a kid or kitten—prob-
ably a streak of physical adjustment and perfection here
and now. I believe I have it in me perennially anyhow.)

Then behind all, the deep-down consolation (it is a

glum one, but I dare not be sorry for the fact of it in the past, nor refrain from dwelling, even vaunting here at the end) that this late-years palsied old shorn and shell-fish condition of me is the indubitable outcome and growth, now near for 20 years along, of too over-zealous, over-continued bodily and emotional excitement and action through the times of 1862, '3, '4 and '5, visiting and waiting on wounded and sick army volunteers, both sides, in campaigns or contests, or after them, or in hospitals or fields south of Washington City, or in that place and elsewhere—those hot, sad, wrenching times—the army volunteers, all States,—or North or South—the wounded, suffering, dying—the exhausting, sweating summers, marches, battles, carnage—those trenches hurriedly heap'd by the corpse-thousands, mainly unknown—Will the America of the future—will this vast rich Union ever realize what itself cost, back there after all?—those hecatombs of battle-deaths—Those times of which, O far-off reader, this whole book is indeed finally but a reminiscent memorial from thence by me to you?

SAIL OUT FOR GOOD, EIDÓLON YACHT!

Heave the anchor short!
Raise main-sail and jib—steer forth,
O little white-hull'd sloop, now speed on really deep
    waters,
(I will not call it our concluding voyage,
But outset and sure entrance to the truest, best, maturest;)
Depart, depart from solid earth—no more returning to
    these shores,
Now on for aye our infinite free venture wending,
Spurning all yet tried ports, seas, hawsers, densities, grav-
    itation,
Sail out for good, eidólon yacht of me!

LINGERING LAST DROPS.

And whence and why come you?

We know not whence, (was the answer,)
We only know that we drift here with the rest,
That we linger'd and lagg'd—but were wafted at last, and
    are now here,
To make the passing shower's concluding drops.

GOOD-BYE MY FANCY.

Good-bye* my fancy—(I had a word to say,
But 'tis not quite the time—The best of any man's word or
    say,
Is when its proper place arrives—and for its meaning,
I keep mine till the last.)

ON, ON THE SAME, YE JOCUND TWAIN!

On, on the same, ye jocund twain!
My life and recitative, containing birth, youth, mid-age
    years,
Fitful as motley-tongues of flame, inseparably twined and
    merged in one—combining all,
My single soul—aims, confirmations, failures, joys—Nor
    single soul alone,
I chant my nation's crucial stage, (America's, haply
    humanity's)—the trial great, the victory great,
A strange *eclaircissement* of all the masses past, the east-
    ern world, the ancient, medieval,

---

*Behind a Good-bye there lurks much of the salutation of another begin-
ning—to me, Development, Continuity, Immortality, Transformation,
are the chiefest life-meanings of Nature and Humanity, and are the *sine
qua non* of all facts, and each fact.
Why do folks dwell so fondly on the last words, advice, appearance, of
the departing? Those last words are not samples of the best, which
involve vitality at its full, and balance, and perfect control and scope. But
they are valuable beyond measure to confirm and endorse the varied
train, facts, theories and faith of the whole preceding life.

Here, here from wanderings, strayings, lessons, wars,
   defeats—here at the west a voice triumphant—justi-
   fying all,
A gladsome pealing cry—a song for once of utmost pride
   and satisfaction;
I chant from it the common bulk, the general average
   horde, (the best no sooner than the worst)—And now
   I chant old age,
(My verses, written first for forenoon life, and for the
   summer's, autumn's spread,
I pass to snow-white hairs the same, and give to pulses
   winter-cool'd the same;)
As here in careless trill, I and my recitatives, with faith
   and love,
Wafting to other work, to unknown songs, conditions,
On, on, ye jocund twain! continue on the same!

MY 71ST YEAR.

After surmounting three score and ten,
With all their chances, changes, losses, sorrows,
My parents' deaths, the vagaries of my life, the many tear-
   ing passions of me, the war of '63 and '4,
As some old broken soldier, after a long, hot, wearying
   march, or haply after battle,
To-day at twilight, hobbling, answering company roll-
   call, *Here*, with vital voice,
Reporting yet, saluting yet the Officer over all.

APPARITIONS.

A vague mist hanging 'round half the pages:
(Sometimes how strange and clear to the soul,
That all these solid things are indeed but apparitions, con-
     cepts, non-realities.)

THE PALLID WREATH.

Somehow I cannot let it go yet, funeral though it is,
Let it remain back there on its nail suspended,
With pink, blue, yellow, all blanch'd, and the white now
     gray and ashy,
One wither'd rose put years ago for thee, dear friend;
But I do not forget thee. Hast thou then faded?
Is the odor exhaled? Are the colors, vitalities, dead?
No, while memories subtly play—the past vivid as ever;
For but last night I woke, and in that spectral ring saw
     thee,
Thy smile, eyes, face, calm, silent, loving as ever:
So let the wreath hang still awhile within my eye-reach,
It is not yet dead to me, nor even pallid.

AN ENDED DAY.

The soothing sanity and blitheness of completion,
The pomp and hurried contest-glare and rush are done;
Now triumph! transformation! jubilate!*

*NOTE.—Summer country life.—Several years.—In my rambles and
explorations I found a woody place near the creek, where for some rea-

OLD AGE'S SHIP & CRAFTY DEATH'S.

From east and west across the horizon's edge,
Two mighty masterful vessels sailers steal upon us:
But we'll make race a-time upon the seas—a battle-contest
    yet! bear lively there!
(Our joys of strife and derring-do to the last!)
Put on the old ship all her power to-day!
Crowd top-sail, top-gallant and royal studding-sails,

---

son the birds in happy mood seem'd to resort in unusual numbers. Especially at the beginning of the day, and again at the ending, I was sure to get there the most copious bird-concerts. I repair'd there frequently at sunrise—and also at sunset, or just before . . . Once the question arose in me: Which is the best singing, the first or the lattermost? The first always exhilarated, and perhaps seem'd more joyous and stronger; but I always felt the sunset or late afternoon sounds more penetrating and sweeter—seem'd to touch the soul—often the evening thrushes, two or three of them, responding and perhaps blending. Though I miss'd some of the mornings, I found myself getting to be quite strictly punctual at the evening utterances.

ANOTHER NOTE.—"He went out with the tide and the sunset," was a phrase I heard from a surgeon describing an old sailor's death under peculiarly gentle conditions.

During the Secession War, 1863 and '4, visiting the Army Hospitals around Washington, I form'd the habit, and continued it to the end, whenever the ebb or flood tide began the latter part of day, of punctually visiting those at that time populous wards of suffering men. Somehow (or I thought so) the effect of the hour was palpable. The badly wounded would get some ease, and would like to talk a little, or be talk'd to. Intellectual and emotional natures would be at their best: Deaths were always easier; medicines seem'd to have better effect when given then, and a lulling atmosphere would pervade the wards.

Similar influences, similar circumstances and hours, day-close, after great battles, even with all their horrors. I had more than once the same experience on the fields cover'd with fallen or dead.

Out challenge and defiance—flags and flaunting pen-
    nants added,
As we take to the open—take to the deepest, freest waters.

TO THE PENDING YEAR.

Have I no weapon-word for thee—some message brief
    and fierce?
(Have I fought out and done indeed the battle?) Is there
    no shot left,
For all thy affectations, lisps, scorns, manifold silliness?
Nor for myself—my own rebellious self in thee?

Down, down, proud gorge!—though choking thee;
Thy bearded throat and high-borne forehead to the gut-
    ter;
Crouch low thy neck to eleemosynary gifts.

SHAKSPERE-BACON'S CIPHER.

I doubt it not—then more, far more;
In each old song bequeath'd—in every noble page or text,
(Different—something unreck'd before—some unsus-
    pected author,)
In every object, mountain, tree, and star—in every birth
    and life,
As part of each—evolv'd from each—meaning, behind
    the ostent,
A mystic cipher waits infolded.

LONG, LONG HENCE.

After a long, long course, hundreds of years, denials,
Accumulations, rous'd love and joy and thought,
Hopes, wishes, aspirations, ponderings, victories, myriads of readers,
Coating, compassing, covering—after ages' and ages' encrustations,
Then only may these songs reach fruition.

BRAVO, PARIS EXPOSITION!

Add to your show, before you close it, France,
With all the rest, visible, concrete, temples, towers, goods,
machines and ores,
Our sentiment wafted from many million heart-throbs,
ethereal but solid,
(We grand-sons and great-grand-sons do not forget your
grand-sires,)
From fifty Nations and nebulous Nations, compacted,
sent oversea to-day,
America's applause, love, memories and good-will.

INTERPOLATION SOUNDS.

[General Philip Sheridan was buried at the Cathedral, Washington, D.C., August, 1888, with all the pomp, music and ceremonies of the Roman Catholic service.]

Over and through the burial chant,
Organ and solemn service, sermon, bending priests,

To me come interpolation sounds not in the show—
    plainly to me, crowding up the aisle and from the
    window,
Of sudden battle's hurry and harsh noises—war's grim
    game to sight and ear in earnest;
The scout call'd up and forward—the general mounted
    and his aides around him—the new-brought word—
    the instantaneous order issued;
The rifle crack—the cannon thud—the rushing forth of
    men from their tents;
The clank of cavalry—the strange celerity of forming
    ranks—the slender bugle note;
The sound of horses' hoofs departing—saddles, arms,
    accoutrements. *

*NOTE.—CAMDEN, N. J., August 7, 1888.—Walt Whitman asks the
New York Herald "to add his tribute to Sheridan:"

"In the grand constellation of five or six names, under Lincoln's Presi-
dency, that history will bear for ages in her firmament as marking the
last life-throbs of secession, and beaming on its dying gasps, Sheridan's
will be bright. One consideration rising out of the now dead soldier's
example as it passes my mind, is worth taking notice of. If the war had
continued any long time these States, in my opinion, would have shown
and proved the most conclusive military talents ever evinced by any
nation on earth. That they possess'd a rank and file ahead of all other
known in points of quality and limitlessness of number are easily admit-
ted. But we have, too, the eligibility of organizing, handling and officer-
ing equal to the other. These two, with modern arms, transportation,
and inventive American genius, would make the United States, with
earnestness, not only able to stand the whole world, but conquer that
world united against us."

TO THE SUN-SET BREEZE.

Ah, whispering, something again, unseen,
Where late this heated day thou enterest at my window,
    door,
Thou, laving, tempering all, cool-freshing, gently vitaliz-
    ing
Me, old, alone, sick, weak-down, melted-worn with
    sweat;
Thou, nestling, folding close and firm yet soft, companion
    better than talk, book, art,
(Thou hast, O Nature! elements! utterance to my heart
    beyond the rest—and this is of them,)
So sweet thy primitive taste to breathe within—thy sooth-
    ing fingers on my face and hands,
Thou, messenger-magical strange bringer to body and
    spirit of me,
(Distances balk'd—occult medicines penetrating me from
    head to foot,)
I feel the sky, the prairies vast—I feel the mighty north-
    ern lakes,
I feel the ocean and the forest—somehow I feel the globe
    itself swift-swimming in space;
Thou blown from lips so loved, now gone—haply from
    endless store, God-sent,
(For thou art spiritual, Godly, most of all known to my
    sense,)
Minister to speak to me, here and now, what word has
    never told, and cannot tell,
Art thou not universal concrete's distillation? Law's, all
    Astronomy's last refinement?
Hast thou no soul? Can I not know, identify thee?

OLD CHANTS.

An ancient song, reciting, ending,
Once gazing toward thee, Mother of All,
Musing, seeking themes fitted for thee,
Accept for me, thou saidst, *the elder ballads*,
And name for me before thou goest each ancient poet.

(Of many debts incalculable,
Haply our New World's chiefest debt is to old poems.)

Ever so far back, preluding thee, America,
Old chants, Egyptian priests, and those of Ethiopia,
The Hindu epics, the Grecian, Chinese, Persian,
The Biblic books and prophets, and deep idyls of the
     Nazarene,
The Iliad, Odyssey, plots, doings, wanderings of Eneas,
Hesiod, Eschylus, Sophocles, Merlin, Arthur,
The Cid, Roland at Roncesvalles, the Nibelungen,
The troubadours, minstrels, minnesingers, skalds,
Chaucer, Dante, flocks of singing birds,
The Border Minstrelsy, the bye-gone ballads, feudal tales,
     essays, plays,
Shakspere, Schiller, Walter Scott, Tennyson,
As some vast wondrous weird dream-presences,
The great shadowy groups gathering around,
Darting their mighty masterful eyes forward at thee,
Thou! with as now thy bending neck and head, with cour-
     teous hand and word, ascending,
Thou! pausing a moment, drooping thine eyes upon
     them, blent with their music,

Well pleased, accepting all, curiously prepared for by
    them,
Thou enterest at thy entrance porch.

A CHRISTMAS GREETING.

From a Northern Star-Group to a Southern. 1889-'90.

Welcome, Brazilian brother—thy ample place is ready;
A loving hand—a smile from the north—a sunny instant
    hail!
(Let the future care for itself, where it reveals its troubles,
    impedimentas,
Ours, ours the present throe, the democratic aim, the
    acceptance and the faith;)
To thee to-day our reaching arm, our turning neck—to
    thee from us the expectant eye,
Thou cluster free! thou brilliant lustrous one! thou, learn-
    ing well,
The true lesson of a nation's light in the sky,
(More shining than the Cross, more than the Crown,)
The height to be superb humanity.

SOUNDS OF THE WINTER.

Sounds of the winter too,
Sunshine upon the mountains—many a distant strain
From cheery railroad train—from nearer field, barn,
    house,
The whispering air—even the mute crops, garner'd
    apples, corn,

Children's and women's tones—rhythm of many a farmer
    and of flail,
An old man's garrulous lips among the rest, *Think not we
    give out yet,*
Forth from these snowy hairs we keep up yet the lilt.

A TWILIGHT SONG.

As I sit in twilight late alone by the flickering oak-flame,
Musing on long-pass'd war scenes—of the countless
    buried unknown soldiers,
Of the vacant names, as unindented air's and sea's—the
    unreturn'd,
The brief truce after battle, with grim burial-squads, and
    the deep-fill'd trenches
Of gather'd dead from all America, North, South, East,
    West, whence they came up,
From wooded Maine, New-England's farms, from fertile
    Pennsylvania, Illinois, Ohio,
From the measureless West, Virginia, the South, the Car-
    olinas, Texas,
(Even here in my room-shadows and half-lights in the
    noiseless flickering flames,
Again I see the stalwart ranks on-filing, rising—I hear the
    rhythmic tramp of the armies;)
You million unwrit names all, all—you dark bequest from
    all the war,
A special verse for you—a flash of duty long neglected—
    your mystic roll strangely gather'd here,
Each name recall'd by me from out the darkness and
    death's ashes,

Henceforth to be, deep, deep within my heart recording,
    for many a future year,
Your mystic roll entire of unknown names, or North or
    South,
Embalm'd with love in this twilight song.

WHEN THE FULL-GROWN POET CAME.

When the full-grown poet came,
Out spake pleased Nature (the round impassive globe,
    with all its shows of day and night,) saying, *He is
    mine;*
But out spake too the Soul of man, proud, jealous and
    unreconciled, *Nay, he is mine alone;*
—Then the full-grown poet stood between the two, and
    took each by the hand;
And to-day and ever so stands, as blender, uniter, tightly
    holding hands,
Which he will never release until he reconciles the two,
And wholly and joyously blends them.

OSCEOLA.

[When I was nearly grown to manhood in Brooklyn, New York, (middle of 1838,) I met one of the return'd U.S. Marines from Fort Moultrie, S.C., and had long talks with him—learn'd the occurrence below described—death of Osceola. The latter was a young, brave, leading Seminole in the Florida war of that time—was surrender'd to our troops, imprison'd and literally died of "a broken heart," at Fort Moultrie. He sicken'd of his confinement—the doctor and officers made every allowance and kindness possible for him; then the close:]

When his hour for death had come,
He slowly rais'd himself from the bed on the floor,
Drew on his war-dress, shirt, leggings, and girdled the
    belt around his waist,
Call'd for vermilion paint (his looking-glass was held
    before him,)
Painted half his face and neck, his wrists, and back-hands.
Put the scalp-knife carefully in his belt—then lying down,
    resting a moment,
Rose again, half sitting, smiled, gave in silence his
    extended hand to each and all,
Sank faintly low to the floor (tightly grasping the toma-
    hawk handle,)
Fix'd his look on wife and little children—the last:

(And here a line in memory of his name and death.)

A VOICE FROM DEATH.

(The Johnstown, Penn., cataclysm, May 31, 1889.)

A voice from Death, solemn and strange, in all his sweep
    and power,
With sudden, indescribable blow—towns drown'd—
    humanity by thousands slain,
The vaunted work of thrift, goods, dwellings, forge,
    street, iron bridge,
Dash'd pell-mell by the blow—yet usher'd life continuing
    on,
(Amid the rest, amid the rushing, whirling, wild debris,
A suffering woman saved—a baby safely born!)

Although I come and unannounc'd, in horror and in
    pang,
In pouring flood and fire, and wholesale elemental crash,
    (this voice so solemn, strange,)
I too a minister of Deity.

Yea, Death, we bow our faces, veil our eyes to thee,
We mourn the old, the young untimely drawn to thee,
The fair, the strong, the good, the capable,
The household wreck'd, the husband and the wife the
    engulf'd forger in his forge,
The corpses in the whelming waters and the mud,
The gather'd thousands to their funeral mounds, and
    thousands never found or gather'd.

Then after burying, mourning the dead,
(Faithful to them found or unfound, forgetting not, bear-
    ing the past, here new musing,)

A day—a passing moment or an hour—America itself
    bends low,
Silent, resign'd, submissive.

War, death, cataclysm like this, America,
Take deep to thy proud prosperous heart.

E'en as I chant, lo! out of death, and out of ooze and slime,
The blossoms rapidly blooming, sympathy, help, love,
From West and East, from South and North and over sea,
Its hot-spurr'd hearts and hands humanity to human aid
    moves on;
And from within a thought and lesson yet.

Thou ever-darting Globe! through Space and Air!
Thou waters that encompass us!
Thou that in all the life and death of us, in action or in
    sleep!
Thou laws invisible that permeate them and all,
Thou that in all, and over all, and through and under all,
    incessant!
Thou! thou! the vital, universal, giant force resistless,
    sleepless, calm,
Holding Humanity as in thy open hand, as some
    ephemeral toy,
How ill to e'er forget thee!

For I too have forgotten,
(Wrapt in these little potencies of progress, politics, cul-
    ture, wealth, inventions, civilization,)

Have lost my recognition of your silent ever-swaying
    power, ye mighty, elemental throes,
In which and upon which we float, and every one of us is
    buoy'd.

A PERSIAN LESSON.

For his o'erarching and last lesson the graybeard sufi,
In the fresh scent of the morning in the open air,
On the slope of a teeming Persian rose-garden,
Under an ancient chestnut-tree wide spreading its
    branches,
Spoke to the young priests and students.

"Finally my children, to envelop each word, each part of
    the rest,
Allah is all, all, all—is immanent in every life and object,
May-be at many and many-a-more removes—yet Allah,
    Allah, Allah is there.

"Has the estray wander'd far? Is the reason-why
    strangely hidden?
Would you sound below the restless ocean of the entire
    world?
Would you know the dissatisfaction? the urge and spur of
    every life;
The something never still'd—never entirely gone? the
    invisible need of every seed?

"It is the central urge in every atom,
(Often unconscious, often evil, downfallen,)

To return to its divine source and origin, however distant,
Latent the same in subject and in object, without one
    exception."

THE COMMONPLACE.

The commonplace I sing;
How cheap is health! how cheap nobility!
Abstinence, no falsehood, no gluttony, lust;
The open air I sing, freedom, toleration,
(Take here the mainest lesson—less from books—less
    from the schools,)
The common day and night—the common earth and
    waters,
Your farm—your work, trade, occupation,
The democratic wisdom underneath, like solid ground for
    all.

"THE ROUNDED CATALOGUE DIVINE COMPLETE."

*[Sunday,——.—— —Went this forenoon to church. A college profes-
sor, Rev. Dr.——, gave us a fine sermon, during which I caught the
above words; but the minister included in his "rounded catalogue" let-
ter and spirit, only the esthetic things, and entirely ignored what I name
in the following:]*

The devilish and the dark, the dying and diseas'd,
The countless (nineteen-twentieths) low and evil, crude
    and savage,
The crazed, prisoners in jail, the horrible, rank, malignant,
Venom and filth, serpents, the ravenous sharks, liars, the
    dissolute;

(What is the part the wicked and the loathesome bear
    within earth's orbic scheme?)
Newts, crawling things in slime and mud, poisons,
The barren soil, the evil men, the slag and hideous rot.

MIRAGES.

*(Noted verbatim after a supper-talk out doors in Nevada with two
old miners.)*

More experiences and sights, stranger, than you'd think
    for;
Times again, now mostly just after sunrise or before sun-
    set,
Sometimes in spring, oftener in autumn, perfectly clear
    weather, in plain sight,
Camps far or near, the crowded streets of cities and the
    shop-fronts,
(Account for it or not—credit or not—it is all true,
And my mate there could tell you the like—we have often
    confab'd about it,)
People and scenes, animals, trees, colors and lines, plain
    as could be,
Farms and dooryards of home, paths border'd with box,
    lilacs in corners,
Weddings in churches, thanksgiving dinners, returns of
    long-absent sons,
Glum funerals, the crape-veil'd mother and the daugh-
    ters,
Trials in courts, jury and judge, the accused in the box,
Contestants, battles, crowds, bridges, wharves,
Now and then mark'd faces of sorrow or joy,

(I could pick them out this moment if I saw them again,)
Show'd to me just aloft to the right in the sky-edge,
Or plainly there to the left on the hill-tops.

L. OF G.'S PURPORT.

Not to exclude or demarcate, or pick out evils from their
    formidable masses (even to expose them,)
But add, fuse, complete, extend—and celebrate the
    immortal and the good.

Haughty this song, its words and scope,
To span vast realms of space and time,
Evolution—the cumulative—growths and generations.

Begun in ripen'd youth and steadily pursued,
Wandering, peering, dallying with all—war, peace, day
    and night absorbing,
Never even for one brief hour abandoning my task,
I end it here in sickness, poverty, and old age.

I sing of life, yet mind me well of death:
To-day shadowy Death dogs my steps, my seated shape,
    and has for years—
Draws sometimes close to me, as face to face.

THE UNEXPRESS'D.

How dare one say it?
After the cycles, poems, singers, plays,

Vaunted Ionia's, India's—Homer, Shakspere—the long,
    long times' thick dotted roads, areas,
The shining clusters and the Milky Ways of stars—
    Nature's pulses reap'd,
All retrospective passions, heroes, war, love, adoration,
All ages' plummets dropt to their utmost depths,
All human lives, throats, wishes, brains—all experiences'
    utterance;
After the countless songs, or long or short, all tongues, all
    lands,
Still something not yet told in poesy's voice or print—
    something lacking,
(Who knows? the best yet unexpress'd and lacking.)

GRAND IS THE SEEN.

Grand is the seen, the light, to me—grand are the sky and
    stars,
Grand is the earth, and grand are lasting time and space,
And grand their laws, so multiform, puzzling, evolution-
    ary;
But grander far the unseen soul of me, comprehending,
    endowing all those,
Lighting the light, the sky and stars, delving the earth,
    sailing the sea,
(What were all those, indeed, without thee, unseen soul?
    of what amount without thee?)
More evolutionary, vast, puzzling, O my soul!
More multiform far—more lasting thou than they.

UNSEEN BUDS.

Unseen buds, infinite, hidden well,
Under the snow and ice, under the darkness, in every
    square or cubic inch,
Germinal, exquisite, in delicate lace, microscopic, unborn,
Like babes in wombs, latent, folded, compact, sleeping;
Billions of billions, and trillions of trillions of them wait-
    ing,
(On earth and in the sea—the universe—the stars there in
    the heavens,)
Urging slowly, surely forward, forming endless,
And waiting ever more, forever more behind.

GOOD-BYE MY FANCY!

Good-bye my Fancy!
Farewell dear mate, dear love!
I'm going away, I know not where,
Or to what fortune, or whether I may ever see you again,
So Good-bye my Fancy.

Now for my last—let me look back a moment;
The slower fainter ticking of the clock is in me,
Exit, nightfall, and soon the heart-thud stopping.

Long have we lived, joy'd, caress'd together;
Delightful!—now separation—Good-bye my Fancy.

Yet let me not be too hasty,

Long indeed have we lived, slept, filter'd, become really
blended into one;

Then if we die we die together, (yes, we'll remain one,)

If we go anywhere we'll go together to meet what hap-
pens,

May-be we'll be better off and blither, and learn some-
thing,

May-be it is yourself now really ushering me to the true
songs, (who knows?)

May-be it is you the mortal knob really undoing, turn-
ing—so now finally,

Good-bye—and hail! my Fancy.

*

A BACKWARD GLANCE
O'ER TRAVEL'D ROADS.

Perhaps the best of songs heard, or of any and all true love, or life's fairest episodes, or sailors', soldiers' trying scenes on land or sea, is the *résumé* of them, or any of them, long afterwards, looking at the actualities away back past, with all their practical excitations gone. How the soul loves to float amid such reminiscences!

So here I sit gossiping in the early candle-light of old age—I and my book—casting backward glances over our travel'd road. After completing, as it were, the journey—(a varied jaunt of years, with many halts and gaps of intervals—or some lengthen'd ship-voyage, wherein more than once the last hour had apparently arrived, and we seem'd certainly going down—yet reaching port in a sufficient way through all discomfitures at last)—After completing my poems, I am curious to review them in the light of their own (at the time unconscious, or mostly unconscious) intentions, with certain unfoldings of the thirty years they seek to embody. These lines, therefore, will probably blend the weft of first purposes and specu-lations, with the warp of that experience afterwards, always bringing strange developments.

Result of seven or eight stages and struggles extend-

682

ing through nearly thirty years, (as I nigh my three-score-
and-ten I live largely on memory,) I look upon "Leaves of
Grass," now finish'd to the end of its opportunities and
powers, as my definitive *carte visite* to the coming gener-
ations of the New World,* if I may assume to say so. That
I have not gain'd the acceptance of my own time, but have
fallen back on fond dreams of the future—anticipations—
("still lives the song, though Regnar dies")—That from a
worldly and business point of view "Leaves of Grass" has
been worse than a failure—that public criticism on the
book and myself as author of it yet shows mark'd anger
and contempt more than anything else—("I find a solid
line of enemies to you everywhere,"—letter from W. S. K.,
Boston, May 28, 1884)—And that solely for publishing it
I have been the object of two or three pretty serious spe-
cial official buffetings—is all probably no more than I
ought to have expected. I had my choice when I com-
menc'd. I bid neither for soft eulogies, big money returns,
nor the approbation of existing schools and conventions.
As fulfill'd, or partially fulfill'd, the best comfort of the
whole business (after a small band of the dearest friends
and upholders ever vouchsafed to man or cause—doubt-
less all the more faithful and uncompromising—this lit-
tle phalanx!—for being so few) is that, unstopp'd and
unwarp'd by any influence outside the soul within me, I
have had my say entirely my own way, and put it unerr-
ingly on record—the value thereof to be decided by time.

In calculating that decision, William O'Connor and

---

*When Champollion, on his death-bed, handed to the printer the revised
proof of his "Egyptian Grammar," he said gayly, 'Be careful of this—it is
my *carte de visite* to posterity."

Dr. Bucke are far more peremptory than I am. Behind all else that can be said, I consider "Leaves of Grass" and its theory experimental—as, in the deepest sense, I consider our American republic itself to be, with its theory. (I think I have at least enough philosophy not to be too absolutely certain of any thing, or any results.) In the second place, the volume is a *sortie*—whether to prove triumphant, and conquer its field of aim and escape and construction, nothing less than a hundred years from now can fully answer. I consider the point that I have positively gain'd a hearing, to far more than make up for any and all other lacks and withholdings. Essentially, *that* was from the first, and has remain'd throughout, the main object. Now it seems to be achiev'd, I am certainly contented to waive any otherwise momentous drawbacks, as of little account. Candidly and dispassionately reviewing all my intentions, I feel that they were creditable—and I accept the result, whatever it may be.

After continued personal ambition and effort, as a young fellow, to enter with the rest into competition for the usual rewards, business, political, literary, &c.—to take part in the great *mêlée*, both for victory's prize itself and to do some good—After years of those aims and pursuits, I found myself remaining possess'd, at the age of thirty-one to thirty-three, with a special desire and conviction. Or rather, to be quite exact, a desire that had been flitting through my previous life, or hovering on the flanks, mostly indefinite hitherto, had steadily advanced to the front, defined itself, and finally dominated everything else. This was a feeling or ambition to articulate and faithfully express in literary or poetic form, and uncompromisingly, my own physical, emotional, moral, intellectual,

and æsthetic Personality, in the midst of, and tallying, the
momentous spirit and facts of its immediate days, and of
current America—and to exploit that Personality, identi-
fied with place and date, in a far more candid and com-
prehensive sense than any hitherto poem or book.

   Perhaps this is in brief, or suggests, all I have sought
to do. Given the Nineteenth Century, with the United
States, and what they furnish as area and points of view,
"Leaves of Grass" is, or seeks to be, simply a faithful and
doubtless self-will'd record. In the midst of all, it gives
one man's—the author's—identity, ardors, observations,
faiths, and thoughts, color'd hardly at all with any
decided coloring from other faiths or other identities.
Plenty of songs had been sung—beautiful, matchless
songs—adjusted to other lands than these—another spirit
and stage of evolution; but I would sing, and leave out or
put in, quite solely with reference to America and to-day.
Modern science and democracy seem'd to be throwing
out their challenge to poetry to put them in its statements
in contradistinction to the songs and myths of the past. As
I see it now (perhaps too late,) I have unwittingly taken
up that challenge and made an attempt at such state-
ments—which I certainly would not assume to do now,
knowing more clearly what it means.

   For grounds for "Leaves of Grass," as a poem, I aban-
don'd the conventional themes, which do not appear in it:
none of the stock ornamentation, or choice plots of love or
war, or high, exceptional personages of Old-World song;
nothing, as I may say, for beauty's sake—no legend, or
myth, or romance; nor euphemism, nor rhyme. But the
broadest average of humanity and its identities in the
now ripening Nineteenth Century, and especially in each

of their countless examples and practical occupations in the United States to-day.

One main contrast of the ideas behind every page of my verses, compared with establish'd poems, is their different relative attitude towards God, towards the objective universe, and still more (by reflection, confession, assumption, &c.) the quite changed attitude of the ego, the one chanting or talking, towards himself and towards his fellow-humanity. It is certainly time for America, above all, to begin this readjustment in the scope and basic point of view of verse; for everything else has changed. As I write, I see in an article on Wordsworth, in one of the current English magazines, the lines, "A few weeks ago an eminent French critic said that, owing to the special tendency to science and to its all-devouring force, poetry would cease to be read in fifty years." But I anticipate the very contrary. Only a firmer, vastly broader, new area begins to exist—nay, is already form'd—to which the poetic genius must emigrate. Whatever may have been the case in years gone by, the true use for the imaginative faculty of modern times is to give ultimate vivification to facts, to science, and to common lives, endowing them with the glows and glories and final illustriousness which belong to every real thing, and to real things only. Without that ultimate vivification—which the poet or other artist alone can give—reality would seem incomplete, and science, democracy, and life itself, finally in vain.

Few appreciate the moral revolutions, our age, which have been profounder far than the material or inventive or war-produced ones. The Nineteenth Century, now well towards its close (and ripening into fruit the seeds of the two preceding centuries*)—the uprisings of national masses and shiftings of boundary-lines—the historical and other prominent facts of the United States—the war of attempted Secession—the stormy rush and haste of nebulous forces—never can future years witness more excitement and din of action—never completer change of army front along the whole line, the whole civilized world. For all these new and evolutionary facts, meanings, purposes, new poetic messages, new forms and expressions, are inevitable.

My Book and I—what a period we have presumed to span! those thirty years from 1850 to '80—and America in them! Proud, proud indeed may we be, if we have cull'd enough of that period in its own spirit to worthily waft a few live breaths of it to the future!

Let me not dare, here or anywhere, for my own purposes, or any purposes, to attempt the definition of Poetry, nor answer the question what it is. Like Religion, Love, Nature, while those terms are indispensable, and we all give a sufficiently accurate meaning to them, in my opinion no definition that has ever been made sufficiently encloses the name Poetry; nor can any rule of convention ever so absolutely obtain but some great exception may arise and disregard and overturn it.

Also it must be carefully remember'd that first-class literature does not shine by any luminosity of its own; nor

---

*The ferment and germination even of the United States to-day, dating back to, and in my opinion mainly founded on, the Elizabethan age in English history, the age of Francis Bacon and Shakspere. Indeed, when we pursue it, what growth or advent is there that does not date back, back, until lost—perhaps its most tantalizing clues lost—in the receded horizons of the past?

do its poems. They grow of circumstances, and are evolutionary. The actual living light is always curiously from elsewhere—follows unaccountable sources, and is lunar and relative at the best. There are, I know, certain controlling themes that seem endlessly appropriated to the poets—as war, in the past—in the Bible, religious rapture and adoration—always love, beauty, some fine plot, or pensive or other emotion. But, strange as it may sound at first, I will say there is something striking far deeper and towering far higher than those themes for the best elements of modern song.

Just as all the old imaginative works rest, after their kind, on long trains of presuppositions, often entirely unmention'd by themselves, yet supplying the most important bases of them, and without which they could have had no reason for being, so "Leaves of Grass," before a line was written, presupposed something different from any other, and, as it stands, is the result of such presupposition. I should say, indeed, it were useless to attempt reading the book without first carefully tallying that preparatory background and quality in the mind. Think of the United States to-day—the facts of these thirty-eight or forty empires solder'd in one—sixty or seventy millions of equals, with their lives, their passions, their future—these incalculable, modern, American, seething multitudes around us, of which we are inseparable parts! Think, in comparison, of the petty environage and limited area of the poets of past or present Europe, no matter how great their genius. Think of the absence and ignorance, in all cases hitherto, of the multitudinousness, vitality, and the unprecedented stimulants of to-day and here. It almost seems as if a poetry with cosmic and dynamic features of magnitude and limitlessness suitable to the human soul, were never possible before. It is certain that a poetry of absolute faith and equality for the use of the democratic masses never was.

In estimating first-class song, a sufficient Nationality, or, on the other hand, what may be call'd the negative and lack of it, (as in Goethe's case, it sometimes seems to me,) is often, if not always, the first element. One needs only a little penetration to see, at more or less removes, the material facts of their country and radius, with the coloring of the moods of humanity at the time, and its gloomy or hopeful prospects, behind all poets and each poet, and forming their birth-marks. I know very well that my "Leaves" could not possibly have emerged or been fashion'd or completed, from any other era than the latter half of the Nineteenth Century, nor any other land than democratic America, and from the absolute triumph of the National Union arms.

And whether my friends claim it for me or not, I know well enough, too, that in respect to pictorial talent, dramatic situations, and especially in verbal melody and all the conventional technique of poetry, not only the divine works that to-day stand ahead in the world's reading, but dozens more, transcend (some of them immeasurably transcend) all I have done, or could do. But it seem'd to me, as the objects in Nature, the themes of æstheticism, and all special exploitations of the mind and soul, involve not only their own inherent quality, but the quality, just as inherent and important, of *their point of view*,* the time

---

*According to Immanuel Kant, the last essential reality, giving shape and significance to all the rest.

had come to reflect all themes and things, old and new, in the lights thrown on them by the advent of America and democracy—to chant those themes through the utterance of one, not only the grateful and reverent legatee of the past, but the born child of the New World—to illustrate all through the genesis and ensemble of to-day; and that such illustration and ensemble are the chief demands of America's prospective imaginative literature. Not to carry out, in the approved style, some choice plot of fortune or misfortune, or fancy, or fine thoughts, or incidents, or courtesies—all of which has been done overwhelmingly and well, probably never to be excell'd—but that while in such æsthetic presentation of objects, passions, plots, thoughts, &c., our lands and days do not want, and probably will never have, anything better than they already possess from the bequests of the past, it still remains to be said that there is even towards all those a subjective and contemporary point of view appropriate to ourselves alone, and to our new genius and environments, different from anything hitherto; and that such conception of current or gone-by life and art is for us the only means of their assimilation consistent with the Western world.

Indeed, and anyhow, to put it specifically, has not the time arrived when, (if it must be plainly said, for democratic America's sake, if for no other) there must imperatively come a readjustment of the whole theory and nature of Poetry? The question is important, and I may turn the argument over and repeat it: Does not the best thought of our day and Republic conceive of a birth and spirit of song superior to anything past or present? To the effectual and moral consolidation of our lands (already, as materially establish'd, the greatest factors in known history, and far, far greater through what they prelude and necessitate, and are to be in future)—to conform with and build on the concrete realities and theories of the universe furnish'd by science, and henceforth the only irrefragable basis for anything, verse included–to root both influences in the emotional and imaginative action of the modern time, and dominate all that precedes or opposes them— is not either a radical advance and step forward, or a new verteber of the best song indispensable?

The New World receives with joy the poems of the antique, with European feudalism's rich fund of epics, plays, ballads—seeks not in the least to deaden or displace those voices from our ear and area—holds them indeed as indispensable studies, influences, records, comparisons. But though the dawn-dazzle of the sun of literature is in those poems for us of to-day—though perhaps the best parts of current character in nations, social groups, or any man's or woman's individuality, Old World or New, are from them—and though if I were ask'd to name the most precious bequest to current American civilization from all the hitherto ages, I am not sure but I would name those old and less old songs ferried hither from east and west—some serious words and debits remain; some acrid considerations demand a hearing. Of the great poems receiv'd from abroad and from the ages, and to-day enveloping and penetrating America, is there one that is consistent with these United States, or essentially applicable to them as they are and are to be? Is there one whose underlying basis is not a denial and insult to democracy? What a comment it forms, anyhow, on this era of literary fulfilment, with the splendid day-rise of science and resuscitation of history, that our chief religious and poetical works are not our own, nor adapted to our light, but have been furnish'd by far-back ages out of their arriere and darkness, or, at most, twilight dimness! What is there in those works that so imperiously and scornfully dominates all our advanced civilization, and culture?

Even Shakspeare, who so suffuses current letters and art (which indeed have in most degrees grown out of him,) belongs essentially to the buried past. Only he holds the proud distinction for certain important phases of that past, of being the loftiest of the singers life has yet given voice to. All, however, relate to and rest upon conditions, standards, politics, sociologies, ranges of belief, that have been quite eliminated from the Eastern hemisphere, and never existed at all in the Western. As authoritative types of song they belong in America just about as much as the persons and institutes they depict. True, it may be said, the emotional, moral, and aesthetic natures of humanity have not radically changed—that in these the old poems apply to our times and all times, irrespective of date; and that they are of incalculable value as pictures of the past. I willingly make those admissions, and to their fullest extent; then advance the points herewith as of serious, even paramount importance.

I have indeed put on record elsewhere my reverence and eulogy for those never-to-be excell'd poetic bequests, and their indescribable preciousness as heirlooms for America. Another and separate point must now be candidly stated. If I had not stood before those poems with uncover'd head, fully aware of their colossal grandeur and beauty of form and spirit, I could not have written

"Leaves of Grass." My verdict and conclusions as illustrated in its pages are arrived at through the temper and inculcation of the old works as much as through anything else—perhaps more than through anything else. As America fully and fairly construed is the legitimate result and evolutionary outcome of the past, so I would dare to claim for my verse. Without stopping to qualify the averment, the Old World has had the poems of myths, fictions, feudalism, conquest, caste, dynastic wars, and splendid exceptional characters and affairs, which have been great; but the New World needs the poems of realities and science and of the democratic average and basic equality, which shall be greater. In the centre of all, and object of all, stands the Human Being, towards whose heroic and spiritual evolution poems and everything directly or indirectly tend, Old World or New.

Continuing the subject, my friends have more than once suggested—or may be the garrulity of advancing age is possessing me—some further embryonic facts of "Leaves of Grass," and especially how I enter'd upon them. Dr. Bucke has, in his volume, already fully and fairly described the preparation of my poetic field, with the particular and general plowing, planting, seeding, and occupation of the ground, till everything was fertilized, rooted, and ready to start its own way for good or bad. Not till after all this, did I attempt any serious acquaintance with poetic literature. Along in my sixteenth year I had become possessor of a stout, well-cramm'd one thousand page octavo volume (I have it yet,) containing Walter Scott's poetry entire—an inexhaustible mine and treasury of poetic forage (especially the endless forests and jungles of notes)—has been so to me for fifty years, and remains so to this day.*

Later, at intervals, summers and falls, I used to go off, sometimes for a week at a stretch, down in the country, or to Long Island's seashores—there, in the presence of outdoor influences, I went over thoroughly the Old and New Testaments, and absorb'd (probably to better advantage for me than in any library or indoor room—it makes such difference *where* you read,) Shakspere, Ossian, the best translated versions I could get of Homer, Eschylus, Sophocles, the old German Nibelungen, the ancient Hindoo poems, and one or two other masterpieces, Dante's among them. As it happen'd, I read the latter mostly in an old wood. The Iliad (Buckley's prose version,) I read first thoroughly on the peninsula of Orient, northeast end of Long Island, in a shelter'd hollow of rocks and sand, with the sea on each side. (I have wonder'd since why I was not overwhelm'd by those mighty masters. Likely because I read them, as described, in the full presence of Nature, under the sun, with the far-spreading landscape and vistas, or the sea rolling in.)

Toward the last I had among much else look'd over Edgar Poe's poems—of which I was not an admirer, tho'

---

*Sir Walter Scott's COMPLETE POEMS; especially including BORDER MIN-STRELSY; then Sir Tristem; Lay of the Last Minstrel; Ballads from the German; Marmion; Lady of the Lake; Vision of Don Roderick; Lord of the Isles; Rokeby, Bridal of Triermain; Field of Waterloo; Harold the Dauntless; all the Dramas; various Introductions, endless interesting Notes, and Essays on Poetry, Romance, &c.
Lockhart's 1833 (or '34) edition with Scott's latest and copious revisions and annotations. (All the poems were thoroughly read by me, but the ballads of the Border Minstrelsy over and over again.)

I always saw that beyond their limited range of melody (like perpetual chimes of music bells, ringing from lower *b* flat up to *g*) they were melodious expressions, and perhaps never excell'd ones, of certain pronounc'd phases of human morbidity. (The Poetic area is very spacious—has room for all—has so many mansions!) But I was repaid in Poe's prose by the idea that (at any rate for our occasions, our day) there can be no such thing as a long poem. The same thought had been haunting my mind before, but Poe's argument, though short, work'd the sum out and proved it to me.

Another point had an early settlement, clearing the ground greatly. I saw, from the time my enterprise and questionings positively shaped themselves (how best can I express my own distinctive era and surroundings, America, Democracy?) that the trunk and centre whence the answer was to radiate, and to which all should return from straying however far a distance, must be an identical body and soul, a personality—which personality, after many considerations and ponderings I deliberately settled should be myself—indeed could not be any other. I also felt strongly (whether I have shown it or not) that to the true and full estimate of the Present both the Past and the Future are main considerations.

These, however, and much more might have gone on and come to naught (almost positively would have come to naught,) if a sudden, vast, terrible, direct and indirect stimulus for new and national declamatory expression had not been given to me. It is certain, I say, that, although I had made a start before, only from the occurrence of the Secession War, and what it show'd me as by flashes of lightning, with the emotional depths it sounded and arous'd (of course, I don't mean in my own heart only, I saw it just as plainly in others, in millions)—that only from the strong flare and provocation of that war's sights and scenes the final reasons-for-being of an autochthonic and passionate song definitely came forth.

I went down to the war fields in Virginia (end of 1862), lived thenceforward in camp—saw great battles and the days and nights afterward—partook of all the fluctuations, gloom, despair, hopes again arous'd, courage evoked—death readily risk'd—*the cause*, too— along and filling those agnostic and lurid following years, 1863-'64-'65—the real parturition years (more than 1776- '83) of this henceforth homogeneous Union. Without those three or four years and the experiences they gave, "Leaves of Grass" would not now be existing.

But I set out with the intention also of indicating or hinting some point-characteristics which I since see (though I did not then, at least not definitely) were bases and object-urgings toward those "Leaves" from the first. The word I myself put primarily for the description of them as they stand at last, is the word Suggestiveness. I round and finish little, if anything; and could not, consistently with my scheme. The reader will always have his or her part to do, just as much as I have had mine. I seek less to state or display any theme or thought, and more to bring you, reader, into the atmosphere of the theme or thought—there to pursue your own flight. Another impetus-word is Comradeship as for all lands, and in a more commanding and acknowledg'd sense than hitherto. Other word-signs would be Good Cheer, Content, and Hope.

The chief trait of any given poet is always the spirit he brings to the observation of Humanity and Nature—the mood out of which he contemplates his subjects. What kind of temper and what amount of faith report these things? Up to how recent a date is the song carried? What the equipment, and special raciness of the singer—what his tinge of coloring? The last value of artistic expressers, past and present—Greek æsthetes, Shakspere—or in our own day Tennyson, Victor Hugo, Carlyle, Emerson—is certainly involv'd in such questions. I say the profoundest service that poems or any other writings can do for their reader is not merely to satisfy the intellect, or supply something polish'd and interesting, nor even to depict great passions, or persons or events, but to fill him with vigorous and clean manliness, religiousness, and give him *good heart* as a radical possession and habit. The educated world seems to have been growing more and more ennuyed for ages, leaving to our time the inheritance of it all. Fortunately there is the original inexhaustible fund of buoyancy, normally resident in the race, forever eligible to be appeal'd to and relied on.

As for native American individuality, though certain to come, and on a large scale, the distinctive and ideal type of Western character (as consistent with the operative political and even money-making features of United States' humanity in the Nineteenth Century as chosen knights, gentlemen and warriors were the ideals of the centuries of European feudalism) it has not yet appear'd. I have allow'd the stress of my poems from beginning to end to bear upon American individuality and assist it—not only because that is a great lesson in Nature, amid all

her generalizing laws, but as counterpoise to the leveling
tendencies of Democracy—and for other reasons. Defiant
of ostensible literary and other conventions, I avowedly
chant "the great pride of man in himself," and permit it
to be more or less a *motif* of nearly all my verse. I think this
pride indispensable to an American. I think it not incon-
sistent with obedience, humility, deference, and self-ques-
tioning.

Democracy has been so retarded and jeopardized by
powerful personalities, that its first instincts are fain to
clip, conform, bring in stragglers, and reduce everything
to a dead level. While the ambitious thought of my song is
to help the forming of a great aggregate Nation, it is, per-
haps, altogether through the forming of myriads of fully
develop'd and enclosing individuals. Welcome as are
equality's and fraternity's doctrines and popular educa-
tion, a certain liability accompanies them all, as we see.
That primal and interior something in man, in his soul's
abysms, coloring all, and, by exceptional fruitions, giving
the last majesty to him—something continually touch'd
upon and attain'd by the old poems and ballads of feu-
dalism, and often the principal foundation of them—
modern science and democracy appear to be
endangering, perhaps eliminating. But that forms an
appearance only; the reality is quite different. The new
influences, upon the whole, are surely preparing the way
for grander individualities than ever. To-day and here
personal force is behind everything, just the same. The
times and depictions from the Iliad to Shakspere inclusive
can happily never again be realized—but the elements of
courageous and lofty manhood are unchanged.

Without yielding an inch the working-man and working-woman were to be in my pages from first to last. The ranges of heroism and loftiness with which Greek and feudal poets endow'd their god-like or lordly born char- acters—indeed prouder and better based and with fuller ranges than those—I was to endow the democratic aver- ages of America. I was to show that we, here and to-day, are eligible to the grandest and the best—more eligible now than any times of old were. I will also want my utter- ances (I said to myself before beginning) to be in spirit the poems of the morning. (They have been founded and mainly written in the sunny forenoon and early midday of my life.) I will want them to be the poems of women entirely as much as men. I have wish'd to put the com- plete Union of the States in my songs without any prefer- ence or partiality whatever. Henceforth, if they live and are read, it must be just as much South as North—just as much along the Pacific as Atlantic—in the valley of the Mississippi, in Canada, up in Maine, down in Texas, and on the shores of Puget Sound.

From another point of view "Leaves of Grass" is avowedly the song of Sex and Amativeness, and even Animality—though meanings that do not usually go along with those words are behind all, and will duly emerge; and all are sought to be lifted into a different light and atmosphere. Of this feature, intentionally palpable in a few lines, I shall only say the espousing principle of those lines so gives breath of life to my whole scheme that the bulk of the pieces might as well have been left unwrit- ten were those lines omitted. Difficult as it will be, it has become, in my opinion, imperative to achieve a shifted attitude from superior men and women towards the thought and fact of sexuality, as an element in character, personality, the emotions, and a theme in literature. I am not going to argue the question by itself; it does not stand by itself. The vitality of it is altogether in its relations, bearings, significance—like the clef of a symphony. At last analogy the lines I allude to, and the spirit in which they are spoken, permeate all "Leaves of Grass," and the work must stand or fall with them, as the human body and soul must remain as an entirety.

Universal as are certain facts and symptoms of communities or individuals all times, there is nothing so rare in modern conventions and poetry as their normal recognizance. Literature is always calling in the doctor for consultation and confession, and always giving evasions and swathing suppressions in place of that "heroic nudity"[*] on which only a genuine diagnosis of serious cases can be built. And in respect to editions of "Leaves of Grass" in time to come (if there should be such) I take occasion now to confirm those lines with the settled convictions and deliberate renewals of thirty years, and to hereby prohibit, as far as word of mine can do so, any elision of them.

Then still a purpose enclosing all, and over and beneath all. Ever since what might be call'd thought, or the budding of thought, fairly began in my youthful mind, I had had a desire to attempt some worthy record of that entire faith and acceptance ("to justify the ways of God to man" is Milton's well-known and ambitious phrase) which is the foundation of moral America. I felt it all as positively then in my young days as I do now in my old ones; to formulate a poem whose every thought or

[*]"Nineteenth Century," July, 1883.

fact should directly or indirectly be or connive at an implicit belief in the wisdom, health, mystery, beauty of every process, every concrete object, every human or other existence, not only consider'd from the point of view of all, but of each.

While I can not understand it or argue it out, I fully believe in a clue and purpose in Nature, entire and several; and that invisible spiritual results, just as real and definite as the visible, eventuate all concrete life and all materialism, through Time. My book ought to emanate buoyancy and gladness legitimately enough, for it was grown out of those elements, and has been the comfort of my life since it was originally commenced.

One main genesis-motive of the "Leaves" was my conviction (just as strong to-day as ever) that the crowning growth of the United States is to be spiritual and heroic. To help start and favor that growth—or even to call attention to it, or the need of it—is the beginning, middle and final purpose of the poems. (In fact, when really cipher'd out and summ'd to the last, plowing up in earnest the interminable average fallows of humanity— not "good government" merely, in the common sense— is the justification and main purpose of these United States.)

Isolated advantages in any rank or grace or fortune— the direct or indirect threads of all the poetry of the past— are in my opinion distasteful to the republican genius, and offer no foundation for its fitting verse. Establish'd poems, I know, have the very great advantage of chanting the already perform'd, so full of glories, reminiscences dear to the minds of men. But my volume is a candidate for the future. "All original art," says Taine, anyhow, "is self-regulated, and no original art can be regulated from without; it carries its own counterpoise, and does not receive it from elsewhere—lives on its own blood"—a solace to my frequent bruises and sulky vanity.

As the present is perhaps mainly an attempt at personal statement or illustration, I will allow myself as further help to extract the following anecdote from a book, "Annals of Old Painters," conn'd by me in youth. Rubens, the Flemish painter, in one of his wanderings through the galleries of old convents, came across a singular work. After looking at it thoughtfully for a good while, and listening to the criticisms of his suite of students, he said to the latter, in answer to their questions (as to what school the work implied or belong'd,) "I do not believe the artist, unknown and perhaps no longer living, who has given the world this legacy, ever belong'd to any school, or ever painted anything but this one picture, which is a personal affair—a piece out of a man's life."

‣ "Leaves of Grass" indeed (I cannot too often reiterate) has mainly been the outcropping of my own emotional and other personal nature—an attempt, from first to last, to put a *Person*, a human being (myself, in the latter half of the Nineteenth Century, in America,) freely, fully and truly on record. I could not find any similar personal record in current literature that satisfied me. But it is not on "Leaves of Grass" distinctively as *literature*, or a specimen thereof, that I feel to dwell, or advance claims. No one will get at my verses who insists upon viewing them as a literary performance, or attempt at such performance, or as aiming mainly toward art or æstheticism.

I say no land or people or circumstances ever existed so needing a race of singers and poems differing from all others, and rigidly their own, as the land and people and circumstances of our United States need such singers and poems to-day, and for the future. Still further, as long as the States continue to absorb and be dominated by the poetry of the Old World, and remain unsupplied with autochthonous song, to express, vitalize and give color to and define their material and political success, and minister to them distinctively, so long will they stop short of first-class Nationality and remain defective.

In the free evening of my day I give to you, reader, the foregoing garrulous talk, thoughts, reminiscences,

> As idly drifting down the ebb,
> Such ripples, half-caught voices, echo from the shore.

Concluding with two items for the imaginative genius of the West, when it worthily rises—First, what Herder taught to the young Goethe, that really great poetry is always (like the Homeric or Biblical canticles) the result of a national spirit, and not the privilege of a polish'd and select few; Second, that the strongest and sweetest songs yet remain to be sung.

Notes

p. 5 *"Eidólons"*: "images" or "idols" in Greek. Whitman's eidólons are immaterial and unchanging, "everlasting," "ever the permanent life of life." By contrast, people and things are "mutable" and "evanescent"; material things are ever "changing, crumbling, re-cohering" while "[i]ssuing eidólons" that survive their passing.

p. 12 *"Me imperturbe"*: a Whitman coinage meaning "I am serene."

p. 13 *"I Hear America Singing"*: this oft-anthologized poem, criticized for its sentimentality and "folksy nationalism," roots the joy and strength of the American character in the material details of the country's productivity (*Encyclopedia*, p. 294*). Like Whitman, who called many of his poems "songs," the catalogued figures contribute their unique, "varied," individual voices to an implicit national chorus.

p. 16 *"Paumanok"*: *paumanok* means "fish-shaped"; it is a Native American name for Long Island, where Whitman was born in 1819 and spent much of his youth.

p. 18, line 13 *a programme of chants*: "Starting from Paumanok" can be regarded "a programme" that introduces many of the themes and images of *Leaves of Grass* as a whole. Whitman began writing "Starting from Paumanok" soon after the volume's first publication in 1855, evidently intending that it replace that edition's Preface (*Encyclopedia* 687).

p. 33, line 1 *camerado*: a Whitmanism derived from Old Spanish, meaning "comrade."

*For references to specific titles, see the Bibliography.

line 10 *my soul:* in *Leaves of Grass,* the "soul" is sometimes the poet's soul, and sometimes a larger universal soul with links to creativity and nature.

line 11 *a spear of summer grass:* the spear or leaf of grass is a key symbol in *Leaves of Grass,* a part of the poetic landscape that also stands for nature, fertility, the earth, the individual, a poem, creativity and procreativity (as a symbol of the phallus and of fertility), love, and death ("the beautiful uncut hair of graves" [sec 6]).

p. 34, line 1 *Creeds and schools in abeyance:* logic, philosophy, law, society, and civilization in general are opposed to poetry, freedom, the soul, transcendence, and "Nature without check with original energy."

line 3 *harbor:* offer refuge.

line 13 *love-root, silk-thread, crotch and vine:* references to plants and insects that are also suggestive allusions to male genitalia.

p. 38, line 10 *loose the stop from your throat:* the soul is cast as a singer, like a traditional poetic muse, but of pure sound (which may stand for unmediated experience) rather than of the actual language of poetry.

p. 39, line 6 *kelson:* a beam or beams bolted to the keel of a ship to give it structural strength. Love is thus the backbone of the creation.

line 9 *worm fence:* a zigzag fence made of interlocking rails supported by crossed poles. *mullein:* a woolly-leaved herb of the snapdragon family. *poke-weed:* a perennial American herb.

line 10 *A child said* What is the grass?: the lines that follow explore the different meanings of the grass or its connection to various aspects of existence. Grass's ubiquity makes it a symbol of universality and equality, and of the eternity of life.

p. 42, line 13 *The little one sleeps in its cradle:* in sections 8 through 18 the poet presents examples of the people he can now see. They link him to birth, sexuality, and death, and to urban and rural scenes; they include people on the borders of civilization, of different races, classes, and professions, as well as animals.

p. 50, line 13 *king-pin:* a vertical pin connecting two parts of a knuckle joint (as in a steering joint).

p. 51, line 3 *jour printer:* "jour" is short for "journeyman," meaning a worker who has mastered a trade and works for someone else, usually during the day.

p. 51, line 4 *quid:* a wad.

line 14 *pate:* the crown of the head.

p. 56, line 1 *These are really the thoughts of all men:* the extended exploration of the symbol of the grass focuses on the notions of equality and ubiquity. Thus sections 18 and 19 include failures, outcasts, and unfortunates (as do sections 33 through 37).

line 12 *embouchures:* the mouthpieces of wind instruments.

p. 58, line 13 *truckling:* acting in a subservient manner.

p. 60, line 2 *tenon'd and mortis'd:* a tenon and mortise is a joint (a tenon is the projecting member in a piece of wood, and a mortise is the cavity into which the tenon is inserted). "Tenon'd and mortis'd," then, means "joined securely" in the manner of a tenon and mortise.

p. 61, line 6 *vitreous:* glassy.

p. 62, line 5 *amies:* friends, from the French *ami,* "friend."

line 13 *scrofula:* a disease characterized by the swelling of the lymph nodes, especially of the neck.

p. 63, line 16 *cartouches:* gun cartridges containing an explosive charge and a bullet.

p. 64, line 5 *I but enter by them to an area of my dwelling:* material facts and objects are not ends in themselves but are important in allowing transcendent truths to find expression in the physical world. For example, the power of the soul is revealed in part by its manifestation in animals, such as the stallion in section 32.

p. 66, line 13 *sweet-flag:* a perennial marsh herb. *pond-snipe:* a bird that frequents riverbanks.

p. 69, line 7 *Now I will do nothing but listen:* the poet explores his senses. The exploration culminates in section 29 (page 73), where the personified sense of touch bribes the other senses to "go and graze at the edges" of his awareness while touch brings him to a sexual climax. In a sense he runs a systems test of his body, as part of the confirmation of his "new identity" (section 28, p. 71).

p. 71, line 5 *quahaug:* a large thick-shelled clam.

p. 74, line 2 *omnific:* all-creating.

line 5 *pismire:* the ant.

line 11 *gneiss:* a variety of slatelike rock composed of quartz, feldspar, and mica.

p. 77, line 7 *gulch:* a ravine or gully.

p. 78, line 11 *trip-hammers:* a hammer operated by a tripping mechanism that causes the head of the hammer to drop.

p. 92, line 3 *Enough! enough! enough!:* the poet escapes from an overwhelming catalogue of experience that ends in death, pain, and ignominy by remembering the divinity of suffering.

p. 93, line 1 *eleves:* from the French *élèves,* "students."

p. 95, line 14 *I am he bringing help:* in this section, the poet compares the divinity of his immortal self or soul with a series of traditional divine figures.

p. 100, line 8 *gymnosophist:* a member of a sect of ascetics in ancient India who went naked and meditated.

line 10 *teokallis:* usually spelled "teocalli," a temple of ancient Mexico, built on a the top of a pyramid-shaped mound.

p. 111, line 13 *accoucheur:* a man who assists women in childbirth, an obstetrician.

p. 112, line 10 *soughing:* a soft murmuring sound, like the sound of the surf.

line 15 *debouch:* to emerge.

p. 113, line 1 *Wrench'd and sweaty:* here, the poet leaves his state of mystical discovery.

p. 114, line 7 *yawp:* loud or coarse talk.

p. 116 *"Children of Adam":* the poems of this section principally celebrate heterosexual love, as opposed to the homoerotic or "manly love" which is the focus of *Calamus.*

line 1 *To the garden the world:* reading a comma after "garden" helps clarify the sense of the phrase.

p. 119, line 15 *engirth:* surround.

line 13 *the charge of the soul:* electricity represents both the soul, or spirituality, and sexuality.

p. 123, line 6 *nimbus:* a circle of radiant light.

p. 125, line 9 *Is it one of the dull-faced immigrants:* as hinted in "Starting from Paumanok," the theme of love shades into the theme of democracy. Every individual body, regardless of social status, has its "place in the procession" of humanity and of the larger cosmos. Stanzas 7 and 8 go on to attack slavery for demeaning the perfection of human bodies.

p. 128, line 6 *O my body!:* the critical "notoriety" of the catalogue of human anatomy takes various forms (*Encyclopedia,* p. 298). G. W. Allen dismisses the "somewhat mechanical descriptions of the parts of the body added in 1856" (*Handbook,* p. 123). H. Gutman cites T. Nathanson, who describes the catalogue as "a struggle against alienation . . . [that] the poet seems to lose. What ought to be a ritual of repossession . . . comes to seem instead like an obsessive enumeration" (Nathanson, quoted in *Encyclopedia,* p. 296). Conversely, H. J. Waskow contends that the section "fulfills the logic of the rest of the poem"; he writes that for Whitman, "the describing of things . . . [is not] the best the poet can do; naming things, simply noting their existence, will be more true to reality" (p. 87).

line 14 *neck-slue:* "to slue" is to turn about on a fixed point. Presumably, Whitman is referring here to the joints connecting the neck to the shoulders.

p. 133, line 2 *Beautiful dripping fragments:* "Whitman's sexiest poem" contains numerous precise, lightly metaphorical allusions to sexual acts and anatomy, as well as more explicit descriptions (Schmidgall, p. 127). Note "The hairy wild-bee"; "The no-form'd stings"; "The sensitive, orbic, underlapp'd brothers"; "The limpid liquid"; "The souse upon me"; and the culminating image of "this bunch pluck'd at random."

p. 134, line 15 *The pulse pounding through palms:* while the poem offers evocations of heterosexual and homosexual desire, the autoerotic dominates through the image of the aroused boy. M. Mullins argues that the boy and his ilk "suffer from unquenched desire for physical contact," and claims, "Their desire culminates only in frustrated acts of 'torment' " (*Encyclopedia*, p. 684). However, the end of the poem suggests a different reading of the masturbation theme, one that casts the boy more as a novice than as blocked.

p. 135, line 8 *The wholesome relief:* early on, the poem links the phallus and poetry; here, the autoerotic, the artistic, and the procreative unite in the image of the bunch—"of semen, of words, of poems"—that is tossed "carelessly" into the world in a manner perhaps best described as polysexual (*Encyclopedia,* p. 684). For further examples of striking sexual imagery with political and spiritual implications, see the *Calamus* poems.

p. 139 *Hymen:* the membrane that covers part of the vagina; also, the Greek god of marriage.

p. 143 *"Calamus":* this section is concerned with "adhesiveness" and "manly love." The term "adhesiveness," meaning "friendship" or "comradeship," was used in phrenology, a pseudoscientific discipline that associated individual human behaviors, such as adhesiveness, with specific parts of the brain. In a letter Whitman defined "calamus," writing, "It is the very large & aromatic grass, or rush, growing about water-ponds in the valleys—spears about three feet high, often called 'sweet flag'—grows all over the Northern and Middle States—(see *Webster's Large Dictionary—Calamus—* definition 2). The recherché or ethereal sense of the term, as used in my book, arises probably from the actual Calamus presenting the biggest & hardiest kind of spears of grass— and their fresh, aquatic, pungent bouquet" (*Selected Letters,* p. 128). As a symbol it stands for the phallus, the speaking tongue, the musical reed, and permanence; its fragrance, like other natural fragrances, also has a spiritual valence for the poet.

The *Calamus* poems are thoroughly homoerotic, but the assertion that Whitman was or considered himself to be a homosexual is not uncontested. A number of critics argue at length that the *Calamus* poems represent homosocial but not homosexual desire. E. Crawley, for example, writes, "It is to [the] vibrant, sincere love of man for man as the true spirit of democracy that the 'Calamus' poem are dedicated" (p. 102). G. W. Mathews argues that the poet "thought in pictures, not in ideas, and hence when he portrays affection it tends to run into terms of contact" (Mathews, p. 39, quoted in Crawley, p. 106). Many other scholars, however, are less chary of accepting that the biographical Whitman was attracted to men, that he acted to an unknown degree on his feelings, and that this is reflected in his amorous tableaux at the same time that they symbolically link his "greatnesses" of love, democracy and religion (or spirituality). Thus R. K. Martin describes "In Paths Untrodden" as a "text of 'coming out,' both literal and metaphorical," and asserts that "the love evoked is seen as both physical and metaphysical" (*Encyclopedia,* p. 306). Those who take similar positions on Whitman include G. Schmidgall, who asserts "the reality of his homosexuality," and the poet Allen Ginsberg, who depicts Whitman in a store, "eyeing the grocery boys" (Schmidgall, p. xiii; Ginsberg, p. 136).

line 1 *In paths untrodden:* sometimes called the program poem of the *Calamus* section, the poem retreats from the public, procreative themes of the *Children of Adam* verses. The phallic calamus plant is not ubiquitous like the grass in the book's title; rather, it is found principally in secluded places, "[i]n the growth by margins of pond-waters."

lines 3–11 *Escaped from the life that exhibits itself . . . Strong upon me the life that does not exhibit itself:* the speaker leaves behind public themes in order to "tell the secret of [his] nights and days" and to direct his art to "young men" and readers who are in the know, rather than to the whole world. He arguably rejects the "standards" of larger society in order to bask in the delight of forbidden homosexual love—"manly attachment," "athletic love"—and more generally to enjoy, in D. Cavitch's words, "the wonder and beauty of intimate privacy" (p. 126). Note also that "[i]n seeming to withdraw from open view, he is giving expression to something he positively wants for the fullness of love's satisfaction; he is not merely reflecting social taboo" (Cavitch, p. 127).

p. 144, line 5 *Tomb-leaves:* the image of calamus growing over the dead recalls the grass of "Song of Myself," section 6 (p. 40, line 6): "And now it seems to me the beautiful uncut hair of graves." It is also an image of chest or other body hair.

p. 147, line 8 *gawk:* a fool.

p. 151, line 8 *systole and diastole:* rhythmically recurrent contraction and expansion, especially of the heart.

p. 154 *"When I Heard at the Close of the Day":* with its thirteen lines and a progression from dissatisfaction to contentment, the poem is often called a free-verse sonnet. It is one line shorter than a traditional sonnet and lacks a fixed meter or rhyme pattern, but it does offer a poetic "turn" at the word "But" in the third line.

p. 159, line 11 *rude, unbending, lusty:* originally intended for a cycle about homosexual love called "Live Oak with Moss," the poem retains the phallic or at least erotic symbol of the live oak. The poem portrays "a tension between homoerotic emotions unrepresentable in poetry and Whitman's stance of poetic self-sufficiency" (*Encyclopedia*, p. 296).

p. 170, line 4 *sharing the earth with all:* this first poem of the so-called song section introduces the themes of the journey and of internationalism, which will be taken up by "Song of the Open Road," "Song of the Rolling Earth," and others. It also uses the catalogue "for the first time in *Leaves of Grass* as the basic poetic technique for an entire long poem" (Crawley, p. 122).

p. 171, line 7 *emulous:* eager to imitate.

line 8 *rebeck:* a three-stringed fiddle.

line 15 *muezzin:* a man who, from a tower in the mosque, calls Muslims to prayer.

p. 175, line 13 *sabian:* an adherent of the Sabian religion who worships the stars.

p. 176, line 4 *Kneph:* the ram-headed god of ancient Egypt, also called Khnum.

p. 177, line 2 *tumuli:* ancient grave mounds. *Kalmucks:* a branch of the Mongolian race inhabiting parts of Russia and China. *Baskirs:* the natives or inhabitants of a region in southwest Russia in the southern Ural Mountains.

line 9 *vaquero:* cowherd.

line 14 *Samoiede:* Samoyed, a native or inhabitant of northwest Siberia.

p. 179, line 1 *Kruman:* a native or inhabitant of Kuruman, an oasis town in the middle of the dry expanse of the Kalahari Desert in South Africa. *Dahoman:* a native or inhabitant of Dahomey, a republic in West Africa, formerly part of French West Africa. *Ashantee:* a native or inhabitant of Ashanti, a former kingdom and British colony in West Africa, now a region in Ghana.

line 2 *Aleppo:* a city in northwest Syria.

line 3 *Khiva:* a city located in the Khorezm oasis of the Kara-Kum Desert in Uzbekistan, Russia. *Herat:* a city of northwest Afghanistan on the Hari Rud east of Kabul.

line 4 *Muscat:* the capital of Oman. *Medina:* a city of west Saudi Arabia north of Mecca.

line 8 *fall'n Theban:* Thebes was a capital of ancient Egypt, sacked by the Assyrians in 663 B.C. Whitman perhaps refers to the king of Egypt, Tanwetamani, at the time Thebes fell; the hands-folded-across-the-breast pose of the statue described is typical of statues of pharaohs.

p. 180, line 15 *Swabian:* a native or inhabitant of a historical region of southwest Germany that originally included parts of present-day France and Switzerland. *Wallachian:* a native or inhabitant of Wallachia, a former principality in southeast Europe that united with Moldavia to form Romania in 1861.

p. 181, line 1 *Bokh:* a native or inhabitant of Bokhara, or Bukhara, a city of south Uzbekistan in Russia, west of

Samarkand. It is one of the oldest cultural and trade centers of Asia.

p. 184 *"Song of the Open Road":* the road symbolizes movement, progress, the vagabond or itinerant mind-set, and the outdoor life. It also leads to consideration of opposed kinds of travel: movement along the conventional "highway . . . well-beaten and undenied" (section 4) versus travel in general, which allows for independent movement outside of established routes. The speaker's imagination soon moves off the road into "the open air" (section 4); he ordains himself "loos'd of limits and imaginary lines, / Going where I list" (section 5). The poet shakes loose of "the road as a limited symbol," making it "an expanding symbol" (Waskow, p. 192).

line 13 *I carry them, men and women:* H. Waskow argues that the speaker initially carries his readers along as burdens as he introduces them to the life of constant movement. The burdens may also be read as old emotional pains and joys.

p. 187, line 5 *I think I could stop here myself and do miracles:* Crawley notes the poem's scattered Christ symbolism, e.g., "Whoever accepts me he or she shall be blessed and shall bless me" (section 5); "Here a great personal deed has room (. . . Its effusion of strength and will overwhelms law and mocks all authority and all argument against it)" (section 6); "Allons! . . . From your formules, O bat-eyed and materialistic priests" (section 10); "Camerado! . . . I give you myself before preaching or law; Will you give me your self?" (section 15). Note also the fisherman who the speaker sees in section 7.

p. 198 *"Crossing Brooklyn Ferry":* in *Specimen Days* Whitman wrote, "I have always had a passion for ferries; to me they afford inimitable, streaming, never-failing, living poems."

line 10 *Flood-tide below me!:* throughout *Leaves of Grass* the poet uses the sea as a symbol for death and for the mystical "womb of time" where all souls are eternally united (Allen and Davis, p. 11). The water is both fluid and permanent, symbolizing both the spiritual oneness of humanity and the ongoing nature of time and human existence. This figure of moving stasis recurs in the image of the ferry passenger: "Just as you stand and lean on the rail, yet hurry with the swift current, I stood yet was hurried" (section 3). See also "Out of the Cradle Endlessly Rocking" and "As I Ebb'd with the Ocean of Life."

p. 202, line 6 *What is it then between us?:* D. Cavitch takes a psychological approach: Whitman, he writes, "meditates on the clash between his intense separateness, which he finds an irrefutable fact of nature, and his need for acknowledgment as a living person" (p. 106). In this reading the speaker's curious glances and his thoughts about the ferry passengers underline his apparent disconnection from them. He then comes to understand that "only rancorous feelings . . . could cause isolation," leading him to the litany of evils that makes up section 6 (p. 110).

p. 207 *"Song of the Answerer":* the two sections of the poem both work to name the characteristics that identify the "Answerer" or poet. But they also offer something of a "paradox": in the first section he is the ultimate common man—"His welcome is universal"—while in the second he is "the master among philosophs," the capital-*P* Poet who is uniquely able to sum up existence in "true poems" (*Encyclopedia*, p. 658). He is both common and uncommon.

line 3 *romanza:* a romantic song or story.

p. 213, line 3 *feuillage:* a bunch or row of leaves.

p. 217, line 4 *arriere:* the rear. *calumet:* a kind of pipe used by North American Indians for smoking tobacco. The bowl is usually made of soft red stone, and the tube is a long reed often ornamented with feathers.

line 5 *sachem:* a chief of a tribe of American Indians.

p. 218, line 9 *windlass:* a machine for raising weights.

line 11 *sporades:* stars not included in any constellation.

p. 226, line 8 *O the joy of my soul:* this passage helps clarify an understanding of Whitman's relation of the soul and the physical world. The soul "receiv[es] identity through materials . . . observing characters and absorbing them." It expresses and enjoys itself using a body, and by observing the spirituality of other people and of objects. But the body is ultimately only a tool: "it is not my material eyes which finally see."

p. 229, line *odium:* hatred, dislike.

p. 230, line 3 *Weapon shapely, naked, wan:* the first six lines, with their rhymes, near-rhymes (bone/one), and trochaic tetrameter couplets, constitute a rare interval of relatively traditional verse for Whitman. (A trochee is a two-syllable foot with the emphasis on the first syllable: WEAPon SHAPely NAked; tetrameter means that four feet make up line. Splitting lines 3 and 4 makes the meter clearer.) This poem within the poem has been described as a riddle whose symbolism invites interpretation.

line 4 *Head from the mother's bowels drawn:* the phallic imagery suggests a reading of the poem as "an Oedipal drama compounded of admiration for the potency of the father . . . and fear of castration" (*Encyclopedia,* p. 661). In a different but related interpretation, the ax stands for "man's law and masculine power," symbolically opposed to "an inner core of feminine power, which expresses nature's law" (Cavitch, p. 90).

p. 234, line 15 *lictors:* a lictor was a Roman officer who bore an ax and rods as ensigns of his office, and whose duty was to attend the chief magistrates when they appeared in public and also to apprehend and punish criminals.

line 16 *The antique European warrior with his axe in combat:* one progression to note in this richly meaningful poem is the ax's transformation from an Old World instrument of primitive violence to a democratic, New World instrument of creation. The ax sums up the great American project in Whitman's eyes (while eliding the ongoing violence of the nation's settlement).

p. 242, line 12 *hackmatack-roots:* a hackmatack is a coniferous tree with slender deciduous leaves.

line 14 *auger:* a tool for boring holes larger than those that can be bored by a gimlet. *adze:* a tool like an ax with the blade at an angle of approximately ninety degrees to the handle, which is used for cutting and shaping wood.

p. 244, line 7 *Her shape arises:* arguably, the maternal forces of Nature and stability triumph. However, a number of critics observe a difficult psychological conflict over the course of the poem. In Cavitch's biographical analysis, this section reveals Whitman's suppressed distress over his own mother, who, while "best belov'd," is also "more guarded than ever"; the poet supposedly sees in her what Cavitch calls a "withering complacency" toward her children's emotional and even material needs (p. 96).

p. 247, line 8 *Castaly's fountain:* a fountain of Parnassus, sacred to the Muses; those who drank from it were inspired with the gift of poetry.

line 11 *Calliope . . . Clio . . . Melpomene . . . Thalia:* Calliope is the Muse that presides over eloquence and heroic poetry and is chief of the nine Muses; Clio is the Muse who presides over history; Melpomene is the Muse of tragedy; and Thalia is the Muse of comedy.

line 12 *Una and Oriana:* Una, who stands for truth (because truth is one), is the heroine of Spenser's *The Faerie Queene.* Oriana either refers to Queen Elizabeth I, the Fairy Queen Gloriana in Spenser's allegory, or to the beloved of Amadis in *Amadis of Gaul* (see next note, below).

line 15 *Amadis, Tancred:* Amadis is the hero of *Amadis of Gaul,* a famous prose chivalric romance. Tancred was a Norman soldier and renowned late-ninth-century crusader.

line 16 *Palmerin . . . Usk:* Palmerin is the hero of another prose chivalric romance, *Palmerin of England.* The Usk is a river in Wales.

p. 248, line 4 *charnel:* a tomb, vault, cemetery, or other place where the bones of the dead are deposited.

p. 249, line 13 *Rhenish:* pertaining to the river Rhine, or to Rheims in France.

line 14 *Columbia:* the United States; "Columbia" is a poetical appellation given in honor of Christopher Columbus, the discoverer.

p. 253, line 21 *longeve:* long-lived.

p. 254, line 8 *rondure:* circle.

p. 258, line 8 *A California song:* as expressed in a number of the "song" poems, Whitman thought human progress followed a course from east to west, from the Old World to America, culminating in the development of the "lands of the Western shore" (section 1). See also "Passage to India."

line 10 *hamadryads:* tree nymphs whose lives ends with that of the particular tree, usually an oak, that each inhabits.

p. 259, line 10 *I heard the mighty tree:* in his sympathy with nature, the poet "in [his] soul" hears the tree prophesy human accomplishments. The poem seems to contain two speakers; however, "the thought of the tree and the poet are so nearly alike that to all practical intents the poet identifies himself with the tree . . . and projects his program of literary nationalism through the tree's song" (Allen and Davis, p. 30).

p. 260, line 8 *Nor yield we mournfully:* the trees go to death "[w]ith Nature's calm content, with tacit huge delight" in order that humans, "a superber race," may supplant them. Conservationism was not unknown in the 1870s when Whitman wrote the poem; he may not have taken such concerns seriously, or perhaps he thought the poetic vision of civilization's advance gave a transcendent value to the destruction of the western forests (*Encyclopedia*, pp. 664–65).

p. 264, line 10 *A song for occupations!:* although the poem celebrates numerous kinds of work in section 5, it is in a sense more concerned with the basic humanity that transcends one's occupation or social position. The speaker wants to undo the tendency for this humanity to be forgotten in the pursuit of wealth; he "seeks to recover wholeness by affirming the dignity of human labor, as the process that generates both the material and the social world" (*Encyclopedia*, p. 653).

p. 270, line 7 *exurge:* rise up.

p. 271, line 11 *derrick:* a mast, spar, or tall frame, supported at the top by stays or guys, with suitable tackle for hoisting heavy weights.

line 12 *smutch'd:* blackened with smoke, soot, or coal.

p. 272, line 1 *loup-lump:* a pasty mass of iron gathered into a ball for the tilt hammer or rolls.

line 7 *gutta-percha:* the sap of a tall tree, native to the Malayan archipelago, and a natural latex that is widely used in medicine, to insulate underground and marine cables, to cover golf balls, and for adhesives.

p. 277, line 1 *Accouche:* French for "be delivered [of a child]."

p. 287 *"Pioneers! O Pioneers!":* originally placed among the Civil War verses in "Drum-Taps," this poem shares their greater conventionality in form and style. It uses a fixed stanza form, with a basically trochaic meter and a refrain, as well as frequent alliteration (repeated consonant sounds) and assonance (repeated vowels), e.g., "resistless restless race," "Lo, the darting bowling orb!", "clustering suns."

p. 288, line *Have the elder races halted?:* Whitman sees Americans, who constitute a new race, as fulfilling human evolutionary destiny and creating democracy following the failures of Europe.

p. 290, line 2 *By those swarms upon our rear:* G. W. Allen notes that the title of this part of the book is *Birds of Passage,* "suggesting that the divine scheme of creation is accomplished by transitory flights of the soul—or souls" (*Handbook,* p. 291). The swarms, the "ghostly millions," are thus the birdlike souls in endless, progressive, cosmic flight.

p. 291, line 8 *We, a curious trio:* the "mind of the poet, accompanied by his soul and body," marches along with the other pioneers (Allen and Davis, p. 32).

p. 296, line 3 *hopples:* fetters for horses or cattle when they are turned out to pasture.

p. 297, line 1 *battues:* bloodbath.

p. 302, line 7 *skald:* an ancient Scandinavian poet or bard.

p. 304, line 8 *Niphon:* Nippon, that is, Japan.

line 10 *barouches:* a barouche is a four-wheeled carriage, with a folding top, a seat on the outside for the driver, and two double seats on the inside arranged so that the sitters on the front seat face those on the backseat.

p. 305, line 1 *Libertad:* liberty.

p. 306, line 7 *eld:* a poetic term for old times or former days.

line 12 *cantabile:* a musical piece, vocal or instrumental, peculiarly adapted to singing.

p. 307, line 7 *bonze:* a Buddhist or Fohist priest, monk, or nun.

p. 311, line 2 *A man, yet by these tears a little boy again:* the narrative frame of the poem, as set up in the initial twenty-two-line sentence, has the grown poet recalling a boyhood experience.

p. 313, line 5 *now translating the notes:* within the frame of memory, the boy hears the lament of the bird, his "brother."

p. 316, line 8 *The colloquy there, the trio:* the three speakers or singers are the soul of the "ecstatic boy," the bird, and the sea, which is described as "the fierce old mother incessantly moaning." The word "trio" plays on the bird's song as "aria" (an operatic solo performance). Whitman was a frequent and enthusiastic operagoer.

p. 317, line 17 *death, death, death, death:* the maternal sea finally calms the boy by telling him of death and implicitly of the universality and permanence of loss. By their participation in this greater natural fact, his own disappointments take on a greater resonance, which is "delicious," mollifying, and worthy of poetry. In one psychological reading, Whitman's acknowledgment of an essential sadness—due to a solitary loneliness or parental estrangement, or to a romantic disappointment for the adult poet—strips him of his innocence but also awakens him to a truth about life. Having found that paternal and romantic affection end in sadness, he succumbs to the qualified comfort of an enveloping, maternal model of love. This figure unites the concepts of love and death: the boy/poet "fuse[s] the song of [his] dusky demon and brother," the lovelorn bird, with "the word up from the waves." Cavitch writes that this "reconceptualization of himself . . . commits Whitman to a consistently elegiac mode of expression in the best of his subsequent works. He will remain the poet of death . . ." (p. 152).

p. 319, line 1 *windrows:* a long row of cut hay or grain left to dry in a field before being bundled.

p. 320, line 11 *friable:* easily crumbled, pulverized, or reduced to powder.

p. 321, line 1 *I throw myself upon your breast my father:* turning away from "the fierce old mother" (section 1), the sea, the speaker seeks comfort in the paternal land, the "fish-shaped" Long Island of his youth, the phallic Paumanok. The speaker "cling[s]" to his father-figure and asks for a kiss, desiring closeness to a "murmuring" that may represent the sounds of a marriage bed (*Encyclopedia,* p. 33). Cavitch finds in the poem a biographical narrative of Whitman's desperate effort to win signs of paternal affection, and his failure to do so, as indicated by his sudden, resigned return to the figure of the ocean in section 4.

p. 325, line 10 *Pleiades:* a star cluster in the constellation Taurus. The seven daughters of Atlas and the nymph Pleione were fabled to have been made by Jupiter into a constellation in the sky to save them from being chased by Orion.

p. 327, line 8 *clef:* French for "key."

p. 332 *"A Boston Ballad":* as a journalist and essayist, Whitman frequently wrote on political topics, but "A Boston Ballad" is one of the rare satires that survived through to the final edition of *Leaves of Grass.* He wrote it following the 1854 capture and return of a slave who had escaped Virginia for Boston. This occasion of the enforcement of the federal Fugitive Slave Law caused first a riot and later a huge protest by opponents.

p. 334, line 4 *Dig out King George's coffin:* the arrival of the monarch's bones completes the return of centralized tyranny.

343, line 7 *The clinching interlocking claws:* as R. K. Martin observes, this short poem contains "a remarkable series of fifteen present participles, a rushing progression," and uses rhythms that "enact the subject matter" (*Encyclopedia,* p. 161).

line 10 *Till o'er the river pois'd:* the moment of mating and of stasis is represented by an absence of participles and only one verb at all, "pois'd."

line 12 *their separate diverse flight:* the egalitarian sexual politics of the poem proposes a "way to *preserve* the self at the same time that one *merges* the self, the same problem on a personal level as the democratic dilemma of maintaining individual freedom in the midst of universal equality" (Miller, p. 151).

p. 353 *"Beat! Beat! Drums!":* Whitman wrote the poem after the July 1861 battle of Bull Run, the first major clash of the Civil War and a defeat for the Union. "Beat! Beat! Drums!" supports the war, though with ambivalence, as reflected in the "the cries of opposition . . . from the weak, the aged, the child, and the mother" in stanza 3 (Allen and Davis, p. 201). The poet saw the conflict as "an unwelcome but necessary means of redeeming a divided and increasingly materialistic democracy" (*Encyclopedia*, p. 52).

p. 354, line 13 *trestles:* horizontal beams or bars held up by two pairs of sloping legs and used as supports.

p. 360, line 1 *halyards:* ropes used to raise or lower a sail, flag, or yard.

p. 386, line 3 *To sit by the wounded and soothe them:* Whitman worked as a volunteer in Washington-area military hospitals from 1862 until the end of the war, giving gifts and offering comfort to wounded and dying soldiers and occasionally serving as a "wound-dresser" (*Encyclopedia*, p. 800). Unlike the speaker of the poem, he was never a soldier or a nurse in a field hospital.

p. 388, line 2 *open doors of time!:* the narrative is framed as the recollections of an old man speaking to "maidens and young men." However, Allen and Davis contend that "the poet presents his reminisces not as history or truth but as an imaginative projection into the future" (p. 211). The speaker calls them "dreams' projections" in sections 2 and 4.

p. 389, line 12 *Many a soldier's kiss dwells on these bearded lips:* the suffering Whitman saw "did not embitter or disillusion him but aroused his great motherly compassion"; the poem's speaker calls his experiences "sweet and sad" (section 2) (Allen, *Handbook,* p. 167). Furthermore, Whitman's hospital work allowed him to enjoy a socially permissible "manly love" toward a huge number of young soldiers. As Allen observes, "His *Calamus* love found an outlet in his activities as a 'wound-dresser'."

p. 398, line 12 *guidons:* the flags or standards of a troop of cavalry, or the standard-bearer.

p. 402, line 11 *cerulean:* blue azure.

p. 407, line 1 *leaven'd:* the blood of the Civil War dead has permeated and revivified the American soil and spirit. Reading a comma between "trod" and "calling" clarifies the meaning of the line.

line 4 *to the South and the North:* with the war ended, Whitman does not celebrate the Northern victory but emphasizes the unity of the rejoined halves of the nation. The "Alleghanian hills and the tireless Mississippi" geographically link the two regions, and the "Northern ice and rain" cooperate with "the hot sun of the South" to "fully ripen [the poet's] songs" (*Encyclopedia,* p. 730).

p. 408, line 6 *And thought of him I love:* President Abraham Lincoln was assassinated on April 14, 1865. Whitman, a longtime admirer, began writing the poem soon thereafter. In the tradition of the poetic elegy, the person mourned is never named.

line 7 *O powerful western fallen star!:* Lincoln came from Illinois, and his body was returned there by train from Washington; thus the star is in the "western sky," a "great star early droop'd" in correspondence with the president's premature death. It is actually the planet Venus (symbolizing love), which shined from the west that spring. The star also represents the poet's grief.

p. 409, line 4 *the lilac-bush tall-growing:* the lilac, with its heart-shaped leaves and strong fragrance, often stands for love or nature in Whitman's poems. It blooms in the spring.

line 11 *Solitary the thrush:* the hermit thrush sings only during its breeding season, providing another association with spring (Allen and Davis, p. 231). In the poem's basic symbolic trinity, the bird represents the poetic soul that struggles to sublimate grief into art. It sings "the carol of death" (section 14), which like the ocean and moon in other poems, soothes the speaker.

p. 412, line 6 *As my soul in its trouble dissatisfied sank, as where you sad orb:* the star stands for his personal grief, which remains painful; he cannot find calm within himself. Cavitch has a psychological reading rooted in Whitman's biography: he argues that the poet is trying to reach out to his distant, troubled, dead father ("Now I know what you must have meant"), but that the father-figure continues to fail him (pp. 164–65).

line 12 *The star my departing comrade holds and detains me:* the tug-of-war between the star (personal grief) and the singing bird (artistic expression of the experience) for dominance in the poet's sentiments provides the poem's tension or drama. Cavitch sees an "old conflict" over "emotional authenticity" as Whitman tries move from feeling to writing without misrepresenting his experience (p. 162).

p. 415, line 3 *Now while I sat:* the narrative switches back to the past tense of section 1, as if the speaker is recalling his initial reaction to the news of Lincoln's death.

p. 420, line 4 *Lilac and star and bird twined with the chant of my soul:* in the last stanza, the poet is able to summon all his symbols and experiences at once and to turn mourning into an uplifting experience. Note that the end of the poem evokes the moon's "silver face" (as in "Dirge for Two Veterans") and leaves the speaker in the swamp.

p. 420 *"O Captain! My Captain!":* although now usually described as conventional and trite, this elegy to Lincoln is Whitman's most widely read work. It metaphorically describes the post–Civil War United States as a ship that has arrived safely in port but with its captain dead.

p. 427, line 15 *canebrake:* a thicket of canes.

p. 429, line 14 *lambent:* gliding over, flickering, playing on the surface.

p. 445, line 3 *reticulations:* netlike patterns.

p. 447, line 8 *parturient:* bringing forth, or about to bring forth, young; fruitful.

p. 448, line 8 *demesne:* domain.

p. 452, line 18 *kine:* cows.

p. 458, line 16 *morbific:* infectious; causing disease.

p. 467, line 2 *peculation:* embezzlement.

p. 477, line 13 *burin'd:* a burin is the cutting tool an engraver on uses on metal in line engraving.

p. 481, line 5 *trottoirs:* footpaths.

p. 490, line 13 *salaams:* to greet someone by bending deeply from the waist with the front of the right hand against the top of the face.

p. 497, line 2 *George Fox:* (1624–1691), an English preacher and founding member of the Society of Friends (or Quakers); he documented the birth of the Quaker movement in his autobiography.

p. 498, line 14 *Sonnambula . . . Norma . . . Poliuto: Sonnambula* (1831) is an opera by Bellini in which Amina, who is betrothed to one man but found on the night before the wedding in the bed of another (because she sleepwalks). Norma is a vestal in another Bellini opera, *Norma* (1831), who had been seduced, and discovers her lover trying to seduce a sister vestal, and who, despairing, contemplates murdering her children borne of the seducer. Poliuto is a character in Donizetti's opera of the same name (composed in 1838 but not performed for the first time until 1848), based on Corneille's *Polyeucte,* a story about the martyrdom of an early Christian saint.

p. 500 *"Proud Music":* the poem functions as a fanfare and inspiration for a change in Whitman's poetic goals. G. W. Allen writes that it announces the poet's intention to begin a new collection of "Poems bridging the way from Life to Death" (section 6), which was to start with "Passage to India" (*Handbook,* p. 201).

p. 502, line 3 *minnesingers:* one of a class of German poets and musicians who flourished from about the middle of the twelfth to the middle of the fourteenth century.

p. 503, line 1 *Tuttti!:* (Italian for "all") a direction for all to play in full concert.

p. 504, line 8 *Lucia:* a character in Donizetti's opera *Lucia di Lammermoor* who is in love with her brother's bitter enemy.

line 10 *Ernani:* Ernani is the robber-captain, duke of Segorbia and Cardona, lord of Aragon, and count of Ernani in Verdi's operi *Ernani* (1844).

line 19 *Fernando:* a character in Donizetti's opera *La Favorita* (1840) to whom Alfonzo XI promises Leonora in marriage.

line 20 *Amina:* Amina the character who walks in her sleep in Bellini's *La Sonnambula* (1831).

p. 505, line 3 *Alboni:* Marietta Alboni (1826–1894), the celebrated Italian contralto.

p. 506, line 1 *Corybantian:* Corybantians, attendents or priests of the goddess Cybele, who were know for their extremely emotional rites.

line 2 *flageolets:* a small flute resembling a recorder.

line 11 *vina:* A stringed instrument of India that has a long, fretted fingerboard with resonating gourds at each end.

line 12 *bayaderes:* Indian dancers.

p. 508, line 1 *diapason:* a stop in the organ, so called because it extends through the scale of the instrument; also a burst of sound.

line 9 *Haply:* by chance.

line 16 *Poems bridging the way from Life to Death:* during this period (the late 1860s and later), Whitman's "concept and expectation" of death became "joyous, personal liberation" (*Handbook,* p. 199).

p. 509, line 4 *Our modern wonders:* the underwater telephone cable across the Atlantic Ocean was laid in 1866; 1869 saw the completion of the transcontinental railroad in the United

States and the Suez Canal between the Mediterranean Sea and the Red Sea. The poem was first published in 1871.

p. 510, line 22 *You, not for trade or transportation only:* while the poem sanctifies the accomplishments of science as signs of God's plan, for Whitman material objects are principally ways for the soul and spirituality to be expressed and not ends in themselves. He sings his "worship new" of explorers and engineers "in God's name" and for the sake of the soul.

p. 512, line 9 *Ah Genoese:* a reference to Christopher Columbus.

p. 513, line 17 *Who justify these restless explorations?:* Adam and Eve were banished from Eden for their "questionings"; the poet seeks to justify the curiosity of the first couple (and of the rest of humanity) as the first step toward mastery of the earth and union with God. The poet uses the verb "justify" three times in "Passage to India," echoing John Milton's effort in *Paradise Lost* to "justify the ways of God to men" (I.26). In this way Whitman emphasizes the epic and holy nature of the spiritual journey his poem delineates.

p. 515, line 7 *terraqueous:* consisting of land and water, like the Earth.

p. 516, line 4 *Tamerlane:* Timur Lenk, Mongol emperor of Tartary, who invaded India in 1398. *Aurungzebe:* a Mughal (Persian for "Mongol") emperor (1658–1707) who imposed Muslim orthodoxy in India and expanded the empire.

line 6 *Batouta:* Ibn Battutah (1304–1368), Arab traveler who explored Africa, the Middle East, and India.

line 14 *And who art thou sad shade?:* Columbus is called a "visionary," "the chief histrion," and "the Admiral." Whitman briefly mentions his voyages, his return to Spain as a prisoner, and his death in neglect. Like the poet, Columbus sought a "Passage to India," and like him he suffered as much or more "slander" than success. The explorer is Whitman's hero; see also the next poem, "Prayer of Columbus."

p. 521, line 15 *A batter'd, wreck'd old man:* at the time of the writing of the poem, Whitman himself had recently suffered a stroke. His mother, a sister-in-law to whom he was close, and a male friend all died that year, and his literary work was not well received.

p. 522, line 16 *emprises:* a chivalrous or adventurous undertaking.

p. 523, line 19 *Old, poor, and paralyzed:* Whitman's January 1873 stroke left him partly paralyzed.

p. 525, line 1 *I wander all night in my vision:* H. Waskow calls the poem a "monodrama" in which "we meet a speaker who describes an action happening in himself at the present time"; "we must *see* the action happen, not merely be told about it" (p. 142). We must observe "the change in the speaker's manner, his *actual* shifting from one position to another," rather than just depend on his "overt statements about his movement."

line 8 *onanists:* masturbators.

p. 527, line 5 *douceurs:* a gift for service done or to be done; an honorarium; sometimes, a bribe.

line 6 *cache:* A hole in the ground or hiding place.

p. 528, line 2 *My truant lover has come:* the speaker becomes a woman waiting for her lover.

p. 529, line 11 *I see a beautiful gigantic swimmer:* the speaker may identify with the swimmer but does not become him, as he became various people in sections 1 and 2. Waskow argues that having experienced love through the woman in section 1, and death through the shroud in section 2, the speaker fears that he "will be destroyed by the buffets of experience," like the swimmer (p. 149). To save his identity, he places the swimmer outside himself, affirming his ultimate commitment to the external day world over the dream.

p. 534, line 12 *erysipalite:* a person afflicted with a disease called St. Anthony's fire, which causes inflammation of the skin, primarily on the face (one species of erysipelas is shingles).

line 13 *antipodes:* one meaning of "antipodes" is "anything exactly opposite or contrary"; here Whitman seems to use it to mean "a contrary person."

p. 549, line 4 *Brahm:* Brahm is a force or spirit in Hinduism in which the three major Hindu gods—Brahma (the Creator), Vishnu (the Preserver), and Shiva (the Destroyer and the Regenerator)—are one. *Saturnius:* Whitman is probably referring to the Roman god Saturn, who is often identified with Greek god Kronos (see next note).

line 7 *Kronos:* a son of Uranus and Gaia, and father of Zeus, Kronos was god of harvests.

p. 550, line 14 *sudra:* the lowest of the four great castes among the Hindus.

p. 556, line 3 *tutti:* here, the simultaneous playing of strings, brass, and woodwind.

line 7 *cons:* direct the steering or course of a vessel.

line 14 *It launch'd forth filament, filament, filament:* As Allen and Davis note, "The length of the word, the *f*'s and *l*'s, and the repetition emphasize the 'patient' effort, and the approximation of internal rhyme in line 5 ('unreeling'—'speeding') is suggestive of the action" (p. 199). They also observe that line 8 and 9 are the poem's longest, "suggesting the throwing out of the filament into space."

p. 557, line 1 *And you O my soul:* The second stanza, an address by the poet to his soul, is not a complete sentence, "in accordance with the incompletion of the soul's search" (Allen and Davis, p. 199).

p. 569, line 7 *seine-ends:* a seine is a large net, one edge of which is provided with sinkers, and the other with floats. It hangs vertically in the water, and when its ends are brought together or drawn ashore it encloses the fish.

p. 573, line 6 *caoutchouc:* India rubber, a tenacious, elastic, gummy substance obtained from the milky sap of several plants of tropical South America. See *gutta-pereha,* note to p. 272.

p. 579, line 3 *alembic:* an apparatus formerly used in distillation, usually made of glass or metal; also something that purifies or transforms.

p. 581, line 13 *Thee for my recitative:* a recitative is a passage in an opera with a rhythmically free vocal style that imitates the natural inflections of speech. The first 17 lines of the poem emulate this style.

p. 582, line 15 *(No sweetness debonair of tearful harp or glib piano thine):* the poem's celebration of the locomotive's dissonant, "modern" music asserts that "any subject may be poetical— and cacophony may be beautiful" *(Encyclopedia,* p. 726).

p. 593, line 3 *mummeries:* pretentious or hypocritical shows or ceremonies.

p. 594, line 13 *ambuscade:* ambush

p. 603.9 *reveillé:* the beat of drum, or bugle blast, to give notice that it is time for the soldiers to rise.

p. 617, line 6 *To conclude:* other than the annexes, which were added later, this has been the final poem of *Leaves from Grass* from 1860.

line 15 *I have sung the body and the soul:* "So Long!" serves as a companion peace to "Starting from Paumanok," once again summing up the themes of his poetic career.

p. 618, line 6 *I announce the justification of candor:* Whitman and his publishers several times faced problems with censors and decency crusaders. With these considerations in mind, Ralph Waldo Emerson once tried to convince him to omit the *Children of Adam* poems from an edition of *Leaves of Grass,* but Whitman declined to follow Emerson's advice.

p. 619, line 20 *(death makes me really undying):* the soul, and the poet's verses, are immortal.

p. 624, line 10 *nonpareil, brevier, bourgeois, long primer:* old names for type sizes, listed from smallest to largest.

p. 625, line 2 *querilities:* Whitman perhaps meant some form of "querulous," that is, of a complaining nature. "Querilities" could be "complaints."

p. 634 *"With Husky-Haughty Lips, O Sea!":* when it tells the "tale of cosmic elemental passion" the sea may be describing "the eternal struggle of the elemental spirit of freedom against the elemental spirit of law in nature," either as a topic in itself or in sympathy with the sick, old poet, the sea's "kindred soul," who feels similarly "lonely," his heart "chain'd and chafing" (Stovall, p. 414).

p. 636, line 8 *Ossian:* Oisín, legendary Gaelic warrior-bard, son of Finn.

p. 640, line 8 *Fernando . . . Manrico . . . Ernani . . . Gennaro:* for Fernando and Ernani, notes to page 504. Manrico is a character in Verdi's opera *Il Trovatore* (1852); allegedly the son of Azucena the gypsy, but in fact the son of Count Luna, Leonora is in love with him. Gennaro is a character in Donizetti's opera *Lucrezia Borgia* (1834), the natural son of Lucrezia Borgia (daughter of pope Alexander VI) before her marriage with Alfonso d'Este, duke of Ferrara.

p. 649, line 9 *green-hand:* novice.

p. 656 *"Good-Bye my Fancy!":* two of Whitman's late poems use this name. This longer, 18-line work is the true conclusion to the final version of *Leaves of Grass.* The fancy is an artist's power to conceive or imagine; Whitman personifies Fancy as a muse figure who "usher[s]" him "to the true songs."

p. 664, line 9 *eleemosynary:* given in charity; given or appropriated to support the poor.

p. 680, line 15 *The slower fainter ticking:* Whitman unhappily imagines himself dying. The poem was first published in 1891; he died the following year.

Selected Bibliography

For references to *Encyclopedia*, see LeMaster and Kummings. For references to Allen and Davis, see *Walt Whitman's Poems: Selections with Critical Aids.*

Allen, Gay Wilson. *A Reader's Guide to Walt Whitman.* New York: Farrar, Straus & Giroux, 1970.

———. *Walt Whitman Handbook.* Chicago: Packard and Company, 1946.

Black, Stephen A. *Whitman's Journeys into Chaos: A Psychoanalytic Study of the Poetic Process.* Princeton: Princeton University Press, 1975.

Cavitch, David. *My Soul and I: The Inner Life of Walt Whitman.* Boston: Beacon Press, 1985.

Crawley, Thomas Edward. *The Structure of Leaves of Grass.* Austin: University of Texas Press, 1970.

Fone, Byrne R. S. *Masculine Landscapes: Walt Whitman and the Homoerotic Text.* Carbondale: Southern Illinois University Press, 1992.

Ginsberg, Allen. *Collected Poems, 1947–1980.* New York: Harper & Row, 1984.

LeMaster, J. R., and Donald D. Kummings, eds. *Walt Whitman: An Encyclopedia.* New York: Garland, 1998.

Mathews, Godfrey W. *Walt Whitman.* Liverpool: "Daily Post" Printers, 1921.

Miller, James Edwin. *A Critical Guide to Leaves of Grass.* Chicago: University of Chicago Press, 1957.

Nathanson, Tenney. *Whitman's Presence: Body, Voice, and Writing in Leaves of Grass.* New York: New York University Press, 1992.

Schmidgall, Gary. *Walt Whitman: A Gay Life*. New York: Dutton, 1997.

Waskow, Howard J. *Whitman Explorations in Form*. Chicago: University of Chicago Press. 1966.

Whitman, Walt. *Poetry and Prose*. Selected and with notes by Justin Kaplan. New York: Library of America, 1982.

———. "Specimen Days." in *The Collected Writings of Walt Whitman*, vol. 2 *Prose Words 1892*, edited by Floyd Stovall. New York: New York University Press, 1963.

———. *Walt Whitman: Representative Selections with Introduction, Bibliography, and Notes*. Edited by Floyd Stovall. New York: American Book Company, 1939.

———. *Selected Letters of Walt Whitman*. Edited by Edwin Haviland Miller. Iowa City: University of Iowa Press, 1990.

———. *Walt Whitman's Poems: Selections with Critical Aids*. Edited by Gay Wilson Allen and Charles T. Davis. New York: New York University Press, 1955.

*

COMMENTARY

RALPH WALDO EMERSON

CHARLES DANA

WALT WHITMAN

RUFUS GRISWOLD

HENRY JAMES

WILLIAM DOUGLAS O'CONNOR

EDWARD DOWDEN

WILLIAM DEAN HOWELLS

PAUL ELMER MORE

VAN WYCK BROOKS

AMY LOWELL

GAY WILSON ALLEN

RANDALL JARRELL

IRVING HOWE

DONALD HALL

RALPH WALDO EMERSON

Emerson's letter to Whitman on receiving a complimentary copy of the first edition of Leaves of Grass *from the poet is one of the most famous letters in literary history.*

I am not blind to the worth of the wonderful gift of *Leaves of Grass.* I find it the most extraordinary piece of wit & wisdom that America has yet contributed. I am very happy in reading it, as great power makes us happy. It meets the demand I am always making of what seemed the sterile and stingy Nature, as if too much handiwork or too much lymph in the temperament were making our western wits fat & mean. I give you joy of your free & brave thoughts. I have great joy in it. I find incomparable things said incomparably well, as they must be. I find the courage of treatment, which so delights us, & which large perception only can inspire. I greet you at the beginning of a great career, which yet must have had a long foreground somewhere for such a start. I rubbed my eyes a little to see if this sunbeam were no illusion; but the solid sense of the book is a sober certainty. It has the best merits, namely, of fortifying & encouraging.

The original of the letter is in the Library of Congress.

CHARLES DANA

Charles Dana (1819–1897) was an American journalist and newspaper editor and the author of several books, including Recollections of the Civil War *(1898) and* The Art of Newspaper Making *(1895).*

Leaves of Grass are doubtless intended as an illustration of the natural poet. They are certainly original in their external form, have been shaped on no pre-existent model out of the author's own brain. Indeed, his independence often becomes coarse and defiant. His language is too frequently reckless and indecent, though this appears to arise from a naive unconsciousness rather than from an impure mind. His words might have passed between Adam and Eve in Paradise, before the want of fig-leaves brought no shame; but they are quite out of place amid the decorum of modern society, and will justly prevent his volume from free circulation in scrupulous circles. With these glaring faults, the *Leaves of Grass* are not destitute of peculiar poetic merits, which will awaken an interest in the lovers of literary curiosities. They are full of bold, stirring thoughts—with occasional passages of effective description, betraying a genuine intimacy with Nature and a keen appreciation of beauty—often presenting a rare felicity of diction, but so disfigured with eccentric fancies as to prevent a consecutive perusal without offense, though no impartial reader can fail to be impressed with the vigor and quaint beauty of isolated portions.

From "The Leaves of Grass" in the *New York Daily Tribune*, July 23, 1855

WALT WHITMAN

Whitman wrote a number of anonymous reviews of the 1855 edition of Leaves of Grass.

An American bard at last! One of the roughs, large, proud, affectionate, eating, drinking, and breeding, his costume manly and free, his face sunburnt and bearded, his posture strong and erect, his voice bringing hope and prophecy to the generous races of young and old. We shall cease shamming and be what we really are. We shall start an athletic and defiant literature. We realize now how it is, and what was most lacking.

From "Walt Whitman and His Poems," in *The United States Review*, September 1855

RUFUS GRISWOLD

Rufus Griswold (1819–1857) was a newspaper editor, writer, and anthologist. He is best known for his anthology The Poets and Poetry of America *(1842); he also published* The Prose Writers of America *(1847) and* The Female Poets of America *(1849).*

An unconsidered letter of introduction has oftentimes procured the admittance of a scurvy fellow into good society, and our apology for permitting any allusion to [*Leaves of Grass*] in our columns is, that it has been unworthily recommended by a gentleman of wide repute, and might, on that account, obtain access to respectable people, unless its real character were exposed.

Mr. Ralph Waldo Emerson either recognizes and accepts these 'leaves,' as the gratifying result of his own peculiar doctrines, or else he has hastily indorsed them, after a partial and superficial reading. If it is of any importance he may extricate himself from the dilemma. We, however, believe that this book does express the bolder results of a certain transcendental kind of thinking, which some may have styled philosophy.

As to the volume itself, we have only to remark, that it strongly fortifies the doctrines of the Metempsychosists, for it is impossible to imagine how any man's fancy could have conceived such a mass of stupid filth, unless he were possessed of the soul of a sentimental donkey that had died of disappointed love. This *poet* (?) without wit, but with a certain vagrant wildness, just serves to show the energy which natural imbecility is occasionally capable of under strong excitement.

From " 'Leaves of Grass' " in the *New York Criterion*, November 10, 1855

HENRY JAMES

[Drum-Taps] exhibits the effort of an essentially prosaic mind to lift itself, by a prolonged muscular strain, into poetry. Like hundreds of other good patriots, during the last four years, Mr. Walt Whitman has imagined that a certain amount of violent sympathy with the great deeds and sufferings of our soldiers, and of admiration for our national energy, together with a ready command of picturesque language, are sufficient inspiration for a poet. If this were the case, we had been a nation of poets.

From "Mr. Walt Whitman" in *The Nation*, 1865

WILLIAM DOUGLAS O'CONNOR

William Douglas O'Connor (1832–1889) was a close friend and early biographer of Whitman; he secured a job for Whitman in the Department of the Interior in 1865 and wrote The Good Gray Poet *in 1866 as a defense of Whitman after he was fired by Interior Secretary James Harlan, who found a copy of* Leaves of Grass *on Whitman's desk and considered it obscene.*

Walt Whitman's [*Leaves of Grass*] is a poem which Schiller might have hailed as the noblest specimen of naïve literature, worthy of a place beside Homer. It is, in the first place, a work purely and entirely American, autochthonic, sprung from our own soil; no savor of Europe nor of the past, nor of any other literature in it; a vast carol of our own land, and of its Present and Future; the strong and haughty psalm of the Republic. There is not one other book, I care not whose, of which this can be said.

From *The Good Gray Poet: A Vindication*, 1866

EDWARD DOWDEN

Edward Dowden (1843–1913) was an Irish-born literary critic, Shakespearean scholar, and poet. He wrote a well-received biography of Shelley (1886), a number of critical works on Shakespeare, and produced editions of the works of Shelley, Shakespeare, and Wordsworth.

At last steps forward a man unlike any of his predecessors, and announces himself, and is announced with a flourish of critical trumpets, as Bard of America, and Bard of democracy. What cannot be questioned after an hour's acquaintance with Walt Whitman and his "Leaves of Grass," is that in him we meet a man not shaped out of old-world clay, not cast in any old-world mould, and hard to name by any old-world name. In his self-assertion there is a manner of powerful nonchalantness which is not assumed; he does not peep timidly from behind his works to glean our suffrages, but seems to say, "Take me or leave me here I am, a solid and not an inconsiderable fact of the universe." He disturbs our classifications. He attracts us; he repels us; he excites our curiosity, wonder, admiration, love; or, our extreme repugnance. He does anything except leave us indifferent. However we feel towards him we cannot despise him. He is "a summons and a challenge." He must be understood and so accepted, or must be got rid of. Passed by he cannot be.

From "The Poetry of Democracy: Walt Whitman" in
The Westminster Review, July 1871

WILLIAM DEAN HOWELLS

[Whitman's goal in *Leaves of Grass* was] the emancipation of poetry from what he felt to be the trammels of rhyme and metre. He did not achieve this; but he produced a new kind in literature, which we may or may not allow to be poetry, but which we cannot deny is something eloquent, suggestive, moving, with a lawless, formless beauty of its own. He dealt literary conventionality one of those blows which eventually show as internal injuries, whatever the immediate effect seems to be. He made it possible for poetry hereafter to be more direct and natural than hitherto.

From "Editor's Study: 'Leaves of Grass' " in *The Harper's
New Monthly Magazine,* February 1889

PAUL ELMER MORE

Paul Elmer More (1864–1937) was an American critic and philosopher, associated with Irving Babbitt and the movement called the New Humanism, which rejected what Babbitt saw as the excesses of romanticism, calling for moderation and reliance on classical literature as a model. He was a leading au-

thority on Greek philosophy; one of his major works was The Greek Tradition *(5 vols., 1921–31).*

Unfortunately, in breaking away from much that was undoubtedly a sham, [Whitman] forgot too often those eternal conventions which grow out of the essential demands of human nature. Rhythm is such a convention, and where his broken prose is of a kind to strain the ear in the search for cadences which are not to be found, he simply, as Ben Jonson said of Donne, deserves hanging for not keeping accent. To bawl out that things unlike are like, is not to make them so, and a manly egotism, if too noisy, may sink into mere fanfaronade. For page after page Whitman is rather a preacher of poetry than a poet; and this perhaps may be his final condemnation, that he is persistently telling us how the true poem of to-day should be written instead of making such a poem. Preaching has its uses and may arouse the loftiest emotions, but its uses and emotions are not those of poetry. The simple truth is that a large number of Whitman's so-called poems are not only sermons, but dull and amorphous sermons.

From "Walt Whitman" in *Shelburne Essays,*
fourth series, 1906

VAN WYCK BROOKS

Van Wyck Brooks (1886–1963) was an American critic and biographer whose early work focused on the Puritan influence on the development of American culture. He won the Pulitzer Prize in 1936 for The Flowering of New England, *the first book in his well-known series* Makers and Finders: A History of the Writer in America, 1800–1915, *a history of American literature that appeared in five volumes between 1936 and 1952.*

Whitman—how else can I express it?—precipitated the American character. All those things that had been separate, self-sufficient, incoördinate—action, theory, idealism, business—he cast into a crucible; and they emerged, harmonious and molten, in a fresh democratic ideal, based upon the whole personality. Every strong personal impulse, every coöperating and unifying impulse, everything that enriches the social background, everything that enriches the individual, everything that impels and clarifies in the modern world owes something to Whitman.

From "The Precipitant" in *America's Coming-of-Age,* 1915

AMY LOWELL

Amy Lowell (1874–1925) was an American poet best known for introducing Imagism to the United States. Her book What's O'Clock *was awarded the Pulitzer Prize in 1926, a year after her death.*

I believe that [Whitman] fell into his own peculiar form through ignorance, and not, as is commonly supposed, through a high sense of fitness; in this point he is at complete issue with the moderns who are supposed to derive from him, since they are perfectly conscious artists writing in a medium not less carefully ordered because it is based upon cadence and not upon metre. Whitman never had the slightest idea of what cadence is, and I think it does not take much reading to force the conviction that he had very little rhythmical sense.

Whitman was a great poet whether he invented his form consciously or whether he stumbled into it while endeavoring to avoid the obvious pitfalls of an older practice.

From "Walt Whitman and the New Poetry" in
The Yale Review, April 1927

GAY WILSON ALLEN

Gay Wilson Allen (b. 1903) is one of the best-known biographers of Whitman (The Solitary Singer, *published in 1955, is still considered a standard reference) and one of the most influential Whitman critics of the postwar period.*

A careful study of Whitman's punctuation will also reveal that it was not erratic or eccentric, as many readers have thought, but that it was an accurate index to the organic rhythm, the musical effects which the poet hoped to have brought out in the reading. We have already noticed that the comma at the end of nearly every line except the last is an indication not of the usual sense-pause but of the end of a prosodic unit—usually ending in a cadenza or falling of the voice. Perhaps it might be called a final caesura—a slight pause before the voice continues with the recitative. In the first edition Whitman frequently used semicolons at the end of lines which were grammatically complete (either complete predications or elliptical sentences), but later he adopted commas. Inside the line he was still forced to punctuate somewhat according to thought, but his internal commas and dashes are also often caesural pauses.

Whitman has a great variety of caesuras, and an exhaustive study of them would reveal much about his word-music that is still little known. Only a few examples can be given here. We might begin with one of the most rudimentary effects, which may be called a catalog-caesura:

> The blab of the pave, / tires of carts, / sluff of boot-
>   soles, / talk of the promenaders, /
> The heavy omnibus, / the driver with his interrogat-
>   ing thumb, / the clank of the shod horses on the
>   granite floor, / . . .

Notice the cumulative effect of the cadences, aided by the slight caesural pauses:

> $\overset{x}{\text{The}}$ $\overset{\prime}{\text{blab}}$ $\overset{x}{\text{of}}$ $\overset{x}{\text{the}}$ $\overset{\prime\,(x)\,\prime}{\text{pave, tires}}$ $\overset{x}{\text{of}}$ $\overset{\prime\,(x)\,\prime}{\text{carts, sluff}}$ $\overset{x}{\text{of}}$ $\overset{\prime}{\text{boot-}}\overset{\grave{}}{\text{soles,}}$

the omitted unaccented syllable before "tires" and "sluff" breaking the monotony of the pattern and emphasizing the beat, presently giving way to longer sweeps in the following line,

> . . . the driver with his interrogating thumb,
> the clank of the shod horses on the granite floor. . . .

A similar caesura, but with many subtle variations:

> I hear bravuras of birds, / bustle of growing
>   wheat, / gossip of flames, / clack of sticks cooking
>   my meals.//
> I hear the sound I love, / the sound of the human
>   voice,//
> I hear all sounds running together, / combined, fused
>   or following, /
> Sounds of the city and sounds out of the city—
>   / sounds of the day and night, . . .

Notice how much the shortening or lengthening of the pause can contribute to both the rhythm and the thought. The first line is cumulative in effect, the second balanced, the third suggestive or illustrative, the fourth is emphatic.

Sometimes the caesura divides the parallelism and is equivalent to the line-end pause:

> There is that in me—//I do not know what it is—
>   / but I know it is in me.
> Wrench'd and sweaty— / calm and cool / then my
>   body becomes, /
> I sleep—// I sleep long.//
> I do not know it—//it is without name—//it is a
>   word unsaid,//
> It is not in any dictionary, / utterance, / symbol.

Another caesural effect Jannaccone calls "thesis" and "arsis" because the second half line echoes the thought of the first and receives a weaker stress and perhaps a lower pitch:

> Great are the myths—// I too delight in them;
> Great are Adam and Eve—//I too look back and
>   accept them. . . .

From *The Walt Whitman Handbook*, 1946

RANDALL JARRELL

They might have put on his tombstone WALT WHIT-MAN: HE HAD HIS NERVE. He is the rashest, the most inexplicable and unlikely—the most impossible, one wants to say—of poets. He somehow is in a class by himself, so that one compares him with other poets about as readily as one compares *Alice* with other books. (Even his free verse has a completely different effect from anybody else's.) Who would think of comparing him with Tennyson or Browning or Arnold or Baudelaire?—it is Homer, or the sagas, or something far away and long ago, that comes to one's mind only to be dismissed; for sometimes Whitman *is* epic, just as *Moby Dick* is, and it surprises us to be able to use truthfully this word that we have misused so many times. Whitman *is* grand, and elevated, and comprehensive, and real with an astonishing reality, and many other things—the critic points at his qualities in despair and wonder, all method failing, and simply calls them by their names. And the range of these qualities is the most extraordinary thing of all. We can surely say about him, "He was a man, take him for all in all. I shall not look upon his like again"—and wish that people had seen this and not tried to be his like: one Whitman is miracle enough, and when he comes again it will be the end of the world.

From "Some Lines from Whitman" in
Poetry and the Age, 1953

IRVING HOWE

There are passages in his long poems, and whole shorter ones, in which the struggle of the self to locate a principle of movement, or a place of rest, comes to a momentary stop. A quietness begins; the language becomes hushed and completely controlled; the poet, not Walt the *kosmos* but Whitman the solitary, exposes himself in all his vulnerability. It is the moment after the struggle between the self and everything that resists and hurts and destroys the self, the blessed moment when anxiety has not been suppressed or dispelled but brought to its proper subordination. He reaches such moments in occasional passages of *Song of Myself* and for almost the whole of *Crossing Brooklyn Ferry*, which seems to me his single greatest poem. One thinks of them as moments of twilight, somewhat similar to those shadowy intervals between sleeping and waking, when the unconscious is still active and free yet we are not without some capacity to extricate ourselves from it, and when the will is present to our sense of things yet is relaxed and uncensorious. These are moments of rare psychic balance, everyone knows them in one way or another, but few writers have managed to create verbal equivalents as beautiful as those Whitman has.

From "Walt Whitman" in *Modern Literary Criticism: An Anthology*, 1958

DONALD HALL

The familiar doubleness is here—"the world I see," and "the Invisible World"—and emphasis falls upon the latter phrase as it must. Many of Whitman's admirers, I think, consider that he chiefly concerns himself with the world he sees. They speak of his catalogues, his multiplication of *things*. Yet, the seen world hardly exists for him, because he spiritualizes everything. He is the ultimate poet of dream. When he sings of him*self*, he is removed from egotism precisely through inwardness; this self that he observes through imagination has become all selves; he *is* the multitude he called himself. The outer world, the world of jobs and brothers, is passage which songs can cheer you through, and songs, when the truth is out, are

all dedicated to the Invisible World. Appearances in po-
etry are the colors and shapes of spirit by which Whitman
brings us into his Invisible World, which he insists is also
ours if we will only discover it.

From "The Invisible World" in *A Choice of*
Whitman's Verse, 1968

Reading Group Guide

1. Critic and poet Lewis Turco maintains that, contrary to the otherwise nearly universally accepted view, Whitman is not America's most innovative and important poet. He did nothing new, Turco argues, and "the level of his competence was not very high—he retained his poor ear throughout his life; his poems are too long, too disorganized, too pompous, too repetitious, too boring." Do you agree or disagree with this assessment?

2. Although *Leaves of Grass* might appear to be an amorphous, unstructured mass (as Turco suggests above), Whitman spent nearly forty years carefully revising it, reordering the poems, deleting poems or sections of poems, and adding new poems and cycles. He insisted that there was an overall unity and structure to the book (and stated that the ninth and final edition, the "Death-bed" edition published in 1892, was the last word on it). Do you perceive an overall unity in the book? Is there a discernible structure to it?

3. Walt Whitman is often called the poet of democracy and of America; one of the best-known and most often quoted poems in *Leaves of Grass* is "For You O Democracy" in "Calamus." How does *Leaves of Grass* answer the question of what democracy is and what it means to be an American?

751

4. In *The Good Gray Poet*, one of the first biographies of Whitman, William Douglas O'Connor explained in words that Whitman himself acknowledged that one of the primary purposes of *Leaves of Grass* was to save sexuality "from the keeping of blackguards and debauchees, to which it has been abandoned"—by which he meant rescue it from libertines, whose dissolute behavior made sex disrespectable to middle-class Victorian sensibilities. One American reviewer of the 1855 edition described Whitman as having "a degrading, beastly sensuality, that is fast rotting the core of all the social virtues" and a British reviewer asked, "Is it possible that the most prudish nation on earth will adopt a poet whose indecencies stink in the nostrils?" How is sexuality represented in *Leaves of Grass*?

5. There are many recurrent themes, symbols, images, and motifs in *Leaves of Grass* as a whole, as well as in particular poems and cycles of poems. Consider, for example, the following: a) The use of the star, the lilac, and the bird in "When Lilacs Last in the Dooryard Bloom'd" (What do they symbolize and how do they relate to each other? How do they contribute to the structure of what many critics consider to be one of the finest poems ever written in the English language?); b) The recurrence of the word "mother" or "mothers" (more than one hundred times) in the book; and c) the repeated invocation of odor, fragrance, and perfume throughout the book.

6. The Civil War was a defining event in Walt Whitman's life, and the poems in "Drum-Taps" are a testimony to the impact the time he spent as a nurse to both Northern and Southern soldiers in the army hospitals of

Washington, D.C. had on him. What view of the war is expressed by the narrative persona, and does the perspective of the persona change over the course of the cycle of poems?

7. Discuss the following stylistic aspects of *Leaves of Grass:* a) lists and catalogues; b) the extensive use of parentheses; c) parallelism (the development of rhythm via a repetition of ideas and sentences rather than through accents and syllables); d) the repetition of sounds and words; and e) punctuation.

A NOTE ON THE TYPE

The principal text of this Modern Library edition
was composed in a digitized version of Palatino,
a contemporary typeface created by Hermann Zapf,
who was inspired by the sixteenth-century calligrapher
Giambattista Palatino, a writing master of Renaissance Italy.
Palatino was the first of Zapf's typefaces
to be introduced in America.